THE
BURNING
TIGRIS

The Armenian Genocide and

America's Response

PETER BALAKIAN

HarperCollins*Publishers*

HarperCollins books may be purchased for educational, business, or sales promotional use. For information please write: Special Markets Department, HarperCollins Publishers Inc., 10 East 53rd Street, New York, NY 10022.

FIRST EDITION
Designed by Joseph Rutt

Printed on acid-free paper
Library of Congress Cataloging-in-Publication Data

Balakian, Peter
    The burning Tigris : the Armenian genocide and America's response /
                    Peter Balakian.
                        p. cm.
            Includes bibliographical references and index.
                    ISBN 0-06-019840-0
  1. Armenian massacres, 1915–1923.   2. Armenian massacres, 1915–1923—
Foreign public opinion, American.   3. Genocide—Turkey.   4. Human rights.
                    DS 195.5.B353 2003
956.6'2015—dc21   2003044986

  03   04   05   06   07   NMSG/RRD   10 9 8 7 6 5 4 3 2 1

To the victims and survivors
of genocide everywhere

CONTENTS

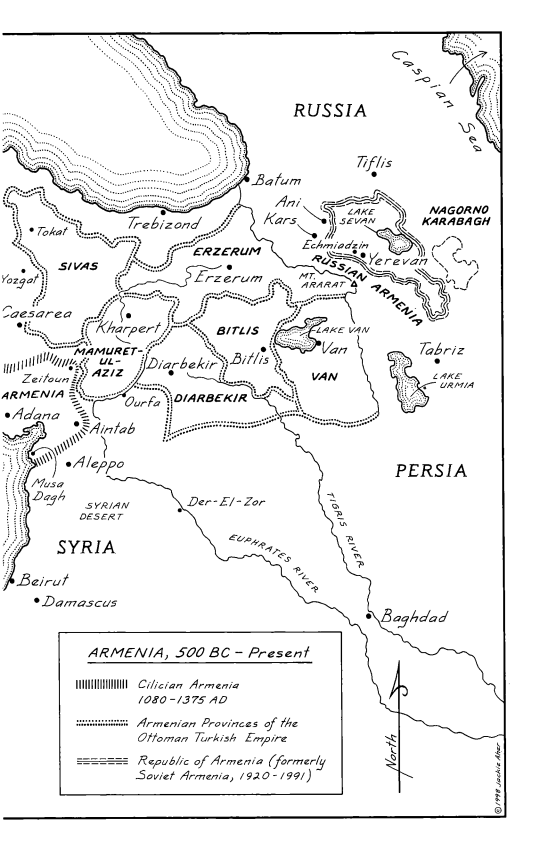

RUSSIA

Caspian Sea

Tiflis

Batum

Ani
Kars
LAKE
SEVAN

NAGORNO
KARABAGH

Trebizond

Tokat

ERZERUM

Echmiadzin

RUSSIAN
Yerevan

SIVAS

Erzerum

MT.
ARARAT

ARMENIA

Yozgat

Caesarea

Kharpert

BITLIS

LAKE VAN

Tabriz

Van

MAMURET-
UL-
AZIZ

Diarbekir

Bitlis

VAN

LAKE
URMIA

Zeitoun

ARMENIA

DIARBEKIR

Ourfa

Adana

Aintab

PERSIA

Musa
Dagh

Aleppo

SYRIAN
DESERT

Der-El-Zor

TIGRIS RIVER

SYRIA

EUPHRATES RIVER

Beirut

Damascus

Baghdad

North

ARMENIA, 500 BC – Present

|||||||||||||| Cilician Armenia
1080–1375 AD

:::::::::::::::: Armenian Provinces of the
Ottoman Turkish Empire

======= Republic of Armenia (formerly
Soviet Armenia, 1920-1991)

© 1998 Jackie Aher

PREFACE

———— ∞ ————

In recent decades, the Armenian Genocide has often been referred to as "the forgotten genocide," the "unremembered genocide," "the hidden holocaust," or "the secret genocide." However, such epithets convey little sense of how large the massacres of the Armenians in the 1890s and the genocide of the Armenians in 1915 loomed in American (as well as European) consciousness and social and political life during a span of four decades. The U.S. response to the Armenian crisis, which began in the 1890s and continued into the 1920s, was the first international human rights movement in American history and helped to define the nation's emerging global identity. It seems that no other international human rights issue has ever preoccupied the United States for such a duration. Looking back at the World War I era, President Herbert Hoover noted that "the name Armenia was in the front of the American mind . . . known to the American schoolchild only a little less than England."[1] The breadth and intensity of American engagement in the effort to save the Armenians of the Ottoman Empire is an important chapter in American history, and one that has been lost. It is also one from which Americans today can learn a great deal.

In the past decade there has been much focus on and debate about the issue of United States engagement, response, and responsibility for crimes of genocide committed in other parts of the planet. What is the role of the

most powerful nation in the world when the ultimate crime is being perpetrated in plain view? Why was there no U.S. activist response to the Holocaust, or to Pol Pot's genocide in Cambodia in 1978, or to the Rwandan
genocide in 1994, when in fact the State Department, media, and general
public often knew what was happening in those killing fields? Why is U.S.
policy evasive, sluggish, resistant to action (of various and creative kinds,
not simply or only military intervention), and often tinged with denial?
Why has there been so little political will at the top when media coverage
and popular knowledge and empathy are often large and dramatic?

A deeper understanding of these questions and of the history of
America's confrontation with genocide must begin with a study of the
Armenian Genocide. For the Armenian Genocide is—as historians and
genocide scholars Yehuda Bauer, Robert Melson, Howard M. Sachar,
Samantha Power, and others have noted—the template for most of the
genocide that followed in the twentieth century. In the world after
September 11, 2001, Americans and U.S. leaders may find that the Armenian lesson has much to teach about the moral accountability of
bystanders, trauma and survivor experience, and the immediate and far-
reaching impact of mass violence committed against innocent civilians.

A hundred years ago, in 1903, the feminist writer and social critic
Charlotte Perkins Gilman believed that the Armenian massacres of
1894–96 should prompt a new age of American international leadership.
"The most important fact in this new century is the rapid kindling of the
social consciousness; and among the shocks of pain which force that wak-
ening the archetype is to be found in the sorrows of Armenia." The word
"Armenian," she wrote, "has a connotation of horror; we are accustomed
to see it followed by 'atrocities,' 'massacre,' 'outrage'; it has become an
adjective of incredible suffering." Gilman's appeal to international ethics
in the Armenian case was adamant. "America has heard and responded to
a certain degree," but there must be more engagement in order to prevail
"on the Turkish government to desist from its criminal conduct."
Human rights crimes such as the Armenian massacres, Gilman noted,
"demand international law, to restrain, prohibit, punish; best of all, to
prevent.

"Who is to do it?" she demanded. "The world . . . of civilized nations
. . . advancing in united action for the common good. And America," she
answered, "with the blended blood of all peoples in her veins, with inter-

ests in every land, and duties with the interests; America, who leads in so many things, can well afford to lead in this; not only allowing human liberty here, but using her great strength to protect it everywhere."[2]

Less than two decades later, during and after World War I, former president Theodore Roosevelt berated President Wilson for his refusal "to take effective action on behalf of Armenia. . . . The Armenian massacre," Roosevelt concluded, "was the greatest crime of the war, and failure to act against Turkey is to condone it; because the failure to deal radically with the Turkish horror means that all talk of guaranteeing the future peace of the world is mischievous nonsense; and because when we now refuse war with Turkey we show that our announcement that we meant 'to make the world safe for democracy' was insincere claptrap."[3]

Had Theodore Roosevelt answered Charlotte Gilman's question? The dialogue posed by their statements is one that still haunts us.

During the 1890s Sultan Abdul Hamid II ordered massacres against the Armenians—the largest Christian minority culture in the Anatolian part of the Ottoman Empire—that took the lives of about two hundred thousand Armenians. In response to the Hamidian massacres taking place halfway around the globe, Americans from all classes and walks of life organized philanthropic and relief programs. Women's groups, churches, synagogues, and civic organizations around the country organized to protest the massacres—which were covered boldly and regularly in U.S. newspapers and magazines—and to raise money. The National Armenian Relief Committee, headed by influential American industrialists—including John D. Rockefeller, Spencer Trask, and Jacob Schiff—raised hundreds of thousands of dollars in money, services, and goods, and recruited the venerable elder stateswoman Clara Barton to take her Red Cross relief teams, for the first time, out of the country—to the Armenian provinces nearly six thousand miles away. In 1896 Congress passed the Cullom resolution—the first international human rights resolution in American history—condemning the sultan for the massacres.

American intellectual and cultural leaders articulated their opinions on the Armenian atrocities and often worked for Armenian relief. Julia Ward Howe, Isabel Barrows, Alice Stone Blackwell, William Lloyd Garrison Jr., Charlotte Perkins Gilman, and Stephen Crane all lent their voices and deeds. At the forefront of the movement were women who had been abolitionists and were now at the head of the woman suffrage movement. By the second decade of the twentieth century, public figures as varied as Theodore Roosevelt, Ezra Pound, H. L. Mencken, William Jennings Bryan, and President Woodrow Wilson addressed and assessed the century's first genocide.

Much of America's moral sentiment emanated from the near century of Protestant missionary presence in the Ottoman Empire. American missionaries had first gone to Turkey in the second decade of the nineteenth century in an effort to convert the Muslim Turks, but they found more fertile ground with the Christian minorities. By the middle of the century, the missionaries had set up a network of missions, colleges, schools, and hospitals throughout Turkey for the Armenians, Greeks, and Assyrians. From their deeply entrenched place, the Protestant missionaries became witnesses to atrocities against Armenians, and often rescuers and administers of relief. But American Catholics and Jews, as well as secular intellectuals, all worked to alleviate the Armenian crisis. The Zionist rabbi Stephen Wise, along with Wall Street financier Jacob Schiff, were prominent Jewish-Americans leading the Armenian relief campaign. The Central Conference of American Rabbis went so far as to pass a proclamation in 1909 urging the European powers to protect the Armenians from Turkish barbarism.[4]

The Armenian Genocide of 1915 spawned extraordinary heroism on the part of American foreign service officers—from consuls posted in remote areas to the U.S. ambassador in Constantinople, Henry Morgenthau. These U.S. State Department officials often risked their lives to save men, women, and orphaned children. Ambassador Morgenthau went beyond the duty of his job as he became the crucial nexus between the killing fields and the American relief community and the press back home. A man of high moral conscience, Ambassador Morgenthau was most likely the first high-ranking diplomat to confront boldly the leaders of the Ottoman government about its treatment of the Armenians. When he left his post in 1916, he wrote, "My failure to stop the destruction of the Armenians had made Turkey for me a place of horror."[5]

Eyewitness accounts of the Armenian Genocide from American foreign service officers stationed in the heart of the massacre and deportation zones quickly became the first body of U.S. diplomatic literature about a major foreign human rights tragedy. Their narratives were eloquent in their clean language and clinical images, and provided a certain detachment and perspective on events that might otherwise seem to surpass description. In their consistency, their narratives also corroborated one another as they disclosed the plan and process of the Turkish final solution for the Armenians.

By the early 1920s, the American response to the Armenian Genocide was divided between a passionate popular appeal for aid and justice, and the limits of the federal government—the State Department, the White House, and a powerful segment of the Senate, which was isolationist and Republican. The post–World War I power alliance with Kemal Atatürk's new Turkish republic, and the American drive for oil in the Middle East, led to the abandonment of Armenia. In some sense this paradox would haunt the United States through the twentieth century and beyond.

In many ways it is a propitious time to study the Armenian Genocide. In the past two decades scholars have unearthed and translated a large quantity of official state records documenting the Committee of Union and Progress's (Ottoman Turkey's governing political party) finely organized and implemented plan to exterminate the Armenians. I have studied hundreds of U.S. State Department documents (there are some four thousand documents totaling about thirty-seven thousand pages in the National Archives) written by American diplomats that report in depth the process and devastation of the Armenian Genocide. The extermination of the Armenians is also illuminated in British Foreign Office records, and in official records from the state archives of Germany and Austria-Hungary, Ottoman Turkey's World War I allies. The foremost scholar of the Armenian Genocide, Professor Vahakn Dadrian, has made available in translation a body of Turkish sources both primary and secondary. Dadrian has also translated and annotated the issues of *Takvimi Vekayi*, the Ottoman parliamentary gazette, that record the proceedings of post–World War I Ottoman military tribunals, with court-martial testimony that documents the process of the genocide and confessions of guilt from the Turkish perpetrators.

As scholars of the Holocaust have made clear, survivor accounts are a profound part of history and allow us into regions we would not otherwise come to know. I have found Armenian survivor narratives and memoirs, as well as oral histories on audio- and videotape, to be of great value. I have also included a broad selection of historical photographs. Some of them, such as those from the *London Graphic* in the 1890s, are landmarks in photojournalism, bringing an unprecedented human rights atrocity to the vivid view of the general public. The most important group is that of the German military medic Armin T. Wegner, who risked his life photographing extraordinary scenes of the massacres and deportations and then smuggling them out of Turkey. A comprehensive demographic map of the massacres and deportations, and a map of President Wilson's post–World War I award to Armenia, also provide a graphic view of a lost history.

Unfortunately, writing a history of the Armenian Genocide still entails addressing the Turkish government's continued denial of the facts and the moral dimensions of this history. As Richard Falk, the eminent professor of international law at Princeton University, has put it: The Turkish campaign of denying the Armenian Genocide is "sinister," singular in the annals of history, and "a major, proactive, deliberate government effort to use every possible instrument of persuasion at its disposal to keep the truth about the Armenian Genocide from general acknowledgment, especially by elites in the United States and Western Europe."[6]

Today Turkey would like the media and the public to believe there are "two sides" to the Armenian Genocide. When scholars and writers of Armenian descent write about the Armenian Genocide, the Turkish government calls this a biased "Armenian point of view." This accusation is as slanderous as it would be for the German government to claim that the work of Jewish scholars and writers represented merely a "Jewish side" of the Holocaust, which is to say a biased and illegitimate version of history.

The most notable scholar of genocide denial, Professor Deborah Lipstadt of Emory University, has written: "Denial of genocide—whether that of the Turks against Armenians, or the Nazis against Jews—is not an act of historical reinterpretation. Rather, it sows confusion by appearing to be engaged in a genuine scholarly effort." Lipstadt also notes that deniers claim that all documents are "forgeries and falsehoods." She calls denial of genocide the "final stage of genocide," because it "strives to reshape history in order to demonize the victims and rehabilitate the perpetrators."[7]

That the Turkish government today and a small group of its sympathizers work hard (spending time and money) in order to undermine and distort the history of the Armenian Genocide does not, Deborah Lipstadt concludes, comprise a legitimate debate, and certainly not an intellectual conversation worth reporting. In short, she argues, it is morally wrong to privilege the deniers by according them space in the classroom or in the media. Elie Wiesel, too, has called denying genocide, and in particular the Armenian Genocide, a "double killing," because it murders the memory of the event.

It is troubling to find in the press today the echoes of Turkish denial when references to the Armenian Genocide use phrases like "Armenians claim" that more than a million died in the Armenian Genocide. This effort to present the Armenian Genocide as a history that has two legitimate sides, and one that can be reduced to ethnic perspectives—the victims' and the perpetrators'—trivializes and defames a human rights crime of enormous magnitude. It is doubly ironic when one notes that in 1915 alone, the *New York Times* published 145 articles on the Armenian massacres (one about every 2.5 days). The conclusive language of the reportage was that the Turkish slaughter of the Armenians was "systematic," "deliberate," "authorized," and "organized by government"; it was a "campaign of extermination" and of "systematic race extermination."[8]

The Association of Genocide Scholars and the community of Holocaust scholars—which is to say, the professional scholars who study genocide—affirm that the extermination of the Armenians *was* genocide, and that this genocide took the lives of about two-thirds of the Armenian population of Ottoman Turkey. Genocide scholars are comfortable putting the number of dead at more than a million (some estimates put it at 1.5 million). Out of exasperation with Turkish denial, the Association of Genocide Scholars in 1997 passed unanimously a resolution stating the facts of the Armenian Genocide. In June 2000, 126 leading Holocaust scholars, also deeply troubled by Turkey's campaign of denial, published a statement in the *New York Times:* "126 Holocaust Scholars Affirm the Incontestable Fact of the Armenian Genocide and Urge Western Democracies to Officially Recognize It." Among the signatories were Elie Wiesel,

Yehuda Bauer, Israel Charny, Stephen Feinstein, and Ward Churchill. Inevitably, progressive Turkish scholars are also beginning to acknowledge the Armenian Genocide. Professor Taner Akçam's several recent books on the Armenian Genocide, published in Turkey, may be a signal light for a new era.

The Armenian Genocide prompted two historic responses in the evolution of international ethics. In May 1915 in the midst of World War I, the Allies meeting in London conceived of what they termed "crimes against humanity," in warning the Ottoman government that massacring the Armenian population would violate a fundamental standard of humanity and would have consequences. And during the 1930s and 1940s, when the Polish jurist Raphael Lemkin was studying and writing about what he would term *genocide*, he articulated his definition in large part by what had happened to the Armenians in 1915 and by what was happening to the Jews of Europe.

In many ways, then, the Armenian Genocide emerges as a landmark event—and one that deserves its proper place in modern history.

Part I

THE EMERGENCE OF INTERNATIONAL HUMAN RIGHTS IN AMERICA:

The Armenian Massacres in the 1890s

—⤫—

A GATHERING AT

FANEUIL HALL

Ah, Mrs. Howe, you have given us a prose Battle Hymn.
—Frederick Greenhalge,
governor of Massachusetts

The light in New England in late fall is austere and clean and rinses the white steeples of Boston's Congregational and Unitarian churches, the red brick of the State House, and the gray stone of the Back Bay town houses. Even the gold dome on the white cupola of Faneuil Hall reflects its luster. It's November 26, 1894, the Monday before Thanksgiving, a windy and clear evening, as men and women file into Faneuil Hall from all over Boston and from the suburbs of Cambridge, Watertown, Winchester, and as far out as Quincy and Andover. They have come to this public meeting place near the harbor to talk about the most pressing international human rights issue of the day.

Schooners and sloops and oyster scows make a grid of rigging that glows in the sunset. The sound of squawking gulls. Buckets of cod and haddock on the docks. The outline of the giant masts of the USS *Constitution* fading in the twilight of the Charlestown Naval Yard. Across the street the stalls of Quincy Market are closed, the awnings rolled up for the night.

Faneuil Hall was known as the Cradle of Liberty because Samuel Adams and James Otis and the Sons of Liberty had met here in the decade before the American Revolution to form their opposition to the sugar tax, the stamp tax, and other forms of British oppression. The Boston Tea Party was conceived here. The space itself was made even more dramatic when the architect Charles Bulfinch redesigned it in 1805. Even after government by town meeting ended in Boston in 1822, the hall continued to be the main forum for political and social debate. Here in the 1840s William Lloyd Garrison, Wendell Phillips, Charles Sumner, and Frederick Douglass gave some of their most important antislavery speeches to overflowing crowds.

By 1873 women were speaking from the podium, and suffragists Lucy Stone and Julia Ward Howe were among the first to address the movement for woman suffrage on that stage beneath George A. Healy's dramatic painting of Daniel Webster exhorting, "Liberty and union, now *and* forever" on the Senate floor. In keeping with that spirit of reform, a group of prominent New Englanders filled Faneuil Hall on that blustery late-November evening.

All that summer and fall, news of the massacres of the Armenians at the hands of the Turks in the Ottoman Empire reached Americans through news reports and bold headlines in the *New York Times,* the *Washington Post,* the *Boston Globe,* the *Chicago Tribune,* the *San Francisco Chronicle,* and in the nation's leading magazines—*The Nation, The Century,* and *Harper's.* The news came from American missionaries who were teaching Christians at missionary colleges all across the Anatolian plain of central and eastern Turkey; it came from American and British diplomats stationed in the Armenian provinces of the Ottoman Empire, from European and American journalists, and from Armenian survivors and refugees. And recently it came by way of a new invention—the wireless telegraph.

The outrage over the Armenian massacres emerged in a culture that was just beginning to look outward to the international arena in which the United States would define a global identity in the coming decade. In the first years of the 1890s, there had been a near war with Chile over the killing of two American sailors in Valparaiso, and U.S. involvement in a border dispute between British Guiana and Venezuela that brought jingoism to a new level. Americans such as Theodore Roosevelt began to broadcast their feeling that the country needed a war. The question of annexing the Hawaiian Islands dominated a tug-of-war between the imperialists and anti-imperialists that lasted throughout the decade.

Americans also expressed great sympathy for the Cubans in their struggle for independence from Spain. By 1895, when Cuban rebels rose up against the deplorable conditions to which they were subjected by their Spanish rulers, the Cuban crisis became a Western Hemisphere liberation cause for Americans. By 1898 the Cuban struggle would lead to the Spanish-American War—the war that consummated the jingoist spirit and launched the United States as a colonial force in the world. With the defeat of Spain, in a war that lasted ten weeks and gave Cuba its independence, the United States acquired Puerto Rico, the Philippines, and Guam, giving the nation a rising sense of global power.

The 1890s were a transformative time for U.S. foreign policy—a decade in which it would embrace imperialism and assert itself, at times, with a rhetoric of Protestant Anglo-Saxon superiority over the "backward" peoples of the world. The Armenian Question emerged, in some ways uniquely, as a humanitarian project at a time when imperialist designs were governing most American international interventions.

Sultan Abdul Hamid II, the Turkish caliph, had begun to implement his solution to what was now internationally known as the Armenian Question. In short, the Armenian Question revolved around the issue of much-needed reform for the oppressed Armenians—the largest Christian minority living under Ottoman Turkish rule in Anatolia. As the British journalist and longtime resident of Constantinople—Sir Edwin Pears— put it, all the Armenians "desired was security for life, honour, and property."[1] But, the sultan's lifetime friend and confidant, the Hungarian scholar Arminius Vambery, wrote, the sultan had decided that the only way to eliminate the Armenian Question was to eliminate the Armenians themselves. The means would be government-sanctioned mass murder on a scale never before seen.[2] The Turkish massacres of some fifteen thousand Bulgarians in 1876 (a response to the Bulgarian uprising for independence) had been an unprecedented act of state-sponsored mass murder that riveted Europe and the United States. Yet even that atrocity paled beside what happened in 1894, when the very sultan who came to power in the midst of the "Bulgarian horrors," as they were soon known, began a campaign of mass slaughter against his Armenian subjects. By the end of 1896 the sultan's campaign had taken the lives of about two hundred thousand Armenians—approximately one hundred thousand killed by direct massacre and the rest dying of disease and famine.[3] In a two-year period, in the middle of what in the U.S. was called the Gay Nineties, the sultan refined the idea of state-sponsored murder, creating a new and ominous political weapon for the modern age.

That evening at Faneuil Hall was marked by a distinguished company of social reformers that included William Lloyd Garrison Jr. (the son of the great abolitionist); Henry Blackwell and his poet daughter, Alice Stone Blackwell; Julia Ward Howe; the Reverend Samuel June Barrows, publisher of the *Christian Register;* Massachusetts governor Frederick Greenhalge; and a score of other leading civic figures.

Julia Ward Howe, in her seventies, was beginning to feel the effects of another year on the national lecture circuit. For decades she had lectured on woman suffrage, world peace, freedom in Russia—and on literary and cultural topics. A leading abolitionist, she continued to be a national and international voice of conscience. By the nineties Mrs. Howe was a figure of such national stature that the *New York Times* compared her with Queen Elizabeth I and Queen Victoria, claiming that these English monarchs never inspired "the spontaneous, instinctive, chivalric obeisance which American audiences now pay to Julia Ward Howe, who fills the national imagination as no other woman has, by her identification with a great chapter in human liberty"—the abolition of slavery.[4]

Soon to become the first woman elected to the American Academy of Arts and Letters, Howe had risen to national prominence in the wake of her famous poem, "The Battle Hymn of the Republic," which had helped to galvanize the Union cause with its vision of sacrifice for human liberty. By 1868, when she became the first president of the New England Woman Suffrage Association, she was a figure in American public life of the same stature as Ralph Waldo Emerson and Mark Twain. No woman in American history had ever equaled the breadth of her moral and intellectual concerns or the radius of her voice in the national and international arenas.

Although Howe was not feeling her spunky self that Monday in November, she confessed when she reached the podium that she "could not stay away from this meeting. . . . I have to pray God night and morning that He would find some way to stay this terrible tide of slaughter."[5] A meeting about a human rights issue that had gripped America for the past two months was more than she could resist.

Dressed in her usual lilac satin gown, black flowered silk cloak, and small lace cap, Julia Ward Howe was eloquent:

> Now, the fleets of the Western nations are waiting for some diplomatic development which shall open the way for action. I think that we, the United States of America, are now called upon to play the part of Florence Nightingale; to take our stand and insist upon it that the slaughter shall cease. Oh! let us give money, let us give life, but let us stand by our principles of civil and religious liberty.

With rising passion, she went on:

> It may be asked, where is the good of our assembling here? what can a handful of us effect against this wicked and remorseless power, so far beyond our reach . . . ? The walls of this old hall should answer this question. They saw the dawn of our own larger liberties. They heard the first indignant plea of Wendell Phillips when, in the splendor of his youth, he took the field for the emancipation of a despised race which had no friends. So, on this sacred arena, I throw down the glove which challenges the Turkish Government to its dread account. What have we for us in this contest? The spirit of civilization, the sense of Christendom, the heart of humanity. All of these plead for justice, all cry out against barbarous warfare of which the victims are helpless men, tender women and children. We invoke here the higher powers of humanity against the rude instincts in which the brute element survives and rules.[6]

Governor Greenhalge was so moved by Mrs. Howe's words that he embraced her afterward, declaring: "Ah, Mrs. Howe, you have given us a prose Battle Hymn!"[7] The analogy was lost on no one. Now, three decades after the Civil War, Howe saw the plight of the Armenians as yet another chapter in the struggle for human liberty and human rights. Throughout the rest of the nineties, the phrase "Spoke for Armenia" would be a frequent entry in Julia Ward Howe's diary.[8]

Howe's was not the only voice resounding that night. The leading Unitarian minister Samuel Barrows exclaimed: "We are appealing to the ears of the whole civilized world. We want you, Armenian citizens, and Armenians all over the world, to know and feel that from our heart of hearts we sympathize with them tonight in the deep wrong, in the terrible crimes, that have been committed in the name of government." Social reformer Henry B. Blackwell—perhaps best known today as the husband of Lucy Stone and the brother of Elizabeth Blackwell, the first woman to earn a medical degree in the United States—spoke in terms that seem prescient, looking back at the dawn of the twentieth century's age of genocide.

"It is literally true," he exclaimed, "that an attempt is being made to exterminate the whole Armenian race and put an end to the whole Armenian question. All the horrors in Bulgaria that led to a great war have now been repeated, and we are here, not only to protest, but to demand of our government that it shall send its delegates to Turkey and ascertain the facts and demand explanation." Blackwell was equally insightful in characterizing the American dilemma and appealing to an idea of foreign policy that transcends national self-interest:

> It will be said that the traditional policy of the United States is one of non-intervention, and I approve of that principle, but there are times and places when every nation owes to human nature itself an expression of sympathy with those who have been so wronged. The people in Turkey who are governed are civilized; the government is barbarous. . . . What we want to do is to move not only our own government, but the governments of Europe.

Another speaker, Col. Albert Clarke, declared that "Turkey might govern as she pleased, but she was not to be permitted to outrage the sense of humanity."[9]

The next day the *Boston Globe* headline reported: CRY FOR JUSTICE COMES FROM FANEUIL HALL, and the *Boston Herald*'s headline: TURKISH ABUSE AND THE SLAUGHTER AT SASSOUN ROUNDLY CONDEMNED. The article called the speeches "the opening shot of a fusillade of popular indignation that bids fair to be heard around the world."[10]

But some Americans had been introduced to the tyranny of Turkish rule decades before the meeting at Faneuil Hall, when the most famous American novelist and wit, Mark Twain, recorded in his memoir *Innocents Abroad* his revulsion toward the autocracy of the sultanate. Writing about his travels to Europe, Turkey, and the Holy Land in 1867, he viewed other cultures through the lens of his democratic perspective. His encounter in Paris with Sultan Abdul Aziz, Abdul Hamid's uncle and predecessor, spurred him to reflect on the brutality of monarchial rule in the Ottoman Empire. Twain called the sultan a "representative of . . . a government whose Three Graces are Tyranny, Rapacity, Blood. Here in brilliant Paris," he reflected, "under this majestic Arch of Triumph, the First Century greets the Nineteenth!" He spared no words in attacking Abdul Aziz—who was known for his despotism, decadence, and cowardice. Of the sultan, Twain wrote:

> a man who sits upon a throne . . . who holds in his hands the power of life and death over millions—yet who sleeps, sleeps, eats, eats, idles with his eight hundred concubines, and when he is surfeited with eating and sleeping and idling, and would rouse up and take the reins of government and threaten to *be* a Sultan, is charmed from his purpose by wary Fuad Pacha with a pretty plan for a new palace or a new ship—charmed away with a new toy, like any other restless child; a man who sees his people robbed and oppressed by soulless tax-gatherers, but speaks no word to save them; . . . a man who found his great empire a blot upon the earth—a degraded, poverty-stricken, miserable, infamous agglomeration of ignorance, crime, and brutality . . .[11]

Twain also recorded his sympathy with the plight of the Syrians, whom he encountered on his trip, and noted that they were an oppressed race living "under the inhuman tyranny of the Ottoman empire," and had been "ground down by a system of taxation" that would destroy most peoples.[12] Although *Innocents Abroad* first appeared in 1869, its reissue in 1897, a year after the Armenian massacres, was timely, and twenty-five years before the Armenians rebelled against the unjust tax system, Twain's observations would come to seem prophetic.

Julia Ward Howe's understanding of Ottoman Turkish history had been formed in part by her husband, Samuel Gridley Howe, a social reformer who had founded the Clark Institute for the Blind. In 1825, after graduating from Brown University and Harvard Medical School, he decided to emulate his favorite poet, Lord Byron, and join the Greek army in its war for independence from the Turks. As a surgeon in the Greek army, he spent the next two years in battle giving medical aid to Greek soldiers. Byron loomed large for both Julia and Sam Howe. Not only had Byron himself died fighting at Missolonghi in 1824 for the cause of Greek freedom, but in his passion for the classical cultures of Asia Minor, he had studied the Armenian language in the winter of 1816–17 at the Armenian monastery in Venice.

In 1828, when Sam Howe returned home to Boston to raise money for the Greek cause, he carried with him Byron's helmet, which he had bought at an auction. As he rode down Beacon Street on a black stallion draped with a crimson saddlecloth, his fellow Bostonians welcomed him as if he were Byron's brother. Indeed, with his strong features, piercing blue eyes, jet black hair, and soldierly demeanor, he was Byronesque. He had little trouble raising the money, and within a few months he was back in Greece helping the war-ravaged country begin a new era. In appreciation of his work, the Greek government later bestowed on him the title Chevalier of the Greek Legion of Honor, and thereafter his friends dubbed him "Chev."[13]

Under Julia Ward Howe's leadership on that evening at Faneuil Hall, the United Friends of Armenia—which had formed a year earlier, in 1893—began a process of activism and international relief, becoming a primary conduit for raising consciousness about the Armenian massacres as well as money for food, clothing, and medical supplies for Armenian relief work in Turkey. Before the 1890s were over, the organization would bring scores of refugees and orphans to the United States and was instrumental in finding employment for Armenian refugees in America.[14]

By September 1894, America's major newspapers carried the names of faraway Armenian villages and romantic-sounding places like Sasun, Moush, Bitlis, and Zeitun, as reports of massacres on an unprecedented scale reached American readers—just as a hundred years later, the names *Cambodia, Pol Pot, Rwanda, Hutu, Tutsi, Bosnia,* and *East Timor* would be insignias of atrocity in the headlines of the late twentieth century. *Harper's Weekly* featured large, dramatic illustrations of Armenians being massacred in the streets of Constantinople or on the rocky plateaus of Anatolia.

In the *New York Times* alone, often on the front page, headlines read: THE WORST WAS NOT TOLD, THE ARMENIAN ATROCITIES, EIGHT THOUSAND BUTCHERED, THE HORRORS OF THE ARMENIAN MASSACRES ONLY JUST BEGINNING TO BE REALIZED BY THE WORLD. And also DENYING ARMENIAN ATROCITIES, and TURKEY'S REPLY DEFIANT. Perhaps the first use of the word "holocaust" to describe a human rights disaster was on the front page of the *New York Times* on September 10, 1895, in the headline ANOTHER ARMENIAN HOLOCAUST. The article describes the mass murder of more than five thousand Armenians by a force of one thousand Turkish troops in the Erzinjan district of eastern Turkey. The beginning of modern human rights reporting had begun, and Americans were responsive.

"THERE IN THE WOODS"

lice Stone Blackwell was among those in the audience at Faneuil Hall that evening. She was the daughter of the social reformers and suffrage activists Henry Blackwell and Lucy Stone. At thirty-seven she might have thought of herself a single woman for life, except that the previous summer she had fallen in love with Ohannes Chatschumian (o-ha-NESS ka-choom-YAHN), a young Armenian theology student, who was visiting Isabel and Samuel June Barrows, friends of the Blackwell family.

Isabel Barrows had befriended Chatschumian when she was visiting Leipzig in the winter of 1893. Chatschumian, a brilliant but penniless graduate student, had been studying theology for the past several years at the University of Leipzig, where he was sent, with the help of some patrons, from his native town of Elizavetpol in Russian Armenia. Isabel, her young daughter, Mabel, and her friend Rose Hollingsworth met Chatschumian at the boarding house near the university, where they were staying. Isabel, a pioneering woman doctor like Elizabeth Blackwell, had received her M.D. from the University of Vienna in 1870, and returned frequently to Germany and Austria.

On their first evening in Leipzig, when the three women came down to dinner, the three young men seated at their table rose and remained standing until the women sat down. Isabel remarked to her friend Rose on the good manners of the young Germans. She soon learned that they were Armenians.

Isabel liked one of the men instantly. Finding Ohannes "exceptionally brilliant and lovable," as she later described him, she soon discovered that he could converse about theology, history, and politics, and that he could speak and read half a dozen languages. She was moved also by his passion for the ancient history of his people and his acute sense of their worsening plight under Turkish rule. She found a quality of gentleness and soulfulness in him that she ascribed to his idealistic vision of human justice and Christian compassion, and she also noted how fiercely proud and opinionated he was. A staunch follower of the Armenian Apostolic Church, Ohannes had little goodwill for the American Protestant missionaries who had come to Turkey with the hope of converting Muslims and were instead converting his countrymen and women to Protestantism.[1] Through Isabel Barrows, however, he would discover another side of Protestantism.

Not long after meeting Ohannes, Isabel scribbled a note to him: "He would have a cold heart who could not be warmed into loving 'poor Armenia' after knowing an Armenian idealist."[2] By the end of her stay in Germany, Isabel was doing her best to persuade Ohannes to come to the United States to represent the Armenian church at the World Congress of Religions, which was to be part of the World's Columbian Exposition in Chicago that summer.

By the time she left Germany in April, she was writing to Ohannes regularly, addressing her letters "My beloved son" and signing them "Your loving Mayrig" (the Armenian word for "mother") and referring to her husband as *Hyrig* (Armenian for "father"). On board the *Cameo,* sailing the North Sea toward Scotland, she wrote again to urge him to come to the United States: "What would be the earliest that you could leave Leipzig if you stay for the semester? But why discuss it all again when by the time I reach Aberdeen I may hear the glad news that you are going with us." Fatigued by travel, she wrote: "[Right now] I have not energy enough to study Armenian. The very thought of it makes me giddy. Nevertheless I love my Armenian son and for his sake I will yet be able to read his mother tongue."[3]

"I felt more like weeping to think how poor you are if I am all you have, save your country," she wrote Ohannes shortly after leaving Ger-

many on that same trip. Alarmed by Ohannes's anguish over the deteriorating conditions for the Armenians, she continued:

> I am grateful for your love and your trust and wish I were more
> worthy of it. And, oh, how I wish I could do something for your
> country. But that is impossible. I can only help you to help her.
> We are all hopelessly and helplessly ignorant about Armenian
> details. You know the facts. What you must do is to acquire the
> English and German with such accuracy that you can put the
> truth in a telling way. I have often said I would help you about
> this. There is no weapon stronger than the press.[4]

It didn't take long for Isabel to learn the facts about Armenia, and
by the spring of the next year, as the news of the Sasun massacres
shocked the West, Isabel and Samuel June Barrows were involved in the
United Friends of Armenia movement in Boston. It wasn't surprising for
Isabel Barrows to urge the young Armenian divinity student to come to
the United States and be, for a short time, a son to them. For the Barrowses were among the most internationally oriented social reformers
of their time, and their devotion to public service and philanthropy was
unique. Traveling back and forth across the Atlantic by steamship for
various social causes, including prison reform in Europe and human
rights in Russia and Turkey, they were acquainted with a wide spectrum
of international problems as well as international colleagues and
friends.

Although Isabel Barrows was a trailblazing woman in the late nineteenth
century and a presence in New England culture, today she is all but forgotten. The daughter of Scottish immigrants, Katherine Isabel Hays was
born in 1845 and grew up in the small towns of Irasberg, Vermont, and
Hartland and Derry, New Hampshire, where she learned to be a compe-
tent physician's aide, accompanying her father on his medical rounds and
house calls. Her mother, Anna Gibb, was a schoolteacher, and Isabel's
childhood was never far from the reach of books. With her turned-up
nose, red curls, and Scottish burr, she rode through New England towns
on her father's medicine box in their two-wheeled carriage.[5] Raised by

progressive parents, she was initiated by her father into two professions—
stenography and ophthalmology.

By virtue of her talent at the new "science" of stenography, she was
called on in 1868 to fill in for her ill husband, June, then secretary to
William Seward, President Andrew Johnson's secretary of state (and
Abraham Lincoln's earlier). Known as "that little woman" around the
White House, she did such good work for Seward that she earned a
salary equal to any man of her rank, and it appears that she was the only
woman to earn equal pay in that world until well into the twentieth century. As Seward's stenographer and secretary, she observed the complexities of American diplomacy in the years after the Civil War. This
experience, along with her first marriage, to a missionary who took her
to India (where he died), were formative in shaping her international
interests.

Eager to complete her medical training at the new Woman's Medical
College of New York Infirmary for Women and Children, she moved to
New York City in 1869, while her husband continued his job in Washington. The Woman's Medical College had been founded by America's first
woman physician, Elizabeth Blackwell, the aunt of Alice Stone Blackwell,
to whom Isabel herself would become a surrogate aunt and mother figure
in the coming years. Later that year Isabel traveled to Austria to study
ophthalmic surgery at the University of Vienna, and then returned to
Washington to begin a private practice in ophthalmology. She was the
first woman in the nation's capital to have a private practice in medicine,
and while she was practicing, she also lectured at Howard University's
School of Medicine and ran their clinic for indigent Negroes. And to add
one more job, she worked as a stenographer for congressional committees on Capitol Hill—again, the first woman ever to do so.

By 1881 she had decided to leave Washington with her husband, who
had since graduated from Harvard Divinity School and had accepted the
post of pastor in Boston's oldest Unitarian Church, Meeting House Hill in
Dorchester. Shortly after their arrival June was asked to become the editor
of the Christian Register—the weekly organ of the Unitarian Church—and
Isabel agreed to join him in the venture as associate editor. For the next sixteen years, until June was elected to Congress, the two of them ran the
Christian Register, and with their broad humanitarian interests, which
included Native American education, education for the blind, science,

public health reform, environmental issues, and human rights, they turned the paper into one of the country's leading progressive publications.[6]

Arriving in the United States in June 1893, Ohannes Chatschumian spent several weeks in Chicago, where he represented the Armenian Apostolic Church at the World Congress of Religions. His first taste of America agreed with him, and by the end of the month he found himself eight thousand miles from his home in Russian Armenia, amid a group of reform-minded New Englanders. He was the new guest at the Barrowses' summer camp on the shore of Lake Memphremagog, just over the Maine border in the Province of Quebec. The camp was a cultural retreat where like-minded progressives gathered each year to commune with the restorative powers of the mountains and the sky, the forest and the lake. At camp, men and women shared work equally, and daily discussion groups about new books and reform-oriented ideas shaped the week's activities. No Barrows summer camp was ever without the presence of the Blackwells, who were like family to Isabel and June. From the time she was young, Alice always wrote to "Aunt Isabel" and signed her letters "your niece Alice."[7]

Perched on a peninsula of the thirty-mile lake, with a mountain known as Owl's Head rising across the water, the camp looked out on sloping sandy beaches and forests of cedar, spruce, hemlock, and birch. Into "the wild luxurious freedom" of camp life, as June Barrows called it, Ohannes arrived dressed in a white shirt and a black suit, wearing a straw hat, and carrying one worn suitcase with his life's possessions. A slight, fine-featured young man with a head of dark curly hair and a beard, his penetrating eyes and gentle smile were immediately appealing to Alice, who saw in him both a worldly graduate student and a slightly ascetic Armenian monk.[8]

Alice recalled that for the first couple of weeks, she and Ohannes couldn't speak to each other for lack of a common language, but because he had with him some copies of *L'Armenie* (a paper published in French and edited by the writer and influential public figure Professor Minas Tcheraz), she began to learn in greater detail about the worsening plight of the Armenians. A gifted linguist, Ohannes was speaking English quite well by the end of July.

Because men and women shared the housework at the Barrowses' camp, one evening, while Alice was washing dishes and Ohannes was drying them, he began to practice his English by telling her the story of the famous Battle of Avarayr—a fifth-century battle in which the now sainted Armenian general Vartan Mamigonian and his nobles were slain by the Persians (the most important martyrdom in classical Armenian history). In her journal Alice recalled the scene as if it were something out of Edith Wharton: "We were both of us so absorbed in the story that we made but slow progress with the work. Mrs. Barrows, bursting with silent laughter, watched us for some time, and finally came and took the dishes out of our hands."[9]

As Alice became captivated by Ohannes—his stories of the classical Armenian past and his knowledge of the present issues surrounding the Armenian Question—the two became inseparable. On long walks into the Canadian woods, rides in Uncle June's boat, and picnics on the beach, they talked endlessly about politics and history, literature and human liberty. Ohannes always had with him his well-worn volume of Eghishé, one of Armenia's major classical historians. Daily he would read from it aloud, translating into his newly learned English.[10]

By the beginning of August their relationship had blossomed, and conversations about the Armenian Question seemed to be inextricable from the passion between them. Amid the white pines and Douglas firs, and the cries of the loons from Lake Memphremagog, Alice Stone Blackwell—whose life had been shaped by her family's commitment to reform, especially woman suffrage—fell in love with this brilliant, handsome theology student who seemed to have dropped out of the blue from his embattled old world into her New England.

As the summer progressed, Isabel suggested that Alice and Ohannes collaborate in translating "some of Armenia's touching and beautiful poetry into English verse." Alice, who had studied English literature at Boston University and who wrote and translated poems, found it an irresistible suggestion. In her lifetime she would bring a large body of foreign poetry into English from Russian, Spanish, Hebrew, Hungarian, Armenian, and French, becoming the same sort of international presence for poetry that Henry Wadsworth Longfellow had been in the middle of the nineteenth century.

One evening after dinner, Mrs. Barrows brought Ohannes to the door of Alice's tent with pencil and paper, and left him there. (These summer camp "tents" had wooden walls and canvas roofs, were well lit with candles and kerosene lamps, and were furnished with a bed, some rustic chairs, an

Oriental throw rug, and a small table.) The two sat down and began to work on "The Tears of Araxes," a poem by one of the most popular nineteenth-century Armenian poets, Raphael Patkanian, who had died the year before.

On a summer night in a candlelit tent, "there in the woods," as Alice put it, Alice Stone Blackwell and Ohannes Chatschumian founded "a little society" they called "Friends of Armenia."[11] When they returned to Boston in the fall, Julia Ward Howe agreed to be its president, and before long Friends of Armenia expanded and became central to launching America's first international human rights movement. This movement would help define American ideas about international human rights and responsibilities, and over the next four decades it would permeate American culture. Intellectuals, politicians, businessmen, churches, civic organizations, and schoolchildren who sold ice cream and lemonade to raise money, would all work in various ways to help save the Armenians from slaughter at the hands of the Turks.

The poem they translated that night, "The Tears of Araxes," is a sentimental Victorian poem in quatrains, in which a poet talks to the great river of his nation. The Araxes flows from the Ararat Plateau, making a border today between Turkey, Armenia, and Iran, and like Mount Ararat, it is a mythic place in the Armenian landscape. In the poem a young man asks the river why it is sad and why it is not refreshed by nature and the singing shepherds and gamboling lambs. The river's answer is an allegory about the pain of political oppression and colonialism that has dominated Armenia's history.

> *My own Armenian nation*
> *Is banished far away;*
> *A godless, barbarous people*
> *Dwells on my banks today.*
>
> *Still while my sons are exiled,*
> *Shall I be sad, as now.*
> *This is my heart's deep utterance*
> *My true and holy vow.*[12]

The place where Ohannes Chatschumian found himself in that summer of 1893 could not have been more propitious. The New England

intellectual community of the 1890s—especially the one centered around
Julia Ward Howe, Isabel and June Barrows, Lucy Stone, Henry Blackwell
and Alice Stone Blackwell, William Lloyd Garrison Jr., and writer and abolitionist Thomas Wentworth Higginson—carried on the grand tradition
of New England social reform that began in the 1840s in Boston, Lexington, and Concord with Ralph Waldo Emerson, educator Horace Mann,
feminist and writer Margaret Fuller, and the prominent abolitionists
William Lloyd Garrison and Wendell Phillips. Two crucial members of
Friends of Armenia, Julia Ward Howe and William Lloyd Garrison Jr.,
were direct bridges to that era.

Julia Ward Howe and her husband had been among the inner circle of
Garrison's and Phillips's abolitionist movement, which had been Julia's
political seedtime. She and Sam had been close friends with reformers like
Mann, Fuller, and Dorothea Dix. Julia had known Garrison's son, William
Lloyd Jr., since his childhood, and the younger Garrison had been raised to
carry on his father's commitment to reform.

As leaders in the suffrage movement since its beginning in the 1850s,
Lucy Stone and Henry Blackwell had worked shoulder to shoulder with
Elizabeth Cady Stanton and Susan B. Anthony, and were close friends with
Henry Ward Beecher, Thomas Wentworth Higginson, Mary Livermore,
and the Howes for most of their lives. Devotion to human rights—to
woman suffrage, abolitionism, and now to international human rights—
was their lifetime project.

Ohannes had come to the right place at the right time, and he had so
inspired Isabel Barrows, Alice Stone Blackwell, and Julia Ward Howe that
before the summer was over Isabel and Alice had persuaded him to stay a
while longer in the United States and apply to Harvard Divinity School as
a special student for the coming year.

There were no more than ten thousand Armenians in the United States by
the middle of the 1890s, and one could say that Ohannes was a "first."
Never before had an Armenian figure appeared on the American scene
with such charisma and intelligence, such political fervor and spiritual
piety. June Barrows said that he knew no other Armenian in the United
States who had made so many friends in so short a time.[13]

Ohannes's application for admission to Harvard Divinity School reveals some facts about his life. He was born in 1869 in the mountain town of Elizavetpol, in the historic Armenian region of Nagorno Karabagh in the Russian Caucasus, and he grew up in poverty. His father, a carpenter, died when he was five, and his mother, who was from an old and wealthy family, died when he was eleven. "Through treachery," he wrote, "we lost our property. My mother 'cut the bread from her mouth,' working day and night by the fire-light, she sent me to the public school." At the age of twelve, he was the one student chosen by his town to attend college in Etchmiadzin, the seat of the Armenian church.

With about fifty dollars his brother had borrowed for him, he set out alone on foot and sometimes on horseback, "passing near Mount Ararat," he wrote, on his journey to Etchmiadzin—several hundred miles north of Elizavetpol, in the mountains. He attended the academy in Etchmiadzin, which he called "as rigorous an institution as any in Russia," and after a year in the academy, became the youngest person ever to graduate.

For the next three years Ohannes taught religion at a girls' school in Elizavetpol, wrote several religious handbooks, and began translating books from Russian into Armenian. So impressed were the people of his community that he was able to gain several patrons, and at the age of twenty he went off to begin graduate study at the University of Leipzig.[14]

In his application he informed Harvard Divinity School that he knew Russian, French, German, Greek, and English, modern and classical Armenian, and was acquainted with Hebrew, Persian, Georgian, and Slavonic. In a letter on his behalf to Professor Francis G. Peabody of the Divinity School, Alice Blackwell noted that he "began life as a barefooted peasant boy of illiterate parents" and at twenty-four was "able to read fourteen languages."[15] Isabel Barrows praised Ohannes as "high-minded," "remarkable," "lovable," and "warm in character." She went on, calling him "one of the purest, most unselfish men I have ever known."[16] Isabel reminded Professor Charles C. Everett, dean of the Divinity School, that Ohannes was a poor foreign student who "is so accustomed to simple living that he could subsist on what most Harvard students waste."[17]

As an Armenian who came of age in the Caucasus in the last decades of the nineteenth century, Ohannes had been shaped by the new cultural renaissance in Russian Armenia. During this period of cultural awakening, Armenian intellectuals in the czar's empire were most inclined to study in Moscow, St. Petersburg, Leipzig, and Berlin, and like their Russian counterparts, they discovered Marxism and socialism. The two main Armenian political organizations of the new era, the Hunchak and Dashnak Parties, were formed by Russian Armenian intellectuals of the 1880s. The Russian Armenians had been cut off from the Armenians of Persia and the Ottoman Empire since the annexation of eastern Armenia by Russia in the 1820s. In Russia an industrial elite and bourgeoisie developed among the Armenians. By the 1880s a Russian Armenian intelligentsia had emerged, and in Tiflis, which had become its center, literary and political circles formed around Grigor Artsruni's newspaper *Mshak* (The Cultivator), which espoused a moderate brand of liberal nationalism.[18]

The impact of modern social thought on the Armenian intelligentsia impelled Russian Armenians to devote their newfound ideas to help solve Armenia's political problems. As Russian Armenians became articulate opponents of political oppression, their outrage against Russian autocracy was outstripped by their commitment to social change and reform for their fellow Armenians living over the border under the Turkish yoke. It was out of this intellectual climate that Ohannes Chatschumian grew before he found himself in Boston in 1894—an eloquent spokesman for the Armenian Question.

YANKEES IN ARMENIA

M ore than a hundred years later, it may seem surprising that prominent Bostonians filled Faneuil Hall in 1894 to discuss the Armenian Question, or that Ohannes Chatschumian was greeted with such affection by a group of New England's intellectual elite. But in the late nineteenth century, Armenia resonated with Americans, and Armenian civilization held a place of fascination in the Western mind because it was an ancient culture of the Near East and the first Christian nation in the world.

American interest in the Armenian Question was inseparable from the legacy of the Protestant missionary movement, which had brought American culture, and in particular New England Protestant culture, to the Armenians of the Ottoman Empire by the second quarter of the nineteenth century. American Protestants were not the only missionaries in Turkey in the nineteenth century: Catholics and Protestants from Great Britain, France, Germany, Austria, Denmark, and other countries had found their way to the Christian interior of Anatolia, some as early as the late eighteenth century. But the American Protestant missionaries had, by the 1880s, created an organized network of institutions that surpassed those of European Christians.

The American missionary movement grew out of the Second Great Awakening that swept through the United States in the early nineteenth century; it spread with particular intensity through New England, upstate New York, and the new Ohio Territory. A Christian revival movement, the Awakening was a response to growing secularization in American life and a fear that the American Christian ethos was waning. Charles Grandison Finney, Lyman Beecher, and Samuel Hopkins were among the dynamic clergy who propelled the new wave of religious enthusiasm across the various "burned-over districts," as they came to be called, of the Northeast. At the same time enthusiasm grew for missionary work abroad.

In 1806 Samuel Mills Jr. formed the Society of Brethren, which was dedicated to foreign missions, at Williams College, and two years later he took his society to the newly founded Andover Theological Seminary, renaming it the Society of Inquiry on the Subject of Missions.[1]

The founding of Andover Theological Seminary in 1808 by the Calvinist minister Samuel Hopkins would become a bedrock of the Protestant foreign mission movement. Hopkins believed that Christian spirit and duty should inspire evangelists to convert non-Christians around the world—the essence of the missionary zeal that led Americans to Turkey in the 1830s, or as the historian Suzanne Moranian has put it, to "export Jesus and America to the 'cradle of civilization.'"[2] Within years Princeton, Yale, Dartmouth, Union, and Andover Theological Seminaries became leading forces behind the foreign missions movement, and colleges like Mount Holyoke Female Seminary, Smith, Bowdoin, Middlebury, Williams, Amherst, Hamilton, and Oberlin sent their graduates out to foreign missions, many of them in the Armenian provinces.[3]

The earliest missionaries had millennial views, and hopes that the conversion of the world to Christianity would bring about the Second Coming of Christ and thus the fulfillment of history. But it became clear to them that the Muslims of Turkey were not going to become Christian, and so most of their energy became focused on modernizing the already existing Christian cultures of the Near East and converting those who were willing to Protestantism. By 1812 the American Board of Commissioners for Foreign Missions (ABCFM) had been founded in Boston by Congregationalists and to a lesser degree Presbyterian and Dutch Reform churches, which later went out on their own. The first missions were set up in 1812 in India and in 1816 in Ceylon, and a year later, on native ground, the ABCFM began its program among the Cherokee and the Choctaw. By 1818, evangelizing the Holy Land and the Near East became a priority, and by 1819 two missionaries who were Middlebury College classmates, Levi Parsons and Pliny Fisk, shipped out for Smyrna on the western coast of Turkey.[4]

Parsons and Fisk were sent on an exploratory mission to the Ottoman Empire with the millennial hope of converting the Jews of Palestine, and then the Turks, Arabs, and the Orthodox Christians of the Near East, such as the Armenians, Greeks, Assyrians, Maronites, Nestorians, and Copts. In his send-off speech to the two young men, Samuel Worcester, a founder of Andover Theological Seminary, told Parsons and Fisk to search "from the heights of the Holy Land, and from Zion" for "variegated scenes presenting themselves on every side to Christian sensibility." The young missionaries were to ask themselves: "WHAT GOOD CAN BE DONE? and BY WHAT MEANS?"[5]

Parsons and Fisk, reporting back to Boston, noted that of all the Christians in the Ottoman Empire, the Armenians seemed among the most welcoming to the Protestant mission. In 1831 the ABCFM established missions for the Armenians in Smyrna and in Constantinople, where later that year Mr. and Mrs. William Goodell became the first American missionaries to set up shop in Turkey. Delighted with this success, the American Board soon opened missionary stations in Brusa, Trebizond, and Erzurum—part of the heartland of the historic Armenian *vilayets*, or provinces. And by 1863 Protestant missions had spread from Asia Minor and Anatolia to northern Syria and Mesopotamia. By the end of the century, the ABCFM had twelve stations and 270 outstations in Asiatic Turkey; about 150 missionaries and 114 organized churches had already made more than thirteen thousand converts to Protestantism. The missionaries taught more than sixty thousand students in their 132 high schools and eleven hundred elementary schools, and ran six colleges and various theological academies.[6]

Although the Yankee Congregationalists never lost hope of converting the Turks—who regarded Christians as *gâvur*, meaning "infidel" and "unbeliever"—when they realized that the Ottoman authorities and Turkish families punished and sometimes even killed Muslims who showed an interest in Christianity, they directed their energy toward the Armenians, the Greeks, and the Assyrians. The missionaries were further galvanized by the fact that there was already a reform movement afoot in the Armenian Apostolic Church (Armenia's original church), which, they believed, had made the ground fertile for their mission. But, for the Armenians, the missionaries created further complexity and often damage. While the Armenian church leaders were interested in improving their mother church, they were not interested in abandoning it. Thus the missionaries, with their zeal for converting Armenians to the Protestant way, became agents of divisiveness: They were often imperialistic in their attitudes at the same time as they were forces for progressive change and democratic ideas.

The clergy, and the wealthy Armenian community that often con- trolled the clergy, saw the missionaries as powerful threats to their authority. Now Armenians were often forced to choose between being Armenian Apostolic or this new thing—Armenian Protestant. In the city of Chemeshgezek, the Armenian community referred to converts as "Protes," which was a pun on "the first syllable of Protestant, but also meant leper in Armenian."[7] The missionary Henry Otis Dwight reported that the Armenian Apostolic patriarch and the wealthy class of Armeni- ans called for "the expulsion of Protestantism from the land." There were even cases of Armenian Protestant converts being imprisoned or exiled. By 1846 the Armenian patriarch was so enraged by the havoc created by the missionaries that he excommunicated all Armenian Protestant evan- gelicals. Within days his decree led to the founding of the First (Protes- tant) Evangelical Armenian Church of Constantinople.[8] Even the sultan remarked—from a slightly different vantage point—in 1847 that the American missionaries were "turning the world upside down."[9]

While the relationship between the new Protestantism and the ancient Armenian church remained tense throughout the nineteenth cen- tury, the American missionaries and the Armenian Protestants activated social change for Armenians throughout the Ottoman Empire. The mis- sionaries emphasized the importance of learning, and their educational projects included making the Bible available to the Armenian populace through translation from classical into modern Armenian. As a campaign for total literacy was essential to modernizing Armenian culture, the mis- sionaries not only established schools and colleges but promoted Sunday School, Bible study, prayer meetings, and youth organizations—all of which conveyed the democratic ideas of human liberty and individualism embodied by Protestantism.

Because many of the missionaries were women who had graduated from progressive colleges, they stressed the idea of equality for women in their educational mission and curriculum. Educating women was such a primary goal for many of the missionaries that by the later part of the nineteenth century, women's schools and colleges had cropped up in Armenian cultural centers from Constantinople to as far east as Van and Bitlis. Euphrates College at Harput, Central Turkey College in Aintab, the Girls' College and Theological Seminary at Marash, Anatolia College of Marsovan, the International College of Smyrna, and Robert College in Constantinople were some of the major institutions the missionaries created.

At Mount Holyoke, for example, women were trained for foreign missions and to crusade against the subjugation of their sex; and they were trained to be teachers. Mary Lyon, founder of Mount Holyoke Female Seminary in 1837, formulated feminist ideas about education that fueled, among other things, an interest in educating women in foreign lands, and especially Christian women who were living under the yoke of patriarchal societies.[10] Opposed to the idea of educating privileged women to be the refined wives of wealthy men, Lyon believed in training women to be independent, intellectually rigorous, and capable of professionally sustaining themselves. In the spirit of Lyon's motto—"Go where no one else will go, do what no one else will do"—her graduates were fast creating the first generation of American women teachers, many of whom went to the American West or to far parts of the world to practice their new profession. Their progressive ideas about teaching had come from Lyon's notions, some of which sound contemporary: "If you cannot teach without scolding," she wrote, "lay aside your office; let certainty rather than severity inspire dread; Never ask categorical questions that could be answered by 'yes' and 'no.' Know your students personally and sympathetically. Never let a dull pupil know that she was thought dull. Never mortify one before the others."[11]

By 1888 Mount Holyoke had sent 178 graduates to work in foreign missions, and had transported Mary Lyon's philosophy of activist education to Turkey, which meant to the Christian minorities, and most particularly the Armenians. This new force of educated women missionaries was an extraordinary aspect of what was evolving as a groundbreaking experiment in nineteenth-century education.[12] By the 1880s a network of international education had been established between elite colleges and universities in the United States and the Armenian cities and provinces of the Ottoman Empire.

The impact on Armenian life was dramatic. The missionaries chipped away at Armenian patriarchal customs in the church and family and made it possible for women to attend church services in public rather than listen to them from an adjacent chamber. And, because the missionaries trained women to become teachers, by the end of the nineteenth century most of the women teaching in Armenian elementary schools were Armenian graduates of American missionary schools.

Along with these liberal American notions, the missionaries also planted ideas about freedom of expression and justice in the face of oppression— ideas that fostered resistance to the existing structures of Ottoman author- ity, as well as pride in Armenian cultural values. As the missionary Edwin Bliss wrote in 1896: "We have no political ends to serve; we want not to square a foot of the sultan's domains. . . . But we stand, as we have always stood, for freedom for the oppressed, for the right of every man to wor- ship his God in the light of his own conscience."[13]

Activities at Robert College, the Christian college in Constantinople, reveal the impact of the new liberalism on the Christian minorities. Because Turks were generally forbidden to attend the missionary schools, the students were Christian, primarily Armenian, Bulgarian, and Greek. Among the college's official goals was the promotion "of the use of the English language and the influence of Protestant . . . and American ideas in the East."[14] In 1881 alone the college sponsored public debates on such topics as "Christianity and Patriotism," "Free Thought," "Representative Government," and "Violation of Popular Rights." George Washburn, soon to be president of Robert College, remarked, "There was certainly no other place in Constantinople where such subjects could have been publicly discussed," though he maintained that "there was nothing sedi- tious in any one of them."[15] At first the Ottoman government watched the missionaries with "a curious and nonchalant eye, and cared not a straw what particular form of worship the infidel dogs preferred,"[16] but as the progressive American influence began to vitalize Armenian society and culture, the Turks grew suspicious and finally hostile to the new reality that had been created. This would make for more complexity as the Armenian dilemma unfolded.

*   *   *

Although the missionaries had planted a vivid sense of Armenia in the American mind by the end of the nineteenth century, Europeans and Americans already had a sense of Armenia's place in Near Eastern history and Western civilization. An Indo-European civilization, Armenia emerged from Urartu, the ancient civilization that spanned eastern Anatolia and western Transcaucasia, around the sixth century B.C. In the classical period the Greek historian Herodotus, the Greek writer Xenophon, and the Persian king Darius depicted Armenia as a rugged highland culture bridging Asia Minor and Europe. English travelers to Armenia in the seventeenth century John Cartwright and John Freyer wrote about the Armenians as excellent entrepreneurs, defined by tight-knit family structures, and as a people who were keepers of both ancient Christian civilization and the Hebraic past. The eighteenth-century English historian Edward Gibbon in *The Decline and Fall of the Roman Empire* noted the prominence of the Armenian Empire under King Tigran I during the first century B.C.[17]

Certain facts about Armenia continued to be significant for European and later American intellectuals and cartographers. On maps of the Roman Empire in and around the era of Caesar's rule, Armenia is the most formidable kingdom abutting the Roman Empire on the east. At the peak of its power between about 65 and 55 B.C., Armenia extended midway across Anatolia into the Russian Caucasus, from the Black Sea to the Caspian, and encompassed what is now northernmost Iran. It was large and powerful enough for Caesar to send his generals Pompey and Lucullus to conquer it in 63 B.C. After killing the Armenian king, Tigran the Great, the soldiers of Marcus Antonius kidnapped his talented son, Artavazd II—who wrote plays in Greek and founded a Greek theater— and put him and his family to death.

For the Christian West it was of no small significance that in the early fourth century A.D. (the traditional date celebrated by the Armenian church is A.D. 301) Armenia became the first nation to adopt Christianity as its official religion. (A century later Armenia's reigning monarch commissioned the monk Mesrop Mashdots to invent an alphabet so that people who could not read Greek or Syriac would be able to read the Bible in their native language.) In the European imagination Armenia would be continuously associated with the place and landscape of the Bible. Armenia's national symbol, Mount Ararat, was the site of

God's covenant with Noah, and cartographers of the Renaissance depicted Mount Ararat, the Garden of Eden, and other sacred sites in or near Armenia.

But upholding a Christian civilization amid invading tribes from the East proved more than difficult. In the seventh century Arab tribes came from Arabia, and by the eleventh century nomadic hordes from central Asia started their journey south and west, sweeping through the lands of the Arabs, Armenians, and Byzantine Greeks. Saracens, Seljuks, Mongols, Tatars, and lastly the Ottoman Turks, who were by now predominantly Muslim, rode in by the tens of thousands. For several centuries Armenia persisted in the wake of the Turkic invasions.

In the early medieval period, from about A.D. 861 until the first attacks by the Seljuk Turks in 1064, Armenia flourished under the Bagratid dynasty, which negotiated delicate diplomacy between the Byzantines and the Muslim rulers to the east. Thus by the tenth century Armenia was socially cohesive, prosperous from its commerce and agrarian productivity, and culturally vital. Music, poetry, and architecture flourished. The most important poet of the era, Krikor Narekatsi (Gregory of Narek), anticipated Dante with his epic poem, *Book of Lamentations: Conversations with God from the Depths of My Heart.*

Armenians built hundreds of churches in the rocky highlands during this period, many of them innovative in their structure and artistically sophisticated with their decorative stone carvings and inscriptions. The city of Ani, the capital of the kingdom, was so refulgent with churches, cathedrals, and chapels that it was known as the city of a thousand and one churches.[18] Today the remains of those churches lie in ruins in Turkey, just yards from the Armenian border. (Thousands of other Armenian churches throughout Turkey also lie in ruins and are used as stables or army barracks, while others are demolished by local people or destroyed by dynamite).[19] Not far from Ani, on the island of Achtamar in Lake Van, the Church of the Holy Cross (915–21) is another monument of the Armenian imagination, with its elegantly drawn and carved iconography, bas-reliefs, and friezes.[20]

But in the eleventh century the Seljuk Turkish invasions drove a good portion of the Armenian population southwest to what came to be known as Lesser Armenia, also known as Cilician (Kilikian) Armenia, in what is now south-central Turkey. An important geopolitical zone in the European quest to recover the Holy Land, it quickly became "a symbol of Christian hope."[21] The Armenian kings of Cilicia made strong alliances with the Crusaders and the Crusader states in the Levant, and by the late twelfth century an Armenian-Frankish alliance was exerting cultural and political impact on both Armenia and Europe. Cilician Armenia was also an important trading zone from which dyes, textiles, coffee, and spices came into Europe.

The Armenian king Levon II was a close friend of King Richard I (the Lion-Hearted), who was a passionate Crusader himself, and Levon aided him in the Third Crusade. The significance of Armenia was embedded deeply enough in the cultural and political milieu of the late Middle Ages that the great English poet Geoffrey Chaucer wrote about or made allusions to Armenia in the prologue to *The Canterbury Tales* and in "The Squire's Tale," "The Man of Law's Tale," and "The Monk's Tale," as well as in *Anelida and Arcite*.[22]

The last Armenian king, Levon VI, was close to King Richard II and was involved in English court politics. In the last decades of the fourteenth century, he worked assiduously as a mediator trying to bring about peace between the French and the English in the midst of the Hundred Years' War.[23] When Cilician Armenia was destroyed by the Muslim Mamluks in 1375, it became an emblem of the failure of European Christianity to save its "Eastern brothers." Philippe de Mézières, the fourteenth-century French diplomat and writer, described the fall of Armenia as "a great disgrace to all of Christianity."[24] It was a statement that would foreshadow the European and American concern for Armenia in the early twentieth century.

In May 1453 the Ottoman Turks brought down the Byzantine Empire, sacking Constantinople, which they made the seat of the new Ottoman Empire. After this the Armenians of Anatolia lived in a complex relationship with their new Muslim rulers. Like the other non-Muslims of the empire, the Armenians were legally designated "infidels" and subjected to a set of oppressive social and political rules that would remain at the center of the Armenian Question when it finally emerged more than four hundred years later.

The imprint of Armenia deepened in the nineteenth century. Lord Byron—who later fought and died in the Greek War for Independence, and was a champion of the Christians living under Ottoman rule—spent 1817 studying and learning classical Armenian at the Armenian monastery on the island of San Lazzaro in Venice. So passionately did he feel about Armenia that he wrote:

> If the Scriptures are rightly understood, it was in Armenia that Paradise was placed—Armenia, which has paid as dearly as the descendants of Adam for that fleeting participation of its soil in the happiness of him who was created from its dust. It was in Armenia that the flood first abated, and the dove alighted. But with the disappearance of Paradise itself may be dated almost the unhappiness of the country; for though long a powerful kingdom, it was scarcely ever an independent one, and the satraps of Persia and the pachas of Turkey have alike desolated the region where God created man in his own image.[25]

In the United States the bard of the new age, Walt Whitman, attuned to the mythic power of ancient Armenia, allotted the Armenians one of the more extensive meditations in his poem to the peoples of the world, "Salut au Monde":

> *You thoughtful Armenian pondering by some stream of the*
> *Euphrates! you peering amid the ruins of Nineveh!*
> *you ascending mount Ararat!*[26]

Whitman envisioned Armenia in the same geocultural realm as Greece, Egypt, and Syria and located the Armenians on their native homeland of 2,500 years. Defining Armenia by iconic landmarks of Western civilization, including the Armenian national symbol, Mount Ararat, the poet sees the Armenians amid the debris of historical struggle ("the ruins of Nineveh") but also creates a hopeful image—"ascending" the great mountain.

To Americans of the 1890s, then, the Armenians were a Christian people who had survived on the battleground of empires for centuries and were known for their endurance. As the first Christian nation and the easternmost indigenous Christian culture in the world, the Armenians held a unique place in the American mind. As a Bible land civilization that was now in need of rescue (as it had been in the late fourteenth century), Armenia was an inspiring reminder of the continuity and typology of the Judeo-Christian tradition as it evolved from its origins in the Near East through Europe and then to the Puritan wilderness of New England.

While Armenians in the late nineteenth century were in the middle of a cultural revival on their own terms, rediscovering their history and creating a new body of literature and music, the American missionaries remained an important force in this renaissance. In the end the Protestant missionaries embodied the dual nature of imperialist attitudes. Fiercely proud of doing God's work in the wilderness, they brought beneficial change and reform to the Armenians. Yet they were arrogant about their superior role in the so-called backward parts of the world, and too often oblivious to the dangerous situation they were creating for the people they were so dedicated to helping. That paradoxical situation would unravel in increasingly tragic and ironic ways as the fate of the Armenians became bound up in the power struggles surrounding President Wilson's foreign policy during and after World War I. But in the 1890s, as Armenian relief movements sprang up around Turkey, the missionaries were working day and night to help the Armenians.

THE SULTAN AND THE

ARMENIAN QUESTION

THE ARMENIAN QUESTION

At the end of the nineteenth century, Sultan Abdul Hamid II had become the most notorious despot known to the Western world. (The brutality of Belgian king Leopold II's treatment of the Africans in the Congo had not yet come to full public awareness.) The "Bulgarian horrors," and the sultan's policy of wholesale massacre of the Armenians between 1894 and 1896 led Prime Minister William Ewart Gladstone and the press in Great Britain to refer to him as "the bloody Sultan" and "the great assassin," while the French press and President Georges Clemenceau denounced him as *"le Sultan rouge"* and *"Monstre de Yildiz."* Not only was the sultan making headlines in the Western press, but dozens of cartoons condemning him and his ruthless policies appeared in the British magazine *Punch* in the 1890s and on into the early years of the twentieth century.

By 1890, Arminius Vambery reported, the one issue that obsessed Abdul Hamid more than any other was Armenia. In his memoir Vambery recalled a night at Yildiz Palace, when he and the sultan were peacefully sipping their after-dinner coffee; the sultan suddenly turned to him with a look of cold determination and said, "I tell you, I will soon settle those Armenians. I will give them a box on the ear which will make them smart and relinquish their revolutionary ambitions." The remark upset Vambery, who wrote later that by "this 'box on the ear,' he meant the massacres which soon after were instituted. The Sultan kept his word."[1]

Sir Edwin Pears—the distinguished British writer and journalist who had lived in Constantinople since the 1870s—noted that "the very name of Armenia" had become "anathema" to the sultan. "He had long since given orders that it should never be employed in the newspapers, and the order had to be strictly obeyed. By an imperial decree Armenia ceased to exist."[2] He closed Armenian schools on the slightest pretext and prohibited the entry into the empire of any books that mentioned Armenia or that dealt with its history. Armenian teachers, in particular, were loathed and were constantly arrested without reason, imprisoned without trials, tortured, and often killed. Clarence Ussher, an American physician and missionary who went to the Armenian provinces in 1899, upon entering the country was searched by Ottoman customs officials who confiscated his dictionary because it contained the words "liberty" and "revolution," and who then proceeded to cut the maps out of his Bible because the name "Armenia" appeared on them.[3] So pathological was the sultan's obsession with expunging the name of Armenia from public consciousness that he demanded that the State of Massachusetts change the name of the missionary college in Harput from Armenia College, and so it became Euphrates College.[4]

There is speculation that the Armenian Question was even more complex for the sultan because it was rumored that his mother was Armenian. Her name was Pirimujan. A former dancer who was only nineteen when he was born, she has been referred to as either Circassian or Armenian. Further mystery was added to the circumstances of his birth when it took the harem officials three days of record checking to verify his mother's identity. For the rest of her short life, Pirimujan was assiduously ignored by Hamid's father, Sultan Mejid. The young prince, who was close to his mother, watched her slowly die of consumption, and after her death, when he was seven, he fell into inconsolable grief. Some said he had an Armenian-looking face, but Abdul Hamid always denied vigorously that he had any "Armenian blood in his veins."[5]

In the last two decades of the nineteenth century, the Armenian Question emerged as an international issue. The Armenian Question had grown out of the Ottoman reform movement known as Tanzimat, meaning the restructuring of Ottoman society. Two Tanzimat reform acts, in 1839 and 1856, proposed constitutional and social change within the Ottoman Empire. Among the serious problems with which the Tanzimat reforms grappled were the issues of more equitable treatment for the non-Muslim minorities, which were discriminated against at every social and political level.

The Ottoman scholar Roderick Davison has noted that the 1839 imperial edict, Hatt-i Sherif of Gulhane, made an official declaration of equality for all the nationalities of the empire; and the Hatt-i Hümayan of 1856 promised equal opportunity in the administration of justice, taxation, military service, education, and government appointments. In short it promised to end prejudice and discrimination against non-Muslims.[6] Understandably the Armenians were encouraged by these Tanzimat proclamations. Correspondingly, between 1850 and 1870, the Armenian patriarch sent 537 notes to the Sublime Porte (office of the grand vizier) requesting and often pleading for protection from the daily abuses of violence and social and political injustice to which Armenians were subject. The patriarch asked for his people's protection from brigandage, murder, abduction and rape of women and children, confiscatory taxes, and fraud and extortion by local officials.[7]

In certain salient ways the Armenian reform movement was also inseparable from the tangle of Russo-Turkish relations that were so flammable in the nineteenth century that four Russo-Turkish Wars broke out (1806–12, 1828–29, 1853–56, and 1876–77). While the wars were bound up in national struggles for control and domination of strategic areas in the Balkans, along the Black Sea, and in the Caucasus, the plight of the Christians under Ottoman rule also figured into Russia's concern for its coreligionists across the border.

When the Russians went to war in 1853 in the Crimea—a peninsula jutting into the northern Black Sea—part of their justification was to protect the Ottoman Christians, and to settle a secondary squabble about whether the Latin church or the Greek would have the right to protect holy sites in Palestine. France and Sardinia, both Roman Catholic countries, joined the Ottoman Empire against Russia. Because Prime Minister Benjamin Disraeli could not abide the thought of Russian encroachment into Turkey, British forces also joined the war on the Turkish side.

After three years of bloodshed, the British had helped the Ottoman army to win.

Following the Crimean War, the Russians were forbidden from protecting the Armenians in Turkey, and the Armenians stayed within the realm of the sultan's "own sovereign will." The Hatt-i Hümayan was inserted into the peace treaty, thus promising more equitable treatment of Christian subjects, prohibiting mistreatment and discrimination against them. It also explicitly forbade the major powers "either collectively or individually" from interfering in relations between the sultan and his subjects.

But continual struggles between Turkey and Russia brought them to war again in 1877–78. This Russo-Turkish War was inspired by a Russian freedom cry for the subject peoples of Eastern Europe, who were predominantly Christian, and who were seeking more autonomy from Ottoman rule. The Greeks had already broken free of Ottoman rule in 1832, and now the Balkan nationalities felt that they too had the right to free themselves from oppressive Ottoman rule. In 1876 Serbia and Montenegro joined Bosnia and Herzegovina in seeking independence, and a year later Bulgaria too rebelled. Ottoman reprisals against Bulgarians— which took the lives of more than fifteen thousand innocent people—were well covered in the British press and brought outcries across England against the "Bulgarian horrors" and against entering another war on the side of Turkey.[8]

Czar Alexander II, who saw himself as a Christian liberator, called the Sublime Porte "immovable in its categorical refusal of every effectual guarantee for the security of its Christian subjects." The czar invoked "the blessing of God" upon his armies as he ordered them to "cross the frontier of Turkey" on April 24, 1877.[9] The Russians defeated the Turks quickly, making extraordinary gains. By the terms of a preliminary armistice, signed by the Turks in January 1878 in order to prevent the Russians from marching on Constantinople, Bulgaria was to be autonomous; Montenegro, Romania, and Serbia independent; and Bosnia and Herzegovina to have autonomous administrations.

Russian gains were considerable in the East as well, and the Russian army now occupied the heavily populated Armenian territories including Kars, Ardahan, and Batum, and as far west as Khorasan. For the Armenians the peace treaty signed at San Stefano, near Constantinople, in March

1878 offered brightening prospects: Article 16 stated that Russian troops would evacuate the Armenian provinces they were occupying once the Sublime Porte implemented "the improvements and reforms demanded by local requirements in the provinces inhabited by Armenians, and to guarantee their security from Kurds and Circassians."[10]

But the Turks were angry over their losses in the Treaty of San Stefano and appealed to the British to intervene. Lord Salisbury, Disraeli's foreign secretary, was sympathetic to the sultan's request and demanded that Russo-Turkish issues be settled by the European powers. In Salisbury's mind the Russian gains were a threat to Europe and in particular to British interests in the Near East and Asia. He was particularly hostile to the Russian gains in the Armenian territories because European trade that passed from Trebizond to Persia would now be subject to Russian governmental jurisdictions. With commercial and political interests at stake, Salisbury and Disraeli insisted that a new treaty be drawn up at a congress that would meet in Berlin later the same year.

The Treaty of Berlin returned thirty thousand square miles of territory and 2.5 million Europeans to the sultan's administration. Disraeli managed to have article 16 of the Treaty of San Stefano nullified and reversed, ironically, by article 61 of the new Treaty of Berlin. Article 61 authorized the return of just two Armenian provinces, with neither Russian forces nor an organization of European militia remaining there to protect the Armenians. Article 61 in fact contained the identical reasoning of the earlier Hatt-i Hümayan reforms, which put the very sultan who had been abusing the Armenians in charge of protecting them from himself— a classic case of having the fox guard the henhouse. Disraeli agreed to establish British consulates in the region to try to restrain the Turks, and after signing the treaty, the Sublime Porte disclosed "to the amazement of the delegates" that it was giving Cyprus, which happened to be populated mostly by Greeks, to England.[11]

Notwithstanding the success of Turkish pressure on Great Britain to reverse the Treaty of San Stefano, the fact remained that in the aftermath of the Russo-Turkish War, the treatment of the Armenians had been made an international issue. Not only Russia but the other European powers were to oversee the Armenian reforms. An angry Abdul Hamid II now referred to European concern and demands for the improvement of life for the Armenians as "the everlasting persecutions and hostilities of the

Christian world."[12] Consequently, in the period after 1878, social and political conditions for the Armenians in the Ottoman Empire grew worse;
and the question of what it meant to be a Christian and an Armenian in
the Ottoman Empire grew more acute.

The French ambassador to Turkey, Paul Cambon, assessed the Armenian plight:

> The masses simply yearned for reforms, dreaming only of a nor-
> mal administration under Ottoman rule. . . . The inaction of the
> Porte served to vitiate the good will of the Armenians. The
> reforms have not been carried out. The exactions of the officials
> remained scandalous and justice was not improved . . . from one
> end of the Empire to the other, there is rampant corruption of
> officials, denial of justice and insecurity of life. . . . The Armenian
> diaspora began denouncing the administrative misdeeds, and in
> the process managed to transform the condition of simple admin-
> istrative ineptness into one of racial persecution.[13]

INFIDEL STATUS IN THE OTTOMAN EMPIRE

From the time they first came under Ottoman rule in the fourteenth century, the Armenians as Christian subjects were designated under Ottoman
law as *dhimmi*—that is, non-Muslim subjects living under the protection of
the Muslim Turkish ruling order—and were ostracized as *gâvur*. By the
eighteenth century the Turks had organized the Armenians, as a conquered people, into communities known as *millets*, and within the *millets*,
the Armenians had permission for limited self-governance. They were
allowed to run their communities' internal affairs, such as the institutions
of marriage and inheritance, and the building of schools and hospitals. But
the payback for this autonomy was often severe, and the arrangement of
being protected as *dhimmi* has been described by one historian as closer to
racketeering.[14]

Perhaps nothing was so discriminatory as the fact that Christians and
Jews had almost no legal rights in Turkey's pre-Tanzimat Muslim society.
While Armenians had courts and prisons for their own communities and
could conduct civil cases for conflicts between a Christian and a Muslim,

an Armenian had no recourse in the Islamic court system. A Muslim could apply to have his case heard in the religious court (the *sheriat mehkeme*), but there non-Muslim testimony was either disallowed or accorded significantly less value. A Muslim need only swear on the Koran and the case was settled. In this way the deck was powerfully stacked against the Armenians and all other *dhimmi*. The amount of theft and extortion, as well as rape and abduction of Armenian women, that was allowed under this Ottoman legal system placed the Armenians in perpetual jeopardy.

Armenians were made vulnerable by other policies that often rendered them incapable of defending themselves. They were not allowed to own weapons, which made them easy prey for Turks and Kurds. Since only Muslims were allowed to join the army to defend Islam, Christians were exempt from military service; if this spared them from warfare, it also kept them out of positions of military power and removed them from the warrior class, with its knowledge and skills. Notwithstanding all that, Christians were also subjected to what was known as boy collection or *devshirme,* which meant that Ottoman officials would take children from their Christian families, convert them to Islam, and put them to work in the Ottoman military and civil service.[15]

The Ottoman system of taxation further burdened and exploited Christian subjects. The Armenians and other Christians, along with Muslim peasants, were subjected to the tax-farming system—a system in which the right to collect taxes was sold to the highest bidder, who then farmed out the actual collection duties to an array of underlings, which resulted in corruption and extortion. Christians also were forced to pay a special head or poll tax, which was later converted into a military exemption tax to compensate for their exemption from the service. Armenians paid a "hospitality tax" to the *vali* (governor) that entitled "government officials, and all who pass as such," to free lodging and food for three days a year in an Armenian home.

Another burden solely for the Armenians was the *kishlak,* or winter-quartering obligation, which enabled Kurds and Turks to quarter themselves, their families, and their cattle in Armenian homes during the long winter months. The fact that the Kurdish way of life was nomadic and rough and the Armenian dwellings did not allow for much privacy made the intrusion unbearable, and knowing that the unarmed Armenians had

neither physical nor legal recourse, a well-armed Kurd or Turk could not
only steal his host's possessions but could rape or kidnap the women and
girls of the household with impunity. The *dhimmi* were also required to
follow institutionalized codes of behavior. Armenians, for example, had to
be deferential before Muslims in public; they could not ride a horse when
a Muslim was passing by; they were to wear dress that made them easily
identifiable; they were forbidden to own weapons.[16]

In a basic way the lives of the Armenians were in the capricious hands
of the ruling *vali*, feudal lords, or tribal chieftains, who, if they chose,
could exert a degree of control over the local Muslim populations. Thus in
one province, under a relatively kindhearted *vali*, the Armenians might
have a period of respite, while in another their fate could be exceptionally
cruel—as in districts such as Afyon Karahisar, where the ruling official had
at one time decreed that an Armenian could speak his native language
only at the risk of having his tongue cut out, so generations of Armenians
learned to speak only Turkish.[17]

In the late nineteenth century, with much encouragement from the
sultan, the authorities in the eastern provinces also allowed the collection
of illegal levies; official tax collectors would come around a second time
insisting that the taxes had never been paid, or the Kurdish chieftains
would impose taxes, claiming they were representing the central government. In addition the Turkish chieftains demanded protection money to
prevent their people from attacking and kidnapping Armenian women,
and when two Kurdish clans were at odds, or claimed to be, the chiefs of
each side demanded payment to protect the Armenians from the other.
The Armenians were well aware that these were not taxes at all—
although they passed as such—but outright extortion.

The British vice-consul stationed in Adana, P. H. Massy, put it perceptively:

> The Armenian population is everywhere oppressed by a system
> of government which takes from them the means of circulating
> freely, of earning a livelihood, and of enjoying a feeling of secu-
> rity to life and property, even on the most frequented highway.
> Taxes are levied without mercy, even from the poorest. The pris-
> ons are filled with innocent men, who lie there for months with-
> out trial.[18]

The British ethnographer William Ramsay—who spent more than a decade in Turkey doing fieldwork and was fond of the Turks—described what it meant to be an infidel:

> Turkish rule . . . meant unutterable contempt. . . . The Armenians (and the Greeks) were dogs and pigs . . . to be spat upon, if their shadow darkened a Turk, to be outraged, to be the mats on which he wiped the mud from his feet. Conceive the inevitable result of centuries of slavery, of subjection to insult and scorn, centuries in which nothing that belonged to the Armenian, neither his property, his house, his life, his person, nor his family, was sacred or safe from violence—capricious, unprovoked violence— to resist which by violence meant death.[19]

At the heart of the problem—whether in the Balkans or in the Armenian provinces of the east—was the legal, political, and social status of Christians in the Ottoman Empire. On one front the fundamental question was: Can a Christian be the equal of a Muslim? The question was raised again and again by the Christian minorities and by the European powers, and in the end the answer from the Ottoman ruling elite was a resounding no. And the Armenians, as well as the Assyrians and the Greeks, all paid dearly for that answer.

ARMENIANS RESPOND

In the aftermath of 1878, as Armenian frustration grew, a new Armenian activism emerged. Because article 61 of the Berlin treaty was an obvious hollow clause, Armenian expectations for reform were dashed and, in fact, conditions grew worse. With the Treaty of Berlin signed and sealed, Abdul Hamid felt emboldened to send masses of Muslim refugees (*muhajirs*), whom the Russo-Turkish wars had driven from the Balkans and the Caucasus, into eastern Anatolia. This led to open violence against the Armenians—as murdering, looting, and pillaging were sanctioned. Enraged that the Armenian Question had become an international issue, the sultan by 1890 had created the *Hamidiye,* a well-trained force made up of Kurds whom he armed and had clothed in distinctive uniforms.

Hamidiye regiments were responsible only to the sultan and were fanatically loyal to him.[20]

In forming the *Hamidiye* (literally, "belonging to Hamid") regiments the sultan could both control the unruly Kurds and at the same time use them to deal with the Armenians as he wished. The lands over which the Kurdish nomads roamed bordered on and often dovetailed with those of the Armenian peasants, whom the Kurds resented for their relative prosperity. It was the old scheme of divide and conquer.

Thrown back into misrule and wanton violence, Armenians began to take matters into their own hands. Even at the time of the Treaty of Berlin, the Armenians had eagerly, even if naively, sent a delegation to Berlin, headed by the venerated and popular former archbishop, Mugerditch Khirmian (known affectionately to the Armenian people as Khirmian Hairig—Father Khirmian). The Armenian delegation hoped to secure some agreements for security of life and property and some governance reform. Khirmian Hairig and his delegation were ignored as they stood outside the conference hall in Berlin. When the Armenian delegation read article 61 of the new Treaty of Berlin, which declared that the Sublime Porte would carry out "improvements and reforms" in the Armenian provinces, they were furious about the hollow clause and wrote a formal protest, boldly stating that the Armenians had "been deceived" and that "their rights [had] not been recognized."[21] On returning home Archbishop Khirmian gave a sermon in the Armenian Cathedral in Constantinople and expressed his sense of betrayal over what had happened in Berlin. In short, he likened the peace conference to a "big cauldron of Liberty Stew," into which the big nations dipped "iron ladles" for real results, while the Armenian delegation had but a "Paper Ladle."

"Ah, Dear Armenian people," Khirmian said, "could I have dipped my Paper Ladle in the cauldron it would sog and remain there! Where guns talk and sabers shine, what significance do appeals and petitions have?"[22]

In Turkish Armenia the rising tide of progressive ideas about liberty, human rights, and equality came both from the Armenian intellectuals in Russia and from a long-standing intellectual relationship with Europe and its Enlightenment. Western ideas had come to Armenians either in the course of travel or study in Europe, if their families were well-to-do, or because they had been educated at one of the many American Protestant schools in Anatolia, where they were instilled with the egalitarian ideas of the American Revolution.

But the formation of three political parties gave voice to Armenian aspirations in ways that were unprecedented for them and their Turkish rulers. The fall of 1885 saw the founding of the Armenakan Party in Van— that Armenian cultural center near the Russian border. It was a secret society and had its first meetings literally underground in a burrow used for pressing grapes. The party espoused self-defense in the face of violence, and it affirmed Armenia's right to self-rule, trusting that the European Powers would eventually come to Armenia's aid. More vociferous and centralized was the Hunchak Party, founded in 1887 by a group of Russian Armenians in Geneva. A socialist party with a strong Marxist orientation, its members believed that a new and independent Armenia would initiate a worldwide socialist revolution.[23]

By the summer of 1890, Dashnaktsutiun (Armenian Revolutionary Federation) was founded in Tiflis. Dedicated to a revolutionary struggle for Armenian advancement and freedom, this third party evolved into a more nationalist platform that involved a commitment to engage in armed struggle in the face of wholesale violence and oppression; eventually it would become the best known and most controversial of the three.[24]

As the political parties evolved so did civic protest. In the summer of 1890 in Erzurum, about two hundred Armenians met in the cathedral yard to draw up a petition to protest the conditions under which Armenians were living throughout the empire. The police interrupted the rally and before long an Ottoman battalion was dispatched to Erzurum. Before it was over, the Armenian quarter was attacked and looted, and there were more than a dozen dead and 250 wounded. A month later in Constantinople, Armenians demonstrated outside their cathedral in the Kum Kapu section of the city, and again violence broke out between the police, some soldiers, and the Armenian demonstrators. Of the fracas that followed, the British ambassador, Sir William White, noted what seemed to him the historical importance of the occasion by referring to it as "the first occasion since the conquest of Constantinople by the Turks on which Christians have dared resist soldiers in Stamboul."[25]

By 1893 Armenian activists were placing *yaftas*—placards—on the public walls of certain towns in western and central Anatolia. The placards were addressed to Muslims around the world asking them to stand up to the sultan, an incompetent oppressor. Instead of instigating Muslim rebellion, however, the plan, which had come from Hunchak cells throughout Anatolia, instigated a mass of arbitrary arrests and torture across the empire. Nonetheless, by the early nineties the Armenians were making themselves heard, which further enraged the already paranoid sultan.[26]

The Armenian Question was received by a sultan who—notwithstanding his cunning—was mentally unstable.[27] The Armenian quest for reform also dovetailed with the rule of a sultan whose empire was collapsing at an accelerating pace, causing him and his empire a crisis of self-esteem. The Ottoman Empire had been dubbed the "sick man of Europe" in the middle of the nineteenth century, when Sultan Abdul Aziz escalated the empire's plunge into debt with a decadence and profligacy that had become scandalous. Now his nephew Abdul Hamid plunged his empire deeper into crisis. Under Hamid's reign the debt grew worse, misgovernment and political corruption became further institutionalized, and the condition of his subject peoples, particularly the Christians, grew disastrous. "In one of the worst periods of his reign," Sir Edwin Pears wrote, "one of the ablest of his Ministers remarked that if Abdul Hamid could be removed better government could be secured for the Empire."[28]

As the state of the empire and the state of the sultan were tightly intertwined, Abdul Hamid's paranoia had a profound and complex impact on the infrastructure of his empire. His residence in Constantinople was an apt emblem of that entanglement. After his ascension to power in 1876, the sultan began building a fortress and a maze around himself. Having moved permanently to Yildiz Palace overlooking the Bosporus, he appropriated contiguous houses and grounds for miles, including two Christian cemeteries, and built a rambling patchwork of gardens and high walls around him. On every vantage point he then built a chalet or a kiosk fully furnished for sleeping, and had powerful telescopes installed in each so his guards could survey the outside world.[29]

Against a second large encircling wall he ensconced his imperial guards in barracks, making Yildiz a kind of arsenal. He assembled a private, self-contained world inside the walls that included a farm, a small artificial lake, stables, workshops, a menagerie, and an aviary. With the women of his harem and his servants, there were about five thousand people in residence, along with another seven thousand men in the Imperial Guard.[30] A police office and a prison were in operation close to the palace grounds, and as Edwin Pears put it, "There can be no reasonable doubt that many persons suffered tortures for offences committed in and around Yildiz, for the details given of these horrors are too many and too detailed not to have in them a large amount of truth."[31]

An early riser, the sultan had a simple breakfast, after which he devoted himself to the reports of his spies, who were part of an enormous surveillance network he had created to keep tabs on things. Deeply superstitious, he took advice from fortunetellers and soothsayers, one of whom had told him when he was a young man that he would come to his death from cholera or poison unless he drank from one pure spring at Kiat-hane, which he did every day for the rest of his life.[32]

Apart from being a heavy smoker and coffee drinker, Abdul Hamid was, unlike his predecessors, frugal and almost austere in his habits and meals. He preferred a good pilaf and stuffed squash and cucumber to the elaborate concoctions prepared by his Greek chef. Yet, however simple his food, the most elaborate precautions were taken in its preparation. His special kitchens had barred windows and iron doors. Before it was served, each dish had to be tasted by the chief chamberlain, Osman Bey, whose title was Superintendent of the Kitchens and Guardian of the Sultan's Health and Life.[33] The sultan's meals were transported from the kitchens to Little Mabeyn, the tightly guarded kiosk adjoining the palace that was now his private apartment. Then two officials in gold-embroidered uniforms wheeled a trolley holding the imperial dinner service. Covered with a black cloth, a second trolley held the various dishes on an enormous silver tray. A lackey followed carrying a covered bread basket, and last came the water carrier, bearing a sealed bottle of water from the springs of Kiat-hane.[34]

His staff lived in fear of him. He was an insomniac for whom his physician's sedatives seemed not to work. He often dismissed—long before dawn—the harem woman who was to share his bed on a given night, and the palace eunuchs reported seeing him wandering from room to room inspecting various couches to sleep on. He kept a gold-and-mother-of-pearl pistol in his pocket and had been known to fire spontaneously on anyone if startled: A palace gardener was shot dead when he inadvertently surprised the sultan, who thought he was alone in a secluded part of the

garden. A little slave girl who had strayed from her mother and was playing with one of the jeweled firearms she'd found in the palace was killed
on the spot.[35] As one historian put it, the "entire Hamidian system had but
one aim: the security of the Sultan himself."[36]

From the start, as historian Bernard Lewis has noted, the sultan was "bitterly hostile" to constitutional ideas and reform.[37] In the aftermath of the
treaties of San Stefano and Berlin, when constitutional reform was being
urged by the Europeans and by liberal forces within Turkey, the newly
installed sultan grew angry and intransigent. In short, "He hated the very
word 'constitution' and everyone who approved of it."[38]

The idea of reforms for the Armenians was part of the sultan's aver-
sion to change. The British ambassador in Constantinople, Sir Henry
Layard, a Disraeli appointee and a Turcophil, worked hard to get the sultan to implement the proposed reforms for Armenia but came to see that
his efforts were futile. When Gladstone's Liberal Party came to power in
1880, there was an outcry to recall Ambassador Layard because of his failure to negotiate reforms for the Armenians and other Christians in the
empire. The sultan was delighted because he believed he had won a victory over Great Britain—a country which he was coming to despise, in
large part because of its concern for the Armenians.[39] But, in assiduously
ignoring the efforts of the European powers to implement article 61 of
the Treaty of Berlin—and in ignoring the demand for constitutional government by disbanding parliament after one session and in dismissing his
most able and reform-minded minister, the grand vizier, Midhat Pasha—
Abdul Hamid made it clear that his reign would be autocratic. In 1880
one British official summed it up: "There is less security for life and property; poverty has increased, while crimes of oppression and corruption
have increased proportionately with the impoverished state of the
Empire."[40]

A protomodern autocrat in some sense, the sultan was attracted to
those aspects of modernization that would facilitate his power and control. He saw in the railroad and the telegraph powerful tools for central-
izing his authority more efficiently. His pragmatic interests in education
were, in part, motivated by his fear that, due to the impact of the missionary colleges on the Armenian, Greek, and Assyrian populations, his

Christian subjects were far outstripping the Muslim majority. Thus he promoted professional (meaning for the professions) education for the Muslim elite.[41]

But the sultan's response to the new age of information also bordered on the absurd. He declared numerous words and subjects taboo and illegal. Beyond his strict censorship of all words and references to Armenia, he ordered a ban on any form of expression that referred to regicide or the murders of heads of state. The name of the deposed Sultan Murad V was banned; the king and queen of Serbia were reported to have died of indigestion; Empress Elizabeth of Austria was said to have died of pneumonia, French president Carnot of apoplexy, and President William McKinley of anthrax.[42] In his fear of his non-Turkish subjects, he outlawed all historic Anatolian geographic names, at the center of which was the name *Armenia,* whose use was also forbidden in the press.[43] So far did his paranoia carry him that he ordered his censors to expunge all references to H_2O from science textbooks because he feared the symbol would be read as meaning "Hamid the second is nothing."[44]

The French writer Paul Fesch in 1907 summed up the state of the press under the sultan: "For thirty years the press has ceased to exist in Turkey. There are indeed newspapers, many of them even, but the scissors of censorship cut them in so emasculating a manner that they no longer have any potency. If I dare, I would call them gelded newspapers—or rather, to keep the local color, eunuchs."[45] Correspondingly, intellectual expression and book publishing were also under strict censorship.[46]

It is not surprising, then, that Armenian political activism was met with rage by the sultan. Anyone suspected of sedition—which meant a genuine part of the population, in a society that was enveloped in the sultan's network of espionage and surveillance—was arrested, tortured, killed, or exiled. It was in this climate that a group of liberal Turkish intellectuals and politicos known as the Young Turks created a movement that demanded reform and constitutional government. As it grew in power, Abdul Hamid did what he could to tighten the muzzle on all political opposition. But the empire-wide corruption and the sultan's own paranoia had corroded even the military, so that what was supposed to be the army of the sultan's protection became the seat of discontent and the seed ground for the Young Turk movement.

Since the army was a "police force" designed to maintain "control of the Turkish overlords over their subject peoples,"[47] the sultan's loss of control of it would have consequences for the Armenians as well—ironically, not positive ones. Caught between his "desire to maintain a strong army and the fear of allowing it to become too powerful," the sultan let his army deteriorate. Pay for soldiers and officers was so poor and conditions for the men so harsh that bribery and other forms of corruption became part of Ottoman army life. Because the sultan had subjected the army to his surveillance system, soldiers found ways of gaining advancement by framing their fellow soldiers. By the end of the century, small mutinies riddled army life throughout the empire, and dislike of the sultan was so rampant that, as one historian put it, "it was difficult to find a Turkish officer in all European Turkey who was not pledged to overthrow the government he served."[48] Similarly, the navy was in disrepair because the sultan let the ships founder where they were moored in the Golden Horn below his palace. While he was nervous to be out of sight of his guns, he was also afraid of his ships having guns. Thus when new ships were acquired, he often ordered parts of them to be dismantled and often had the ammunition removed from the vessels.[49]

Afraid of his military forces and obsessed with the growing unrest among his subjects, the sultan continued to enlarge the *Hamidiye* as the political tensions of the 1890s unfolded. As he sent his special army into the trouble spots of the empire, the Armenian provinces became the top priority. The British consul Charles Hampsun, reporting from Erzurum in the winter of 1891, disclosed something of the impact of the *Hamidiye* on the Armenians:

> The measure of arming the Kurds is regarded with great anxiety here. This feeling is much increased by the conduct of the Kurds themselves, many of whom openly state that they have been appointed to suppress the Armenians, and that they have received assurances that they will not be called to answer before the tribunals for any acts of oppression committed against Christians.
>
> The Armenians in this town are very uneasy, and very many of those who are in a position to be able to do so have expressed their intention of leaving Erzerum as soon as the roads are open.[50]

While the *Hamidiye* made the sultan feel more secure, the Armenians in the interior were now living under their impact, as the troops pillaged, looted, and terrorized the region. At the end of 1892 a British military attaché reported that there were thirty-three *Hamidiye* regiments, each with five hundred men, and that more were being formed under a new commander, Zeki Pasha, who would play an important role in the empire-wide massacres of the Armenians that were only a few years away.[51]

KILLING FIELDS:

THE MASSACRES OF THE 1890s

*I asked no privileges for them, but simple justice between man
and man.*

—Lord Salisbury

I t was in the region of Sasun that the simmering cauldron of Armenian frustration finally boiled over. There in the remote highlands of the eastern plateau, the Armenians had finally had enough of tax fleecing and extortion by the *vali* and enough of Kurdish winter quartering in their homes—which often brought with it the rape and abduction of the women of the house—and they decided that it was time to protest for tax reform.

The landscape of the Armenian highlands of the Sasun region in eastern Turkey has been compared by nineteenth-century travelers to that of Montenegro in the Balkans. Frequent earthquakes in both regions had in prehistoric times thrown up a series of high-ridged mountains and deep valleys, which created dramatic views for those brave enough to reach them. Numerous ancient Armenian villages, overseen by Kurdish tribal chieftains, dotted these valleys, while the larger cities of Bitlis (the capital of the *vilayet*) and Moush flanked the Sasun Plain on the east and north respectively. Less than fifty miles east of Bitlis, Lake Van lay, with its scores of Armenian villages and the ancient Armenian city of Van on its eastern shore.

Sasun, and the larger Moush Plain around it, was a place where Armenians had lived for more than two millennia,[1] and in the late nineteenth century they made up close to half the population of the region. In winter, when even the rough footpaths might be covered with snow, it would have been nearly impossible to travel in the region other than on foot. In the spring the hills and valleys were thick with fig, mulberry, and walnut trees, oaks and willows, and grapevines. The abundant streams eventually gathered to join the upper Tigris after it wound through an even more treacherous terrain, where thousands more Armenians lived.

This and the surrounding region was the home of ancient Armenia—the oldest civilization to have survived in that part of the world. Mount Ararat and the Ararat Plain were to the northeast, and the great Arax River flowed along the border where ancient Armenia, Persia, and Russia came together. In the highlands of Sasun, according to legend, lived the epic hero of Armenian myth, David of Sasun. A David and Goliath in one, he was an indefatigable fighter with the strength of ten and a hearty sexual appetite, whose story was passed along by oral tradition until the epic poem *David of Sasun* was finally written down in the nineteenth century.

In 1891 and 1892, reformers of the Hunchak Party came to Sasun to help the Armenian agrarian community—farmers of millet, wheat, barley, tobacco, and herders of cattle and sheep[2]—organize resistance to tax extortion. The system of double taxation that involved paying both the government and the Kurdish chieftains was ruining the Armenian agrarian community. It was yet another example of both feudal oppression and of the *gâvur* being exploited by the Muslim majority. This time, when the Kurdish *aga* (chieftain) came through Sasun with his entourage for his usual take, an Armenian spokesman confronted him. In the ensuing fight, at least one Kurd was killed, and a new sense of enmity was established. Early in the following year, 1893, Turkish officials arrested a Hunchak from Constantinople whom they blamed for the previous year's disturbance and accused of distributing arms to Armenians in the region. Shortly after, the sultan ordered an invasion of nomadic Kurds into Sasun and Moush. The *mutassarrif* (governor of a *sanjak,* or county) gave his backing to an anti-Armenian fanatic, the Kurdish sheikh of Zeilan, and in a matter of weeks, three or four thousand Kurds launched an attack on the Armenian villages of the Sasun region. The *mutassarrif* of Genje reported falsely that the Armenians were in revolt, when in fact the Armenians had fled into the mountains to hide. With the onset of winter, the Kurdish forces retreated, waiting till spring to return.[3]

As spring broke in the Sasun highlands in 1894, the Armenians were ready to fight for justice, this time with whatever force it might take. In June, in the villages of the Talori *nahiye* (subdistrict), an Ottoman official, accompanied by *zaptiye* (military police), arrived to collect overdue taxes. The Armenian men met them and told them that they were willing to pay government taxes if the government would protect them from Kurdish extortion. According to British consul R. W. Graves in Erzerum, the Ottoman official "proceeded to abuse and maltreat them."[4] Then, as the British consul put it, the Armenian men finally "lost their temper, fell upon him, and, after administering a severe beating, drove him and his zaptiehs from the district." The official reported that he had been the victim of armed rebellion. In this tense situation large numbers of Kurds appeared, in the course of their seasonal migration, and stole some two hundred sheep from the Armenian herders; fighting broke out, and this time the Armenians killed several Kurds. By the middle of August, the sultan had sent in his troops on the pretext of suppressing an Armenian rebellion.[5]

Assisted by *zaptiye* and Kurds, the Ottoman troops attacked and burned villages and "wounded and killed, without regard to age or sex, all who fell into their hands."[6]

In a village called Semal, the Armenians, led by a priest who had received assurances from the colonel of the Turkish forces that they would be unharmed, gave themselves up. But as soon as they surrendered, the colonel gave the order to seize the priest, and they proceeded to gouge out his eyes and bayonet him to death. Then they separated the men from the women and that night raped the women. The next night they bayoneted the men to death, within hearing of the terrified women.[7] As Consul Graves put it, things degenerated "from bad to worse, culminating in a massacre of some three thousand Armenians in the district of Talori."[8]

Instead of dissolving quietly into the Anatolian haze, the massacre at Sasun sent terror through the Armenian provinces, a shock wave throughout the empire, and it became a dramatic human rights issue for

Europeans and Americans. Among other things the massacre at Sasun "was the first instance of organized mass murder of Armenians in modern Ottoman history that was carried out in peace time and had no connection with any foreign war."[9] British vice-consul H. S. Shipley (one of the British members of the Sasun investigative commission) described it this way:

> [The] Armenians were absolutely hunted like wild beasts, being killed wherever they were met, and if the slaughter was not greater, it was, I believe, solely owing to the vastness of the mountain ranges of that district which enabled the people to scatter, and so facilitated their escape. In fact, and speaking with a full sense of responsibility, I am compelled to say that . . . [the object was] extermination, pure and simple.[10]

If protest over taxes had begun the violence, it was soon clear that the issue of taxes had become a pretext for killing the Armenians. As witnesses noted and an official inquiry later confirmed: "No distinctions were made between persons or villages as to whether they were loyal and had paid their taxes or not. The orders were to make a clean sweep. A priest and some leading men from one village went out to meet an officer, taking in their hands their tax receipts, declaring their loyalty and begging for mercy; but the village was surrounded, and all human beings put to the bayonet."[11]

In the aftermath of Sasun the sultan realized that the atrocities his troops had committed had provoked harsh public opinion in Europe and the United States. However, the investigative commission that the Sublime Porte then set up to try to appease world opinion did nothing more than try to cover up the killing. The sultan's commission sent out propaganda that blamed the Armenians for the massacres, and also claimed that the Kurds, who were characterized as wild nomads, got out of control. The sultan's commission refused to allow Armenians to testify and finally did everything it could to obstruct any genuine investigations in the region.[12] The duke of Argyll called the sultan's investigation a "farce" from beginning to end, and the Italian government was so angry with the format of the investigation that it refused to get involved.[13]

Disgusted with the sultan's investigation, the European powers decided to set up their own commission. In particular British consuls Graves in Erzurum and C. M. Hallward in Van, who were appalled, as one historian put it, by "the horror of Ottoman injustice," pushed hard for a legitimate investigation.[14] The British, French, and Russians, who had consuls in the region, provided the decisive leadership for the commission, and began meeting in the remote highland city of Moush in the bitter winter of 1895. When they had finished their investigation, Consul Hallward summarized their findings:

> There was no insurrection, as was reported in Constantinople; the villagers simply took up arms to defend themselves against the Kurds. The statement made to me by an official here of their having killed soldiers and Zaptiches, I found after careful inquiry to be false. Before arriving in Moush, I naturally supposed that something of the sort must have occurred to call for such a display of military force, but neither the Mutesarif nor the Military Commandant with whom I spoke on the subject hinted at anything of the sort, nor did I learn elsewhere that the Armenians had been guilty of any act of rebellion against the Government.[15]

By the spring the European powers were demanding that the sultan implement the reforms that had been set forth in the treaties of San Stefano and Berlin in 1878. Perhaps Lord Salisbury summed up the European mood when he said to the Ottoman ambassador, "The essential matter was that provision should be made for securing equitable government to the Armenians. I repudiated," he went on, "all ideas of autonomy as absurd, and I asked no privileges for them, but simple justice between man and man."[16]

As the sultan stalled on the new demands for reform in the Armenian provinces, the frustration among Armenians grew. By the summer of 1895, the Hunchak Party was planning a demonstration in the capital. The mass rally took place at noon on October 1, 1895, as nearly two thousand Armenians gathered in the Kum Kapu section near the Armenian patriarchate to march to the Sublime Porte. Their goal was to deliver a petition, a "Protest-Demand,"[17] which decried the Sasun massacre, the condition of

Armenians throughout the empire, and the inaction of the central government.

The petition was—especially given its time and place—an extraordinary statement about civil rights. In clear language the Armenians protested "the systematic persecution to which our people has been subjected, especially during the last few years, a persecution which the Sublime Porte has made a principle of government with the one object of causing the Armenians to disappear from their own country." They protested the "state of siege" under which Armenians were forced to live and the recent massacres at Sasun. Peace and security were essential, the text went on, "to a nation which desires to reach by fair means a position of comparative prosperity, which it has certainly a right to aspire to, and to reach the level of progress and civilization towards which other peoples are advancing." The list of Armenian demands was broad and basic: fair taxation; guarantees of freedom of conscience; the right of public meetings; equality before the law; protection of life, property, and honor (this meant the protection of women). The petition also demanded the cessation of mass political arrests and the brutal torture that most often followed them, as well as the right to bear arms for self-defense. The Armenian authors of the petition underscored that the Armenians had waited patiently for the reforms promised them in the Treaty of Berlin in 1878.[18] As one historian put it, it was "the first time in Ottoman history that a non-Muslim, subject minority had dared to confront the central authorities in the very capital of the empire."[19]

As the rally commenced there was tension all over the city. The Sublime Porte was surrounded by cavalry and police, as the huge crowd made its way into the center of the city and approached the Porte. Copies of the Protest-Demand had already been delivered to various embassies. As the Hunchak leaders were about to deliver the petition at the Porte, they were stopped by Maj. Servet Bey, the adjutant to the minister of police, who ordered them to disband. As the soldiers and the police let loose on the protesters, about twenty people were bludgeoned to death and hundreds were wounded. Major Servet was killed, fights broke out and shots were fired, and a massacre began in the clear daylight on the streets of the capital. Foreigners and European diplomats looked on in horror.[20]

Around the city the *softas* (Islamic theological students) in their white turbans and some policemen dressed as *softas* appeared on the streets and alleyways and boulevards and began massacring Armenians. Many of the police and *zaptiyes* either stood by watching or joined in the killing. When the police tried to convince a group of Armenians that it was safe to leave the cathedral where they were hiding from the mob, they replied: "We do not trust the promises of the massacrers of Sasun."[21] The working-class Armenians of the city, mostly porters and day laborers, were the hardest hit. Not only were they the most visible but they were the most vulnerable, as they were despised by their Muslim counterparts because they occupied so many of the city's service jobs.[22]

During the first week of October, massacres continued throughout Constantinople day and night. Horrified by what they were witnessing, the foreign diplomats sent a collective message to the Porte asking for an end to the massacres. British ambassador Philip Currie telegraphed the grand vizier to tell him that conditions were deteriorating by the day and that Armenians were being massacred in the city and throughout the suburbs.[23] As the number of dead piled up on the streets and the hospitals filled with wounded, 2,400 Armenians stayed locked up inside their churches throughout the many sections of the city. Finally, on October 10, with assurances from all six foreign embassies, they agreed to come out into the open air.[24] But by then the Constantinople massacre had set off a new wave of violence against Armenians throughout the empire.

In the autumn of 1895 the map of Armenia in Turkey went up in flames. From Constantinople to Trebizond to Van to Diyarbekir, and across the whole central and eastern plain of Anatolia, where historic Armenia was lodged, the killing and plunder unfolded. One can follow the conflagration by the weeks: October 8, 1895, Trebizond, Akhisar, in the district of Izmit; October 11, Gümüshane in Trebizond Province; October 13, Bayburt in Erzurum Province; October 21, Erzinjan in Erzurum Province; October 25, Diyarbekir in Diyarbekir Province; October 28, Tomarza in Kayseri district, Ankara Province, and Urfa in Aleppo Province; October 30, Erzurum and Khnus in Erzurum Province and Moush in Bitlis Province; November 6, Arabkir in Harput Province; November 8, Tomzara in Kayseri district, Ankara Province; November 10, Gurun in Sivas Province; November 11, Harput; November 12, Sivas; November 15, Moush in Bitlis Province and Aintab in Aleppo Province; November 26, Zile in Sivas Province; November 30, Kayseri in Ankara

Province; December 28–29, Urfa in Aleppo Province; January 1, 1896, Birejik in Aleppo Province.[25]

There were, however, some places where Armenians were able to mobilize and fight back, and they did so with tenacity, courage, and relative success against great odds. Perhaps the most dramatic defense was in the rugged mountainous town and region of Zeitun, in the northeast corner of Cilicia. There, on October 24, 1895, when the sultan's military units began to burn down certain Armenian villages, the people of Zeitun— again urged on by Hunchak representatives—retaliated. As they dared to fight back in self-defense, the military commander sent a telegram to the sultan stating that the Armenians were in open rebellion and were massacring Muslims.[26] As the fighting escalated, the Armenians of Zeitun found themselves in battle with the Ottoman Fifth Army Corps, which had come from its station at Marash. After more than three months in the severe highlands, often in brutal winter weather, twenty-four Turkish battalions with twelve cannons backed by eight thousand men from a division from Smyrna, and about thirty to thirty-five thousand Kurdish, Turkish, and Circassian irregulars, could not put down the fifteen hundred Armenian mountaineers with their flintlock guns and four hundred Martin rifles. By February, the six powers intervened and helped to bring the sultan and the Armenians into negotiations. The sultan, persuaded by the powers, agreed to some tax relief for the Zeituntsi as well as the appointment of a Christian governor for Zeitun county. The Armenian leaders were expelled from the empire, and the fighters of Zeitun were forced to give up all their weapons.[27]

In another region of complex political tensions—Van—Armenians also refused to die without a struggle. Situated near the Turkish-Russian border, Van drew political energy from the reform movements in Russian Armenia, which is why the Turks regarded the ancient Armenian city and the surrounding province with suspicion. And, because it was on the border between competing empires, it was a region that also felt the tug of political tensions between the sultan and the czar.

Although the city had escaped disaster in the recent wave of autumn massacres, by January 1896 there were signs that the situation in Van was tenuous. British vice-consul W. H. Williams wrote to his ambassador in

Constantinople that many Armenian villages had already been "looted," and that the people were "suffering considerable hardships." The situation, he underscored, "is very bad; the Armenians are everywhere in a state bordering on panic, afraid lest the spring will bring still further disasters."[28] Not surprisingly, Williams's prediction proved accurate. By June the Turkish military officers and the local Kurdish chieftains had pooled their strategies and organized a massacre under the pretext of promulgating the reforms for which the six powers had asked. What happened was becoming a pattern for initiating massacre. What clearly seemed to be a staged skirmish would break out between a Turkish gendarme, a soldier, and some unidentified assailants, who were suspected of being Armenian activists or Turkish salt smugglers; this would become a pretext for the killing of Armenians. Vice-Consul Williams confirmed that the skirmish was "begun by a mob of Turks, gipsies and zaptiehs," but that once the violence began, the massacring of Armenians followed.[29]

Between June 3 and 11 the Turks sent four battalions and some cavalry from Erzurum, Harput, and Moush into Van. The Armenians, with six to seven hundred men, defended the Armenian section of Aikesdan (Garden City), adjacent to Van. Vice-Consul Williams reported being astonished at the heroism and skill of the Armenians in defending themselves. By the end of the week the sultan was compelled to seek the assistance of the powers, especially France and England, in putting an end to the violence, and in exchange, he promised the powers that he would guarantee "the lives and safety" of the Armenians in Van.[30]

After several failed negotiations, the Armenian combatants—making clear again that they were only acting in self-defense in the face of continual massacre—agreed to leave Turkey by the Iranian border, to which they were to be escorted by Turkish troops. As nearly a thousand men were marched toward the border—the "crème of the Armenian youth of Van"—they were massacred en masse by the troops and Kurdish tribesmen. When the news reached Van, the townspeople were in shock. Before June was over the revelations about the massacres in the outlying villages of the region sent terror throughout the province. Vice-Consul Williams estimated that some twenty thousand Armenians had been killed, some 350 hamlets and villages destroyed, and "the reports from the villages," he wrote, "are heartrending."[31]

HUMANITY ON TRIAL:

CLARA BARTON AND AMERICA'S

MISSION TO ARMENIA

Has it come to this, that in the last days of the nineteenth century
humanity itself is placed on trial?

—Shelby Moore Cullom, chair
of the Senate Foreign Relations
Committee, January 1896

Writing in her journal in January 1896, Julia Ward Howe recorded her participation in a joint meeting in New York City of the National Woman Suffrage Association and the Boston-based American Woman Suffrage Association, to which she belonged: "[The] time had come in which women were bound to study, assist, and stand by each other. I quoted Christ's saying about the mustard seed. Miss Barton's mission to Armenia I called a mustard seed, and one which would have very important results."[1]

For Howe, Clara Barton's mission to the killing fields of Turkey was exemplary of international feminism. In the last decade of the nineteenth century, Clara Barton was a national hero, the heir to Florence Nightingale, and the first president of the American Red Cross. In the rising tide of the women's movement, Barton had come to personify social work and public service. Until the call to go to Armenia, her work—which meant bringing aid to Americans stricken by floods, hurricanes, or disease—had been done on native ground only. But the mission to the Ottoman Empire and the Armenian provinces was something new. It would be the first international American Red Cross mission, and it would bring Barton and her life's work into a new realm—the realm of global human rights.

Although the United States sent money and provisions to aid Greece during the Greek War of Independence in 1824–25, and Americans aided

Ireland during the potato famine of the 1840s and Russia during the 1892 famine, the movement for humanitarian intervention for the Armenians in Turkey in 1896 commenced what I believe can be called the modern era of American international human rights relief. Americans sent not only large amounts of money and provisions to the Armenian *vilayets* of Turkey but for the first time mobilized sophisticated relief teams, under the auspices of the Red Cross, and sent them to the sites of disaster. Furthermore, another network of American relief and rescue was already at work, for American missionaries were stationed throughout the Armenian *vilayets* and were immersed in relief projects as hundreds of thousands of Armenians were dying of disease and famine in the wake of the massacres. One of the unique dimensions of American philanthropy in 1896 was the synergy between American missionaries, the Red Cross—which was a federally incorporated organization—and the American people. In many ways Barton's mission anticipated the kind of work the Peace Corps would do in the second half of the twentieth century. Barton's voyage to Turkey was also another part, and a bright one, of America's growing global involvement during the decade that would bring the United States a new international identity.

So prominent a place did the Armenian massacres have in the political spectrum of the 1890s that the Republican Party platform of 1896—in the intensely fought election between William McKinley and the populist Democrat William Jennings Bryan—highlighted three international issues: the annexation of the Hawaiian Islands, the Armenian massacres, and the Cuban struggle for independence from Spain. The party platform read:

> The massacres in Armenia have aroused the deep sympathy and just indignation of the American people, and we believe that the United States should exercise all the influence it can properly exert to bring these atrocities to an end. In Turkey, American residents have been exposed to gravest (grievous) dangers and American property destroyed. There, and everywhere, American citizens and American property must be absolutely protected at all hazards and at any cost.[2]

In many ways American women played a crucial role in the movement for Armenian relief, and their work helped to give shape to a new vision of what might be called global sisterhood. As survivor accounts and eyewitness reports came to public knowledge through the press, the magnitude of sexual violence committed against Armenian women—rape and torture, abduction, slavery, and imprisonment in harems—appeared to be unprecedented in modern Western history, and it affected Americans deeply.

In reviewing Frederick Davis Greene's timely book, *The Armenian Crisis in Turkey: The Massacre of 1894, Its Antecedents and Significance,* for the *Woman's Journal* in June 1895, Isabel Barrows excerpted missionary and relief worker reports of the Armenian atrocities. Because the authors of the reports were still living in Turkey near the scenes of the atrocities, Greene published the letters anonymously. A missionary himself, Greene had been born in Turkey and had spent a large part of his life in Van, and so was well acquainted with the treatment of the Armenians in the Ottoman Empire. The authors of the accounts acknowledge that most of their knowledge is from survivor testimony, which they have listened to and recorded. Even in the earliest account in Greene's book, written in April 1893—the author notes that "it seems to be the systematic policy of the government to crush the Armenians, and it looks as though they will be exterminated." While the *Woman's Journal* gave in-depth coverage to Greene's book, it was reviewed widely around the nation and had a large impact on the national consciousness.

The letters in Greene's book reveal a process of systematic massacre and violence. While the men were being murdered outright, thus destroying the Armenian economy and political infrastructure, the women were subjected to extraordinary sexual violence. It is worth noting that the word "outrage" was, in this context, a Victorian euphemism for rape. From letter 5:

A lot of women, variously estimated from 60 to 160 in number, were shut up in a church, and the soldiers were "let loose" among them. Many were outraged to death, and the remainder dispatched with sword and bayonet. Children were placed in a row, one behind another, and a bullet fired down the line, apparently to see how many could be dispatched with one bullet. Infants and small children were piled one on the other and their heads struck off.

From letter 7:

No respect was shown to age or sex. Men, women, and infants were treated alike except that the women were subjected to greater outrage before they were slaughtered. In one place three or four hundred women, after being forced to serve the vile purposes of merciless soldiery, were taken to a valley near by and hacked to pieces with sword and bayonet. In another place about two hundred women, weeping and wailing, knelt before the commander and begged for mercy, but the blood-thirsty wretch, after ordering their violation, directed the soldiers to dispatch them in a similar manner.

From letter 8:

Women were outraged and then butchered; a priest taken to the roof of his church and hacked to pieces; young men piled in with wood saturated with kerosene and set on fire; a large number of women and girls collected in a church, kept for days, violated by the brutal soldiers, and then murdered. It is said the number was so large that the blood flowed from the church door.

From letter 10:

Men, women, and children were most barbarously slaughtered—unnamable outrages were perpetrated on all. The less horrible outrages were some of the following: bayoneting the men, and in this wounded condition either burying or burning them; outraging women and then dispatching them with bayonets or swords; ripping up pregnant women; impaling infants and children on the bayonet, or dispatching them with the sword; houses fired and the inmates driven back into the flames.[3]

Week by week eyewitness accounts and survivor testimony continued to appear in the *New York Times,* the *Boston Globe,* the *San Francisco Examiner,* as well as dozens of major and small-town newspapers around the country. Accounts of children, women, and men being butchered, raped, and hacked to pieces were part of the ongoing narrative that brought home to Americans the meaning of state-sponsored massacre.

An illustrated feature story in the *New York Times* in August 1895 focused dramatically on gender. "The Women of Armenia: The Wives, Mothers, and Daughters of an Afflicted Nation," portrayed Armenian women as counterparts to their American sisters: "intelligent, educated," endowed with grace, civility, and domestic prowess. Given the "condition of perpetual terror" under which Armenians were forced to live, the women had come to be even more essential to maintaining the moral fortress of the family and home. Yet now they were subject to rape and murder by the Turks and Kurds. The story was illustrated with a picture of an Armenian grandmother with her daughter and grandson; fashionably dressed amid Victorian furniture, they look like proper Bostonians. The juxtaposition of the image with the story is shocking.⁴

The word "holocaust" in a *New York Times* headline of September 10, 1895, signaled that something extraordinary was happening to the Armenians. As the coverage of the atrocities became part of the nation's consciousness, Clara Barton felt called to action by "the pent-up sympathies of the people."⁵ For the Armenians, Barton exclaimed, "American enthusiasm is boundless, and its expression limitless."⁶ It was not surprising that the Armenian relief movement looked to Clara Barton. She had become a national figure during the Civil War, when she earned the name Angel of the Battlefield. Now an elder stateswoman, she had become as popular as Mark Twain and Frederick Douglass on the postwar lecture circuit.

In those years her musical voice carried her messages with eloquence through auditoriums and concert halls all over the United States. When she spoke at New York's Steinway Hall in 1867 to more than five hundred Civil War veterans, she walked on to a stage "decorated with an army tent, a stack of muskets, and a small howitzer . . . while the band struck up the 'William Tell Overture.' "⁷ Such scenes had come to define the fanfare that surrounded her. In 1867 she had become friends with Elizabeth Cady Stanton and Susan B. Anthony, and lent her voice to the woman suffrage movement. Although she kept her distance from the more official domains of the movement, she would say many times over what she said to a group of veterans one evening: "Consider the wants of my people. . . . God only knows women were your friends in time of peril—and you should be [theirs] now."⁸

But it wasn't until 1870, while she was traveling in Europe following one of her many bouts with depression, that she witnessed the Red Cross in action during the Franco-Prussian War. Founded by the Swiss philanthropist Jean-Henri Dunant, the Red Cross was established at the First Geneva Convention in 1864. Amazed by the effectiveness of the Red Cross, Barton was angry that her own country had refused to join the organization. On returning home, she told a group of Civil War veterans that she was in awe of "the work of these Red Cross societies in the field, accomplishing in four months under their systematic organization what we failed to accomplish in four years without it."[9] After arduous petitioning of the Hayes and Garfield administrations, she prevailed on President Chester A. Arthur to ratify the congressional resolution for an American Red Cross, as well as the Geneva Convention. In doing so she helped bring the United States one step further in its move toward a new age of internationalism.

But before Barton and the Red Cross were recruited, a culture of activism was fast evolving. What the Friends of Armenia had started at Faneuil Hall the previous year had become a national movement by the summer of 1895. Within months of the Sasun massacres, Louis Klopsch, the editor of the *Christian Herald,* America's largest religious newspaper, began raising money for Armenian relief. Grace Kimball, a missionary physician in the Armenian quarter of Van, reported in December 1895 that she had received ten thousand dollars from the *Christian Herald* and that eight thousand Armenians were being clothed and fed with that money.

Magazines and newspapers from the *Outlook* and Edward Everett Hale's *Lend a Hand* to the *Woman's Journal,* the *New York Times,* and the *Boston Globe* began to run articles about Armenian relief and the need for funds. Although New York City, Boston, and Philadelphia remained the centers of Armenian relief activity, by the end of 1895 relief organizations and committees were cropping up across the country. Syracuse, Worcester, Baltimore, Harrisburg, Washington, Cleveland, Columbus, Detroit, Indianapolis, Chicago, and St. Paul were just a few of the cities now involved in the drive.[10]

In New York what began as a local committee, backed by the New York Chamber of Commerce, grew quickly into the National Armenian Relief Committee. Its board included some of the most powerful men in the United States, including financier and philanthropist Spencer Trask, Supreme Court Justice David Josiah Brewer, railroad executive Chauncy Depew, Wall Street banker Jacob Schiff, and church leaders Dr. Leonard Woolsey Bacon and the Reverend Frederick D. Greene. The prestigious Wall Street banking firm Brown Brothers agreed to be the committee's treasurer.[11]

The movement brought together Democrats and Republicans, conservatives and liberals, Christians and Jews—all believing in their own Victorian American way that each individual could make a difference; each person could be—as Ralph Waldo Emerson put it—a vehicle for "the triumph of principles." According to one Philadelphia relief worker, "Never . . . was so much earnest, energetic, persistent and intelligent work done for any cause as was bestowed upon the Armenians."[12]

Spencer Trask was a key figure behind the National Armenian Relief Committee, bringing it wealth, power, and humanitarian commitment. After graduating from Princeton in 1866, he started his own investment firm, Spencer Trask & Company. Not long after, he befriended Thomas Edison and became a major benefactor of Edison's work and later the director of the Edison Electric Light Company. In 1897 he would help save the *New York Times* by refinancing and reorganizing the company.

Trask was one of those Victorians with a passionate commitment to civic duty, public service, and philanthropy. A founder and trustee of New York Teachers' College, a patron and member of the Municipal Arts Society of New York, the National Arts Club, and the Metropolitan Museum of Art, he was so generous that at the time of his death in a freak train accident in 1909, his own wealth had been greatly diminished. After the death of his wife, Katrina, in 1922, their Victorian mansion and grounds, known as Yaddo, in Saratoga Springs, New York, would become the most important writers' and artists' colony in the country.

The National Armenian Relief Committee was bolstered by other American elites who worked with Trask. John D. Rockefeller gave the first of the hundreds of thousands dollars he and his family would contribute to Armenian relief. The powerful Jacob Schiff, a director of the banking firm Kuhn Loeb, helped mobilize resources quickly.[13] Schiff's interest in the Armenian Question was connected to his work helping Russian Jews escape the pogroms. A Republican who became influential with the Roosevelt and Taft administrations, he would later be a primary force behind

the Galveston movement (1907–14), which brought Russian-Jewish immigrants to communities in the West. Supreme Court Justice David Brewer
brought further distinction to the committee. A moderate in the world of
jurisprudence, he was a liberal on social issues, a proponent of international peace, anti-imperialism, and woman suffrage, and a passionate
believer in justice for the Armenians.

    Religious leaders and organizations around the nation enthusiasti-
cally joined the movement: Protestants, Catholics, Quakers, and Jews,
the Salvation Army, the Women's Christian Temperance Movement
(WCTU), and Chatauqua were among them. Conservative and liberal
religious figures alike became leaders on both the national and local levels.
The conservative Catholic archbishop of New York, Michael Corrigan,
and the Episcopal bishop of Pennsylvania, Alonzo Potter, were both
national committee members.

The Armenian relief movement also was driven by a network of local
committees and organizations. While the local committees were not officially linked to the National Armenian Relief Committee, the national
organization instructed local committees around the country on how to
set up their operations; it provided them with fund-raising pamphlets and
educational materials, and arranged for speakers and public programs.
From John D. Rockefeller to the twenty-five hundred schoolchildren in
Minneapolis who collected more than seven hundred dollars, donations
came in from across the nation in large and small amounts: from the
Worcester Relief Committee; the Ladies Relief Committee of Chicago;
the Citizens of Milton, North Dakota; the Davenport Iowa Relief Committee. By March 1896, ninety-five thousand dollars was raised in New
York City and in Boston forty thousand dollars, and in Philadelphia there
was enough anxiety about not keeping pace with the funds raised in rival
cities that the *Philadelphia Inquirer* reported that the fifteen thousand dollars it had already raised was not nearly enough. By the end of the year-
long drive, Americans had raised more than three hundred thousand
dollars in an age when a loaf of bread cost a nickel.[14]

    So deeply had Armenian relief cut into the popular consciousness that
in 1896, a Thanksgiving appeal was launched nationwide, and Americans
from St. Paul to San Francisco to Boston gave thanks by sending money to

Armenian widows and orphans of the massacres. Citizens of St. Paul boy-cotted buying turkey (the pun could not have been lost on anyone) and gave their Turkey Day money to the cause. Clara Barton prodded Americans that fall: "Unless the open hands of charity be reached out and across and access be secured, hunger and cold will gather victims by the tens of thousands and bury them like the falling leaves beneath the snow."[15]

By December 1895, as Barton was being recruited intensely by Trask and the National Armenian Relief Committee, the Armenian Question had hit Capitol Hill, and Congress became embroiled in debates about how to respond. Wilkinson Call, Democratic senator from Florida, put before Congress a resolution calling for the United States to intervene in order to stop the sultan's massacres. "In the name of religion, humanity, and the principles on which all civilization rests," the resolution affirmed, "the United States should use peaceful negotiations or by force of arms if necessary, to stop the cruelties inflicted on the Armenians."[16] The Call resolution went so far as to include a provision for the establishment of an independent Armenian state, which would be protected by the civilized powers of the world.

However, the resolution proved too activist for the Senate Foreign Relations Committee, and by late January 1896, at the moment when Clara Barton would be leaving for Turkey, the committee's chairman, Shelby Moore Cullom of Illinois, introduced another resolution. This one assured President Cleveland that Congress would support any move he might make to encourage the European powers to uphold their treaty obligations to the Armenian people by putting the appropriate pressure on the Turkish government. Cullom's amendment watered down the Call resolution by maintaining that the United States, as a neutral nation, could not interfere with the affairs of Europe. But it affirmed that America had an obligation to humanity to which it could not be blind, especially in such an extreme case as this one.

Call and others, like Senator Newton Blanchard, a Democrat from Louisiana, called the Cullom resolution weak and insignificant given the enormity of the crisis. William Frye, Republican senator from Maine and the president pro tem of the Senate, raised his voice in disgust at the fact that the Armenian massacres had put an abrupt halt to the decades of

American work and money that had gone into improving living conditions in Turkey. He was, of course, referring to the work of American missionaries; their establishment of high schools and universities mostly for Armenians, Greeks, and Syrians; and to the establishment of an American diplomatic presence during the last half of the century.[17]

Senator Cullom's speech on the Senate floor crystallized much of the sentiment on Capitol Hill:

> Mr. President . . . the concurrent and accumulated testimony of hundreds and thousands of intelligent, humane, honest, and courageous Christians and Jews alike, Catholics and Protestants, Europeans and Americans, makes it absolutely certain as a dreadful truth that a massacre of innocence [sic] unparalleled for ages has been perpetrated in the Armenian provinces of Turkey. . . . the most gigantic and brutal enormities have been committed upon a wholly unoffending people. . . .
>
> We believe . . . that "of one blood God made all the nations of the earth," but I confess that my faith is somewhat shattered in the accepted belief when I see the soldiers of an organized and recognized Government, where there is no war and no enemy, killing, bayoneting, and outraging an unarmed and unoffending people—a Turkish army, under the pay of the Turkish Government. . . .
>
> Has it come to this, that in the last days of the nineteenth century humanity itself is placed on trial?[18]

Senator Cullom blamed the European powers for not forcing Turkey to fulfill its obligations to the Armenians as stated in the 1878 Treaty of Berlin, which stipulated that the Armenians would be governed justly and that Europe would ensure such just rule. As Senator Frye pointed out, it was absurd for the United States to stand by and watch while the lives of Americans were in danger and millions of dollars of American property, including colleges and schools, were being destroyed by the Turks. Would Great Britain be silent in the same situation?[19]

In the final round of debate, Senator Call took the floor and lambasted the Cullom resolution, calling it feeble and emasculated, and reintroduced his original resolution. Call agreed with Frye that "the Armenian people should have the protection of this Government, not because they are citizens of the United States, but because the people of the United States have a duty to civilization, have a duty to the progress of mankind, to perform." Mere expressions of sympathy from the Committee on Foreign Relations, he went on, were not enough "while murder, outrage, and ferocity such as beasts of the forest do not possess are perpetrated upon these Armenian people."[20]

In the end, however, the Senate passed the tame Cullom resolution, and it was sent on to the House, where it was carried by a vote of 143 to 26. The conservative press called the joint resolution mad jingoism and a violation of the Monroe Doctrine, but the House paid no attention to that. In fact, according to a *New York Tribune* reporter who covered the debate, at least seven-eighths of the House favored strong interventionist action.[21] Representative Charles Henry Grosvenor of Ohio, like many in the House, felt that the resolution was too weak: "They have asked us for bread, and we are giving them a stone." We "are falling down," he said indignantly, "at the feet of the Turkish government."[22]

But the powerful condemnations of Turkish atrocities on the floors of the Senate and the House marked a new awareness in Congress about human rights in the global arena. According to historian Merle Curti, the joint resolution concerning the Armenian massacres adopted by Congress in 1896 was the first time in American history that Congress made a statement beyond advocating "temporary relief," urging "political action" in order to ameliorate a human rights tragedy happening thousands of miles from home.[23] If nothing else it created a precedent for human rights legislation in the coming century.

But the resolution was ignored in the White House. Oscar Straus, the former American minister to the Ottoman Empire, appealed to President Cleveland to leave Turkey's internal affairs alone, and he pressured Cleveland too by suggesting that the resolution would so offend the sultan that he wouldn't allow a Red Cross mission to enter the empire because of it. It was the beginning of what would become an ongoing pattern of White House and State Department acquiescence to Turkish human rights violations and, in particular, to Turkey's coercive tactics with the United States government on issues of the Armenian massacres and later the Armenian Genocide. Although Cleveland's refusal to heed the Cullom resolution provoked anger and disappointment across the nation, not even a delegation of prominent Americans including businessman William E. Dodge and former Cornell University president Andrew D. White, who went to the White House to protest, were unable to budge the president on the issue.[24] As one writer for the London *Times* prophetically put it: If security for the Armenians in Turkey is not achieved, then "we are only feeding them now for future massacres."[25]

As Congress was discussing the Armenian atrocities, the National Armenian Relief Committee was focusing on Clara Barton as the only suitable person to lead the arduous effort to bring relief to the Armenians. Trask and his committee reasoned that the Red Cross was the most distinguished humanitarian organization with international standing, and it had a member in Turkey (the Red Crescent). With a celebrity like Barton, the Red Cross would be able to raise money quickly.

But the elderly Barton had to be wooed and recruited, and the Boston community proved once again to be crucial. As snow filled the Public Gardens in Boston on the day before New Year's Eve 1895, Bostonians gathered in City Hall on School Street. In that grand building (modeled on the Louvre), Clara Barton found herself before a room filled with Boston's prominent businessmen and a group of leading women, many of them activists for the Armenian cause. Mayor-elect Josiah Quincy presided that evening in the Council Chamber. The grandson of Josiah Quincy Jr. and the great-grandson of Josiah Quincy, he was heir to a long-standing Boston mayoral tradition. Now in his mid-thirties, he had made his name as a mugwump (Republicans who had jumped parties in the wake of Republican Party corruption of the mid-eighties). A young idealist and a Brahmin Democrat, he was a strong advocate of civil service and urban reform, and his concern for the plight of the Armenians was another dimension of his progressive politics.

The strikingly handsome, newly elected mayor took the podium and spoke plainly: "[V]ery rarely," he noted, "have so many persons been killed outside of a state of actual hostilities as has been the case in Armenia in the last few months." He underscored that as a neutral country, the United States had even more responsibility to save the Armenians. "We are met here today," he declared, to entrust Miss Barton with "the necessary funds to enable her to perform this work of humanity."[26]

When Clara Barton took the podium, she was, at seventy-five, still robust. Her dark hair was parted in the middle and drawn back into a bun, and her broad face, prominent cheekbones, and intense eyes exuded confidence. Photos from the era show her in a black silk dress with a high collar, wearing the official Red Cross field badge and the amethyst and topaz brooches that were a gift from Grand Duchess Louise of Baden in honor of her work. "When I left home to come to Boston," Barton opened, "I had no more idea that I was to face the business men of Boston than that I was to immediately face the country of Turkey."[27]

But "immediate action was urged" by the American people, she later wrote; "human beings were starving and could not be reached, hundreds of towns and villages had not been heard from since the fire and sword went over them, and no one else was so well prepared for the work of field relief, it was said, as ourselves. . . . and as Turkey was one of the signatory powers to the Red Cross Treaty of Geneva," Barton reasoned, "it must consequently be familiar with its methods and humanitarian ideas."[28]

Barton may have launched the phrase "starving Armenians" that evening, creating the term that would come to signify the Armenian plight well into the twentieth century. "It was not until the committee from this city, and also one from New York, brought the matter before me," she said, asking the Red Cross to bring aid "to the starving Armenians, to the people who were suffering so much that the world was shocked by what it read, that it occurred to us that we could be of any use." Addressing the diplomatic problems, she pointed out that the Turkish door had been closed to the outside world, and as American enthusiasm for a Red Cross mission had crescendoed, the Turkish minister in Washington had become increasingly hostile to the idea.[29]

A complex woman, Barton alternated between cycles of depression and the exhilaration of serving the needy in crisis. A combination of insecurity and forthrightness, rigidity and flexibility, she was a woman of charm and charisma, and time and again she proved to be an effective leader of people in trying times.[30] Yet, as she stood at the podium facing a room of hopeful Bostonians, she felt ambivalent about the whole project and recognized the difficulties she might face. Hardy as she was, she was not the young woman who had become a national hero on the battlefields of the Civil War.

Furthermore she had no experience with international relief work.

From the time she became the first president of the American Red Cross in 1882, she had dealt only with domestic natural disasters. In 1882 the Mississippi River flooded, and she and her workers found themselves in New Orleans, Vicksburg, Natchez, and Memphis. In 1884, when the Ohio River flooded and Cincinnati was under water, she went to the towns and cities of southern Indiana and Ohio. An earthquake in Charleston, South Carolina, in 1886; a tornado in Mt. Vernon, Illinois, in 1888; an epidemic of yellow fever in Jacksonville, Florida, that same year were new challenges for her new organization. And in 1889, when the Johnstown Flood in southwestern Pennsylvania shocked the nation, killing more than three thousand people, the Red Cross earned even more national respect as it swiftly arrived on the scene and stayed there for the next five months.

All in all Barton had shown little interest in the global frontier, and seemed diffident about foreign intervention. She had refused to go to Greece during the Balkan War in 1877 and had also refused to send aid to a famine-ravaged Serbia during the same time, claiming that it was beyond the scope of the organization's charter.[31] In fact, the Red Cross's first gesture toward international relief had come in 1891, after the people of Iowa created a movement to send corn to Russia for famine relief. Although Barton did not leave the country for Russian relief, the Iowa corn drive was a step toward the Red Cross's coming age of internationalism. The next venture would be something unprecedented—intervention for the survivors of Armenian massacres six thousand miles away.

Barton's send-off in January 1896 combined a celebrated bon voyage with a moral passion that was unprecedented. In Washington, Barton held press conferences, and Red Cross secretary George H. Pullman felt besieged: "Reporters to the right of us. Reporters to the left of us. Reporters in front of us. Volleyed and thundered." Newspaper men and women, messengers, telegraph boys, women and men eager to volunteer to go to the Armenian provinces of Turkey swarmed the headquarters.[32]

Barton's arrival in New York City was met with headlines in the *New York Times* and *Herald*, such as HEROIC PLANS OF MISS BARTON, and FLYING THE FLAG OF THE RED CROSS. A crowd of dignitaries met her at Penn Station and then whisked her off to breakfast at Delmonico's, the restaurant novelist Theodore Dreiser had called "the sanctum sanctorum of the smart social life of the city." At Delmonico's Barton combined a farewell

breakfast with a business meeting. Politically shrewd—particularly with a
Turkish ban on the Red Cross in place—she made it clear that she was
going to Turkey with a nonpartisan commitment, and she noted that her
purpose was to serve not only Christian Armenians but any and all people
in dire straits.[33]

When she reached the harbor, another large crowd was waiting for
her, and well-wishers included Spencer Trask, Frederick Greene, the
author of *The Armenian Crisis in Turkey,* as well as various Armenian American leaders including Hagop Bogigian and M. H. Gulesian of Boston, the
Reverend H. K. Samuelian, and Dr. Ayvasian.

More speeches were made, and Mrs. Charles H. Raymond, president
of the New York Red Cross chapter, pinned a new, ornate Red Cross badge
on Clara Barton, and Barton in turn pinned a new silver Red Cross pin on
each of the New York Red Cross officers. Bouquets of flowers were
brought on board, and one of them was a flag fabricated of white carna-
tions with a cross of red roses. The SS *New York* sailed shortly after eleven
o'clock in the morning on January 22 with the Red Cross flag rippling
from the mainmast. Dr. Julian B. Hubbell, the general field agent; George
Pullman, Red Cross secretary; Miss Lucy Graves, the stenographer; and
Ernest Mason, the interpreter, completed the Red Cross party. The cheers
of the crowds echoed across the harbor into the Hudson as the ship
slipped out of sight on its way to Constantinople.[34]

It was a maiden voyage in many ways, and Barton wrote with characteristic candor:

> The picture of that scene is still vivid in my memory. Crowded
> piers, wild with hurrahs, white with parting salutes, hearts beat-
> ing with exultation and expectation—a little shorn band of five,
> prohibited, unsustained either by government or other authority,
> destined to a port five thousand miles away, from approach to
> which even the powers of the world had shrunk. What was it
> expected to do or how to do it? Visions of Don Quixote and his
> windmills loomed up, as I turned away and wondered.[35]

A week later Barton and her crew arrived at Southampton at midnight and were met by a messenger from London who informed them
that the sultan had not lifted the prohibition on the Red Cross, but that the

U.S. minister, Alexander Watkins Terrell, would be received by the government in Constantinople. There was such uncertainty that Barton sent Dr. Hubbell on to Constantinople to report back on the Ottoman government's disposition. Although the prohibition was still in place, Hubbell's report was cautiously optimistic, so Barton and her party set out for Constantinople.

Arriving on February 15, Barton was greeted by American officials, who were themselves still in a state of alarm because the Constantinople massacres of the fall had left an atmosphere of terror everywhere. The famous Pera Palace Hotel seemed like the safest place to stay, and Barton was taken there immediately. In the damp February of Constantinople, with the stench of death hanging in the air, amid the splendor of the ancient city's Byzantine architecture, Armenian and Greek churches, and Turkish mosques, Clara Barton, a Yankee from Massachusetts, set up her headquarters. Like an ambassador she would stay in the capital for the next eight months, orchestrating the relief efforts in the provinces of the interior. Here she would receive dispatches, reports, and eyewitness accounts.

Waking the next day at the hotel, she learned that the sultan still had not approved the entry of the Red Cross into the Ottoman Empire. Having made the arduous trip across oceans and continents, Barton now faced a queasy moment of uncertainty. The next day she was escorted, with Minister Terrell and his interpreter, to the office of the minister of foreign affairs, Tewfik Pasha. The meeting would be "the base of all our work," as Barton put it. Tewfik Pasha, whom Barton described as a handsome, cosmopolitan, "genial" man with "polished manners," received them graciously.

Minister Terrell, who would later become a mouthpiece for the sultan, bluntly told Tewfik Pasha how concerned the Americans were about "the suffering condition of the people of the interior in consequence of the massacres." In the United States there was "great sympathy," he added, and also an intense desire to help the missionaries whose burdens were too great. He then assured Tewfik Pasha that Clara Barton's "objects were purely humanitarian, having neither political, racial, nor religious bear[ings]."

The pasha "listened most attentively," and told them that these sentiments were well understood by his government. "We know you, Miss Barton," Tewfik said, "have long known you and your work. We would like to hear your plans for relief and what you desire." Barton's reply was forthright but shrewd. She had come too far to be turned back now. Like Minister Terrell she never once mentioned the word "Armenian." She, too, made it clear that "the condition to which the people of the interior of Asia Minor had been reduced by recent events had aroused the sympathy of the entire American people until they asked, almost to the extent of a demand, that assistance from them should be allowed to go directly to these sufferers, hundreds of whom had friends and relatives in America." Her language was broad and general, and her slant was toward things American.

"It was at the request of our people, *en masse,*" she said, "that I and a few assistants had come." Barton framed her objectives in ways that she hoped would seem beneficial to Turkey. The mission, Barton said, would relieve the suffering people "from continued distress, the State from the burden of providing for them, and other nations and people from a torrent of sympathy which was both hard to endure and unwholesome in its effects."

Everyone would benefit from her mission, she said, because she "had brought skilled agents, practical and experienced farmers whose first efforts would be to get the people back to their deserted fields and provide them with farming implements and material wherewith to put in summer crops and thus enable them to feed themselves." The Red Cross, she made clear, would transform the wasteland of massacre to a fertile land again"—with "plows, hoes, spades, seed-corn, wheat, and later, sickles, scythes."

As the pasha listened, Barton went on to be as reassuring as she could possibly be. "We have brought only ourselves, no correspondent has accompanied us, and we . . . shall not go home to write a book on Turkey. We are not here for that," she said. "Nothing shall be done in any concealed manner." She wanted him to know that all their dispatches would "go openly through your own telegraph, and I should be glad if all that we shall write could be seen by your government." She concluded that she would never permit "a sly or underhand action with your government," and in her no-nonsense Yankee way she said, "and you will pardon me, Pasha, if I say that I shall expect the same treatment in return—such as I give I shall expect to receive."

WALKING SKELETONS

B y the time Clara Barton's relief teams landed in the Armenian provinces in the spring of 1896, the missionary stations had already been giving what aid they could to the survivors. Now American men and women—physicians, nurses, Red Cross field-workers, and missionaries—found themselves working together, bearing witness, and risking their lives. The dozens of narrative accounts that emerged from their ordeal created a bird's-eye view of what it meant to be thousands of miles from home in the aftermath of massacre.

Dr. Julian B. Hubbell, Clara Barton's general field agent, left Constantinople with his relief team on March 10, 1896, by steamer for Alexandretta, a port on the southern Turkish coast, where they arrived eight days later. With the help of U.S. consular agents Daniel Walker and John Falanga, the Red Cross team put together its caravans for the journey to Aintab, the central station for the southern part of the Armenian provinces. With field agents Edward M. Wistar and Charles King Wood, several dragomans (interpreters), and Reverend Dr. Fuller, the president of the American college in Aintab, they set out in the spring weather, with the fear of massacre everywhere. Hubbell wrote: "Alexandretta was in a state of fear. . . . Kirk Khan, the first stopping place on our journey inland, was threatened with plunder and destruction on the night before our arrival there. At Killis we found the town in a state of fear from the recent massacres."[1] In Killis they began their medical relief as they visited the wounded, who were under the care of a young physician who had come down from the college at Aintab.

When they arrived in Aintab they were warmed by the sight of the American school, college, seminary, and hospital buildings, which stood "out in relief and contrast from the native buildings . . . a welcome reminder of home." As hundreds of students came running down the road to welcome back their college president, they recognized the Red Cross flag and turned the greeting into a Red Cross welcome. The city's Western presence also included two tireless American physicians, Shepherd and Hamilton, and a missionary group of Franciscan Brothers, who, Hubbell noted, were "doing excellent work," despite the fact that the father superior had been killed near Zeitun. Staying in a local *khan* (inn) with his crew to get the feel of the place, Hubbell mapped the region for its needs, received "carefully prepared lists of those artisans needing tools and implements for their various trades and callings," and distributed "clothing, new goods for working up, thread, thimbles, needles, medicines, and surgical stores."[2] Hubbell's plan involved apportioning supplies and relief workers for the major devastated cities to the north— Urfa, Marash, Zeitun, and Harput.

An English couple, Rendel and Helen Harris, were also in Aintab, on an investigative mission for the British Quaker Relief Committee, and what they reported back to England reveals something of the horrors Hubbell and his teams encountered. They described the city as a shocking scene where countless numbers of people were helpless, walking around "mutilated, hands and right arms cut off, and eyes gouged out."[3] They continually heard the Turks taunt the Armenians: "Where is your Christ now? Where is your Jesus? Why does He not save you?" And, since the English, who were supposed to be Armenians' rescuers, did not come, the Turks would shout through the marketplace that the queen couldn't save them; "*several times* they led a donkey with a mangy dog tied on its back around the town," shouting: "Make way for Queen Victoria." The Turks "had a somewhat similar demonstration in derision of the Christ," Helen Harris reported.[4] The indignities and the violence were endless, and some of the Turks and Kurds who had pillaged the Armenian houses found they had no use for "the things they stole at the time of the massacres," and now were "bringing them back and selling them boldly to their former owners!"[5]

In the wake of the devastation, the Harrises reported that the Armenians of Aintab were working industriously and "helping one another splendidly" in their efforts to repair their lives and culture. Mrs. Shepherd, the wife of one of the American physicians, had organized two hundred men and women to do embroidery—"a most exquisite industry to which they seem born," Mrs. Harris put it, and the weaving, she noted, would be sent on to Liberty in London. As they left Aintab, she wrote, in the spirit of Gladstone's England, "Tomorrow, we shall have a wonderful day. It is the day of prayer for Armenia in England, and the commencement here of a week of services."[6]

The Harrises seemed to follow Hubbell's route, and as Hubbell's supplies were sent east to Urfa, they confirmed more scenes of disaster. Urfa, "once [a] metropolis of Eastern Christianity . . . now has become its charnel house and sepulchre," wrote Harris. As the English couple walked through the streets of the ruined city they saw "looted shops and battered doors" and widows and orphans everywhere. Here too they were overwhelmed by the spirit of the Armenians, whose "patience is boundless and unutterable, and their charity towards one another abundant," Harris wrote. "What has been done for them in the West has fractional moral value compared with their care for one another. If the problem of living here can be solved they will solve it; but for myself it seems to be the insoluble and impossible problem, the *reductio ad absurdum* of existence."[7]

In Urfa they found another American, the missionary Corinna Shattuck, doing extraordinary work under enormous stress in an environment close to despair. "Miss S. is a truly wonderful woman, and so free from self-life," Helen Harris described her, "but oh, she is so tired! and there is no possible release, not even for a day."[8] Throughout the worst periods of the massacre in Urfa, Corinna Shattuck worked night and day to shelter and hide Armenians, to administer relief, and to seek food for the survivors. There was not one Armenian house, Rendel Harris wrote, in which he and Miss Shattuck did their daily inspection rounds that "does not show marks of violence." In one home with "marble pillars and beautifully carved woodwork on doors and shutters," they found the owner still alive, but the twenty-one members of his family murdered. "Twenty-one! Just think of the desolation of his hearth and home!" Harris wrote back to England. At the infirmary where Miss Shattuck attended to the wounded daily, the maimed survivors looked ghastly: "a man with a great sword gash across his face cutting the nose in two, another shot through the lungs, another with one hand off and the other wounded."[9]

"But it is impossible for me to tell you in detail what goes on in this relief work. I only want you to know that it is splendidly managed, and that you need not have any fear that the help given here will go into wrong or doubtful hands. It is all being used to set the people on their feet again; but this is no slight task," because as Harris emphasized, the massacres were carried out systematically. "[The] work of Armenian eradication has been anything but a random frenzy. The men have been taken, and, amongst the men, the strongest and ablest and wisest."[10]

In a world of orphans and widows, the relief jobs were often staggering. "What is to be done with the great mass of widows," one missionary wrote. There are "probably over 1500, and some say 3000! All have children, without a father to support them."[11] Following a meeting with Armenian widows, Ruth Harris and Corinna Shattuck found themselves overwhelmed by "several hundred" women with "tears in their eyes or running down their cheeks," who stayed to talk about their husbands and children who had been killed. Although the survivors everywhere were consumed by trauma and grief, Corinna Shattuck, with the aid of the Red Cross and the British Westminster Committee, worked tirelessly to help the widows regain some semblance of their former lives, and within months she, like Mrs. Shepherd in Aintab, had many women embroidering colorful felt mats as well as doing traditional embroidery and weaving for themselves and for whatever cottage industry they could make happen.[12]

In Urfa, J. B. Hubbell received a telegram from Clara Barton in Constantinople, reporting outbreaks of typhus and dysentery at Marash and Zeitun. Hubbell and his team immediately started north, and after three days of "rain, snow and mud," they came to Marash, a city with a large Armenian population, a hundred miles northeast of Aintab. After the massacre there in November, typhus, dysentery, and smallpox were spreading, and the city was crammed with refugees. Hubbell described the surrounding country as having been "pillaged, people killed and villages destroyed, and the frightened remnant of people had crowded" into the city for protection. "With insufficient drainage and warm weather coming on," Hubbell wrote to Barton, and with "typhus, dysentery and smallpox already in the prisons, an epidemic was becoming general." The situation was so desperate that the clergy had "requested mothers not to bring children with smallpox to church."[13]

Clara Barton sent for Ira Harris, an American missionary and physician stationed in Tripoli. He arrived with his assistants and with "his well-filled medical chests and surgical supplies in a mule caravan." As Dr. Harris joined Hubbell the relief work was done with greater efficiency. Ira Harris's description of the scenes in Marash and Zeitun are prophetic of concentration camp scenes of the twentieth century:

> I have witnessed scenes of suffering, both in the United States and the Orient, but never, to my dying day, will I be able to dismiss from my mind the horror of the pinched, haggard faces and forms that gathered about me that first day. Before we left the tent one of the doctors said: "We will now see the place is full of walking skeletons." This expressed fully their condition. Just imagine a place having a normal population of 12,500 living all told in 1403 houses, you can see there is not much cubic space to spare; then imagine 7000 or more refugees to be provided for in the town also . . . in fact not a place that even suggested shelter was unoccupied. The smell and presence of human excrement were everywhere, and this, added to diverse other odors, made the air a fit place for the culture of disease germs.[14]

Harris disclosed how the devastation of massacre plays out in the total breakdown of the health and sanitation infrastructure—in short, the rudiments of civilization. He estimated that about 98 percent of the population had chronic dysentery, diarrhea, dropsy (usually those recovering from typhus), rheumatism, bronchitis, dyspepsia, or malaria; and "all were suffering from anemia and debility." As starvation stalked everyone, the survivors became so desperate that many contracted diarrhea "from eating soup made from grass, weeds, buds and leaves of shrubs and trees."[15]

Primitive as conditions were, Harris and Hubbell's relief teams worked with amazing speed, district by district. After hospitalizing those in extremity, Dr. Harris and his team set up a makeshift soup kitchen in the middle of the ruined city. "We hired (for we could get nothing without a system of bargaining as to price) two large copper kettles" for making grape molasses, and bought "two hundred pounds of beef and made a strong, rich soup. We then strained every nerve to get a soup ticket into the possession of every sick person. . . . The second day we added three kettles, and to supply the number we served at ten o'clock clear meat broth; at four o'clock thick soup of beef and rice. By the end of the third day," Harris recorded, "every sick person was receiving food," and before long the "complaints of vomiting the medicine ceased."

As typhus and dysentery began to cease, the daily funerals decreased in number. One lesson Harris wanted to send back to Barton was a dramatic confirmation of the germ theory that Pasteur and Lister had proved only decades earlier. No doubt Barton knew all that, but the laboratory of Armenian devastation demonstrated it to Dr. Harris so clearly. Disease is carried by microorganisms that thrive in unsanitary conditions, and so he wrote Barton that "it is much better for people to risk possible exposure out in the open air, than risk contagion in vile, unwholesome shelter in an overcrowded town."

In closing his letter to Barton, Harris expressed his own pride in the international rescue work they were both part of. "No one but yourself and your associates and those who have lived in Turkey for a number of years, can appreciate the difficulties and perplexities under which you have labored from the very first. . . . believe me, dear Miss Barton, my wife and I shall hold yourself and your associates always in interested remembrance."[16]

After leaving Marash and Zeitun, Hubbell and his team traveled east and north through the mountains for four days to the "garden city of Malatia," which, Hubbell noted, "formerly had a population of 45,000." At Malatia he found the Armenians living in terror, because 1,500 houses had been plundered and 375 of them burned, and thousands had been killed. Stopping briefly at the ruined city, Hubbell left money for the aid of typhus patients, but had to move on quickly to Harput and Mezre, the twin cities just northeast, with large Armenian populations "suffering more than any other part of the interior."

At Harput "the people turned out *en masse* to welcome the Red Cross," and according to the Reverend Mr. Wheeler, who had founded the Mission and American College of Central Turkey in Marsovan, Hubbell's party was only the second group of Americans (other than missionaries) that had been seen in Harput in the past forty years. In that devastated city the scene of welcome was astonishing: "The road was lined, the streets and windows filled, and house roofs covered, and all had words of welcome on their lips." Although their houses and buildings also had been plundered and burned, the missionaries offered "most kindly, the shelter of the remaining roofs and seats at their table as long as we would stay."

Feeling a bit of nostalgia, Hubbell recalled, "We felt at home again, though startled, too, when we stopped to think we were 8000 miles away and fifteen days by horseback to the nearest steamer that might start us on a homeward trip or that could carry a letter for us to the outside world." The tasks were huge, and the sweep of destruction included not only cities such as Harput, Mezre, Arabkir, and Palu, but hundreds of towns and villages, spanning hundreds of square miles in the rugged and often forbidding terrain of the eastern plateau. "Mr. Wistar," Hubbell wrote, took "the Char-Sanjak with Peri as a centre, the Harpoot plain, and later the Aghan villages. Mr. Wood took the Palou district with two hundred villages, and Silouan in the Vilayet of Diarbekir with one hundred and sixty villages, with the town of Palou and the city of Farkin as centers."[17]

Although she was hundreds of miles away, Barton directed the relief work from Constantinople by telegram. When a telegram reached her reporting that "typhus and dysentery [were] raging in Arabkir" northwest of Harput, and asking for help, she telegrammed Hubbell asking him to send a team there. Woefully understaffed, Hubbell enlisted the help of an American-educated Armenian physician, Dr. Hintlian, and Caroline Bush of the mission at Harput. The severe Anatolian terrain made everything more dangerous. Crossing the Euphrates in a "big wooden scoop-shovel ferryboat" with their luggage and horses they hit a rock, almost capsized, and ended up walking on stones and ragged rocks to the shore with their luggage. Because there were no *khans*, they slept in stables with their horses.

In the "cold, pouring rain," they came into "the ruined city of Arabkir," and again, despite the rain, "hundreds of people stood in the streets as we passed to make their 'salaams'" to welcome the Red Cross. The Armenians were overwhelmed by the sight of strangers bringing aid, and with it—hope—to their remote and ravaged city.

Hubbell's description of Arabkir is an image of wasteland:

Nearly the entire city of Arabkir was in ruins, only heaps of stones where houses had been. Out of eighteen hundred homes but few remained; the markets as well as the dwellings were destroyed, and the people, plundered and destitute, were crowded into the few remaining houses, down [infected] with the typhus. We were told that six hundred had already died of the disease, and the [Armenian] people's physician, the only one in that part of the country, was in prison.[18]

Within a day the Armenian church and school buildings that had escaped destruction were turned into a makeshift hospital, and the team worked there as well as in the remaining dwellings, where many of the sick had gone for shelter. With medicine and surgery, "many lives and limbs were saved," and Hubbell estimated that his team was seeing a hundred patients daily. Once medical relief was under way, they began distributing farming tools, food, and clothing, and the Red Cross relief work began to regenerate the population and their economic infrastructure. "A sheep or a goat given where there was a helpless babe or mother would give food for both, and be a permanent property that would grow by the increase of its own young," Hubbell reported to Barton.

Tools were ordered from Harput for blacksmiths, carpenters, tinkers, masons, and stoneworkers, and within days, "the blacksmiths were set to work making sickles for cutting grass and reaping grain; shovels, plows and other implements for farmers." Because Arabkir was the regional center for cotton manufacturing, Hubbell's team put the vast majority of the women, mostly widows, to work at spinning wheels or looms. After the massacre only a handful of looms remained in a city that once had about twelve hundred, so the new looms were revitalizing. Similarly, the Red Cross helped to restart agriculture by distributing large amounts of field and garden seeds, and bringing oxen and cattle for plowing.[19]

As they approached their next destination, Egin, they were delighted to see that villages that six weeks earlier had been laid waste, and where they had distributed seeds, were now full of "gardens green with onions, potatoes, beans, cucumbers, melons, squash, pumpkins." Hubbell wrote to Barton that "the women were in the fields cutting the grass and grain with the sickles which the blacksmith had made from the iron and steel we had furnished." Where everything had been "plundered, houses burned or destroyed," the people were now "plowing with the plows and oxen we had supplied."[20]

Egin—"an old, strangely beautiful city," as Hubbell described it—was reported to be populated by many of the descendants of the noble families of Nineveh. Since it was unsafe for Hubbell and his crew to go into the villages, they stayed in town with the prominent families of Nicoghos Agha Jangochyan and Alexander Effendi Kasabyan—both of whom had been instrumental in saving the city and many of its people from massacre, while all the villages around them were destroyed. Deciding to leave relief money for the eight surrounding villages they were unable to reach, Hubbell and his team turned around and went back to Harput. Only days after leaving Egin, Hubbell wrote, "we learned the sad news" that the Jangochyan and Kasabyan families—"the center of a large community of the most charming and cultivated people we had met—were massacred along with a thousand others"[21] in the spasms of massacres that continued throughout 1896 and even into early 1897.

As June wore on, the blistering heat of the central Anatolian Plain was such that in order to stay cool and maximize their workday, they traveled by moonlight.[22] By mid-June, Hubbell and his crew had returned to Harput, where they arranged for tools and cattle to go to the more than two hundred surrounding villages that had been "either plundered or wholly destroyed."[23] Since wheat was the main crop of the region, they went to work immediately, once again reseeding the infrastructure by supplying harvesting and threshing tools and cattle for plowing. They continued west to Sivas, and then on to the ancient Armenian and Pontic cities of Tokat and Amasia, keeping the relief project going until they returned to Constantinople, and the Red Cross headquarters, some four months and six days from the time they set out.[24]

Hubbell's Red Cross relief journey was a dramatic chapter in the Armenian relief project, but in other parts of the empire, Americans were working in similar ways amid the ruins. In Van, near the Russian border, the American physician Grace Kimball was working under extraordinary conditions. In June 1895 Kimball wrote to her friend Elizabeth Theldberg, a physician at Vassar College: "We've got to go into relief work forthwith, and I suppose I've got to engineer it. As I have only twenty dollars cash capital I am beginning mildly." Kimball's idea was "to buy wool and cotton, and give it to the famine-stricken people to card and spin at so much the pound."[25] As the thread was then made into socks and clothes, the workers would be paid and the refugees would have clothing as winter came. Within months sixteen thousand people were being "fed daily by the wages paid them in the cotton, wool and garment factories" and the six bakeries Grace Kimball had set up.[26]

A native of New Hampshire and, like Clara Barton, Isabel Barrows, Julia Ward Howe, and Alice Stone Blackwell, a fiercely self-reliant New Englander, Kimball went to Van in 1882, after graduating from Vassar, to run the Girl's Boarding and Day School, which belonged to the American Missionary Board. After six years she returned to the United States to study medicine at Elizabeth Blackwell's Woman's Medical College in New York City, and like several other women physicians was drawn back to the Armenian provinces of Turkey to practice medicine. She happened to arrive just as the Armenian situation in Van was deteriorating in the early 1890s.

Even before the province of Van was torn apart by pillage and massacre, the effects of the massacres in the Bitlis region already had ripple effects on Van, causing the breakdown of the economy and creating poverty and depression throughout this Armenian region. "Practically all the small traders and shopkeepers," Kimball wrote, "all the mechanic and artisan class, are in want of daily bread." As the massacres moved eastward in November 1895, she wrote to Theldberg at Vassar that "a campaign of systematic destruction was set on foot." Fifty villages between Van and the Persian frontier "were pillaged in the space of two weeks and their inhabitants driven out helpless and naked. Already the famous Kurdish Pashas, Hussein and Emin, had devastated thirty-eight or forty villages on the north side of the lake."[27] Now the refugees poured into Van city just as winter was beginning.

Kimball described them as "a vast array of wretched men, women and children, [who] bore down on the city, filling every inch of available space . . . stripped of all their property even to the clothing on their backs, driven out from their homes, many of their men killed . . . wanderers on the face of the earth. . . . Who can answer," she asked, "these innocent victims of a political situation of which they are as innocent as the cattle in their stables?"[28]

Working under extraordinary stress, Kimball wrote to Theldberg in December 1895 that she was 700 pounds in debt, but that "to put down brakes and stop the machinery means taking the daily bread from 7,000 people, not to speak of clothing for hundreds of naked refugees. I am going to keep on a few days longer in the faith that some good news will come." As the winter grew bitter Kimball split her days keeping the work projects going and doing from two to four hours of surgery a day, mostly on "frozen feet and gunshot wounds—sword cuts don't count."[29]

As the numbers of refugees mounted, she turned her weaving relief scheme into something she now called the Van Industrial Bureau, and began employing survivors and refugees by paying them with daily rations of food. By the winter of 1896, Kimball had employed more than a thousand refugees, of whom 70 percent were women occupied in spinning cotton and wool; her sewing operation was able to supply about 250 garments a day to refugees. Relief of this kind was far better than "gratuitous charity," she wrote, affirming her belief in self-reliance and the Protestant work ethic—an ethos that fitted well with the Armenians.[30] Kimball's Labour Relief Bureau in Van made such an impact that *The Graphic* magazine—London's major illustrated weekly—ran a full-page illustration of the bureau in action in December 1895.[31]

All that year philanthropy from the United States continued to arrive at crucial moments. When, in November—a devastating month for the Armenians—ten thousand dollars arrived unexpectedly from the *Christian Herald* (in New York), Kimball said she received it "with joy like that of a drowning man at the approach of his rescuers." Forty-eight hours later, Kimball opened a bakery, and within two weeks, a second one. Known as the *"Christian Herald* Bakeries," their ovens produced 3,750 pounds of bread daily for about 2,500 people. With bread in the oven, Kimball then turned her energy to the building of a hospital, as the epidemics of typhus and cholera were spreading.[32]

Long before Senator Hubert H. Humphrey proposed that Congress create a Peace Corps, and John F. Kennedy, campaigning for president, affirmed the idea by declaring that the United States has "enough know-how and knowledgeable people" to help the underdeveloped nations "help themselves,"[33] the American projects in the Armenian provinces of the Ottoman Empire in the late 1890s were a proto–Peace Corps effort. Grace Kimball's Van Industrial Bureau and the Red Cross relief teams

that worked assiduously to rehabilitate the Armenian agrarian infrastructure with seeds, farm tools, and technology were something quite
revolutionary. There were dozens of others like Grace Kimball working
all over the Armenian provinces of Anatolia to save lives and rehabilitate
Armenian society. Had American philanthropic organizations like the
Christian Herald, the American School in Smyrna, *Outlook* magazine, and
the National Armenian Relief Committee not kept funds flowing into the
hands of those tireless workers, the death tolls would have been even
more staggering.

"THE TEARS OF ARAXES":

THE VOICE OF THE

WOMAN'S JOURNAL

In the fall of 1893 Ohannes Chatschumian was studying at Harvard Divinity School and Alice Stone Blackwell was getting more and more involved in Boston's newly arrived Armenian community. It was the beginning of the Armenian part of America's burgeoning melting pot. By the mid-1890s there were about 10,000 Armenians in the United States, most of them coming in the wake of the sultan's massacres. On the eve of World War I, just before the onset of the Genocide, the Armenian American population would grow to about 66,000. In the years following World War I, refugees and survivors would swell the population to about 145,000. By the end of the twentieth century, Armenian tabulations would place the population at about a million.[1]

As a *New York Times* feature of August 1895 pointed out, Armenians seemed to be Near Eastern counterparts to Americans, which was to say they were often professionals, good entrepreneurs, and businessmen; they were Christian, a growing percentage of them Protestant as a result of the work of the missionaries; they were a "people of the Book" who owned an ancient cultural tradition and were oriented toward higher education; they seemed to be, in every way, devoted to what Americans called the "Protestant work ethic." While—like all other immigrant groups—they faced discrimination, they fitted well into their new land and rose quite quickly in their various walks of life.

Alice Stone Blackwell's diary shows that throughout the mid-nineties, she was devoting much of her time to the Armenian crisis. Several times a week she was going to Armenian meetings at the YMCA, the Phillips Street Congregational Church, Arcade Hall, Wellesley Hills Women's Club, Christ Church, Wellesley College, or as far away as Lynn, Worcester, or Providence. The Armenian names *Gulesian, Papazian, Bedrosian, Djelalian, Keljik, Baghdasarian, Torrosian, Ekserdjian, Damgagian,* and *Varzhabedian* float through her daily register; she is meeting with them for tea or dinner, or going to a play or a party. In Boston and its vicinity, there were various clubs, such as United Friends of Armenia and the Armenian Literary Club, to which both Americans and Armenian Americans belonged.[2]

The Armenian human rights movement had homes in many cities, including New York, Minneapolis, Chicago, Philadelphia, and Worcester, but Boston seemed to be its center, and Alice Stone Blackwell, Isabel Barrows, and Julia Ward Howe were at its epicenter. Almost every major newspaper in the United States covered the Armenian massacres with regularity, but the *Boston Globe,* the *Boston Herald,* and the *Boston Transcript* covered the massacres, the Friends of Armenia, and various relief projects to a greater extent than any other papers in the country. But it was the *Woman's Journal,* the organ of the American Woman Suffrage Association, whose offices were located at 3 Park Street, off the Boston Common, that would cover the Armenian crisis in greater depth and with a more activist perspective than all the rest. The timing was right, for Alice had inherited the primary editorial responsibility for the paper in the wake of her mother's death in 1893, just at the moment that she found herself engaged in the Armenian Question.

For Alice equal rights for women was the bedrock on which her life rested, and her passion for Armenian human rights had its origin there. She felt a mission to educate her new Armenian friends about women's rights. The woman who fell in love with Ohannes was born and bred in the woman suffrage movement. Alice's diary from her teenage years shows her arguing passionately with her schoolmates over women's rights. At fourteen her friend Hattie Mann tells her she is wicked because she sews on Sunday, and Alice tells her right back that she is worse because she doesn't believe in women's rights. " 'Why Alice Blackwell,' cried she, 'do you mean to say you think it's as wicked not to believe in Womans Rights as to sew on Sunday?' I said 'I think it's quite as much of a mistake.' " After starting a novel by James Fenimore Cooper, she was quickly disgusted with him when she discovered that he "disapproved of Womans Rights and called Queen Bess a monster because she was strong minded."[3]

Isabel and Alice found in Ohannes Chatschumian "a most sympathetic soldier," as he called himself, in the movement for women's rights and suffrage. Alice taught Ohannes about women's rights, and he learned quickly, so that within weeks he had become an advocate who saw the larger picture. "For me there is no distinction between the freedom of Armenia and the entire freedom of women. These both kinds of freedom rest on the same principle."[4] In Divinity School, when Professor Thayer asked the class why in the story of Jesus feeding the five thousand Matthew doesn't mention women, Ohannes answered: 'Because women had no vote.' "[5] It was no small thing for an Armenian man from a patriarchal religious tradition to have learned with conviction so quickly the moral issues of the woman suffrage movement.

As a precocious adolescent Alice was outspoken and articulate. Tall, a bit awkward, with bad eyesight from girlhood, there was a touch of Emily Dickinson about her. Like Dickinson too, she had struggled with God as an adolescent; in the end she found herself more agnostic than not, but considered herself a Christian in an ethical sense. Alice's parents were cultural radicals and reformers. Her mother, Lucy Stone, was the first woman ever to speak full-time for woman's rights, the first woman from the state of Massachusetts to earn a college degree; the first woman to keep her maiden name. Susan B. Anthony credited Stone with introducing her to the woman's rights movement.[6]

An unusually progressive man for his era, Henry Blackwell was born in England and came to Cincinnati as a young man and soon became a staunch abolitionist. His sisters were trailblazers. In 1849 Elizabeth Blackwell became the first woman to receive an M.D. in the United States, and younger sister, Emily, followed in her older sister's footsteps soon after. Although Lucy had pledged never to marry, she confessed that Henry's sisters tilted the scale in favor of his marriage proposal.

The marriage of Lucy Stone and Henry Blackwell in 1854 was distinguished by the wedding vows they wrote to protest the state of the institution of marriage. The couple rejected the contemporary laws of marriage because they "refuse to recognize the wife as an independent, rational being, while they confer upon the husband an injurious and unnatural superiority, investing him with legal powers which no honorable man would exercise, and which no man should possess." Immediately after the wedding, Lucy announced that she would be known only by her maiden name, and for decades after, women who followed her example were known as "Lucy Stoners."[7]

Lucy had been a brilliant nonconformist student at Oberlin College, where she became an ardent abolitionist. A picture of William Lloyd Garrison was prominently placed in her dorm room,[8] and the abolitionist leader extolled her as "a superior young woman," with a bright future for public lecturing, after meeting her at college graduation.[9] Upon graduating she announced that she was going to pursue a career as a public speaker for human rights, and when her mother fiercely disapproved, she replied in a letter: "Mother. . . . I expect to plead not for the slave only, but for suffering humanity everywhere. ESPECIALLY DO I MEAN TO LABOR FOR THE ELEVATION OF MY SEX."[10] By the spring of 1848, she had become an agent and lecturer for Garrison's abolitionist society, and became the first woman to lecture on both antislavery and women's rights. She was such a sensation that P. T. Barnum tried to hire her in 1854 to do a series of lectures for him. When the fight over equal rights hit Kansas in 1867, a telegraph to the American Equal Rights Association in New York read: "With the help of God and Lucy Stone, we shall carry Kansas."[11]

By 1869, however, she was engaged in bitter ideological and personal conflicts with her colleagues Susan B. Anthony and Elizabeth Cady Stanton. In addition to various differences in sensibility and political strategies, perhaps their most flammable disagreement was over the 15th Amendment to the Constitution. Anthony and Stanton opposed suffrage for the newly emancipated slaves if women weren't also included. Lucy Stone's camp, which included Julia Ward Howe, Henry Ward Beecher, and Mary Livermore, remained firm on the 15th Amendment for Negroes even without suffrage for women. A year later the conflicts resulted in a split in the movement; Anthony and Stanton founded the National Woman Suffrage Association (NWSA) and Lucy Stone and Henry Blackwell were instrumental in the founding of the American Woman Suffrage Association (AWSA). After the schism the Stone-Blackwell family moved from

East Orange, New Jersey, where Alice had been born, to Boston, where they established their new suffrage movement with their Boston friends and colleagues such as William Lloyd Garrison Jr., Julia Ward Howe, Thomas Wentworth Higginson, and Mary Livermore. Alice, then thirteen, felt a sense of permanence in her new house in Dorchester, where she settled into the plot of land she would call home for the rest of her life. Looking down on Boston Harbor to the north, and west out to the Blue Hills of Milton, she was just a fifteen-minute train ride from downtown Boston and the offices of her parents' newly founded newspaper, the *Woman's Journal*.[12]

In 1893, just as Ohannes was settling into his year at Harvard Divinity School, Lucy Stone died, and Alice took over the major responsibilities of the paper. Blackwell's coverage of the Armenian massacres strikes one today as astonishingly modern, and her focus on gender and violence in the Armenian case seems also prophetic. Eyewitness accounts of the massacres, weekly articles about the Friends of Armenia, and news of the national network of relief efforts for the victims filled the pages of the *Woman's Journal*. Week after week headlines read, THE ARMENIAN CRISIS IN TURKEY, THE WOMEN OF ARMENIA, SUFFERINGS OF ARMENIAN PEASANTS, THE HAMIDIE CAVALRY IN TURKEY, and WOMEN'S VIEWS ON ARMENIA. Activist projects were also a steady part of its reportage: settling Armenian refugees in the United States, finding host families for the refugees and new émigrés, helping them find employment.[13]

Having emerged in the wake of her mother's split with Stanton and Anthony, the *Woman's Journal* in some sense was a reply to the NWSA's newspaper, *The Revolutionist*. Financed by members of the AWSA, the *Woman's Journal* had among its founding shareholders an impressive cast of New England intellectuals that included Julia Ward Howe, social reformer Caroline Severance, William Lloyd Garrison Jr., women's rights activists and former abolitionists Sarah Grimké and Angelina Grimké Weld, and the Unitarian minister and advocate of women's rights Samuel May. Mary Livermore became a chief editor and Thomas Wentworth Higginson a contributing editor. In some ways the paper was more conservative than *The Revolutionist*, and in others it was more radical and cosmopolitan. The *Woman's Journal* pledged itself to organize suffrage state by state, and accepted the 14th and 15th Amendments with a commitment that was congruent with the abolitionist past of its members.[14]

For forty-seven years a large and important chapter of the women's movement was recorded in its pages, as it fostered new ideas, was a forum for progressive education, and advocated an international perspective on women's rights and other human rights. Lucy corresponded with women around the world, and her paper covered woman suffragist gatherings in Paris, London, Brussels, and Geneva. Notwithstanding the support of its shareholders, in the end Lucy, Henry, and later Alice did the major share of editing and production. When the first issue appeared on January 8, 1870, its five thousand copies sold out immediately, and by 1875 the paper's subscription list boasted readers in every state in the union and thirty-nine foreign countries.[15]

By the time her mother died in 1893, Alice had been taking the trolley each morning for years from Dorchester to her office at the *Woman's Journal*. There, in a large parlorlike room with a big Victorian fireplace and its newly installed coal-burning stove, Alice and her staff received news about the Armenian massacres from London, Paris, Athens, and Constantinople, and edited the array of articles they would run that week. In many ways it was an early modern moment: liberal Americans in their privileged world, using the modern tools of communication to disseminate news to fellow Americans about human rights crimes being committed thousands of miles away.

Ohannes and Alice saw each other regularly, and among other things continued to translate poems for their anthology. They also continued to speak at various Armenian organizations and were instrumental in creating a growing network of activist interest in the Armenian Question. Ohannes was a regular visitor at the Blackwell house at 45 Boutwell Street in Dorchester, and he seemed to be very much Alice's gentleman caller. Alice's father was fond of Ohannes; Alice noted in a letter to Isabel Barrows that "father was in a miserable mood" until Ohannes arrived for dinner and began telling stories, and then you could see "father's face beam."[16]

In the midst of their translating in the summer of 1894, Ohannes, not in the best of health, decided it was time to return to Germany to finish his studies at the University of Leipzig. Not long after that, with the news of the Sasun massacres breaking in the American press, Isabel Barrows wrote Ohannes:

I knew that your heart would be sore wounded by the terrible sorrows in our dear Armenia. But my dear boy, sad and frightful as this is there is all the more reason for living. It would be base cowardice to die now. You have seen how happy freedom and enlightenment can make a country, for you have seen America. . . . There is a great excitement in this country and we are fanning it all we can. *The Christian World* of London has an excellent editorial. Write an article at once for that paper. . . . Write another for the *London Daily News.* England is the place where we must strike.

Trying to bolster the ailing Ohannes with some American spirit, she informed him that

the citizens of Malden have called a mass meeting for Thursday night. Two hundred Americans met in Boston last night and made an appeal to the Czar to say to Turkey, "hands off Christians." He may not do it but if England know that they have appealed to him because they have lost faith in Great Britain it may stir England up. . . . Mr. Blackwell has about consented to carry the petition to the Czar and says he shall take Alice. They want Mrs. Howe to go too.[17]

Ohannes's health had been failing, and within a year he had taken a turn for the worse. Alice wrote to her new émigré friend, the writer Bedros Keljik, that Ohannes "has been spitting blood occasionally, and we are anxious about him. . . . Mrs. Barrows is greatly distressed, and [she] and I are trying to persuade [him] to come back to America immediately." She urged Keljik to write Ohannes and tell him "how much the Armenians in this country need teaching and inspiration and good counsel. . . . He certainly did good when he was here before. Say anything of that kind that you can think of."[18]

Although Ohannes tried to convince his two protectors that he was getting better, Isabel was relentless and ordered the German physician to send her his diagnosis. Less than two months before Ohannes's death in May 1896, Alice was still hoping against hope that Ohannes didn't really have consumption and that he could "spend a few months in Italy" to recover, or if it should prove too serious, come back to the States to be cured; then, she hoped the catholikos (Supreme Head of the Armenian church) would make him bishop of the Armenian Church in America.[19]

A few days later Alice reported to Keljik that her beloved Ohannes was "so weak from hemorrhage of the lungs that he cannot write," and that he had won the hearts of the staff at the hospital. Now she and Isabel were hoping to get him to "Egypt when he is well enough to be moved."[20]

On April 10, 1896, as the headlines in the American papers continued to report the Armenian massacres, Ohannes wrote Isabel a birthday card: "On your birthday I can't send you anything but love, and that I send a whole heartful. Love to Mayrig, Alice, and to all." And he added a sentimental Mother's Day adage, "God couldn't be everywhere, and therefore he made mothers."[21] By the end of the month, Alice and Isabel were so desperate with anxiety that they decided to sail to Germany to rescue Ohannes and bring him to Arizona or Colorado. On a rainy day in early May, they boarded a ship from Boston. But four days into their voyage they received a telegram informing them that Ohannes had died. Stunned and grief stricken, they arrived two days later with the hope of seeing Ohannes's face one last time and rescuing his papers.

Ohannes was gone, but Alice's torch for the Armenian cause grew even more intense, and his ghost seemed to haunt her continued immersion in the Armenian Question. From Paris she wrote to Isabel, who was still in Leipzig dealing with Ohannes's papers, that she had just spent six dollars and she "reflected with remorse [on] how many starving Armenians the money would have fed." Taking a train back to her hotel, she "looked out and saw pink flowers wavering in the wind along the grassy banks, and felt as if the blood of the martyrs were already turning into flowers."[22]

It is impossible to know how her relationship with Ohannes would have played out. Alice was convinced they would have married, and he would have been free to do so as a teacher or priest, though not as a bishop. Her close friend and secretary, Edna Stantial, wrote—in 1930 as Alice was publishing her biography of her mother—that Alice told her that "if Ohannes had lived they no doubt would have been married." "If Fate had treated her a little more kindly," she believed she would "be including in the story of Lucy Stone the names of Armenian-American grandchildren." Alice never married, and while she confided to Stantial that she had crushes on boys in high school and infatuations at college, the one true love of her life was Ohannes. A lock of his hair was found among her papers.[23] The love between Alice and Ohannes seemed, in some way, inseparable from the Armenian cause, and the two of them made things happen in Boston and then across the nation that might not have happened otherwise.

One of their legacies was the project that brought them together, the anthology of Armenian poetry in English. After Ohannes left for Leipzig, Alice teamed up with Bedros Keljik, who translated the remaining poems with her to finish the anthology. Shortly after Clara Barton arrived in Turkey with her Red Cross team in February 1896, *Armenian Poems* was published. Even before the anthology came out, the poems, which had appeared in magazines and newspapers, had made a stir in Constantinople, where Alice's name was censored by the sultan in the Armenian press. Alice wrote to Keljik that "it is forbidden even to print my name in the papers in Constantinople"; at most they were able to print "that Bedros Tourian's poems have been translated by Miss Alice."[24]

In her preface to *Armenian Poems,* Alice wrote that "the sympathy felt for the Armenians in the unspeakable sufferings at the hands of the Turks would be deepened by an acquaintance with the temper and genius of the people, as shown in their poetry."[25] The anthology presented several dozen poems, most of them by nineteenth-century poets such as Bedros Tourian, Michael Nalbandian, and Raphael Patkanian, who were part of a renaissance in Armenian culture. They also included some classical poets, such as the medieval Krikor Narekatsi (Gregory of Narek) or the eighteenth-century Sayat Nova, to give the reader a sense of a longer standing literary history. Well-armed with appendices, the book had an introduction about Armenian history and the recent massacres, as well as essays about the Armenian church and the advanced status of Armenian women.

Armenian Poems was poetry anthology as cultural emissary; its publication was a literary event that carried with it a vision of a culture in crisis, and it was reviewed well and widely in popular and literary newspapers and magazines. The *San Francisco Chronicle* extolled Armenian poets for their "high poetic powers." The *Chicago Post* called it "a collection of poems revealing unexpected beauties"; the *Boston Transcript* noted, "That a second edition of *Armenian Poems* is already in press, although the first has not yet been out a fortnight shows how strong is the interest in this graceful and forceful interpretation of the life of an oppressed people." A reviewer for *Christian Work* wrote, "We can better understand the *Song of Solomon* after reading these. A tinge of sadness colors many of these exquisite poems, for they have been written in a land desolated by fire and sword. But, beyond all else . . . they are all aglow with love of truth and liberty."[26]

The success of the anthology, which would be reprinted in 1917 during another Armenian crisis, was the symbolic offspring of Alice and Ohannes's relationship. Whether they might have married or not, they had succeeded in transporting a piece of Armenia's ancient literary tradition to the shores of the New World.

THE OTTOMAN BANK INCIDENT AND THE AFTERMATH OF THE HAMIDIAN MASSACRES

Not long after Ohannes died, and just as Clara Barton pulled out of Constantinople with her relief teams in the summer of 1896, another conflagration erupted. This time it was in Constantinople, and the consequences for the Armenians would be disastrous. Although there had been outrage expressed in the United States and Europe, and relief efforts and money sent, the sultan's massacres had gone essentially unpunished, and the Armenians seemed more vulnerable than ever. As the *Daily Telegraph* of London had put it more than a year earlier: "The Armenian population throughout the entire country are exhibiting a marvelous degree of patience under treatment which would rouse any other people to open rebellion."[1]

In August 1896 members of the Armenian reform party, the Dashnaks, were poised to stage a protest of a kind that had never been seen in the Ottoman Empire before. Led by three young, idealistic, and somewhat naive activists, Armen Garo (Karekin Pastermadjian), Papken Siuni, and Hratch Tiryakian, twenty-five armed Dashnak Party activists made a surprise attack on the Ottoman Bank shortly after 1:00 P.M. on August 26—a hot, blue-skied day in the capital. A citadel of European banking, especially British and French finance, the Ottoman Bank was one of the most important financial institutions in the empire and was a stately nineteenth-century neoclassical edifice in the commercial district of the city, not far from the Armenian Patriarchate. The Dashnaks saw it as a perfect site for making a political statement to the European powers.

The mastermind behind the scheme was Papken Siuni (born Bedros Parian), the twenty-three-year-old son of an aristocratic family. He teamed up with his friends Garo and Tiryakian, who had both rushed back to Turkey from Nancy in France, where they were studying, when they learned of the sultan's massacres. Until the summer of 1896, the Dashnak and Hunchak Parties had sponsored demonstrations and generated activist fervor where they could. In fact, the Young Turks seemed more interested in them than in most of the other Armenian organizations. But in the summer of 1896, feeling frustration and outrage in the face of nearly two years of massacres, a group of Dashnaks came up with a new idea.[2]

Before storming the bank, the activists issued several manifestos to the Turks and the European powers. In the name of the Dashnak Central Committee of Constantinople, they addressed the Turkish people, intending the message to be heard loudly and clearly by the powers:

> For centuries our forbears have been living with you in peace and harmony . . . but recently your government, conceived in crimes, began to sow discord among us in order to strangle us and you with greater ease. You, people, did not understand this diabolical scheme of politics and, soaking yourselves in the blood of our brothers, you became an accomplice in the perpetration of the heinous crime. Nevertheless, know well that our fight is not against you, but your government, against which your own best sons are fighting also.[3]

In their appeal to the European powers, the Dashnaks asserted that the Ottoman government's crimes had gone unpunished, and that Europe's inaction had allowed such impunity. "The patience of down-trodden nations has its limits," and Europe's silence, they declared, has enabled "Turkish tyranny" and "Sultan Hamid's . . . murderous vengeance." "The time of diplomatic play is passed. The blood shed by our 100,000 [the death toll to that date] martyrs gives us the right to demand liberty." Their language was strong, and they demanded "judicial reforms according to the European system"; the creation of a post of "High Commissioner" to oversee the Armenian provinces—a European to be "elected by the Six Great

Powers"; genuine "freedom of worship, education, and the press"; and the "restoration of usurped real property."⁴ These were bold and direct words, and this appeal, along with the 1895 Protest-Demand, are landmark texts in the history of civil rights in the Ottoman Empire and certainly look forward to the evolution of civil rights in the twentieth century.

In the early afternoon, Armen Garo walked toward the bank. Several of his comrades, including one named Hovannes, from Baybert, drew their guns and opened fire on one of the Albanian bank guards. The guard fired back, and there was an exchange of gunfire between the Armenians and the bank guards. Then, the bank's armed security force appeared and about twenty Armenians ran for the bank. In the chaos Armen Garo ran up to the second floor, followed by a dozen of his men.⁵

When Papken Siuni was shot and killed, Armen Garo took over as leader. He described the initial scene as pure chaos: shooting, bombs being thrown from windows, plaster falling from the ceiling, the building "filled with clouds of smoke and white dust,"⁶ and then Turkish troops arriving so soon that Garo thought the sultan must have been forewarned.

Garo ordered his men to barricade the doorway with large sacks of heavy coins. So inexperienced were the Armenians that, as they hit the floor to evade gunfire, the explosives they were carrying on their belts went off, and as Garo put it, our "comrades [were] torn to pieces," lying on the floor, "their legs shattered." Soon it became clear to Garo "that the majority of our boys were handling guns for the first time," and Garo found himself giving those still alive "a slap in the face" to awaken them "out of their stupor and fright."⁷

Within a couple of hours they "could hear the howling of the Turkish mob in Galata," which meant that Armenians were being massacred again out in the streets.⁸ Then, from the windows of the second-floor foyer, Garo and his men watched a huge mob heading for the bank: *bashebozuks* (irregulars), *softas*, theological students in long white gowns and white turbans, and some police. The young Armenians looked down as the soldiers pointed their bayonets at the mob and their commander shouted at his men, "Where are you going, you fools? The Armenians have cannons and will mow you down like so many dogs!" The squadron moved a distance away, but the *softas* would not halt and came "like a torrent in a great uproar, pushing one another, holding swords, sticks, and axes." When the *softas* began to break down the doors with axes, Garo gave the signal to drop the bombs. Those who could ran off; the rest lay dead. What could they do, Garo wrote, "Let those wretched ones massacre us?"⁹ Garo implored the people inside the bank not to be afraid. "We're neither murderers, nor bandits. We are Armenians who have come here in defense of our people's cause." An Irishman who worked at the bank shouted back— "I am an Irishman, sir, and I understand you very well. How can I help you?"¹⁰

As the drama escalated inside and outside the bank, the bank's director, Sir Edgar Vincent, who had already escaped from his office through a skylight onto the roof of the adjoining building, the Tobacco Regie, proceeded to the sultan's palace to try to negotiate a deal with the Ottoman Council of Ministers. Simultaneously the first dragoman at the Russian Embassy, M. Maximof, had rushed to the palace and was instrumental in helping Vincent negotiate with the sultan, who agreed to pardon the Armenian activists and give them permission to leave the country unharmed. Inside the bank, a French bank official, Sir Edgar Vincent's deputy, Monsieur Auboyneau, became the mediator for the Dashnaks, and as the drama unfolded over the next thirteen hours, Auboyneau was allowed to leave and relay the Armenians' demands to Maximof and the sultan. Garo and his comrades were demanding an immediate halt to the massacre of Armenians that was in progress on the streets of Constantinople and to the firing on the bank by the *softas* and troops.¹¹

In a letter Garo stated that it was "the criminal indifference of humanity" that drove them to this extreme, and he asked the French chargé d' affaires at Constantinople to secure peace and order in Turkey through "international intervention." While the Armenians threatened to blow up the bank if their demands weren't met, they also continued to assure everyone that they had no interest in the bank's money, and that they had been driven to this action by the desperate need to secure basic human rights, for the sultan's massacres had already resulted in the deaths of one hundred thousand Armenians and the destruction of much of Armenian life and civilization throughout the empire.¹²

As negotiations continued among Maximof, Auboyneau, Ibrahim Hakki (the Ottoman Bank interpreter), and the sultan, the bank was a scene of battle. From the windows, roof, and various nooks and crannies of the facade, the Armenians fought off the Turkish troops and the ad hoc mob led by the *softas*. Dozens were mowed down in the streets, and of the twenty-five Armenians who had occupied the bank, four were now dead and six wounded. Moreover, with ammunition dwindling, morale sinking, and a rather belated realization that the destruction of the bank would provoke the sultan to another round of gigantic vengeance against innocent Armenians in the provinces and result in complete European abandonment of the Armenian Question—the young Dashnaks were ready to give up.

The French ambassador, Paul Cambon, later credited Auboyneau and especially Maximof for their skillful diplomacy, which was crucial in bringing the crisis to resolution. Maximof short-circuited the sultan's plan to bomb the building to rubble by threatening to have the European powers destroy the palace with cannon fire from their battleships, which were anchored in the Dardanelles. He is reported to have said to Garo's men: "I beg you, I go down on my knees, please hurry up and leave the premises. I obtained [the] Sultan's permission with great difficulty. Tomorrow he may change his mind. Think of the enormous responsibility falling on your shoulders, should new waves of massacre further decimate your people."[13]

In the cooler, dark hours of the morning, at about 3:30 A.M., with dust settling over the debris in the street, the fifteen remaining Armenians were escorted by guards into the street that hours earlier had been littered with bullets and slain bodies. In the distance Garo and his men could hear the occasional sound of the mob and screams of people who had been taken from their homes to be killed; Garo had little doubt that the screams were those of innocent Armenians. Garo and his men were taken to Sir Edgar Vincent's yacht and then transferred to the French steamer *Gironde,* which took them into temporary exile in Marseilles. The authorities were more than surprised to find that only twenty-five and not two hundred Armenians had seized the bank, had left behind gunpowder bombs and dynamite, and had not touched a cent of money.[14]

A number of European newspapers, such as *Freie Presse* of Vienna, the *Tageblatt* of Berlin, and *Etoile Belge* of Brussels praised the Armenian activists for their honesty in the face of the great wealth of the bank and their courage in pursuing social change. No doubt the tradition of civil rights and democratic protest that had galvanized Europe during the not so distant past—in Belgium, France, and Poland in the 1830s and 1840s—

was still fresh in European memory. The staff physician on the *Gironde* wrote to *Etoile Belge* that the Armenian activists were "neither thieves nor robbers" but "honorable" and "men with a sense of complete self-sacrifice . . . heroes" working for justice.[15] To much of Europe, the Armenian seizure of the Ottoman Bank was an act of civil resistance in the face of appalling injustice, a political act that evoked the storming of the Bastille, the first shot fired at Lexington and Concord, and the popular uprisings of 1848 in Paris and Berlin.

It was ironic that Clara Barton had recently left Constantinople on a Romanian steamer for the Danube, with a great feeling of accomplishment. As she recalled in her memoir:

> The magnificent new quay in either direction was crowded with people without distinction of nationality, the strange costumes and colors commingling in such variety as only an Oriental city can produce . . . [when] the hoarse whistle sounded and the boat swayed from its moorings, the dense crowd swayed with it and the subdued tones pealed out in tongues many and strange; but all had one meaning—thanks, blessings, and God speed.[16]

But by the time Barton and her Red Cross team arrived in London in the last week of August and were preparing for the last leg of their journey home, news of the Ottoman Bank incident reached them. Barton was "shocked and distressed beyond words," as she put it, and was ready to turn around and go back to Constantinople to begin work again. "The streets where we had passed, the people who had served us," she exclaimed, "the Ottoman Bank where we had transacted business almost daily for nearly a half a year, all in jeopardy if not destroyed."[17] Advised to continue home because the situation was reportedly under control, Barton left England for America not knowing exactly what had happened until she returned home.

For two days following the bank takeover, according to the British chargé, "the Turkish mob," the "Softas and other fanatics" used clubs and iron bars to bludgeon thousands of Armenians to death all over the city. And both he and the French ambassador agreed that the weapons had been furnished by the authorities, with the sultan's backing.[18] The Austrian military attaché, also an eyewitness to many street scenes, affirmed that the central authorities were behind the distribution of cudgels and sticks "fitted with a piece of iron," and instructed the mob "to start killing Armenians, irrespective of age and gender, for the duration of 48 hours." The scenes of Turkish mobs killing Armenians with bludgeons to the head "repeated themselves before my eyes interminably," the Austrian military attaché wrote.[19] The French political scientist Victor Bérard, who conducted a study of the massacre and surveyed the killing sites, also affirmed that "all was prepared in advance, the slaughterers, the sticks, the police informers, and the carts" to remove the corpses of the victims.[20] By September 2, British chargé Michael Herbert wrote to Prime Minister Salisbury in London that on Thursday evening when the sultan ordered the mob to cease, the killing stopped.[21]

In a "Collective Note" to the Porte, the European powers, on the basis of eyewitness evidence, asserted that "it is the positively-established fact" the Ottoman government allowed "savage gangs" to massacre the Armenians, and that such gangs "showed every sign of being a special organization," "dressed and armed alike." And these gangs "were led or accompanied by Softas, soldiers, and even police officers." The note went on to underscore that the killer-gangs "were allowed to circulate freely, and execute their crimes with impunity, before the eyes of the troops and their officers. . . . These facts need no comment."[22]

The fact that the Europeans had helped Garo and his men escape to Europe, while European warships still stood by in the harbor, didn't deter the sultan, who now planned more large-scale massacres throughout the empire. Anyone who has seen Elia Kazan's memorable film *America, America* (1963) will recall that the film opens with scenes of the sultan's reprisal massacres of September 1896. On September 15, less than three weeks after the bank incident, the sultan ordered the local authorities to begin a massacre in the city of Egin in Harput Province—an old and wealthy city founded by Armenians who had migrated from Iran. The sultan appears to have chosen Egin because Papken Siuni, the principal architect of the bank takeover, was its native son. According to French ambassador Cambon, more than two thousand Armenians were killed in a "terrible massacre," and "many women and children" were slaughtered. Nearly a thousand of the fifteen hundred houses in Egin's Armenian quarter were pillaged and burned.[23]

The British vice-consul at Harput, Raphael Fontana, also confirmed that a cipher telegram was issued from the sultan's palace to the military governor to mobilize the imperial troops under the pretext that there might be latent revolutionary tendencies in the city. In fact "there was no revolutionary movement whatever," he wrote, and nothing more than a few pistols were found in the ruins of the Armenian quarter.[24] Once again false charges of provocation were used to rationalize the massacre of thousands of innocent people who had nothing to do with the Dashnak Party or the Ottoman Bank takeover.

THE AFTERMATH OF THE 1890s MASSACRES

When the chain of massacres that had begun in 1894 at Sasun and continued through the end of 1896 was over, the death toll was beyond anything anyone could have imagined. There had never been an event of mass slaughter in modern history like this one. According to Ernst Jäckh, a German Foreign Ministry operative, and a Turcophile, two hundred thousand Armenians were killed and another fifty thousand expelled, and one million Armenian homes were pillaged and plundered. The French historian Pierre Renouvin, president of the commission in charge of assembling and classifying French diplomatic documents, concluded that the number of Armenians who perished in the Sultan's massacres was 250,000.[25] Johannes Lepsius, a German pastor who traveled through the Armenian provinces on an investigative mission in the aftermath of the massacres in the spring of 1896, put forth a cautious estimate of one hundred thousand dead from the immediate killing, but estimated that the aftermath of massacre would bring with it the deaths of another one hundred thousand from famine, disease, and injury.[26]

Lepsius realized that the enormity and significance of the loss could not be measured solely in terms of lives. The cultural destruction of the sultan's program was of genocidal proportions because it so devastated "the social fabric and cultural institutions" of Armenian society and culture. According to the data compiled by Lepsius, by the spring of 1896 the sultan's massacres had resulted in the following: 2,500 towns and villages were left completely desolate; 645 churches and monasteries were destroyed. Survivors in 559 villages, plus hundreds in cities, were forcibly converted to Islam. This included fifteen thousand Armenians in the provinces of Erzurum and Harput who converted under the threat of death. In addition, 328 churches were recast into mosques, 508 churches and monasteries were plundered, and 21 Protestant and 170 Apostolic priests were killed; 546,000 people were reduced to destitution.[27]

William M. Ramsay, the British ethnographer who had spent more than a decade doing research in Turkey, and who admired the Turks and was often critical of the Armenians for their passivity, assessed the trauma of massacre on Armenians and their culture:

> Turkish massacre . . . does not mean merely that thousands are killed in a few days by the sword, the torture, or the fire. It does not mean merely that everything they possess is stolen, their houses and shops looted and often burned, every article worth a halfpenny taken, the corpses stripped. It does not mean merely that the survivors are left penniless—without food, sometimes literally stark naked. . . . Sometimes, when the Turks have been specially merciful, they have offered their victims an escape from death by accepting Mohammedanism.

"That is only the beginning, the brighter and lighter side of a massacre in Turkey," Ramsay goes on with an almost Conradian sense of the horror:

> But as to the darker side of Turkish massacre—personal outrage and shame—take what the more freespoken historians of former times have told; gather together the details of the most horrible and indescribable outrages that occasional criminals of half-lunatic character commit in this country; imagine those criminals collected in thousands, heated with the hard work of murder, inciting each other and vying with each other, encouraged by the government officials with promises of impunity and hope of plunder—imagine the result if you can, and you will have some faint idea of the massacres in the eastern parts of Turkey. There has been no exaggeration in the worst accounts of the horrors of Armenia. A writer with the vivid imagination of Dumas and the knowledge of evil that Zola possesses could not attain, by any description, the effect that the sight of one massacre in the Kurdish

part of Armenia would produce on any spectator. The Kurdish part of Armenia is the "black country." It has become a charnel house. One dare not enter it. One cannot think about it. One knows not how many maimed, mutilated, outraged Armenians are still starving there.[28]

The British consul Henry Barnham, who oversaw Aintab and Birecik in Aleppo Province, made it clear in his account how powerfully the killing of Armenians was motivated by Islamic fanaticism and a *jihad* mentality:

The butchers and the tanners, with sleeves tucked up to the shoulders, armed with clubs and cleavers, cut down the Christians, with cries of "Allahu Akbar!" broke down the doors of the houses with pickaxes and levers, or scaled the walls with ladders. Then when mid-day came they knelt down and said their prayers, and then jumped up and resumed the dreadful work, carrying it on far into the night. Whenever they were unable to break down the doors they fired the houses with petroleum, and the fact that at the end of November petroleum was almost unpurchasable in Aleppo suggests that enormous quantities were bought up and sent north for this purpose.[29]

Muslim clerics played a perpetual role in the massacring of Armenians; imams and *softas* would often rally the mob by chanting prayers; and mosques were often used as places to mobilize crowds, especially during Friday prayers.[30] Christians were murdered in the name of Allah. One survivor, Abraham Hartunian, described the desecration of two Armenian churches (one Gregorian—Armenian Apostolic—and the other Protestant) in the town of Severek in Diyarbekir Province:

The mob had plundered the Gregorian church, desecrated it, murdered all who had sought shelter there, and, as a sacrifice, beheaded the sexton on the stone threshold. Now it filled our yard. The blows of an axe crashed in the church doors. The attackers rushed in, tore the Bibles and hymnbooks to pieces, broke and shattered whatever they could, blasphemed the cross and, as a sign of victory, chanted the Mohammedan prayer: *"La ilaha ill-Allah, Muhammedin Rasula-llah"* (There is no other God but one God, and Mohammed is His prophet). . . . The leader of the mob cried: *"Muhammede salavat!"* Believe in Mohammed and deny your religion. No one answered. . . . The leader gave the order to massacre. The first attack was on our pastor. The blow of an axe decapitated him. His blood, spurting in all directions, spattered the walls and ceiling."[31]

Two letters from a Turkish soldier on duty in Erzurum with the Fourth Company, Second Battalion, Twenty-fifth Regiment, written to his parents and brother in Harput, also lend insights into Turkish attitudes about killing Armenians. The letters came into the hands of a British consul after the massacres in that city and were put in the consular file marked "confidential."

My brother, if you want news from here we have killed 1,200 Armenians, all of them as food for the dogs. . . . Mother, I am safe and sound. Father, 20 days ago we made war on the Armenian unbelievers. Through God's grace no harm befell us. There is a rumor afoot that our Battalion will be ordered to your part of the world—if so, we will kill all the Armenians there. Besides, 511 Armenians were wounded, one or two perish every day. If you ask after the soldiers and Bashi Bozouks, not one of their noses has bled. . . . May God bless you.

In these letters, massacring Armenians is seen as a commonplace occurrence sanctioned by Islam as well as by the government. As Dadrian put it: "Here is a regimental unit of the standing army engaged in broad daylight in peacetime killing operations against unarmed civilian populations."[32]

Among the most ghoulish scenes recorded was the extermination of the Armenians of Urfa. Urfa, once ancient Edessa (the city to which Christ's disciples brought Christianity, in this dry region of southeastern Anatolia), had been the site of massacre in October 1895 during the wave of autumn killings of that year, and the Armenians remained under siege in their quarter of the town for the following two months. Then, on

December 28th at midday, a bugle sounded and Turkish soldiers and civilians invaded the Armenian quarter. Doors of houses and shops were smashed open with axes and clubs, and people were shot on the spot. Their material goods and valuables were stolen, and kerosene was poured on the rest. At sunset, when the bugle sounded again, the killers retreated, and the Armenians who had survived sought refuge in their cathedral. (Traditionally synagogues and churches were to be respected as places of refuge under Islamic law).

The next morning the Turkish troops fired through the church windows and broke down the iron door, mockingly calling on "Christ now to prove himself a greater prophet than Mohammed." They began killing everyone on the floor of the church by hand or with pistols. From the altar they gunned down the women and children in the gallery. Finally the Turks gathered bedding and straw, on which "they poured some thirty cans of kerosene" and set the church ablaze. British Consul G. H. Fitzmaurice's careful description reveals something about the religious ethos underpinning the killings:

> The gallery beams and wooden framework soon caught fire, whereupon, blocking up the staircases leading to the gallery with similar inflammable materials, they left the mass of struggling human beings to become the prey of the flames.
>
> During several hours the sickening odour of roasting flesh pervaded the town, and even to-day, two months and a half after the massacre, the smell of putrescent and charred remains in the church is unbearable. . . . I believe that close on 8,000 Armenians perished in the two days' massacre of the 28th and 29th December. . . . I should, however, not be at all surprised if the figure of 9,000 or 10,000 were subsequently found to be nearer the mark.[33]

The massacres of the 1890s fully inaugurated the modern fate of the Armenians in the Ottoman Empire. Abdul Hamid's policy of massacre began what the social psychologist Irvin Staub has called a "continuum of destruction." As Staub notes, "A progression of changes in a culture and individuals is usually required for mass killing or genocide. In certain instances—the Armenian Genocide, for example—the progression takes place over decades or even centuries and creates a readiness in the culture."[34]

The Hamidian massacres also initiated the idea that massacre could be committed with impunity. While the European powers set up an investigative commission after Sasun and Van, and asked the sultan for reforms, there was no forceful intervention to halt the massacres, nor was there any punishment in the aftermath. There was, to be sure, worldwide coverage of the events and attendant outrage, and there was an outpouring of humanitarian relief and philanthropy for the surviving victims. The sultan was vilified in the European and the U.S. press as the "Bloody Sultan," and depicted as a paranoid despot and a defiler of human freedom. Yet in the face of such world opinion, Abdul Hamid remained unrepentant, continuing to deny his actions and blame the victims.

By the end of the 1890s, the lack of political recourse or punishment let the sultan off the hook, and left Turkish society engaged in a culture of massacre that permanently dehumanized Armenians in an evolutionary process that would culminate in genocide in 1915. As Christian infidels, Armenians had already been marginalized. Now they became fair game.

"OUR BOASTED CIVILIZATION":

INTELLECTUALS, POPULAR CULTURE,

AND THE ARMENIAN MASSACRES

OF THE 1890s

T hroughout the second half of the 1890s—in a decade often referred to as a "gay" era in the United States, or more soberly by American intellectuals as a fin de siècle moment with ominous implications for the future of civilization—the news and images of the Armenian massacres permeated popular and intellectual culture in the United States and in Great Britain. In many ways there were parallel humanitarian movements in the two countries. In Great Britain the International Association of the Friends of Armenia, the Scottish Armenian Association, the Anglo Armenian Association, Friends of Armenia, Armenian United Association were working hard; and such influential figures as Prime Minister Gladstone, Lady Frederick Cavendish, Lady Henry Somerset, the duke of Argyll, James Bryce, and E. J. Dillon (the courageous journalist who traveled to Turkey to report on the massacres) were devoting their energy to the cause, and public opinion for Armenia had a large forum.[1]

The transatlantic dialogue seems to have started in 1881 when James Bryce, then Regius Professor of Civil Law at Oxford, spoke on the Armenian Question at Harvard. Perhaps no single figure more energetically bridged the two cultures than Bryce, who would be the most prominent British intellectual to write about the Armenian Question. For almost forty years, from the 1880s to the 1920s, Bryce's writing and thinking about the Armenian crisis was astute and often prophetic. A brilliant and precocious historian, Bryce had become an Oxford don at twenty-four for his monograph *The Holy Roman Empire*, and by the age of thirty-four had been awarded the Regius Professorship of Civil Law. However, it was not scholarship but rather mountain climbing that led him to Armenia. An avid member of an alpine club, he climbed Mount Ararat in 1876 on a trip through the Transcaucasus. Writing about his experience in a personal essay, "Transcaucasia and Ararat" (1877), he wove a travelogue with topographical observations and political reflections about the region—in particular about the Armenians.[2]

Like Gladstone, he was a liberal with a passion for human liberty. When Bryce wrote a seminal essay, "The Armenian Question," for the American publication the *Century Magazine*, in November 1895, he was already a member of the House of Commons, and by the mid-nineties he would be Gladstone's Under Secretary of State for Foreign Affairs. By then he was also famous for his book *The American Commonwealth* (1889). In this study of the United States, he explored American democracy and American culture for both its complexities and virtues, and the book quickly achieved a reputation as the most important work on American culture by a non-American since Tocqueville. Woodrow Wilson, then a professor of government at Bryn Mawr and a rising star in the new field of American studies, praised Bryce's book. Two decades later President Wilson would know Bryce's important parliamentary "blue book," *The Treatment of the Armenians in the Ottoman Empire, 1915–16.*

Bryce's "Armenian Question" appeared in the United States as the massacres were tearing through the Armenian provinces, and he appealed to the American people to make saving Armenia a goal. Nothing, he argued, was more bound up in the American spirit than rescuing this ancient people from Turkish oppression and brutality. As he was a historian of antiquity, Bryce's understanding of Armenian civilization was considerable and very much at the heart of his appeal. "Alone of all the races that once inhabited the inland regions of western Asia," he wrote, "the Armenians have retained their language, their national feeling, and their hold upon the soil. A race with so much natural vigor, so much tenacity of life, and so much capacity for assimilating and using modern ideas, cannot be destined to extinction."[3]

Angry at the folly of the Treaty of Berlin, Bryce saw the sultan as a corrupt and fiercely anti-Christian autocrat who believed that the way to get rid of the Armenian Question was to get rid of the Armenians. About the recent massacres, Bryce confessed, "Much of what is contained in the British consular reports is too horrible for print." The massacre at Sasun he asserted was "unprovoked," and appeared to be "deliberately planned in order to exterminate" the Armenians.[4] Like Gladstone, Bryce believed Europe was morally responsible for the "sufferings of the subjects of Turkey," and suggested that the Turkish problem could provoke a European war; he agreed with Edmund Burke, who had once claimed that the Turks could never be part of Europe because of their hatred of Christianity.[5]

America's political neutrality toward the Ottoman Empire, Bryce believed, put it in a stronger position to do good than the powers, who were entangled in treaty politics with the Ottoman government. In closing, Bryce urged the U.S. government not to be passive. If the safety of American life or property in Turkey were threatened, Bryce suggested, "the appearance of her gunboats off Turkish ports," along with "firmness" in diplomacy, would do much to protect her citizens.[6]

Bryce's timely essay in an important American publication enraged the sultan, who had already banned *Harper's Weekly* from his empire. This time Abdul Hamid responded by putting pressure on the American ambassador (then called minister) to the Ottoman Empire, demanding a rebuttal to Bryce. Eventually, the *Century Magazine* complied, printing an alleged interview with the sultan conducted by the American minister to Turkey, A. W. Terrell, in the November 1897 issue.

Terrell, a Texan, who had been criticized by the Protestant missionaries for being easily duped by the grandeur of the sultan's court and the gentility of the sultan's public manners, produced not so much an interview as a public relations piece attempting to appease the American public and hide the truth. Laced with fulsome praise, Terrell's article extolled the sultan as someone who "has never failed to win the heart of any European who has been admitted to any degree of intimacy with him. All find in him the noble and attractive qualities which they cannot help but admire. . . . Except in religion, he is more of a European than an Asiatic." And, after all that the American public had learned about repression in Turkey, Terrell tried to convince his readers that the sultan had done a great deal to educate his people and was a ruler of great intellectual ability. "I regard him," he concluded, "as the ablest sovereign in Europe."[7]

As for the Armenian massacres, the American minister announced his refusal to say anything: "My opinion as to whether, and in what degree, he [the sultan] is responsible for the massacres that have desolated his kingdom," Terrell wrote, "was given to Secretary of State [Richard] Olney. It remains unpublished, and will not be repeated here." He defended the sultan and gave the Sublime Porte's official line that because the Armenians had established "revolutionary committees," they had to be massacred. Yet, the sultan "deserves the highest praise," Terrell went on, for "attempting to cleanse his empire from filth and disease, and rivaling the most advanced countries in the world in his efforts to care for the health of his people."[8] Whether intentional or not, the suggestion of ethnic cleansing resonates in Terrell's garbled language. The sultan closed his "interview" by claiming that he has known and liked Armenians, especially those whom the Sublime Porte has employed over the years: Dadian, the head of the imperial powder factory; Kuetzroglian, the interior decorator; Agop Effendi in charge of the imperial mint; Gumushgerdan, the women's clothing maker; and the famous Balians, for generations the architects of palaces and imperial buildings.[9]

To some American readers the sultan's "reply" might have sounded reminiscent of a Southern plantation owner's praise of the Negro, but it was also indicative of how out of touch Abdul Hamid II was with the values and assumptions of a democratic society. To most readers of the *Century Magazine,* the sultan's evasions would have been obvious.

If James Bryce was the intellectual whose voice resonated across the Atlantic, Prime Minister Gladstone was the most vigorous and longest-standing opponent of Ottoman oppression in British government. He had, in some sense, defined the final phase of his political career by his appeals for human rights in the Ottoman Empire. From the time of the Sasun slaughter, Gladstone's stance on the Armenian massacres informed opinion around the world. To understand Gladstone's outrage over the issue of Turkish rule and Christian subjects, one must remember that it was precisely this issue that had catapulted the retired prime minister back into political prominence in 1876 as the "Bulgarian horrors" became an urgent cause.

Gladstone's famous Midlothian campaign of 1879 and 1880, which brought him back into power, was in part centered around the international moral issue of Turkish treatment of Christian subjects and the responsibilities of British foreign policy. Gladstone embodied British Liberalism in the second half of the nineteenth century as no other figure of the era. An opponent of Disraeli's imperialism, a defender of the 1834 Poor Law, he was a tireless campaigner for social and economic equality. With his ethical Christian vision, he campaigned against abuses of power both at home and abroad, and turned the light on the fiscal corruption in Disraeli's Tory government. He was an advocate of home-rule for Ireland, an opponent of the imperious Vatican Council of 1870, and a staunch advocate of self-determination and human rights for Christians in the Ottoman Empire. By the 1870s Gladstone had come to accept the downward trend of his own empire and the growing need for liberty and self-determination among its conquered subjects. "Turkish iniquities," H. C. J. Matthew has noted, obsessed him, and he made them a key part of the humanitarian platform that brought him back to power in 1880.[10]

At the outbreak of the "Bulgarian horrors" in 1876, Gladstone campaigned vigorously to raise consciousness in Great Britain with the hope of forcing the British government to take action. Gladstone's pamphlet *The Bulgarian Horrors and the Question of the East* went through several printings and became a celebrated treatise on Turkish cruelty and Ottoman misrule. If the Ottoman Empire was a member of the "Concert of Europe," as it had been since 1865, it was also responsible for the "Duties of a civilised Community."[11]

Gladstone believed those duties were being ignored, and in *The Bulgarian Horrors* he maintained that governments cannot abuse their power. He wrote that the Turks "exercise a perfectly unnatural domination over their fellow creatures; and arbitrary power is the greatest corrupter of the human mind and heart. There is unfortunately," he wrote, "no restraint of law in Turkey, and in the sight of God and man, much as these Christians are to be pitied, perhaps the Turks, who are the victims of that system, are to be pitied still more. The very worst things that men have ever done have been done when they were performing acts of violence in the name of religion."[12]

For all his Christian self-righteousness, Gladstone refused to stereotype the Muslim world. His political intelligence led to a careful analysis of political systems. "It is not a question of Mohammedanism simply but Mohammedanism compounded by the particular character of Turkish civilization. The Muslims of India, the Saladins of Syria, the Moors of

Spain," he argued, were far different from the Turks, whose system was "government by force as opposed to government by law."[13] Gladstone went on, "God forbid that we should judge them. It is that this wretched system under which they live puts into their hands power which human beings ought not to possess, and the consequences are corruption to themselves and misery to those around."[14] The Turks also suffered, he believed, because they had not been able to learn from the peoples they conquered. "The very least that can be expected is that the conquerors should be able to learn civilization from the conquered as the Romans from the Greeks."[15]

As the news of the Sasun crisis broke in the European press in early 1894, Gladstone once again became a leading spokesman. At the town hall in Chester, on a hot day in August 1895, with the duke of Westminster presiding and a number of parliamentarians in the audience, Gladstone presented a resolution and spoke to a packed room after thousands had been turned away. The resolution, he said, was an expression of "her Majesty's government," and had the support of the "entire nation," regardless of party. He made it clear to his audience that day that the atrocities committed against the Armenians were an issue of universal humanity—or what would later be called human rights. Again he spoke with cultural self-awareness. "If, instead of dealing with the Turkish Government, and impeaching it for its misdeeds towards Christian subjects, we were dealing with a Christian Government that was capable of similar misdeeds towards Mahometan [sic] subjects, our indignation ought to be not less, but greater, than it is now." It was important to Gladstone, as it was to Bryce, that Americans, too, were engaged in the Armenian Question. He told his audience that "our own Transatlantic brethren of the United States" had feelings on the subject as strong, or stronger, "if it can be, than that which beats in the hearts of the people of this country."[16]

The former prime minister assured his audience that when the Sasun massacres broke out, he had remained cautious so as to avoid premature judgment, but as the evidence poured in, the Sasun massacre paled in comparison with the "unspeakable horrors which are being enacted from month to month, week to week, day to day in the different provinces of Armenia."[17] Gladstone called attention to the many American witnesses as especially crucial because "America has no separate or sinister political interest of any kind in the affairs of the Levant." Gladstone spoke about recent British witnesses including E. J. Dillon of the *Daily Telegraph*, who had risked his life in Turkey, "laudably making use of a disguise" in order to investigate the Armenian situation. Dillon's articles, which had appeared in the *Contemporary Review* as well as the *Daily Telegraph,* were shocking, and they confirmed the later reports of "the inquiries of the delegates appointed by the three Powers—England, France and Russia."[18]

Dillon's accounts affirmed that "plunder, murder, rape, and torture" had devastated Armenia; they showed unambiguously that the "Government of Constantinople" was responsible, and that the sultan had organized his Kurdish *Hamidiye,* who along with Turkish soldiers, police, and tax gatherers, had carried out the devastation. There was growing evidence, Gladstone went on, that the Turkish government was bent on "deliberate determination to exterminate the Christians in that Empire."[19] With his years of experience as prime minister, Gladstone appealed to his audience to "accept no Turkish promises," unless they were "supported by efficient guarantees entirely outside the promises of the Turkish Government." If Europe could not prevail against the "irrational resistance of the Sultan," Gladstone closed, it would be "disgraced in the face of the world."[20] Gladstone's speech traveled fast to the United States, where Frederick D. Greene anthologized it (along with other remarks by Gladstone) in his *Armenian Massacres*—the same book that contained the eyewitness accounts of the Sasun massacres.

In his last public speech, on September 24, 1896, in Liverpool, Gladstone spoke about the Armenian massacres and British foreign policy. So adamant was he about breaking off British relations with the Ottoman Empire, that his successor as leader of the Liberal Party, Lord Rosebery, said he had no choice but to step down. Rosebery did not favor severing relations with the Turks but rather believed in acting in unison with the powers. "I find myself," Rosebery wrote to the chief Liberal Whip, "in apparent difference with a considerable mass of the Liberal party, on the Eastern question, and in some conflict of opinion with Mr. Gladstone, who must necessarily always exercise a matchless authority in the party."[21] Conflicting opinion over the Armenian massacres had cut a hole right through British foreign policy and Liberal Party politics, and the British failure to follow Gladstone's path signaled for the aging prime minister a betrayal of the idea of civilization itself. It also signaled the coming resurgence of the politics of empire. Bertrand Russell would later look back at the debate over the Armenian massacres as a decisive turning point in British history.

Transatlantic letters between two eminent brothers—William James, professor of philosophy at Harvard, and his brother, the novelist Henry James, who was living in London—give a perspective on how the Armenian massacres played out in the crosscurrent of Anglo-American issues. Although William was disgusted by the new wave of jingoism sweeping the country under President Cleveland, he made an exception for intervention in Turkey on behalf of the Armenians: "If we could ourselves be putting in some licks for Armenia it would be good," he wrote Henry in December 1895. As he bemoaned American imperialism in the Philippines, "protection humbug, silver, jingoism," and the whole "mob-psychology" of it all, in a letter of June 1896, William observed to his brother the Anglophile that jingoism was an irrational force in any society, and he asked if America's nationalism were any "less damnable than the Russophobia of England which would seem to have been responsible for the Armenian massacres. *That* to me," William went on, "is the biggest indictment 'of our boasted civilization'!! It *requires* England I say nothing of the other powers to maintain the Turks at that business [of massacring the Armenians]."[22]

Henry's reply reflected a similar outrage. Writing back to William from the small town of Rye, in Kent, where he was staying for the summer, Henry called the failure of Europe, and England in particular, to intervene in the Armenian massacres "hideous cowardice & baseness," and confessed to his brother that the failure of the world to stop the Armenian massacres "has been more disillusioning to me on the question of the 'progress of the race' than anything that has happened since I was born." Like his brother, he saw the massacres as a world-defining event. "England is only *ashamed* of herself" but does nothing, he wrote. Like his brother he believed intervention was necessary. "I wish to the 'most high God' she & the U.S. wd. do something TOGETHER," Henry went on; it would, he exclaimed, mean something for "civilization of the future." Even in his "sleepy" town of Rye, the Armenian massacres and the "bloody Sultan," he wrote, had created a "sickening consciousness of something hideous," that by England's general inaction "one seems *one's self* to participate in."[23]

Poets Henry van Dyke and William Watson found the Armenian massacres an irresistible issue for their verse. A prolific Victorian man of letters, Henry van Dyke was the unofficial poet laureate of Princeton University, and the Murray Professor of English Literature there. He later became ambassador to the Netherlands.[24] Van Dyke made "Mercy for Armenia" a central poem in his popular book of 1897, *The Builders and Other Poems*. In the poem, van Dyke blames the European powers for acquiescing to the sultan: "So the false Sultan spoke; And Europe, hearkening to his base command, / Stood still to see him heal his wounded land." In the second part of the poem, "America's Way," van Dyke appeals to the United States to be the righteous nation: "Rise, thou, and show the world the way divine!" Instead of calling for intervention, he urges following the philanthropic path of the kind that Clara Barton and the Red Cross were bringing to Armenia: "Thou canst not loose the captive's heavy chain, / But thou canst bind his wounds and soothe his pain."[25]

In England, William Watson, another late Victorian man of letters, appeared to be the logical successor to Tennyson as England's poet laureate. But when his poems on the Armenian massacres and Great Britain's failure to intercede on behalf of the Armenians earned him the disdain of the Conservatives in power, his public career was ruined.[26] His sixteen-poem sonnet cycle, "The Turk in Armenia," was first published in the *Westminster Gazette* and then in his 1896 collection *The Purple East*. In one sonnet he spares no rhetoric in his condemnation of the British:

> *Never, O craven England, nevermore*
> *Prate thou of generous effort, righteous aim!*
> *Betrayer of a people, know thy shame!*
> *Summer hath passed, and Autumn's threshing floor*
> *Been winnowed; Winter at Armenia's door*
> *Snarls like a wolf; and still the sword and flame*
> *Sleep not; thou only sleepest; and the same*
> *Cry unto heaven ascends as heretofore. . . .*

As the poem closes, "Abdul the Damned" sits "on his infernal throne."[27]

When his next volume, *The Year of Shame*, appeared with an introduction by the bishop of Hereford, it was reviewed and read widely, and as the literary critic Patricia O'Neill has noted, it represented an important instance in British imperial history of "poetic engagement in public affairs in its call for international humanitarian intervention."[28] In pursuing the

Armenian cause, Watson undermined his public career as a writer, and fell into obscurity (the Conservative poet and journalist Alfred Austin was made laureate instead). But Watson's poems stirred up a raw feeling about Britain's moral responsibility that made him an intellectual ally of Lord Bryce and ex–Prime Minister Gladstone.

In the new age of the picture magazine, the Armenian massacres were making history as well. The dramatic rise in newspaper and magazine circulation in the last quarter of the century, the aggressive sensationalist journalism generated by William Randolph Hearst, Joseph Pulitzer, Edward Scripps, and Frank Munsey, and the new temper of muckraking with its emphasis on exposing crime and corruption and promoting reform, created a milieu in which the Armenian story was being heard loudly around the United States.[29] With the evolving technology of image making and photographic reproduction, magazines became increasingly popular, and the depiction of dramatic and sensational current events became an essential appeal to the mass market. The distinguished magazine of politics and culture, Harper's Weekly: A Journal of Civilization, which had brought the American public the Civil War, the impeachment of Andrew Johnson, and the Boss Tweed/Tammany Hall scandal, now found the Armenian massacres, the bloodthirsty sultan, and his trusty Hamidiye a compelling story.

Throughout 1895–96 Harper's ran large eleven-by-sixteen photolithographs and drawings of the massacres, along with continuous written coverage under the heading "The Troubles in Armenia." The editors were as interested in exposing the corruption of the Ottoman government as they were in its slain subjects. A feature story about Abdul Hamid II opens with a prominent drawing of the sultan wearing a fez, his bearded face and sharp features well drawn. Timothy Pitkins, the journalist who wrote many of these pieces, was in the Armenian provinces at the beginning of the atrocities and stayed for some time after. Calling the sultan "the Turkish Nero," Pitkins reported that Hamid had planned "the utter extinction" of the Armenians, and was simultaneously obsessed with denying his deeds and blaming the victims. "A consummate falsifier," Pitkins wrote, the Sultan wanted to convince the world that the Armenians were responsible for the deeds done to them.[30]

On April 18, 1895, an editorial note to a long essay by Pitkins on the corruption of the Turkish legal system read: "The Turkish government has been so greatly disturbed by Timothy Pitkins's articles, and has become so panic-stricken by their disclosures of official corruption in Asia Minor, of the fact that the Sultan himself is responsible for the recent massacres of the unfortunate Armenians, and of the general reign of cruelty throughout the Ottoman Empire, that it has 'permanently debarred HARPER'S WEEKLY from Turkey.'—Editor."[31] The banning of a major American magazine, while shocking to Americans, was very much in keeping with the sultan's repressive policies and widespread censorship.

While the reportage of *Harper's Weekly* was morally engaged and vivid, the magazine's illustrations brought to the American public startling images of the faraway world of Armenia under duress. The painter and photographer Edwin Lord Weeks, who was renowned for his illustrations and writings of the Middle East, did most of the drawings. In one full-page plate, "Refugees Arriving at a Khan, or Road-Side Inn, Among the Mountains," anguished survivors are rendered with touches of local color.[32] The cover of the February 22, 1896, issue, Weeks's drawing "The Troubles in Armenia," is a Frederic Remington–like scene of the sultan's *Hamidiye* reconnoitering in a mountain pass, as they prepare to attack Armenians.[33] Another plate, in the March 14 issue, shows Armenian women running along a steep, rocky mountain path as Kurdish *Hamidiye* pursue them on horseback with flashing swords.[34] A full-page scene on March 28, again with something of a Wild West feel, reads "Wagon Train of Armenian Refugees Attacked and Wrecked by Kurds in a Mountain Pass Near the Persian Border."[35] The continual images of Armenians marooned in remote, rocky mountain landscapes, helpless and pursued by the sultan's cavalry, are both realistic depictions of one aspect of the massacre and a symbolic image of persecuted Christians being sent into exile in remote "desert" places: an image with biblical evocations that would have resonated deeply with the Victorian Christian readership of the era.

In contrast to those images, *Harper's* ran a different kind of scene on the cover of the April 25, 1896, issue. "Armenian Pastoral—Gleaners Near the Village and Fortress of Hasan Kaleh, Beyond Erzerum."[36] American readers would have known that Armenians had been massacred at Erzurum in October of the preceding year, and so this drawing of the golden wheatfields of the Armenian heartland suggests the returning fertility of a

by the action of the Powers in insisting upon an inquiry into the
Sasun atrocities, the soldiery, unchecked by the authorities, have
continued to slaughter their Armenian compatriots, literally in
their thousands, to wreck their homes, and in some cases to
practically annihilate entire village populations. . . . At Erzerum
[October 30] . . . one correspondent brought the camera to bear
upon the results of the massacres, and by this witness, which cannot exaggerate, fully confirmed the truth of his terrible statements. It is the duty of the pictorial as well as the literary
journalist to chronicle all world-important incidents whether
they be agreeable or otherwise, and these photographs are of
such historical importance that we feel bound to reproduce
them, unpleasant as they may appear in many of their details.—
The Editor

The first half-page photograph shows a mass, craterlike grave in the
earth with dozens of Armenian corpses. The caption reads: "The Trench
Dug for the Bodies of the Victims: A Scene in the Cemetery." As the photograph was taken, four gravediggers depositing corpses have just begun
another row of bodies. A ring of grieving men and women look on from
above the pit. A large horizontal photo on the next page gives a beautiful
panorama of Erzurum set against the distant mountains; the caption
notes that it has been an important city for trade and that the principal
buildings there are "the Armenian and Greek churches and schools."
    Juxtaposed with the image of the city before the cataclysm is a photo-
graph of two small children lying dead on the ground; the children are
dressed in their everyday clothes. The legs of their mother's corpse rest on
the body of one child. The large photo on the next page shows the ground
of the cemetery strewn with dozens of corpses, and the caption reads:
"Nothing could be more convincing as to the truth of the reports of massacres than the sight of corpses laid out in the cemetery waiting until one
large common grave had been dug for their reception."
    The final image of the series of ten shows the prison at Erzurum, and
makes its point about Turkish repression. The caption reads: "An Important Factor in Turkish Rule at Erzerum: The Prison as Seen From the Wall
Above," and then goes on to note that among the many prisoners—
Armenian, Kurdish, and Turkish—was a teacher, "an Armenian who had

been imprisoned for eight years simply because he let his Protestant schoolchildren sing 'They Are Gathering From Far and From Near' in honour of a Turkish official who happened to be passing by the school." For this, he was arrested and charged by the court with poisoning the minds of children with "revolutionary" ideas.[39]

As 1895 came to a close, *The Graphic* ran a stream of articles and images about the sultan and his corrupt government, as well as about the *softas*—the theology students who seemed essentially and continually motivated to kill Christians. The editors evinced a tone of cynicism that echoed William James on the other side of the Atlantic: They deemed the whole situation "a mockery of the vaunted power of civilisation."[40]

As the decade came to a close, the massacre and postmassacre deaths of about two hundred thousand Armenians had by now created a new threshold in the violation of human rights. Looking back at the 1890s, Henry Adams noted, in *The Education of Henry Adams,* that as history unwound in the second half of the nineteenth century, war, butchery, and massacre "had become so common that society scarcely noticed them unless they summed up hundreds of thousands, as in Armenia."[41] The powerful record of moral response and opinion on the Armenian mas-sacres, in many ways, forecast the century of genocide to come. But for all the public opinion about the massacres, and for all the philanthropic efforts and missions to save the Armenians, there was no justice meted out to the Ottoman government, and no political solutions to the Arme-nian Questions put in place by the powers. In the end there seemed to be too little political will to create a new future for these people.

The sensational young American novelist of the 1890s Stephen Crane—whose new social realism in *Maggie: A Girl of the Streets* and *The Red Badge of Courage* explored the edgy world of violence—corroborated Glad-stone's feeling when he blamed the European powers for complicity in the Armenian massacres. Instead of dealing with Turkey forthrightly over the Armenian massacres, Crane complained that Turkey was forever able to "mystify and seduce and trick his neighbors," and that Europe fell for it and defended Turkey—the powers "clean his knives and wash his dishes for him." A war correspondent who covered the Greco-Turkish wars over Crete and the Spanish-American War, Crane was astute about interna-

tional politics. "Is it massacres then that the Powers seek to prevent? . . . Why was not Armenia occupied on the proof of massacre?" For
the European powers, Crane wrote with sarcasm, were supposed to be
able to "do anything." Fearing that the Europeans would let the Cretans
flounder too, Crane accused the West of paying mere lip service to justice,
because in the case of the Armenians they did nothing. As he put it:

> With the prevention of massacres they have nothing to do. Dur-
> ing the massacres in Armenia they called upon each other to rec-
> ognize a sacred duty and then they contented themselves with
> this empty expression. As far as their sacred duty was concerned
> they let it be eaten by the dogs. It is proved that the Concert of
> Europe formed for the purpose of preventing bloodshed is an idle
> collation.[42]

While Turkey's crimes went unpunished, as the new century arrived
there were others who felt the Armenian case could prompt a new age of
American international leadership, among them the feminist writer and
social critic Charlotte Perkins Gilman. In 1903 Gilman wrote in the inau-
gural issue of the journal *Armenia*—on which she served as an editorial board member, along with Julia Ward Howe and William Lloyd Garrison Jr.—that the Armenian crisis was the primary symbol for what she
hoped would be America's new age of global leadership. In a decade that
saw the continued growth of various peace movements, as well as the Second Hague Conference, Gilman wrote that international law was essential; "individual sympathy and help have been given: but no amount of
individual sympathy and help prevails on the Turkish government to
desist from its criminal conduct." She went on, "National crimes demand
international law, to restrain, prohibit, punish, best of all, to prevent."

In expressing her view of world order and ethics, Gilman did not
mince words:

> As it would be a disgrace to a civilized city to have within it any
> citizens living in filth, disease, vice and poverty—as it is such a dis-
> grace, so it is a disgrace to a civilized world to have within it any
> nation committing such revolting crimes as those of Turkey. . . . If
> a nation is bankrupt, it should be put in the hands of a receiver

and forcibly improved. If it is frankly criminal, it should be restrained. If it is simply ignorant, it should have compulsory education, and if it has senile dementia it should be confined under treatment, and the estate administered in the interests of the heirs.

"Who is to do it?" she asked, sounding a little like Walt Whitman trumpeting America's promise. "Who will usher in the new age of global social consciousness? . . . America," she answers, "with the blended blood of all peoples in her veins, with interests in every land, and duties with the interests; America, who leads in so many things, can well afford to lead in this: not only allowing human liberty here, but using her great strength to protect it everywhere."[43] In the coming decades Gilman's appeal would be tested.

Part II

———※———

THE TURKISH ROAD
TO GENOCIDE

THE RISE OF THE

YOUNG TURKS

A s the Armenians struggled for basic rights and reforms in the second half of the nineteenth century, Turkish intellectuals were pursuing their own path to reform and political change. The movement that came to be known as the Young Turk movement began in the middle of Tanzimat and was driven by a great passion for constitutional government. In the 1860s Turkish activists and intellectuals who believed in the urgency of reform began to organize. A group led by Namik Kemal began a secret society in 1865, inspired, in part, by the Italian society Carbonari. A year later an Egyptian prince, Mustafa Fazil, wrote an open letter of opposition to the Sultan Abdul Aziz, and not long after, in the pages of a Belgian newspaper, Prince Fazil referred to his supporters as *jeunes Turcs*. The phrase appealed to young liberals like Ali Suavi and Namik Kemal, and they soon began calling themselves jeunes Turcs and Yeni Osmanlilar (Young Ottomans).[1]

By 1868 the Young Ottomans, several of whom were living in exile in Paris, were producing their own newspaper, *Hürriyet* (Freedom). Their disgust with the decadent behavior and authoritarian government of the sultan was coupled with a fierce patriotism and a new idea of nationalism, which led one of the prominent advocates, Ali Suavi, to espouse "for the first time, the idea of a *Turkish* as distinct from an Islamic or Ottoman loyalty."[2]

With the ascendancy of the progressive Midhat Pasha, who served briefly as grand vizier under Abdul Aziz before he was dismissed in 1872, the cause of liberal reform was brought to the high offices of government for the first time since the death of Sultan Abdul Mecid in 1861. An advocate of reform and of implementing a new constitution, Midhat Pasha believed that the empire was "being rapidly brought to destruction," as he told British ambassador Sir Henry Elliott. The only remedy, Midhat believed, lay in instituting controls over the sultan, "especially as regarded the finances," and creating a decentralized "national popular Assembly" that would do away with "all distinctions of classes and religions."[3]

The reform movement that had been underway for several years under the leadership of Midhat Pasha and other liberals seemed to come to fruition in 1876, when the constitution was proclaimed. Shortly before that, Sultan Abdul Aziz was deposed because his decadence had run the empire into such financial ruin (two days later he was found with his wrists slit, either having committed suicide or having been murdered),[4] and Murad, his oldest nephew, ascended to the sultanate. But Murad, who was mentally unstable and an alcoholic, was soon declared non compos mentis and deposed, setting the stage for the appointment of his younger brother, Abdul Hamid, as sultan.[5]

Abdul Hamid II became sultan on August 31, 1876. In December the European powers convened the Constantinople Conference in order to discuss reforms in the Balkans. Turkey was now under great scrutiny because of its brutal treatment of Christians in the Balkans, particularly the Serbs and Bulgarians, who were seeking independence. Abdul Hamid appointed Midhat Pasha grand vizier. Amid much celebration, display, and even cannon fire, the conference opened with a proclamation stating that the Ottoman constitution, which had been drawn up in 1839 and 1856 during Tanzimat, would finally be implemented. In retrospect it seems clear that the entire ceremony was a shrewd public relations scheme. "The timing of the reforms," Bernard Lewis has noted, "and the dramatic manner of their presentation, were no doubt influenced by the desire to secure political advantage from them."[6]

But the liberal moment was so short-lived that two weeks after the conference ended in January 1877, Midhat was again dismissed as grand vizier and exiled. In banishing Midhat and the relatively progressive mood he embodied, Abdul Hamid justified his actions by article 113 of the new constitution, which said that the sultan could "expel from the territory of the Empire those who, as a result of trustworthy information gathered by the police administration, are recognized as dangerous to the security of the state."[7] It was an ominous beginning for the reign of Abdul Hamid II.

The first Ottoman parliament met in March 1877 and included representatives from all over the empire—from "Bagdad, Albania, Armenia, and Syria." As Sir Edwin Pears, then a correspondent in Constantinople, reported, the new representatives were "surprised to learn" that misgovernment was rampant throughout the empire—not just in their own districts—and that "from one end of the country to the other . . . radical reform" was required. As accusations of corruption brought by the new representatives against government ministers mounted, and the "hostility between the Chamber and the pashas became serious,"[8] it seemed clear to many that constitutional government would be short-lived. And indeed it was. In February 1878, less than a year after it was first convened, the sultan himself dismissed the parliament, cleared the few ministers charged with corruption, and made it plain that constitutional government was not for him. During Hamid's reign, parliament would not meet again.

In the wake of the sultan's repression, demand for constitutional government would now become an idée fixe with the next generation of reform-minded Young Turks. With the Russo-Turkish War and the gesture toward constitutional government behind him, Hamid did everything he could to fend off European attention and intrusion on his empire. The interventionist nature of the Treaty of Berlin angered the sultan, and the emergence of the Armenian Question as an international issue enraged him. It is not surprising, then, that pogroms against the Armenians by local Muslim tribes—Kurds, Laz, and Circassians—in the Van and Erzurum areas after the war were sanctioned by the sultan.[9]

As Hamid became increasingly paranoid and obsessed with keeping himself on the throne, he developed what would soon become the most sophisticated espionage system in his country's history. Spying, in Abdul Hamid's reign, was a mode of conducting politics. Along with a vast network of spies came policies of extreme repression aimed at silencing all dissident and liberal voices.[10] Having set the tone by exiling Grand Vizier Midhat on grounds of sedition, he would in the coming decades exile, imprison, and execute scores of activists, intellectuals, and writers whom he deemed dangerous to the state. Having "gagged and tied the press," the sultan had created an atmosphere of repression and was fast turning his country into a "jail of pain," as Paul Fesch put it.[11] Hamid's new Yildiz Palace was an emblem of a man who was ruining his empire for the sake of his paranoid sense of security.[12]

The Imperial Military Medical School in Constantinople turned out to be the seed ground for the next phase of the Young Turk movement. In the spring of 1889 a group of Young Turks began a society they called "Progress and Union," whose aim was to overthrow the sultan and his government. Led by Ibrahim Temo, a young Albanian, they embraced the modes of secret societies, encoding member identity with numerical fractions indicating the order of admission and the cell or branch.[13] Unlike the Christian minorities, who were beneficiaries of the Protestant missionary colleges, the only schools in Turkey that offered higher education for Muslims, other than theological seminaries, were the government-run military and professional schools. Ironically it was at a school whose purpose it was to protect the state where the revolution regenerated among the upwardly mobile young men of the empire.[14]

Sometime in 1892 the sultan's spies learned about "Progress and Union," and Abdul Hamid had the commandant of the school fired, the students interrogated, and a few of them taken into custody. It turned out to be a slap on the wrist because the students were released, and "Progress and Union" continued to grow, attracting influential men such as Haji Ahmet Effendi, a civil servant in the War Office, and Naili Effendi, a Shiite dervish. By 1894 a number of the older members of the group, fearing for their safety, left the country for Paris.[15]

In Paris, Khalil Ghanim, a Christian Syrian who had been a delegate to the first Ottoman parliament in 1878, founded a journal called La Jeune Turquie and a paper in Geneva, Khilal (Crescent), both of which added to the presence of this liberal movement in the international arena. The group of Young Ottomans in Paris continued to grow, especially under the new leadership of Ahmet Riza, who was half Turkish and half Austrian. Riza had been influenced by French positivist philosophy, especially that of Auguste Comte, and his passionate opposition to the government of

Abdul Hamid led him to publish the paper *Mechveret* (Consultation), which was intended for readers inside the Ottoman Empire but included a supplement in French as well.[16]

As these publications came into the country, the government grew increasingly aware of the scope of the movement, and the sultan arrested and exiled a number of its key figures. This wave of arrests seems only to have intensified the commitment of the movement, so that by the spring of 1896, a plot to dethrone the sultan was well under way. Ironically "Progress and Union" had planned its coup d'état within days of the Armenian takeover of the Ottoman Bank. There is no evidence that the Armenian revolutionaries and the Young Turks knew of each other's plots, but the coincidence of these two events suggests something about the malaise and crisis created by the sultan's regime. Far from having any sympathy with the Armenian activists, the Young Turks saw the Armenian Question as something that was creating an unfavorable image of the Turks in European eyes, and the Young Turks had, in the end, no interest in the problems of minority peoples in the empire. And to make matters worse in their eyes, at that very moment there was a European commission meeting to assess the Armenian problem in order to make suggestions to the sultan.[17]

Ironically enough the Young Turks' plot to assassinate the sultan was leaked at one of Constantinople's most famous restaurants, Tokatlian's, which was owned and run by an Armenian family. The drunken father of one of the Young Turks spilled the news to Ismail Pasha, the inspector general of the military schools, who ran immediately to the palace and informed Abdul Hamid. Before the night was over, all the Young Turks involved in the conspiracy were arrested.[18]

By 1897 the movement was back in exile in Paris, Geneva, London, and Cairo. One of the leaders, Murat Bey, summed up the Young Turk hatred of the sultan in these words: *"Ce n'est plus un Sultan, mais Satan qui regne!"* (It is no longer a sultan but Satan who reigns). But it was significant that while Murat Bey endorsed liberal reform, he was adamantly opposed to reform for the Christians. He was blunt when he wrote, "The question of the Christians of Turkey is not a fruit ripened on the soil of the Ottoman Empire," but rather a political issue that "had its birth in the diplomatic chancelleries." Furious at the presence of an Armenian delegation at the Congress of Berlin, Murat Bey had the audacity to say that "the

Christians of the Orient commence to suffer from the time of this inge-
nious and *humanitarian* intervention."[19]

However, by 1899, the sultan had coopted Murat Bey and other influential Young Turk leaders with comfortable government jobs and posts.
Just as things looked to be at their worst for the Young Turk movement,
something dramatic happened. Members of the royal family defected and
went into exile in Europe. Damad Mahmud Jelaleddin Pasha was a grandson of Sultan Mahmud II, and the husband of Abdul Hamid's sister.
Unable to endure the sultan's corrupt regime, the couple made a dramatic
flight to France in December with their sons, Sabaheddin and Lutfullah.
There, they helped to complicate the factions of the Young Turk movement in exile, but they gave a fresh energy to it as well.[20] When Damad
Mahmud, as a member of the royal family, spoke out against the sultan, it
created a new sensation. With his scathing wit, he sounded a bit like Mark
Twain speaking about Sultan Abdul Aziz in 1868.

By the 1890s a dramatic split had evolved in the Young Turk movement: One faction was more pro-European in its democratic thinking,
hence more sympathetic to the Armenians, and the other was deeply
nationalistic with little interest in the plight of the Christian minorities in
the Empire. This nationalistic faction focused on the promise of the
Ottoman constitution, which they believed would solve the problems for
all the peoples and ethnic minorities of the Empire.[21]

In an open letter to the sultan, dated January 21, 1900, Damad Mahmud expressed his view of things from his European exile:

> Let me say to you in all frankness, Sire, that your administrative
> system . . . has certain points of resemblance to that of certain
> tyrants who lived a few thousand years ago. . . . As to Your
> Majesty, like certain despotic and egotistic monarchs, you take
> for the principle of your conduct and make yours the ill-starred
> saying of Louis XV: *Après moi, le déluge.* You think only of your
> own person, you trample on all rights and on all humanitarian
> sentiments. The welfare of the people is your last concern, and
> twenty-four million people are sacrificed to your egotism. . . .
> You are the principal author of the ruin of our country and the
> cause of many basenesses and accumulated crimes. The blood
> which you have caused to be shed, the homes which you have

destroyed and the falsehoods which you have circulated dazzle all eyes.[22]

Without mentioning the word "Armenian," Damad Mahmud's statement alluded to the Armenian massacres in evoking bloodshed and destroyed homes. Damad's open letter was read widely across Europe, especially by the French intellectual community. In that very year Georges Clemenceau, Anatole France, Jean Jaurès, Francis de Pressensé, and E. de Roberty began the journal *Pro-Armenia*, dedicated to the Armenian cause.[23]

In February 1902, under the leadership of Damad Mahmud's son Prince Sabaheddin, the two factions of the Young Turks convened a congress in Paris to coalesce and affirm the movement and clarify its goals. Not surprisingly the Armenian question was a source of divisiveness. Armenians were among some forty-seven delegates who attended the congress, which included Arabs, Greeks, Albanians, Kurds, Circassians, and Jews. The Armenians naturally were strong advocates of European intervention for implementing the long-promised reforms, while the nationalist Young Turks were staunchly opposed to this and other Armenian concerns.

The only vocal advocate of the Armenian platform was the sultan's nephew, Prince Sabaheddin, a cosmopolitan with liberal European ideas. After much squabbling and debate, he was able to influence some of the wording of the congress's resolution. It denounced the sultan's regime of "oppression" and "misdeeds," and it also called for the implementation of the constitution of 1876, which would guarantee rights for all peoples of the empire, and a "firm resolution to respect the international treaties and particularly the Treaty of Berlin, of which the dispositions, insofar as they concern the internal order of Turkey, will be extended to all the provinces of the Empire." In those phrases, something of the Armenian platform was reflected.[24]

To emphasize their loyalty to the integrity of the Ottoman state, representatives of the Dashnak Party and other Armenian groups made a statement to the Young Turks that Armenian political action "is directed against the present regime and not against the unity and organic existence of Turkey," and that their objective was simply to implement the reform mandate in article 61 of the Treaty of Berlin and the reforms stipulated in the memorandum of May 1895.[25]

As Prince Sabaheddin and Ahmet Riza were establishing themselves as the leaders in Paris, inside the empire the movement was developing rapidly. By 1906 another secret society, calling itself Vatan (Fatherland), was founded in Damascus, with a young army captain named Mustafa Kemal as one of its charter members. As Vatan grew it began to attract members of the Ottoman Third Army, and in particular those stationed in Macedonia and in the ancient Greek city of Salonika—the most cosmopolitan city of the Ottoman Empire in Europe.

Another organization formed in Salonika, known as the Ottoman Society of Liberty, boasted as its early members Rahmi Bey, later *vali* of Smyrna; Ismail Janbulat (who would succeed Talaat as minister of the interior); Midhat Shükrü, headmaster of the military school in Salonika and a well-known scholar; Talaat Bey, a chief clerk in the Salonika directorate of posts and telegraphs, who had joined the original "Progress and Union" back in 1889; and General Staff Colonel Jemal Bey. Within a year Salonika was brimming with revolutionary energy.[26]

The Ottoman Society of Liberty grew rapidly, especially among the army officers. Once again secret-society rituals—often based on those of the Freemasons and the secret dervish order of Bektashis—were essential to its nature, and the leaders shrewdly used rituals such as blindfolded initiation rites and cell organizations so that group membership remained as anonymous as possible. Before long the Ottoman Society of Liberty had changed its name to Union and Progress.[27]

It was an inevitable paradox that the Ottoman army had become the arena for the final stage of the revolution. The army, which writer and diplomat Sir Charles Eliot once called the "normal state of the Turkish nation,"[28] had fallen under Abdul Hamid into a state of near chaos. The sultan's paranoia about letting his army (which he needed to protect him) become too strong sank the military almost into dysfunction. With corruption rampant and pay often in arrears, "the Turkish officer was likely to be nearly as down-at-the-heels as the common soldier." The sultan was equally afraid of his navy, which he let rot in the Golden Horn, as he dismantled its machinery and refused to allow ammunition aboard the ships.[29]

By the end of 1906 army mutinies were breaking out all over the country, and they continued to spread from Constantinople to Smyrna to Syria throughout 1907. Officers and common soldiers alike were involved;

and in the east in Bitlis, Van, and Erzurum, Turkish civilians also were rising up against corrupt government officials.[30] Then, in late June 1908, several officers began to disappear from their posts in Salonika into the
rugged hills of Resne. One of them, a twenty-seven-year-old officer named
Enver Bey, a member of what is now known as the Society or Committee
of Union and Progress, did so instead of going to Constantinople for a promotion in rank. He no doubt figured that he was under suspicion and that
the sultan was trying to buy him off. His disappearance created enough
notice that even the correspondent for the *Frankfurter Zeitung* suggested
that Enver might be a victim of the Young Turks themselves.[31]

A few days later a more senior officer, Maj. Ahmed Niyazi, followed
Enver into the hills and brought with him a battalion of about two hundred men, well armed with weapons and money taken from the company
stores. As he led his troops through the countryside he distributed manifestos about the need for insurrection in order to bring justice and save the
fatherland.[32] The news of insurrection and mutiny spread quickly through
the army units and the Young Turk committees in Macedonia, in what
one observer called "a complete though half-unconscious cooperation."[33]
At the height of the drama, Major Niyazi wrote his family a courageous
and romantic declaration: "Rather than live basely, I have preferred to die.
I am therefore going out now, with two hundred patriots armed with
Mausers, to die for our country."[34]

But a less likely event took place. In broad daylight in the town of
Manastir, Shemshi Pasha, who had been sent by the sultan to quell the
insurrection, was shot and killed on the street as he walked out of the telegraph office. The assassin was an officer under the pasha's command, a
Young Turk conspirator, who walked away untouched. A unit of the Third
Army then made an open declaration for the restoration of the 1876 constitution, and in Edirne the Second Army Corps expressed its concur-
rence. A shaken Abdul Hamid sent troops from Smyrna by ship to
suppress the army, but it proved useless, for the troops were already sympathetic with the Committee of Union and Progress. He tried to stonewall
the army in Macedonia with bribery, but his offers of promotions, decora-
tions, and back pay went unheeded by the officers.[35] For the sultan it was
too late.

Finally, on July 21 a telegram from the Committee of Union and
Progress arrived at the palace demanding the immediate restoration of

the constitution. If the sultan did not acquiesce, the insurgents would proclaim the sultan's heir apparent, and the new sultan and an army of one hundred thousand would march on the capital.[36] Backed into a corner, the infrastructure of his empire rotting under him, the sultan had no choice but to give in. Three days later, on July 24, 1908, Abdul Hamid assented to the demands. He would keep the title of sultan and his role as caliph, but he would no longer be head of state or have any effective political power.

The enthusiasm for what appeared to be a velvet revolution was overwhelming. The young, debonair, and now triumphant Enver Bey exclaimed publicly that "arbitrary government [had] disappeared. . . . We are all brothers. . . . There are no longer Bulgars, Greeks, Roumans, Jews, Mussulmans; under the same blue sky we are all equal, we glory in being Ottomans."[37] The word "Armenian" was conspicuously absent. Many Armenians, especially progressive ones and even those in the Dashnak Party, had at first believed that the Young Turks would change the Ottoman Empire and thus implement the longed-for reforms for the Armenians and the other Christian minorities. In the end the Young Turks turned out to be passionately Turkic and nationalistic, and the consequences for the Armenians would be realized in a profoundly ironic reversal of their expectations.

But in the summer of 1908, as one historian put it, the many peoples of the empire seemed to come together: "At Serres [in Macedonia] the president of the Bulgarian Committee embraced the Greek archbishop; at Drama the revolutionary officers imprisoned a Turk for insulting a Christian; in an Armenian cemetery a procession of Turks and Armenians listened to prayers, offered up by their respective priests, for the victims of the Armenian massacres; at Samsum the Turks saluted the beard of a Greek prelate; at Tripoli Turks and Arabs joined in thanksgiving services."[38]

For the moment the future looked brighter.

Turkify the empire. The liberal segment of the movement would forge its most cohesive party in the Liberal Union of 1911, but it was the Committee of Union and Progress (CUP) that coalesced power, taking control of the new regime by unseating two liberal elder statesmen: Grand Viziers Said Pasha and Kamil Pasha. As the crises unfolded in 1909, the CUP was able, often behind the scenes, to increase its control of the government.[2]

In early April the news of a counterrevolution in the capital jolted the new government. It was supported by the Mohammedan Union, a zealous religious organization backed by the *softas* and some of the dervish societies. The counterrevolution called for a new Muslim orthodoxy, demanding the protection and the implementation of the *shari'a,* the sacred Muslim law of the Qu'ran. The assassination of an editor of the anti-CUP newspaper, the *Serbesti,* seems to have ignited the immediate uprising.[3]

On the night of April 12, some units of soldiers in the First Army Corps in Constantinople revolted. As dawn broke on the morning of April 13, there was an astonishing sight: Regiments of soldiers marched in the morning mist across the bridges from the suburbs to the Golden Horn, shooting their rifles into the sky to announce their advent. Several hundred filled the courtyard outside the parliament in Saint Sophia Square, while others poured into the old Byzantine plaza known as the Augusteon.[4]

As the mullahs, *hojas* (religious teachers), and *softas* in their white turbans and robes joined the soldiers, cries of "Down with the Constitution!" and "Long live the *shari'a!"* resounded in the plaza and throughout the streets of the city. The presence of the Muslim zealots created such tension that the chief of the Constantinople police was soon in the streets confronting them as they demanded the dismissal of the minister of war and the president of the chamber. The *softas* and their religious colleagues were also protesting the sight of women in public, a complaint that had become commonplace after the revolution. As the day went on, riots broke out in the streets and the soldiers and the *softas* sacked and looted the CUP's newspaper offices, sending many CUP members into hiding.[5]

In the chaos Grand Vizier Hilmi Pasha resigned, as did other cabinet members. Although the sultan issued an order that the *shari'a* would be protected, for the moment the government was in disarray. By telegraph, the news of the counterrevolution reached the army in Salonika, and within days an "Army of Deliverance" was mobilized and sent to the capital. Enver Bey, who was in Berlin at the Turkish embassy, rushed back to join his army, and on April 23 the Young Turk troops entered Constantinople. After some clashes with the *softas* and soldiers, which were over by about five o'clock in the afternoon, the Deliverance Army quashed the counterrevolution.[6] The CUP was now in a position to increase its influence over the next few years, in what would be an unstable and transitional time for the Ottoman government.

By the eve of World War I, the CUP would gradually become the dominant political force in Turkey, assuming a new and more authoritarian control of the government. With their belief in strong government, the Young Turks now expanded their passion for Turkish nationalism, and the party embraced a Turkification plan for the country and an ideology known as pan-Turkism. Any liberal ideas about Ottoman multiculturalism and minority rights were dashed. Furthermore the CUP militarized the government and "the army became the most important single factor in the politics of the Ottoman Empire."[7] Not unlike the way the Nazi Party would take control of the military and then pass repressive laws in the 1930s, the Committee of Union and Progress tightened its grip on Turkish society with repressive measures. The "Law of Associations" was passed to prevent the formation of political organizations that were ethnic in nature, and all existing ethnic organizations and clubs were ordered shut down. The "Law for the Prevention of Brigandage and Sedition" was passed to create new battalions to put down any forms of rebellion[8]—even any *perceived* rebellion. And in order to bolster the military and exert further control over the minorities, for the first time in Ottoman history non-Muslims were conscripted into the army.[9]

The counterrevolution was felt not only in the capital but all over the country, where riots and protests were staged. But in the Mediterranean region of Adana—the center of the last independent Armenian state (Cilician Armenia, which fell in 1375)—events exploded in an unforeseen way.

Irrigated by three major rivers, Adana was rich in wheat, cotton, barley, and sesame. Much of the grain was exported from the Mediterranean port of Mersin, the city, according to the British historian and journalist H. Charles Woods, through which Armenians of the Cilician Plain fled "when massacres [were] feared."[10] Ancient Armenian towns like Hajin and Zeitun were perched in the Taurus Mountains, which rise sharply to the north of the farmland, and the rugged farmers and mountaineers trekked down from them to the fields at harvesttime to work.

The Turks of the region had stereotyped the Armenians as wealthy merchants—especially those in the cities of Adana and Mersin, where, in fact, there were prosperous Armenian communities. The majority of Armenians in the rural areas, however, were struggling farmers and shepherds who labored under the inequitable Ottoman tax system. But the stereotype persisted, and the Turks, many of whom were poor, resented the smaller group of Armenians for their wealth, education, and economic stability, and many despised them as well because they were Christian infidels. In the capital city of Adana the Armenians made up almost half the population of about forty thousand, and those who were small businessmen and shopkeepers played a key role in the city's economic well-being.[11]

Observing the complex situation of minorities in Adana, Charles Woods noted that the Armenians and the Jews "in spite of oppression and hardship, have never given up their language, customs, and religion," and they "possess many merits," including an "aptitude for finance," an ability to "prosper under the most adverse circumstances."[12]

In the aftermath of the constitutional revolution of 1908, Armenians around the empire were feeling hopeful and cautiously optimistic, and in some cases were celebrating their new sense of slowly growing equality with their Muslim neighbors. In Adana, however, some Armenians were considered provocative because they were asserting cultural pride and nationalism by talking openly about their new rights and freedoms. In short, they were beginning to test the long-asked question: Can a Christian be the equal of a Muslim in Turkey? In the social milieu their Turkish and Kurdish neighbors found this offensive—the familiar story of a disliked minority being perceived as too aggressive or "pushy."

By the second week of April 1909, as the *softas* and the counterrevolutionary soldiers were stirring up activity around the country, matters in Adana had become tense and then treacherous. The events that followed must be seen in the light of many factors, but certainly within the context of the political corruption in the province. While corruption was rampant throughout the empire, the recently replaced governor of Adana, Bahri Pasha, was noted as one of the most corrupt, and his successor was indebted to the same political system. He governed by bribery and extortion in a region that was plagued by excessive political infighting.[13] Furthermore the Muslims of the region were poor and had just endured a season of famine in 1908, creating further resentment toward the more affluent Armenians. To add to the chaos and the Armenians' vulnerability, it was harvest time for barley, and the Armenian workers from the mountains had migrated down to the plain for the harvest, swelling the population of Adana and its surroundings.

On the day the counterrevolution was declared in Constantinople, the British dragoman Athanasios Trypanis in Adana reported to British vice-consul Doughty Wylie in Mersin that some Armenians had been murdered, and that there "was a very dangerous feeling in that town."[14] With terror percolating in the streets, the Armenian shops around the city began to close. Gangs of Turks armed with "clubs and provided with white *saruks*[15] (a band of white cloth), which the Muslims wrapped around their fezzes for the massacre, were seen buying revolvers and brandishing their guns wherever they went. By midday the Christian merchants had closed their shops and were running to their homes.[16]

Alarmed by the report Vice-Consul Major C. H. M. Doughty Wylie took the next train to Adana. "So little had I expected that any massacre was imminent," he wrote, "that I took my wife with me." Two stations from Adana, Doughty Wylie saw a dead body near the tracks and refugees running toward the train. And then abruptly Armenians from the second-class carriage came running into first class, crying that their lives were being threatened. When the vice-consul ran into the second-class carriage, he "saw two armed Turks threatening the refugees," and when they saw him, he reported that "they put away their pistols."[17]

More dead bodies appeared along tracks as they approached Adana. As they rushed out of the train station to Trypanis's house nearby, they saw "several men killed under the very noses of the Turkish guard." At Trypanis's Doughty Wylie changed into his uniform and walked a mile and a half to the *konak* (government building). "I saw several men killed on the way, and the town," Wylie noted, "was full of a howling mob looting the shops," and gunfire was everywhere.[18]

Instead of firing on the Turkish looters, Turkish soldiers were firing on the Armenians, who were trying to protect their lives and property against "a pitiless mob of vandals and fanatics."[19] Armenians were being massacred and firing back as they could, but the streets were already filling up with bleeding bodies and Armenian corpses. Doughty Wylie recorded his shock and then disgust that provincial governor Jevad Bey and the commandant, Mustafa Remzi Pasha, refused to do anything but sit in their offices, seemingly inert. When Doughty Wylie demanded some soldiers and officers in order to help quell the violence, the governor grudgingly gave him some soldiers but refused to send any officers.[20] "It is obvious," Charles Woods later wrote, "that if the Turkish troops actually at the Konak had been sent to stop the plundering of Armenian houses, or from the Turkish point of view 'to protect Moslems' that the whole catastrophe might have been averted."[21] Similarly, for a week before the massacre began, William N. Chambers and his nephew, Lawson Chambers—the missionaries who ran the American school for girls—urged the governor to take action to prevent what seemed to be certain disaster. Then, when the massacres began, the two missionaries worked desperately and ceaselessly to save lives, and in the end may have saved more Armenians than did anyone else.

Through the swirl of gunfire, screaming people, and the wounded and dead in the streets, Doughty Wylie ran to the American mission, where he posted a guard, and then to Trypanis's house. By the time he got back to the konak, he was shocked to find that the governor and commandant were still sitting in their offices doing nothing. Enraged, he told them that he would be back in the morning and that he expected fifty soldiers and an officer.

Throughout the next day the main streets of the city "were lined with bashebozuks armed with clubs, sticks, and pistols and claimed to be in terror of the Armenians, who they said were rising up against the government."[22] Again Doughty Wylie was seeing the old pattern of killing Armenians and then claiming that they were seditious and deserved what they got. As he returned to the konak in the dawn hours of the morning, he witnessed the very soldiers who were supposed to be stopping the massacre engaged in killing Armenians.

All morning the looting of Armenian shops and the killing continued. Doughty Wylie was finally given fifty soldiers and an officer, but when it became clear to him that the governing authorities were not going to do anything to stop the killing, he took the law into his own hands. Using his wits, the British vice-consul decided to lead his fifty men into the mayhem of the streets, and he ordered them to blow their bugles, shoot their rifles

over the heads of the crowds, and charge with bayonets in order to disband the killing mobs. He even sent criers down streets and alleyways
ordering all people back to their houses. At the train station he was able to
disband a crowd of Turkish villagers "who were flocking into the town to
loot and murder."[23] Successful and heroic as Doughty Wylie was, he
couldn't stop the killing everywhere.

When he later arrived at the Armenian Quarter, he wrote, "I found
that two American missionaries were killed. They had been gallantly
working for an hour to put out a fire which was threatening their school,
and were killed at close range by five Turks who had previously promised
to let them alone. The third missionary, Mr. Trowbridge, who was with
them, managed to escape." As they carried the dead and dying bodies
from the street, they were fired on from the minaret of a nearby mosque.
When Doughty Wylie returned to the Armenian Quarter, he found that
the "big bazaar was blazing," and that Turks and Armenians were now
engaged in "house-to-house fighting." Doughty Wylie left his guard
posted by the road to keep it clear, and when he returned a few minutes
later he found that "my own guard had joined in the attack on the nearest
Armenian house and killed everybody in it."[24]

He then proceeded to the Tobacco Régie factory, where it was
reported that the killing was even more intense. At the factory the vice-
consul was shot and wounded by an Armenian who thought he was a
Turkish officer. Realizing that this happened by accident, and aware that it
could create an even more flammable situation, the British vice-consul
took decisive action. He quickly issued a message to the governor that if
the fighting stopped immediately no indemnity or punishment would be
dealt. He then telegraphed for a British warship, and gave an order for the
Armenian Quarter of the city to be closed off and secured by troops. The
rest of the town he ordered to be placed under immediate curfew, with a
notice that those who disobeyed would be shot. Having dispatched these
orders to the commandant, Remzi Pasha, he went home to take care of his
injuries.[25]

Doughty Wylie's continued efforts to reach the outside world were
thwarted as the railway refused to transmit telegraphs for him and the
Adana telegraph office remained closed. Finally, by Saturday, April 17, he

sent a message to the governor ordering him to telegraph the "severest orders to outlying districts to stop the massacres." On Tuesday the twentieth, he had received a telegram from the British ship *Swiftsure,* which was sailing off the coast and agreed to dock at Mersin, news of which put some fear into the Turkish authorities.

But the fact was that in the first forty-eight hours of killing, some two thousand Armenians were dead in the city of Adana alone. The vice-consul further noted that there were "already 15,000 Armenians in desperate need of food" and living in terror as homeless refugees, the "shops have been burnt and gutted," and famine was "imminent."[26] As Armenians took refuge in the American School for Girls and various Catholic schools and papal missionary establishments, they cut holes in the sides of the various buildings so they could pass from place to place without having to go out into the streets. So perilous was walking in public that the Armenian pastor, Hovagim Effendi, was shot and killed as Mr. Chambers attempted to escort him across the street from the American School to his house.[27] Doughty Wylie continued to report his astonishment that the governor Jevad Bey and commandant Remzi Pasha remained passive, and in doing so enabled the massacre to happen.

Within days of the massacres, the counterrevolution was put down in Constantinople, and Abdul Hamid was sent into permanent exile. Immediately Mahmud Shevket, the commander of the liberation army, ordered several Young Turk regiments from Beirut and Damascus to Adana to restore order. What happened, however, was the reverse.

Not long after the Young Turk regiments arrived in Adana on the evening of April 25, the city went up in flames again. This time the killing was even more brutal and well organized because it was conducted by the new Young Turk liberation army. It began with a claim of provocation, a strategy the Turks and the Ottoman government had used before and would use again to justify massacre.

The newly arrived soldiers claimed that they were fired on by Armenians as they were camping in their tents on the bank of the Sihun River; they claimed the fire came from a church tower in town. Quite quickly it was revealed that shots fired from the church tower could not possibly have reached the bivouacked tents.[28] The shots in fact appeared to have been fired by local Muslims with the goal of provoking the troops to go after the Armenians.[29]

The soldiers now invaded the Christian quarter and opened fire on the Armenians. After the recent cease fire, the Armenians had been completely disarmed, and it wasn't difficult to kill them en masse and quickly. For this reason the bulk of the killing in Adana happened in this round of massacre, and what followed was—as one historian has put it—"one of the most gruesome and savage bloodbaths ever recorded in human history."[30] In a couple of days some two thousand people were massacred in the Armenian quarter. The Turkish soldiers then set fire to the Mouseghian School, which housed its students as well as two thousand refugees from the first massacre. As the school went up in flames, hundreds of children and their teachers ran outside in terror, burning alive or killed by gunfire of the soldiers, who were posted in adjacent buildings.

Then, as the fire spread to the Armenian church near the school, more refugees were evacuated by a brave Jesuit priest who took them, half-crazed with terror, to the French College, from which they were taken yet again by Major Doughty Wylie when the Turks set the college on fire.[31] The killing and looting went on uninterrupted, and the fires destroyed the entire Armenian Quarter as well as the outlying Christian districts; the Gregorian, Catholic, and Protestant churches and the Jesuit school for girls were all burned.

In his consular report of Tuesday, April 26, Doughty Wylie wrote: "It appears to me that about one-half of Adana city will be burnt."[32] As the fires engulfed the Armenian section of the city, thirteen thousand Armenian refugees packed themselves into a large cotton factory owned by a Greek, Trypani. There was no space for a body to lie down, and Doughty Wylie was terrified because the danger of fire in that cotton factory was now so great. In a German factory another five thousand took refuge, and the girls at the American school were hurried off to the British consulate to hide.[33] As the weeks of April went by, the massacres spread like a wild fire across the Cilician Plain. Armenian towns and villages along the Gulf of Alexandretta were razed and pillaged. The entire population of the village of Hamidiye sixty miles east of Adana was wiped out. In the mountainous towns of Hadjin and Dortyol in the northern part of the province, Armenians fought tenaciously in resistance, beat back the Turks, and saved themselves from total annihilation.

When it was all over, 4,823 houses in Adana were burned to the ground, of which 4,437 were Armenian.[34] Some two hundred villages were also ravaged. In his report Doughty Wylie noted that as yet the death toll in the region was still unknown, but "the loss has been enormous [and] may be estimated at between 15,000 and 25,000; of these, very few, if any, can be Moslems."[36]

Of the devastation journalist Charles Woods wrote: "When I visited Adana in the month of October (six months after the massacres) the Christian business quarter of the city was practically no more than many heaps of charred remains intersected by numerous semi-destroyed walls. . . . the government had not then attempted to rebuild, or even to allow the people to rebuild, the houses which made up the principal Armenian quarter, and included the Christian bazaar. . . . The burning and destruction were so systematically carried out," Woods recorded, "that more than one Turkish mosque or Moslem house might be clearly distinguished in the very middle of the Christian ruins." Then, as he "wandered through the mass of ruins the horror of the scene became more and more real. So great was the destruction that it was almost impossible to discern where streets once existed and where they did not."[37]

Even more heart-rending were the scenes of once prosperous merchants, workmen, and artisans, persevering amid the ruins. Everywhere, Woods noted, there were "barbers, shoemakers, tailors, or tin smiths . . . sitting amongst ruined walls (where once their shops existed) carrying on their respective trades. In some cases the re-equipped tradesmen were sheltered from the sun or rain by rough roofs made out of bits of kerosene tins—the contents of which had actually been used to burn the city— whilst in others the labourers had not even a canopy above their heads." "Never," Woods wrote, "has the burning of a town been more systematically carried out than at Adana in 1909."[38]

Although gestures toward justice were made by the government in the aftermath of Adana, they turned out to be hollow and only for show. An Ottoman parliamentary representative, an Armenian, Hagop Babikian—who was put on the special investigative commission and was, not surprisingly, the most rigorous of the investigators—died mysteriously, many thought from poisoning.[39] Some Turks and even some Armenians were sentenced to death. But the government officials who were in some sense the most responsible for the massacres were given mere slaps on the wrist. Governor Jevad Bey was debarred from his office, and the military commandant, Remzi Pasha, was sentenced to three months in jail.

Woods, Chambers, and Doughty Wylie, among others, expressed their outrage at these two men for their refusal to do their jobs and bring the massacres under control. So transparently were the two colluding with those massacring Armenians, that when Doughty Wylie insisted that the *Swiftsure* land its men on shore to help quell the violence, the governor protested vehemently.[40] Even the funds designated by the Ottoman government for relief were mostly extorted by the government officials in the region, and an international relief committee formed under Doughty Wylie's direction was similarly fleeced.[41]

The Turkish historian Y. H. Bayur noted that "there are very few movements in the world that have given rise to such great hopes as the Ottoman Constitutional Revolution; there are likewise very few movements whose hopes have been so swiftly and finally disappointed."[42] The Armenian poet Siamanto (Adom Yarjanian) embodied that sense of disappointment and more in a book of poems based on eyewitness accounts he received in letters from an Armenian physician, Diran Balakian, who was doing relief work in the aftermath of the Adana massacres. Siamanto was haunted by the betrayal of the very regime he and other progressive Armenians had supported only a year before.

In this book-cycle of thirteen poems, *Bloody News from My Friend* (1910), Siamanto depicts the massacres with a graphic realism that was somewhat revolutionary for poetry of the late Victorian period. He creates images of what Ambassador Henry Morgenthau would later call the "sadistic orgies" of Turkish massacre that include rape, torture, and even crucifixion. In "The Dance" Armenian women are burned to death while they are forced to circle-dance: "The charred bodies rolled and tumbled to their deaths." In "The Cross" a mother is forced to watch the Turks nail her son to a cross: "We'll do it to you like you did it to Christ." The poems carry a recurrent tone of grief over the betrayal of the Young Turk revolution and its promise of constitutional reform. "I want to testify about what's happening to our orphaned race," Siamanto writes at the opening of "The Cross." And in "The Dagger" the pain of betrayal leads the poet to exclaim: "The olive branch of our hope for brotherhood/will burn again in the flame of all this."[43] Siamanto's hope for brotherhood would see further reversal in 1915, when he, along with hundreds of other intellectuals and leaders, would be arrested and murdered at the onset of the Genocide.

What happened in Adana in 1909 was a kind of testing ground for relations—albeit at their worst—between Armenians and Turks in the new Young Turk era of constitutional government. In the Adana massacres, one can see how flammable the network of social, economic, political, and religious conditions were for Armenians in Turkey less than a year after the Young Turk revolution.

If anything, constitutional rights granted to Christians in 1908 deeply disturbed what in Turkish is called *muvazene,* that is, "social order" or "equilibrium." In the minds of the Muslim population, the social order had gone awry, and the already devalued Christian minorities, especially the Armenians, were now more problematic than ever to the mainstream culture. In Adana in 1909, the issue of equal citizenship for Christians and Muslims in the Ottoman Empire had been tested again, and again it had failed.

This chain of Armenian massacre, which began in its modern instance in 1878 after the Berlin Conference, escalated in 1894–96, and occurred again in 1909, created what the social psychologist Irvin Staub calls a "continuum of destruction"—a history and cultural orientation that can lead to conditions for genocide. For mass killing or genocide, Staub suggests, "a progression of changes in a culture and individuals is usually required." In certain instances, Staub notes, "the progression takes place over decades or even centuries and creates a readiness in the culture."[44] The "long history of devaluation and mistreatment of the Armenians," Staub continues, which includes "large-scale mass killings," was a result of government bureaucracy ordering and encouraging the killings, and of individuals who participate and then become socialized by them. "People learn," Staub explains, "by doing, by participation." People are changed by their participation in destructive and harmful behavior, and the victims are further devalued through this process.[45] Scapegoating of the kind that was apparent at Adana and in the Hamidian massacres was clearly the result of devaluing a subgroup, an ethnic minority in this case, in part in order to raise the sinking self-esteem of the majority group—the Turks, who felt their empire threatened by Christian minorities in Anatolia and in the Balkans.[46]

Again, as in the case of the Hamidian massacres, no justice or punishment was served in the wake of the Adana massacres. And it was this impunity that further devalued an already marginalized group. While there were heroic bystanders and rescuers like Major Doughty Wylie, Lawson, William Chambers, and other missionaries on the scene, there was no foreign intervention. The irony that the warships of seven nations—England, France, Italy, Austria, Russia, Germany, and the United States—were stationed just miles away off the coast and did not intervene only dramatizes the failure.

As the concept of Armenian massacre with impunity was hammered deeper and deeper into the social psychology of Turkish society, the Armenian Question was inculcated as an issue that could only be solved by unmitigated state-sponsored and state-sanctioned violence. The Hamidian massacres and the holocaust at Adana were both monumental acts of organized violence, as well as seminal cultural events for Turkish society in the unfolding continuum of destruction that would have its final chapter in the government's plan for total extermination of the Armenians in 1915. The coming of World War I would provide a new moment for the CUP government—so that Talaat Pasha could say to the U.S. ambassador, Henry Morgenthau, "I have accomplished more toward solving the Armenian problem in three months than Abdul Hamid accomplished in thirty years."[47]

In August 1910 in Salonika, Talaat Bey—by then a rising star in the Committee of Union and Progress—gave a talk to his inner circle outlining a platform for the upcoming party congress meeting. "You are aware," he said, "that by the terms of the Constitution equality of Mussulman and Ghiaur [infidel] was affirmed, but you one and all know and feel that this is an unrealizable idea." The future minister of the interior went on to say: "The Sheriat [*shari'a*], our whole past history and the sentiments of hundreds of thousands of Mussulmans and even the sentiments of the Ghiaurs themselves . . . present an impenetrable barrier to the establishment of real equality."[48] It was a clear and telling expression of how deeply committed to Turkism were Talaat and a growing nationalist faction of the CUP.

Adana was a turning point for the Armenians. The massacres there were another major step in the devaluation of this minority culture, and a step forward on the road to genocide.

THE BALKAN WARS

AND WORLD WAR I:

THE ROAD TO GENOCIDE

In part, the Ottoman Empire's road to World War I and then to the Armenian Genocide began with its alliance with Germany and with the Balkan Wars of 1912–13. Bulgarian premier I. E. Geshof summed up the sentiments of the Balkan states on the eve of the Balkan War of 1912, when he said, "The present war . . . is not a product of panslavist agitation. . . . It is a crusade against unbearable Turkish tyranny that is exploiting and martyrizing the Christians of the Balkan peninsula."[1] Both the Balkan Wars and World War I created a new sense of crisis for the Ottoman Empire and its Committee of Union and Progress leaders. With the loss of the Christian states in the Balkans, the Ottoman government became increasingly unstable and its ruling elite came under attack.

On January 26, 1913, the nationalist faction of the CUP staged a coup d'état in the middle of the day at the Sublime Porte as government business was in progress. Talaat and Enver, both powerful figures in their wing of the CUP, and about two hundred followers, marched into the Sublime Porte and assassinated Minister of War Nazim Pasha.[2] The assassination of Nazim Pasha brought down "the Liberal Party," and the nationalist faction of the CUP took control of the government. In June, when Mahmud Shevket Pasha, the grand vizier, was assassinated, the way was open for Talaat Pasha to become minister of the interior and Enver Pasha to become minister of war; Jemal Pasha was made minister of the navy, and the new ruling triumvirate had emerged. This new Young Turk trio came to power with a sense of anxiety about the empire's future in the wake of the Balkan Wars, and when World War I broke out, their siege mentality escalated.

Like the Anatolian Armenian provinces, the Balkan states were historically Christian, and the population predominantly Christian. Within decades after Ottoman troops led by Sultan Muhammad II captured Constantinople in 1453, the Ottomans had conquered southeastern Europe—Albania, Serbia, Bulgaria, Greece, Macedonia, Montenegro, Bosnia-Herzegovina, Romania, and pieces of Poland and the Ukraine. At the empire's peak in the middle of the sixteenth century, under Sultan Süleyman I, the Turks pushed farther into Europe, conquering Hungary. It wasn't until 1683, when Austrian and Polish troops defeated the Turks at the gates of Vienna, that Ottoman Turkey's imperialist designs on Europe were stemmed. But from the fifteenth century through the end of the Balkan Wars of 1912–13, Turkey in Europe, as it was known, was the empire's western domain.

During that span of about five hundred years, the Christians of the Balkans, the majority of whom were Slavs, lived under Ottoman Muslim rule, and were accorded the traditional Ottoman treatment of those of infidel status. The Balkan Christians, like the Armenians, were subjected to heavy taxation, arbitrary violence, political disenfranchisement, and cultural oppression; some of them converted to Islam. There were constant rebellions and uprisings against the Turks, which were put down by the Ottoman army. Finally, by 1828, Greece had successfully fought its war for independence. In 1876 the Bulgarians staged a rebellion, only to be brutally massacred by Ottoman forces in what quickly became known as "the Bulgarian horrors." In the last quarter of the nineteenth century, the Balkan states petitioned continually for reform. After the Russo-Turkish War of 1877, article 23 of the Treaty of Berlin promised reforms for the Balkan states, especially Macedonia, just as article 61 of that treaty promised reforms for the Armenians. With the Treaty of Berlin the Bulgarians had achieved partial autonomy, and the process of Balkan secession had begun.

By 1912, as new Balkan alliances were formed in opposition to Ottoman rule, the Turks again responded with massacre. In the summer of 1912 the Ottoman army carried out two massacres, one in Ishtib, east of Skopje, and another in Kocani, southeast of Skopje, the capital city of Kosovo. In October 1912, the tiny state of Montenegro began a war of rebellion against Ottoman rule. Five days later the other Balkan states demanded reforms and mobilized their armies. On October 17 the Ottoman Empire had declared war on Bulgaria and Serbia, and the next day Greece declared war on the Ottoman Empire. What ensued was astonishing. Within a day Turkey suffered heavy losses to the combined fronts of the Balkan armies, and was forced to stage an eleventh-hour defense near Constantinople. By October 26 the Serbs had won at Skopje in Kosovo, by November 8 the Greeks had taken Salonika, and by November 29 Albania had declared its independence.

Throughout the period of the Balkan crisis, Turkish sentiment was marked by rage. In the streets of Constantinople on the eve of the war, students and CUP members shouted: "We want war!", "To Sofia, to Sofia!", "Down with Greece! Greeks, bow your heads!" and the hatred of European intervention was clear as they chanted "Down with article 23, down with it!", "Down with equality!", "The Balkan dogs are trampling on Islam."[3]

An editorial in the newspaper *Tanin,* a quasi-official voice of the CUP, declared: "Europe's intervention and Europe's desire to control our internal affairs is a warning to us to ponder the fate not only of Rumelia [Macedonia], but also eastern Turkey, for it will be impossible to spare eastern Turkey the fate awaiting Rumelia."[4] In the Turkish mind, the struggle to keep the Balkans was never far from the Armenian Question.

In December an armistice was declared, and at the London peace conference that followed, the Balkan countries demanded that the Ottoman Empire give up European Turkey and pay a war indemnity. When Turkey refused the terms of the peace agreement, the war started up again and continued through the spring of 1913. Turkey had lost nearly all its territory in Europe. The Montenegrans had taken part of Albania; Serbia had gained large areas of Macedonia; and Bulgaria had acquired Adrianople and other areas as far as the Aegean Sea. Greece had gained Crete and other islands, as well as Salonika and part of Macedonia. Following the brief Second Balkan War, Turkey regained some territory, including Adrianople. But in the end the Turks had lost 70 percent of their European population and 85 percent of their European territory.[5]

In the immediate aftermath of the Balkan Wars, Russia mobilized on the Caucasian frontier and informed Turkey that if there was war in the Balkans again, they could not promise neutrality. Germany, for its part, made it clear that an attack on Turkey might trigger an all-out European war.

ARMENIANS ASK FOR REFORMS

It was at this moment of Turkish vulnerability that the Armenians persuaded the European powers to push the empire to agree to some of the reforms for which they had been clamoring for decades. And, after brief negotiations, the Armenian Reform Agreement of February 8, 1914, was initiated by the European powers—among them Turkey's most hated enemy, Russia. In the wake of its losses in the Far East after the Russo-Japanese War, Russia was now more focused on the Armenian Question than ever. To the Turks the reforms quickly became one more humiliating instance of European intervention in their domestic affairs.[6]

The Young Turks feared that the renewal of Armenian reforms might turn into an eastern version of the recent Balkan humiliation. Abdullah Jevdet, a physician for the military and a CUP leader, pointed his finger at the Armenians when he said: "Don't kid yourself that because of our preoccupations in European Turkey, we should not worry about Anatolia. Anatolia is the well spring of every fibre of our life. It is our heart, head, and the air we breathe."[7] The warning here was clear: Christian reforms led to disaster in the Balkans, so too might they lead to disaster in the east.[8] Jevdet's nationalist fervor was indicative of the new tone of pan-Turkism that was defining the Young Turk regime.

The Armenian Reform Agreement of February 1914, diluted as it was from its original plan, was signed as international law in Constantinople; perhaps its most dramatic aspect was the requirement that Europeans be appointed as inspectors-general in the Armenian provinces to administer and oversee the reforms. For the moment the Armenians were hopeful and delighted because this appeared to be a fulfillment of the promise of article 61 of the Treaty of Berlin, the very article that had launched the Armenian Question as an international issue back in 1878, the very article that catalyzed the cycle of Turkish rage at Armenian appeals for international intervention to oversee reform.

As the Turkish sense of unease and panic increased, the CUP put into motion a sophisticated network of party branches in the provinces, directed by party loyalists who were dedicated to a new Turkification plan.[9] The ideas bound up in Turkification and pan-Turkism reflected a mood of fierce nationalism that had been evolving at lower frequencies ever since the 1908 revolution.

Not unlike Hitler's later nazification programs for German youth, exemplified in the Hitlerjugend, the Young Turks now launched a program of nationalist indoctrination and paramilitary training for Turkish youth. The Association for the Promotion of Turkish Strength (Türk Gücü Cemiyeti) established in 1913, was dedicated to the military training of the youth so that the nation would become again "a warrior nation" in order to avoid disaster and "the decay of the Turkish race." Under Enver's direction the War Ministry also sponsored paramilitary youth groups, supplying them with free rifles and ammunition in order to prepare "for the defense of the fatherland."[10] In establishing the League for National Defense, the Young Turks created a program aimed at preparing its citizens for war. These movements and other CUP militarization plans socialized the domestic population for a new kind of militancy and ethnic hatred, so that when war broke out, there was, as the historian Jay Winter has put it, "the military, political, and cultural space" in which genocide also could occur.[11]

The chief propagandist of the CUP, Ziya Gökalp, played an important role in the dissemination of the new nationalism. While there were other pan-Turkist writers and propagandists, such as Yusuf Akchura and Moiz Cohen (known as Tekinalp), Gökalp's was the pan-Turkist voice that rose the highest in the political arena. He was a Kurd from Diyarbekir, whose family had been involved in massacring Armenians in the 1890s.[12] By 1911 he had become an important member of the CUP's Central Committee. A romantic nationalist and a virulent racist, he wrote propaganda, tracts on nationalism, and jingoistic poems. Eerily foreshadowing the leading Nazi propagandists Alfred Rosenberg and Joseph Goebbels, who propounded the central notion that Germany needed to be *Judenrein* if it was to revitalize itself, Gökalp advocated that Turkey could only be revitalized if it rid itself of its non-Muslim elements. Gökalp hated the Tanzimat reforms that opened the door to minority inclusion in Ottoman political life, and he believed that those who were not Muslim were destined to be servile peoples, not citizens but only subjects, and not part of what he called the "dominant culture"; one of his epithets was "Islam mandates domination."[13]

In ways that were similar and anticipated the Nazi race-hygiene ideology of the 1930s, which depicted the Jew as a "harmful bacillus" and "bloodsucker" infecting the German nation from within (Hitler called the Jew "a maggot in a rotting corpse" and "a germ carrier of the worst sort"), pan-Turkist ideology envisioned the Armenian as an invasive infection in Muslim Turkish society. One Turkish physician, Mehmed Reshid, a staunch party member who was appointed governor of Diyarbekir in 1915—and would be responsible for the deaths and deportations of hundreds of thousands of Armenians—likened the Armenians to "dangerous microbes," asking rhetorically, "Isn't it the duty of a doctor to destroy these microbes?" Known as the "executioner governor," Dr. Mehmed Reshid tortured Armenians by nailing horseshoes to their feet and marching them through the streets, and by crucifying them on makeshift crosses. After the Genocide Reshid confessed, "My Turkishness prevailed over my medical calling."[14] Other physicians, like Dr. Behaeddin Shakir and Dr. Mehmed Nazim, both CUP leaders, also believed that Armenians were *gâvurs* who had become "tubercular microbes" infecting the state.[15]

Gökalp's pan-Turkism was bound up in grandiose romantic nationalism and a "mystical vision of blood and race,"[16] and was influenced by the German nationalism of Herder and Wagner, who were also key influences on Nazi Aryan ideology. Gökalp believed that for Turkey to revitalize itself, it had to reclaim a golden age, which he defined as a pre-Islamic era of Turkic warriors such as Genghis Khan and Tamerlane. It is ironic that Hitler also extolled Genghis Khan in his speech about the future of German world domination and his immediate plan to invade Poland. Speaking to his elite generals eight days before invading Poland in 1939, Hitler praised the virtues of power and brutality, referring to how easy it had been to dispense of defenseless people like the Armenians. "Genghis Khan led millions of women and children to slaughter—with premeditation and a happy heart. History sees him solely as the founder of a state. It's a matter of indifference to me what a weak western European civilization will say about me." And then the führer asked rhetorically: "Who today, after all, speaks of the annihilation of the Armenians?"[17]

For Turkey to be strong again, Gökalp believed, it had to emulate this great military past, and it had to be a pure, homogeneous nation. A nation, Gökalp wrote, must be "a society consisting of people who speak the same language, have had the same education and are united in their religious and aesthetic ideals—in short those who have a common culture and religion."[18]

Gökalp declared with passion that nationalism was the new religion in the twentieth century, and that loyalty to the nation must be, for the healthy state, unqualified and total. "I am a soldier, it [the nation] is my commander/I obey without question all its orders. With closed eyes/I carry out my duty," his doggerel went.[19] Like Mehmet Reshid, he espoused the idea that non-Turks were invasive germs that threatened the health of the state. "Greeks, Armenians, and Jews" were "a foreign body in the national Turkish state."[20] Believing the Armenians and Greeks to be parasites, Gökalp and the other pan-Turkists strove to rid their society of this Christian bourgeois element. Gökalp's theory of national economy advocated a homogenous Turkish bourgeoisie, and during the Balkan Wars, a Turkish boycott of Greek and Armenian businesses was a major manifestation of the new xenophobia. As Tekinalp put it, "The rigorous boycott" created "a feeling of brotherhood . . . in the hearts of people all over the empire."[21] It was only a beginning, for as U.S. Ambassador Henry Morgenthau put it, the boycott with its attack on Christians, especially the Greeks in this case, foreshadowed what would happen to the Armenians later.[22] Turkish rage at the *gâvur* bourgeoisie would explode in more extreme ways when the wholesale theft and pillaging of Armenian wealth became institutionalized during the Genocide.

The Young Turk leaders, especially Enver Pasha, went beyond pan-Turkism and became obsessed with the idea of pan-Turanism, an ideology based on the hope of reclaiming the Caucasus and central Asia—an idea laced with some of the occultlike fantasy characterized by the Nazi belief about ruling the world for a thousand years. For Enver it fueled his desire to wipe out the Armenians, whom he saw as an obstacle to Turkish expansion into the Russian Caucasus and then into central Asia, and it dictated some of his military strategy.[23] The pan-Turanist part of Gökalp's ideology made a special appeal to Turkish fantasies. It was predicated on an irridentist idea that the Ottoman Empire could revive itself by achieving some sort of union among "all peoples of proven or alleged Turkic origins," both inside and outside the Ottoman Empire.[24]

The idea encapsulated a dream of creating an empire among the Turkic peoples from Albania through Anatolia, into the Caucuses and then into central and east-central Asia. As the Turks drove east, Gökalp believed, they would find the mythical origin of their culture, "a Shangri-La-like area in the steppes of Central Asia."[25] By 1910, as the idea of Turkification became increasingly popular, the CUP decided to make the Turkish language compulsory in all schools throughout the empire, and it reiterated this at annual meetings in the ensuing years leading up to World War I.[26]

By 1914, as Turkey positioned itself to join Germany in the war, the Young Turk leadership was embracing various elements of pan-Turkism, pan-Turanism, and Turkification. Obsessed with their mortal enemy, Russia, and angry about Russian rule of the Turkic peoples of central Asia, the Young Turks used pan-Turkic goals as a rationale for entering the war. Throughout the press from *Tâsvir-i Efkâr* and *Sabah* to government organs such as *Tanin,* and opposition papers like *Ikdam* and *Zaman,* pan-Turkist propaganda was very much part of the zeitgeist.[27]

THE GERMAN-TURKISH ALLIANCE AND
THE ROAD TO WAR

As Jay Winter has noted, World War I created for the Turks a condition of total war. In short it created an armed and mobilized society, a heightened sense of national security crisis, a deepened xenophobia, and the sense of chaos that accompanies war. Total war was a political, military, and cultural space in which genocide could occur. All these conditions were used to mobilize the "final solution" for the Armenians. "The Armenian genocide," Winter writes, "opened up a new phase in the history of warfare": The CUP waged a campaign of race annihilation against the Armenians by deeming them "the internal enemy."

World War I made it clear that "the old idea that war is politics by another means is outdated in the twentieth century. Now war would become hatred by other means. And, in the case of the Armenians, hatred meant extermination."[28] As the German vice-consul at Erzurum, Max Erwin von Scheubner-Richter, said bluntly in a diplomatic report—"the conditions of the present war," have been utilized by the CUP "for the solution to the Armenian question."[29] (Scheubner-Richter, an early Nazi Party member, conveyed to Hitler after World War I his firsthand knowledge of the Armenian Genocide, which no doubt contributed to Hitler's sense that a minority population could be dispensed of with impunity.[30])

As the Turks were embroiled first in the Balkan Wars and then in World War I, the CUP found wartime and its necessities an opportunity to take control of the military. Enver, the new minister of defense, did what Hitler would later do when he came to power: kill off the old regime of officers and replace them with a new breed of loyal Nazis. Enver fired eleven hundred officers including generals in January 1914, arrested and imprisoned officers from whom he feared "counteraction," and then promoted hundreds of young loyal CUP members to high-ranking positions. In this way the army was rapidly politicized for the new regime's program.[31]

Turkey's new alliance with Germany and partnership in World War I accelerated the empire's militarization program. By March 1914 the Germans had become an entrenched presence in the empire and in the Ottoman military. High-ranking German officers now found themselves holding commanding positions in the Ottoman army and navy. Gen. Liman von Sanders had arrived in Constantinople in December 1913 and was to become commander of the First Ottoman Army Corps, and also inspector-general of the Ottoman army, while Maj. Gen. Fritz Bronssart von Schnellendorf was to become Enver's chief of staff. Marshal Colmar von der Goltz, Maj. Gen. Friedrich Kress von Kressenstein, Gen. Eric von Falkenhayn, Maj. Gen. Hans von Seeckt all assumed positions of power in the Ottoman army. The German rear admiral Wilhelm Souchon became commander of the Ottoman navy, as did his successor Vice-Adm. Hubert von Rebeur-Paschwitz.[32]

To the new American ambassador to the Ottoman Empire, Henry Morgenthau, the aggressive presence of the German army in Turkey seemed nothing less than evidence of the kaiser's plan "to annex the Turkish army to his own." It was certainly no coincidence that Enver Pasha had been trained in Berlin, where he was military attaché in 1909. He worshipped German *Kultur*, and in Morgenthau's view, was little more than "a cog in the Prussian system."[33] With the new German leadership, Morgenthau found himself witnessing changes in the Ottoman army. "What . . . had been an undisciplined, ragged rabble was now parading with the goose step; the men were clad in German field gray, and they even wore a casque-shaped head covering, which slightly suggested the German *Pickelhaube* [spiked helmet]." Of this the "German officers were immensely proud," for they felt they had transformed "the wretched Turkish soldiers of January into these neatly dressed, smartly stepping, splendidly maneuvring troops."[34]

By the summer of 1914, Morgenthau described the German officers as "rushing through the streets every day in huge automobiles," and filling "all the restaurants and amusement places at night, consuming large quantities of champagne." In particular, General von der Goltz, who had accrued the title of pasha, drove through the streets in a flashy car "on both sides of which flaring German eagles were painted," and a "trumpeter on the front seat" announced them as they barreled down the boulevards.[35]

Although the Ottoman Empire signed a secret treaty with Germany on August 2, 1914, many high-ranking Turks were still pro-British, including Yussuf Izzeddin, the heir apparent to the sultanate, and Grand Vizier Said Halim. Jemal Pasha was a Francophile, the majority of the cabinet were not pro-German, and public opinion was more pro-English than pro-German. But Enver and Talaat had succeeded in engineering the German ascendancy, and this struck Morgenthau as ironic because England, not Germany, had been "Turkey's historic friend."[36]

By the summer of 1914, an aggressive German public relations campaign had coopted the Turkish press and fueled the new Turkish-German alliance. German ambassador Hans von Wangenheim purchased the *Ikdam*, one of Turkey's largest newspapers, and began vigorously promoting Germany at the expense of France and Great Britain. The *Osmanischer Lloyd*, which was published in French and German, became an organ of the German embassy, and a new wave of censorship followed, in which the Turkish press was ordered to publish only pro-German sentiment. Russia was portrayed as Turkey's chief enemy, responsible for Turkey's recent losses, and Germany as its ally. As Morgenthau put it: "The Kaiser suddenly became 'Hadji Wilhelm.' "[37]

Trainloads of Germans from Berlin—some 3,800 of them—began landing in Constantinople. Most of them were mechanics sent by the kaiser to work in ammunition plants and to repair Turkish destroyers for war. Like the military officers, this new crew of Germans also filled the cafés at night and paraded through the streets "in the small hours of the morning, howling and singing German patriotic songs."[38] It was a moment in which the gradual erosion of British dominance seemed to have given way fully to German hegemony in Turkey. To the close-up diplomatic eye of the American ambassador, it seemed that the British had not played the game properly. British ambassador Sir Louis Mallet "had not purchased Turkish officials with money, as had Wagenheim; he had not corrupted the Turkish press, trampled on every remaining vestige of international law, fraternized with a gang of political desperadoes, and conducted a ceaseless campaign of misrepresentations and lies against his enemy."[39]

On November 14, less than two weeks after the Ottoman Empire entered the war, the sheikh-ul-Islam (the chief Sunni Muslim religious authority in the Ottoman world), Mustafa Hayri Bey—who was a CUP appointment and not, as it was traditionally, the sultan's choice—made a formal declaration of *jihad* in Constantinople, followed by well-organized demonstrations in the streets. Even though the Germans and the Austro-Hungarians were the only Christians exempt from the *jihad,* they were uneasy about this aspect of the Ottoman religious war cry.[40] Wagenheim wired the Wilhelmstrasse (Foreign Ministry) that the unleashing of religious passions among the Turks was liable to do more harm than good. He noted that there had already been anti-Armenian violence and other disorder in the city, and he assured the kaiser that he was doing everything "to prevent further troubles for which we would be held responsible."[41] The Entente governments were alarmed about the *jihad,* and the Italians, for example, now bolstered their armies in Libya, where they feared trouble.[42]

To promote the idea of *jihad,* the sheikh-ul-Islam's published proclamation summoned the Muslim world to arise and massacre its Christian oppressors. "Oh Moslems," the document read, "Ye who are smitten with happiness and are on the verge of sacrificing your life and your good for the cause of right, and of braving perils, gather now around the Imperial throne." In the *Ikdam,* the Turkish newspaper that had just passed into German ownership, the idea of *jihad* was underscored: "The deeds of our enemies have brought down the wrath of God. A gleam of hope has appeared. All Mohammedans, young and old, men, women, and children must fulfill their duty. . . . If we do it, the deliverance of the subjected Mohammedan kingdoms is assured." *Jihad* pamphlets appealed to the need to exterminate all the Christians—except those of German nationality. "He who kills even one unbeliever," one pamphlet read, "of those who rule over us, whether he does it secretly or openly, shall be rewarded by God." In the worldwide Islamic revolution that was coming, "India" would be "for the Indian Moslems, the Caucasus for the Caucasian Moslems, and the Ottoman Empire for the Ottoman Turks and Arabs."[43]

At the American embassy the day after the *jihad* proclamation, over tea and cakes, Enver assured Ambassador Morgenthau that *jihad* proclamations would not mean any harm to Americans, nor would there be any massacres. In the midst of his assurances, Morgenthau's secretary came into the room to report that a mob was demonstrating "against certain foreign establishments," and already had attacked an Austrian shop that was advertising "English clothes" for sale. Enver brushed off this news as nothing to worry about, but shortly after he left, a report came to Morgenthau that a mob had looted a French dry goods store, the Bon Marché, and was heading toward the British embassy. A few minutes later the mob marched to "Tokatlian's, the most important restaurant in Constantinople," as Morgenthau called it. That it was run by an Armenian, he noted, made it "fair game." Then Turks broke the mirrors and windows and smashed the marble table tops; within minutes the restaurant was "completely gutted."[44]

If the *jihad* failed to incite a worldwide call for three hundred million Muslims to take arms against Christians, it did fan the flames of Turkish nationalism and continued to escalate what Jay Winter has called "the cultural preparation of hatred."[45] As the American ambassador put it, the *jihad* "started passions aflame that afterward spent themselves in the massacres of the Armenians and other subject peoples."[46]

Although the Turks entered World War I on the side of Germany with some ambivalence, in the end Talaat, Enver, and ruling members of the cabinet were bolstered by their belief that the war would provide the Ottoman Empire with a unique opportunity to solve problems that had aggravated and often humiliated the Turks throughout the nineteenth century. The

CUP's public declaration of war made it clear that the new cries for pan-Turkism were never separable from the hatred of Russia: "Our participation in the World War represents the vindication of our national ideal. The idea of our nation and our people leads us towards the destruction of our Muscovite enemy, in order to obtain thereby a natural frontier to our Empire, which should include and unite all branches of our race."[47] Even Enver's disastrous offensive in the Caucasus at Sarikamish in the winter of 1914–15 is inexplicable without his fanatical commitment to this pan-Turanist vision. If he could wipe out the Armenians in the Caucasus, he could push eastward and unite the Turkic peoples living under Russian rule.[48]

The Turks also saw war on the side of Germany and the Central Powers as a way to end all foreign interventions, especially the system of Capitulations. The Capitulations, which began in the sixteenth century under Süleyman I, were privileges the Ottoman government granted non-Ottoman subjects when they were traveling or living on Ottoman soil. Over the centuries the Capitulations allowed Europeans to exert influence on the Ottoman Empire, and this made the Turks more resentful of foreign presence in their domestic affairs. For the Armenians the Capitulations often played out in a negative way; for as they sought protection and refuge with the Europeans or Americans who had the protection of the Capitulations, they were further resented and seen as using them to further their quest for reform.[49] From the first treaty negotiations of August 1914, Foreign Minister Said Halim pressed Germany to assist Turkey in abolishing the Capitulations and, after the anticipated victory, to help increase Ottoman territory by securing the eastern Aegean islands for Turkey, and by making "a small correction of her eastern border which shall place Turkey into direct contact with the Moslems of Russia," which meant, of course, to take over Russian Armenia.[50] With the abrogation of the Capitulations and two earlier European treaties, Foreign Minister Halil asserted that Turkey had freed itself from the "tutelage of the great powers."[51]

The CUP leadership made it clear that with the help of the Central Powers, particularly Germany, it hoped to enlarge its territories in North Africa, parts of Persia, and in the Caucasus, eliminating Russian Armenia. The Turks concluded their treaty conditions with Germany by insisting that neither country make a separate peace after the war; and that under certain circumstances the Ottoman Empire would be able to reclaim certain parts of Thrace. Furthermore, to underscore the CUP's obsession with Russia and the Armenian *vilayets*, Talaat demanded, if necessary, that Germany offer Russia parts of occupied Poland in order to secure Russia's withdrawal from any part of the Turkish-Armenian *vilayets*. The Turks were also asking that the Germans evacuate parts of Flanders, as a way to get the British to leave Iraq.[52]

With the abrogations of the nineteenth-century treaties, the Young Turks felt free from European intervention, and from Europe's watchful eye on Turkey's human rights problems, particularly the ongoing assault on the Armenians. Both politically and psychologically, this was one more step toward resolving the Armenian Question.

FAILURE OF THE ARMENIAN REFORM AGREEMENT

But even before formal abrogation of the major nineteenth-century treaties had been achieved, the CUP government had freed itself from another shackle—the Armenian Reform Agreement. British historians Arnold Toynbee and James Bryce first saw the historic pattern of the Armenian requests inevitably being followed by sanctioned government violence. "The deportation of 1915," they wrote, "followed as inexorably from the Balkan War and the Project [Armenian Reform Agreement] of 1914 as the massacres of 1895–96 had followed from the Russian War and the Project of 1878 [the Berlin treaty]."[53]

Even before the war Talaat had expressed his outrage over the reform agreement act: "Don't the Armenians realize that the implementation of the reforms depends on us; we shall not respond to the proposals the Inspectors may put forward . . . the Armenians are trying to create a new Bulgaria. They don't seem to have learned their lessons; all the undertakings opposed by us are bound to fail. Let the Armenians wait, opportunities will certainly come our way too. Turkey belongs only to the Turks."[54]

The reform agreement provoked hostility from the Turks at large, and a letter signed "Islam Young Turks," and written in November 1913 as Armenians were pushing for reforms, perhaps written by Huseyin Azmi, director general of the Constantinople Police, made this clear: "You

Armenians . . . never forget where you live . . . you accursed ones have brought many perils on the head of our esteemed government . . . paved the way for foreign assault. . . . You must know that the Young Turks have awakened now . . . Turkish youth . . . shall not delay the execution of their assigned duties." A few days later another letter appeared in the Armenian press warning the Armenians that "The Turkish sword to date has cut down millions of *gâvurs,* nor has it lost its intention to cut down millions more hereafter. Know this: that the Turks have committed themselves, and have vowed to subdue and to clean up the Armenian *gâvurs* who have become tubercular microbes for us."[55]

As much as any reform treaty that was pushed through by European pressure, the Turks detested the Armenian Reform Agreement of 1914. By an imperial rescript of December 1914, a month after Turkey joined the war, the two European inspectors, L. C. Westenenk from the Netherlands and Nicolai Hoff, from Norway, were sent home by Talaat. As Toynbee put it, the inspectors

> had barely reached their provinces when the European War broke out, and the government promptly denounced the contracts and suspended the Scheme of Reforms, as the first step toward its own intervention in the conflict. Thus, at the close of 1914, the Armenians found themselves in the same position they were in 1883. The measures designed for their security had fallen through, and left nothing behind but the resentment of the Government that still held them at its mercy.[56]

What was now clear, as Turkey entered the war, was that the Armenians were a stateless people caught between two empires and so totally vulnerable that something unthinkable could happen to them.

GOVERNMENT-PLANNED GENOCIDE

The relationship between World War I and Turkey's plan to exterminate the Armenians was an evolving narrative of intertwining domestic and international events. From the Adana massacres of 1909 through the Balkan Wars of 1912–13 and then to World War I, which the Ottoman Empire joined in November 1914, the Committee of Union and Progress was engaged in promoting a new Turkish nationalism, a growing and encompassing military culture at home, and a large, complex, and clandestine bureaucracy. All of these were crucial to the CUP's orchestration of the extermination of its Armenian population.

The plan to liquidate the Armenians of the Ottoman Empire was put into motion in the spring and early summer of 1915. It was well orchestrated, and in city and town, village and hamlet, and in the Armenian sections of the major cities of Asia Minor and Anatolia, Armenians were rounded up, arrested, and either shot outright or put on deportation marches. Most often the able-bodied men were arrested in groups and taken out of the town or city and shot en masse. The women, children, infirm, and elderly were given short notice that they could gather some possessions and would be deported with the other Armenians of their city or town to what they were told was the "interior." Often they were told that they would be able to return when the war was over.

The Armenian communities all over Turkey were rendered more

vulnerable by the rapid elimination of the able-bodied men. Another large segment of Armenian men, in the labor battalions of the Ottoman army, was massacred from the late winter of 1915 on. The rest of the Armenian community was left increasingly helpless without those who could resist and offer protection.

A map of the Armenian genocide shows that deportations and massacre spanned the length and width of Turkey. In the west the major cities included Constantinople, Smyrna, Ankara, and Konia. Moving eastward, Yozgat, Kayseri, Sivas, Tokat, and Amasia were among the large cities of massacre and deportation. Along the Black Sea, Samsun, Ordu, Trebizond, and Rize were killing stations where Armenians were often taken out in boats and drowned. In the south, in historic Cilician Armenia, Adana, Hadjin, Zeitun, Marash, and Aintab were part of the massacre network. The traditional Armenian *vilayets* in the east—Sivas, Harput, Diyarbekir, Bitlis, Erzurum, Van—with hundreds of villages and dozens of cities, where the majority of the Armenian population of the empire lived on their historic land, were almost entirely depleted of their Armenian populations. In the southeast such towns and cities as Ras ul-Ain, Katma, Rakka, and Aleppo were both killing stations and refugee spots, where Armenians who had survived long death marches from the north lived in concentration camps, in makeshift tents, or on the desert ground, hoping to stay alive. Farther south, in the Syrian desert, more Armenians died than perhaps anywhere else. There the epicenter of death was the region of Deir el-Zor, with the surrounding towns of Marat, Busara, and Suvar, where Armenians died not only of massacre, starvation, and disease but were stuffed into caves and asphyxiated by brush fires—primitive gas chambers, as the investigative journalist Robert Fisk has noted.[1]

The survivors were dispersed across Syria, Iraq, and Palestine in the south, and Russia and Iran to the north and east. Many survivors stayed in those areas, and many migrated in the following decades to Europe, the United States, India, China, Australia, and South America in what became a major twentieth-century diaspora.

The extermination of the Armenians proceeded from several threshold events and circumstances:

1. At the beginning of World War I, Armenian men between twenty and forty-five years old and months later men between

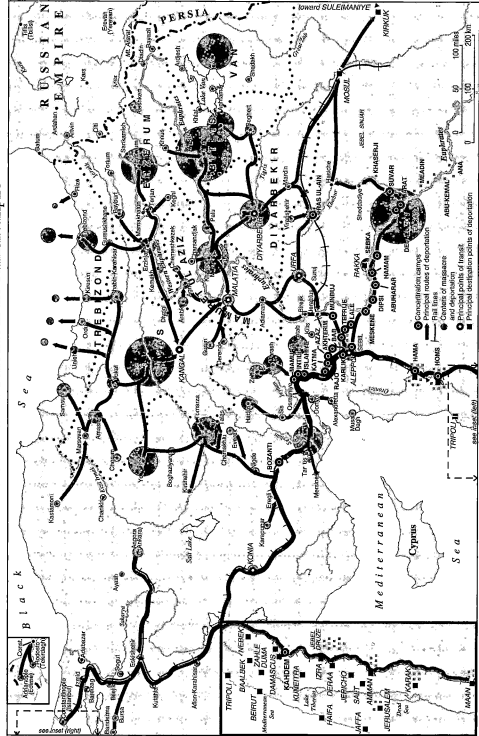

The 1915 Armenian Genocide in the Turkish Empire

forty-five and sixty years old were conscripted into army labor battalions (*amele taburlari*) where they were put to work in munitions and clothing factories, on roads and railway lines, or as bakers or farmers to augment the army's food supply, and often as human beasts of burden (*hamals*) carrying supplies on foot.[2]

But after Enver Pasha's humiliating defeat by the Russians at Sarikamish in December 1914–January 1915, the minister of war and his ruling elite, needing a scapegoat, blamed the Armenians, claiming that they were in sympathy with the Russians. Within a month, by February 25, 1915, all the Armenian men in the Ottoman army were officially disarmed and thrown into labor battalions. Almost immediately thereafter the army began an organized plan of massacring most of the Armenian men in the labor battalions. These killings preceded the beginning of the general deportations and massacres of the spring. Under armed guard, they were taken out into secluded areas where they were killed by gunshot or with bayonets by Turkish soldiers, often with the aid of the gendarmes and the *chetes* (organized auxillary killing squads).[3] In this manner tens of thousands of Armenian men were disposed of. Arnold Toynbee noted that all the disarmed Armenian soldiers doing construction on the Erzurum–Erzindjan road were massacred, as were the Armenian soldiers on the Diyarbekir–Ufra and Diyarbekir–Harput roads.[4]

2. With the devastating military loss at Sarikamish, the CUP not only disarmed the Armenian soldiers but ordered all civilian Armenians who were suspected of possessing arms to surrender them to their regional and local administrators. This resulted in what James Bryce and Arnold Toynbee called a "reign of terror," unleashed by "every administrative center" in the winter and early spring of 1915.[5] It was a preliminary process: Local officials broke into Armenian homes, demanding weapons when often there were none to be found, arresting and executing innocent civilians arbitrarily. (Jay Winter suggests, too, that the landing of British, French, Australian, and New Zealand troops on Turkish soil, at Gallipoli on the Dardanelles in April 1915, propelled Turkey further into a siege mentality, which fueled the zeal for exterminating the Armenians.)[6]

3. By the late winter of 1915, Dr. Behaeddin Shakir took over the leadership of the CUP's Special Organization in the eastern *vilayets*, and organized killing squads for the purpose of exterminating the Armenians.[7]

4. On April 8 the first deportation was ordered in the mountain town of Zeitun, the same place where Armenians had resisted massacre in 1895–96. It was a trial-run deportation, carried out mostly on foot, but for the first time the Turks used the railway for deportation.[8]

5. On April 17 the Armenians in Van refused what they considered to be an unrealistic demand of the *vali*, Jevdet Bey, who had terrorized the region with mass arrests and executions all winter. The *vali* demanded that the Armenian leadership deliver more than four thousand Armenian men for the Ottoman army's labor battalions. The Armenians knew full well that consenting to such a request would result in the mass murder of the men. The altercation led to Turkish attack on the city of Van and corresponding Armenian resistance during the weeks that followed. The resistance at Van became another pretext for the CUP to claim that the Armenians were disloyal during wartime.[9]

6. With the flare-up at Van, the CUP then proceeded the next week to arrest some 250 Armenian intellectuals and cultural leaders in Constantinople. This stunned the community and began the process of liquidating Armenian intellectuals and cultural leaders in every sector of the country.

7. From the spring on through the fall of 1915, the massacres and deportations, which amounted to death marches, were carried out in a deliberate and systematic way and with frenzied competence in all sectors of Turkey. Much of Cilicia was cleared of its Armenians in July and August, the eastern *vilayets* in June and July, the southeast region in August and September.

Scholars and journalists at the time estimated that between eight hundred thousand and a million Armenians died in 1915 alone.[10] Then, in the summer of 1916, there was a new wave of massacres in the Mesopotamian desert (today northern Syria) in a region that included Ras ul-Ain, Rakka, and Deir el-Zor. There, about two hundred thousand Armenians who had survived the death marches were massacred. In addition tens of thousands of women were abducted into harems or Muslim families, and tens of thousands of children were taken into families and converted to Islam, and in this manner of forced conversion another segment of the Armenian population was eradicated. After the war further Armenian massacres took place in Marash in 1920 and in Smyrna in 1922. Thus the death tolls from 1915 through 1922 range from over a million to a million and a half.

THE SPECIAL ORGANIZATION AND THE
FORMATION OF THE KILLING SQUADS

When Richard Rubenstein, in *The Cunning of History*, described the Turkish extermination of the Armenians as the "first full-fledged attempt by a modern state to practice disciplined, methodically organized genocide," he was noting the skill with which the Turks used the bureaucracy of the state to implement mass murder, as well as its historic significance.[11] Like the Nazi Party, the Committee of Union and Progress understood the power that resided in bureaucracy.

As the inheritors of the Ottoman government, the Young Turks were the recipients of an extraordinary bureaucratic infrastructure with which the Turks had ruled a large and complex empire for centuries. The very sultan they had just deposed had expanded the size of Ottoman bureaucracy by creating the most extensive system of surveillance in the empire's history. Although Abdul Hamid's bureaucracy was riddled with corruption and manipulated by bribery, it had been essential to his rule of the empire.

What Rubenstein has noted about the Nazi final solution for the Jews was also true in the case of the Turkish plan for the Armenians. The Armenian Genocide was propelled by "a bureaucratic administration capable of governing with utter indifference [to] human needs."[12] In the end this bureaucracy was allowed to proceed without any external deterrence, and it was able to create, as the Nazis would with the Jews—a totally vulnerable, "expendable, . . . stateless people," as Rubenstein put it. A campaign of genocide, Holocaust scholar Raul Hilberg also underscores, "is a series of administrative measures which must be aimed at a definite group."[13]

The CUP's plan to exterminate the Armenians was made possible by the highest level of government planning: the harnessing of bureaucracy for the organization and implementation of the Armenian deportations; the formation and organization of killing squads; the creation and manipulation of legislation; and the use of technology and communications, such as the railway, the telegraph, and the old-fashioned but ever reliable town crier.

Like its Nazi counterpart after 1933, the CUP's Ministry of the Interior was the key to orchestrating a program of genocide. Talaat Pasha told Ambassador Morgenthau with great candor that "the Union and Progress Committee had carefully considered the matter in all its details and that the policy which was being pursued was that which they had officially adopted." Morgenthau reported, "He said that I must not get the idea that the deportations had been decided upon hastily; in reality, they were the result of prolonged and careful deliberation."[14] The Interior Ministry created another bureau called the Special Organization (SO) (*Teshkilât-i Mashusa*). The brainchild of the party's Central Committee, it was fueled by the ever-tightening relationship between the ascending military and quasi military leaders and the Committee of Union and Progress.[15]

Designed to be a clandestine operation, the Special Organization was very much in the tradition of the politics of secrecy which had defined the Young Turk movement from its origins. The Turkish political scientist Tarik Zafer Tunaya noted that the entire CUP in certain ways was "a power-wielding monopolistic clique . . . operating behind a mysterious curtain of secrecy."[16] The surviving head of the SO later stated that it was "a secret body designed to achieve the internal and external security of the Ottoman State," and that its power was greater than that of the "official government." He confessed that the Armenian "massacres were carried out on order from the Central Committee," and that the SO was at the center of the operation.[17]

One of the SO leaders, Esref Kuscubasi, noted that the new bureau's focus was on the "non-Turkish and non-Muslim races and nationalities" in the empire because their loyalty was "suspect."[18] Throughout the war Ottoman intelligence issued propaganda to scapegoat Armenians, with statements such as: "The Armenians are in league with the enemy. They will launch an uprising . . . , kill off the Ittihadist [CUP] leaders and will succeed in opening up the Straits [Dardanelles]."[19]

While the Secret Organization included many high-ranking party officials such as Mehmed Nazim, Ziya Gökalp, and Talaat Pasha, Dr.

Behaeddin Shakir seems to have been the most influential. In late fall and winter of 1914–15, he successfully lobbied for the autonomy of the SO in the eastern provinces and succeeded in placing the killing squads under the complete authority of the SO. Under his direction, in the late winter and early spring of 1915, the major phase of the Armenian extermination program was launched.[20] Colonel Düzgören Seyfi, director of the Political Department at the Ottoman General Headquarters (the Intelligence Department), worked closely with Dr. Shakir in mapping the strategy of the massacres and mobilizing the Special Organization's killing squads.[21]

THE KILLING SQUADS

The plan to exterminate the Armenians was accelerated and shaped by the rapid rise of military officers to crucial positions of power. This new military authority remained free from the restraints of the Ottoman legislature.[22] With the proclamation of the Temporary Law of Deportation of May 27, 1915, which ordered the forcible deportation of the Armenians, Ottoman officers were given the power to take charge of the wholesale removal of the Armenian population, and the Ministry of War under Enver was authorized to administer the details.[23]

In creating an efficient killing process the Special Organization systematically recruited, organized, and deployed tens of thousands of convicted criminals for the purpose of massacring the Armenian population. In this astonishing use of the nation's criminal manpower, the military authorities were given autonomy to authorize the release of thousands of convicts from the prisons.[24] While the Ottoman government had deployed convicts in small numbers in the Balkan War of 1913, and the sultan had also emptied some prisons for the sake of killing Armenians in the 1890s, the harnessing of the criminal element of Ottoman society was brought to an entirely new threshold in 1915.

The organization of the *chetes*—the ex–convict killer bands—was similar to the Reich Security Main Office's *Einsatzgruppen,* or mobile killing units. While Raul Hilberg claims that the Reich Security Main Office conducted "for the first time in modern history . . . a massive killing operation,"[25] it appears in fact that the CUP's Special Organization was the first state bureaucracy to implement mass killing for the purpose of race extermination. Arnold Toynbee was among the first to assess the role of these killing squads when he wrote that: "Turkish 'political' *chettes* . . . made their debut on the western littoral, and in 1915, after being rein-forced by convicts released for the purpose from the public prisons, they carried out the designs of the Union and Progress Government against the Armenians in every province of Anatolia except the vilayet of Aidin."[26]

The CUP's killing program also involved a hierarchy of command. At the top of this chain, Dr. Shakir played a role not unlike that of Nazi Reich Security Head, Reinhard Heydrich. The military hierarchy was essential to the operation, and accordingly the Special Organization units were mostly directed by active or reserve officers. The small detachments were commanded by lieutenants and captains, the larger ones by majors. In order to ensure that the officers would lead the killing efficiently, they were given incentives of Armenian booty and spoils. The killing squads and their leaders were motivated by both the ideology of *jihad*, with its Islamic roots, and pan-Turkism influenced by European nationalism.[27] The confession made by a Turkish gendarmerie captain named Shükrü to the Armenian priest Krikoris Balakian in Yozgat in 1916 dramatizes the role of *jihad* in the killing process. Captain Shükrü admitted to Balakian, a deportee he assumed would soon be dead, that he had been ordered to massacre all the Armenians of Yozgat because it was a "holy war." When it was over, he told the priest, he "would say a prayer and his soul would be absolved."[28]

The killer bands, or *chetes*, who played such a significant role in the killing process, were estimated to be about thirty to thirty-four thousand in num-ber.[29] While Talaat, Shakir, Enver, Gökalp, Nazim, and the others found the idea of using ex-convicts to be an effective means of carrying out geno-cide, there was another hidden agenda. Using ex-convicts, they believed, would enable the government to deflect responsibility. For as the death tolls rose, they could always say that "things got out of control," and it was the result of "groups of brigands."[30]

But the *chetes* were only part of a killing operation that involved mili-tary police and the provincial police, known as gendarmes. They were the ones who carried out the rigorous process of arrest and deportation city by city, town by town, village by village. Staff officers were assigned to the

Ottoman army corps and became chiefs of staff in the interior, where they were put in command of their respective killing units in order to assist in "the liquidation of the Christian elements." One reserve officer put it bluntly when he said the aim of the whole process "was to destroy the Armenians and thereby to do away with the Armenian question."[31]

Because Germany was the Ottoman Empire's closest wartime ally, there is a large body of extraordinary German testimony about the Armenian Genocide.[32] For example, Colonel Stange, the highest-ranking German guerrilla commander in the Russian-Turkish border region, referred to the *chetes* as "scum" (*Gesindel*), who "in the area of Tercan killed without exception all the Armenians of the convoy coming from Erzurum." This "incontestable fact," he wrote, was carried out "with the assistance of the military escort."[33] Similarly, German consul Scheubner-Richter, reporting on the massacres from Harput to Erzinjan, also referred to the killing squads as "the scum."[34] The German consul in Aleppo, Dr. Walter Rössler, in a July 27, 1915, report, noted that the killing squads were created by "the Turkish government which released convicts from the prisons, put them in soldiers' uniforms and sent them to areas through which the deportees are to pass."[35]

While the killing squads and provincial gendarmerie were consumed with massacring and deporting the civilian Armenian population, they also aided the Ottoman army in its scheme to dispose of all able-bodied Armenian men. Christians had first been conscripted into the Ottoman army in 1909, after the implementation of new constitutional reforms, and so, at the outbreak of World War I, Armenian men between the ages of twenty and forty-five were drafted into the Ottoman army.[36] It was an army with numerous problems, among them severe ethnic discrimination. Arabs, Kurds, Armenians, Greeks, Assyrians, and others were subjected to brutal treatment. Arab soldiers, for example, were often sent to the front lines shackled in chains and escorted by Turks at gunpoint.[37]

After Enver's humiliating defeat by the Russians at Sarikamish in December 1914–January 1915, Enver and his ruling elite, looking for a scapegoat, blamed the Armenians, claiming they were in sympathy with the Russians. Within a month, by February 25, 1915, all the Armenian men in the Ottoman army were officially disarmed and thrown into labor battalions. Almost immediately thereafter, the army began an organized plan of massacring the Armenian men in the labor battalions. These killings preceded the beginning of the deportations and massacres of the later part of the spring. As the historian Erik Zurcher has noted, "Once the massacres started, the unarmed recruits in the labor battalions were sitting ducks." Under the guard of armed soldiers, the Armenian soldiers were taken out into secluded areas where they were killed by gunshot or with bayonets by Turkish soldiers, often with the aid of the gendarmes and the *chetes*.[38] In this manner tens of thousands of Armenian men were disposed of.

If the able-bodied Armenian men were not massacred in the labor battalions of the Ottoman army, they were most often taken out and shot in groups in the first stage of the deportation. As the Armenians were forced from their homes and organized into caravans to be marched out of town, the men were separated from the women and children and taken out into the fields outside their towns and villages and shot en masse. By killing the men quickly in these ways, the Turks rendered the rest of the Armenian community increasingly helpless without those who could best resist massacre and offer protection.

A FINE-TUNED BUREAUCRACY

Much like the hierarchical relationship between the *Sonderkommandos*, who carried out the executive orders in the Nazi bureaucracy, and the *Einsatzgruppen* killing squads, the CUP created a hierarchical administration to carry out the Armenian killing operations. Three levels of bureaucrats were given a supreme authority that superseded the traditional government structure in the provinces, and through this network the details of the deportations and mass killings were carried out. The hierarchy consisted of *Katibi Mesul*, "Responsible Secretaries"; *Murahhas*, "Delegates"; and *Umumi Müfettish*, "General Inspectors." Most of the men who held these positions were former army officers; as loyal party members their job was to maintain the chain of command in the provinces so that the orders for arrests, deportations, and massacre were implemented strictly, and to do this they worked closely with the local CUP clubs, known as Ittihad Clubs.[39]

In his report of July 28, 1915, from Erzurum, Vice-Consul Scheubner-Richter actually referred to this operation as a "shadow, or a parallel government" (*Nebenregierung*) assuming power over the provincial government. He attributed the severity of the deportations to the party administrators, who vetoed the governor-general's decree exempting the sick, families without men, and women living alone. The Responsible Secretaries, Delegates, and Inspectors admitted, Scheubner-Richter reported, that their job was to see the total obliteration (*die ganzliche Ausrottung*) of the Armenians.[40] Colonel Stange reported that in Trebizond Province, Dr. Shakir and Gen. Mahmud Kamil "ruthlessly and constantly pushed for the expediting of the deportations" with the knowledge that the convoys were being massacred on order.[41] From Adana, German consul Eugen Buge reported to his embassy in Constantinople that the local party chief (*der hiesige Komiteeführer*) promised to massacre all the Armenians of Adana if any of them were spared deportation.[42]

Perhaps nobody put it more comprehensively than German ambassador Count Paul von Wolff-Metternich. Reporting back to the chancellor in Berlin, he expressed his exasperation at the power held by the CUP's Central Committee, hence the SO, in the process of the Armenian massacres:

> Nobody has any more power to restrain the multi-headed hydra of the Committee, and the attendant chauvinism and fanaticism. The Committee demands the extirpation of the last remnants of the Armenians and the government must yield. The authority of the Committee is not limited to the Ottoman capital where Ittihad [CUP] is organized and functions as a party in power. That authority of the Committee reaches into all the provinces. A Committee representative is assigned to each of the provincial administrations, from *vali* down to kaymakam, for purposes of assistance or supervision . . . Turkification means license to expel, to kill or destroy everything that is not Turkish, and to violently take possession of the goods of others. . . .[43]

ACTS OF LEGISLATION

In order to accelerate the extermination plan and to give it a further sense of governmental legitimacy, Talaat Pasha requested that the grand vizier, through the cabinet, pass a special law authorizing the deportations. Like the Nazis, who created "a legal solution to the Jewish problem"—as historian Lucy Dawidowicz put it—with their various anti-Jewish legislation of the 1930s, the CUP also implemented legislation to legitimize the Armenian extermination plan. The memorandum was endorsed on May 29, 1915, by the grand vizier, and the cabinet acted on it the next day, after an eager, chauvinistic wartime press had already announced this new emergency law on May 27. The members of the CUP Central Committee were always cautious about leaving traces of their genocidal plan, and so the law, called the Temporary Law of Deportation, made no overt reference to the Armenians. The commanders of armies, army corps, and divisions and commandants of local garrisons were now authorized to deport any groups of the population "on suspicion of espionage, treason, [or] military necessity."[44]

The crucial word in the law was "sensing" (*hissetmek*), which gave the authorities the power to order deportations if they had so much as a feeling or a sense that an individual or a group of people might be dangerous to the state.[45] This concept gave the legislation total license for the administrative network and the killing squads to round up, deport, and massacre Armenians. At the end of the war the Temporary Law of Deportation was repealed by the Ottoman parliament on the grounds that it was unconstitutional. By then it had served its purpose.

Because expropriating Armenian wealth and property was vital to the plan to destroy the Armenians, the CUP devised legal as well as purely coercive and violent means of stealing, plundering, and appropriating Armenian movable and immovable wealth. In another legislative maneuver, the Temporary Law of Expropriation and Confiscation (September 1915) was passed. This law was allegedly designed to register the properties of the deportees, safeguard them, dispose of them at public auctions, with the revenues to be held in trust until the deportees' return. It was such a transparent scheme aimed at confiscating all Armenian property and wealth that when Arthur von Gwinner, the director of the Deutsche Bank, described the new law to the German Foreign Office, he remarked with scorn that the eleven articles might be reduced to two: "1. All goods of the Armenians are confiscated. 2. The government will cash in the credits of the deportees and will repay (or will not repay) their debts."[46]

Only one senator, Ahmed Riza, protested the law on the grounds that it had been proposed in an unconstitutional way and that "it was inimical to the principles of law and justice." In an eloquent statement, Senator Riza said:

> It is unlawful to designate the Armenian assets and properties as "abandoned goods," for the Armenians, the proprietors, did not abandon their properties voluntarily; they were forcibly, compulsively removed from their domiciles and exiled. Now the government through its officials is selling their goods. . . . Nobody can sell my property if I am unwilling to sell it. Article 21 of the Constitution forbids it. If we are a constitutional regime functioning in accordance with constitutional law we can't do this. This is atrocious. Grab my arm, eject me from my village, then sell my goods and properties, such a thing can never be permissible. Neither the conscience of the Ottomans nor the law can allow it.[47]

Most of the eyewitness accounts testify to the rapaciousness of the killers and of the bystanding Turkish and other Muslim populations, who plundered the Armenian wealth left behind in the chaos and terror of the arrests, executions, and deportations. In an investigative hearing in the Ottoman Chamber of Deputies after the war in 1920, several Turkish deputies took former Justice Minister Ibrahim to task for the illegality of the expropriation and for the massive "robberies and plunders."[48] American consul Jesse B. Jackson in Aleppo, in a report to Ambassador Morgenthau in August 1915, assessed the role of the government's confiscation scheme calling it "a gigantic plundering scheme as well as a final blow to extinguish the [Armenian] race."[49] Turkish historian Dogan Avjioglu noted that "among those who enriched themselves in the process of the expropriation of the Armenians were party influential, ex-officers serving as party operatives, and Turkish immigrants."[50]

Henry H. Riggs, an American missionary in Harput, wrote that in July 1915 "You could not look out of the window without seeing some one walking down the street carrying some sort of load of booty, bought or stolen from Armenian houses."[51] Armenian real estate was confiscated by the government. As Morgenthau put it, the government officials told the Armenians that "since their deportation was only temporary . . . they would not be permitted to sell their houses," and as soon as the Armenians were deported, "Mohammedan *mohadjirs*—immigrants from other parts of Turkey—would be moved into the Armenian quarters . . . all the [Armenian] valuables—money, rings, watches, and jewelry—would be taken to the police stations for 'safe keeping' . . . and then parcelled out among the Turks."[52]

One remarkable document was discovered and translated in early 1919 by British officials in Turkey, who labeled it "The Ten Commandments." It is a blueprint of the Armenian extermination operation and appears to have been the centerpiece of a secret party meeting, which took place sometime in late December 1914 or in January 1915. The document was obtained by Comm. C. H. Heathcote Smith, the right-hand man of Adm. Somerset Calthorpe, the British high commissioner in Constantinople. Fluent in Turkish, Smith had served as British consul in Smyrna before the war, and he first learned of the "Ten Commandments" from the former British intelligence agent Percival Hadkinson, in Smyrna.[53]

The document (along with several others) came into British hands through Ahmed Essad, the wartime head of the Ottoman Ministry Department II, Intelligence. Essad had served as secretary at the conference at which the "Ten Commandments" were issued—a conference presided over by Talaat Pasha, the minister of the interior, and Drs. Nazim and Behaeddin Shakir, the masterminds of the Special Organization.

One page of a nine-page correspondence between the British High Commission in Constantinople and the Foreign Office in London in early 1919 is headed "DOCUMENTS RELATING TO COMITE UNION AND PROGRESS ORGANIZATION IN THE ARMENIAN MASSACRES." The subtitle reads: "The 10 commandments of the COMITE UNION AND PROGRES." A note following the text of the ten-point document, added by the British High Commissioner's Office in Constantinople, suggests that that office translated the document into English: "Above is a verbatim translation—dated December 1914 or January 1915."

> (1). Profiting by the Arts: 3 and 4 of Comite Union and Progres, close all Armenian Societies, and arrest all who worked against Government at any time among them and send them into the

provinces such as Bagdad or Mosul, and wipe them out either on the road or there.

(2). Collect arms.

(3). Excite Moslem opinion by suitable and special means, in places as Van, Erzeroum, Adana, where as a point of fact the Armenians have already won the hatred of the Moslems, provoke organised massacres as the Russians did at Baku.

(4). Leave all executive to the people in provinces such as Erzeroum, Van, Mamuret ul Aziz, and Bitlis, and use Military disciplinary forces (i.e., Gendarmerie) ostensibly to stop massacres, while on the contrary in places as Adana, Sivas, Broussa, Ismidt and Smyrna actively help the Moslems with military force.

(5). Apply measures to exterminate all males under 50, priests and teachers, leave girls and children to be Islamized.

(6). Carry away the families of all who succeed in escaping and apply measures to cut them off from all connection with their native place.

(7). On the ground that Armenian officials may be spies, expel and drive them out absolutely from every Government department or post.

(8). Kill off in an appropriate manner all Armenians in the Army—this to be left to the military to do.

(9). All action to begin everywhere simultaneously, and thus leave no time for preparation of defensive measures.

(10). Pay attention to the strictly confidential nature of these instructions, which may not go beyond two or three persons.[54]

THE RAILWAY

Of the Nazi deportation of the Jews, Terrence Des Pres writes, "It began in the trains, in the locked box cars, eighty to a hundred people per car—crossing Europe to the camps in Poland."[55] Similarly, the century's first genocide began in part in the cattle cars of the Anatolian and the Baghdad Railway. In many cities and towns part of the Armenian population was piled into freight cars—around ninety in a car that "had a standard capacity for the military transport of 36 men or 6 horses." Crammed behind slatted bars, they were starving, in terror, and defecating on themselves. Most of the rail cars went south and east, most often to the city of Konia, where the deportees were often let out to continue on foot before they were robbed, raped, and murdered, by the killing squads. Sometimes they were shipped all the way through to Aleppo, where those who survived arrived emaciated and near death, only to confront more massacre. With the rail deportations of the Armenians, "the Ottoman government introduced into modern history," historian Hilmar Kaiser writes, "railway transport of civilian populations" as part of the plan of race "extermination."[56]

Some of the most striking evidence of the use of the railway for deporting the Armenians comes from the German eyewitness accounts of the Baghdad Railway Company. Germany's most important foreign project, the company was at the center of the kaiser's imperial designs in the Near East. It is ironic that the Turks used the railway in ways that the Nazis would later, and that Germans in Turkey in 1915 were on site to testify. Franz Günther, a delegate of the Deutsche Bank who headed the project's office in Constantinople and worked closely with the German embassy, reported that the Ottoman government was acting with "bestial cruelty" and noted that it was hard to justify the company's passivity in the face of what they were witnessing. When Günther sent a photograph of a deportation train to Deutsche Bank director Gwinner, Günther also noted the irony that the railway was billed as "an upholder of civilization in Turkey."[57]

The railway deportations were directed by the Ottoman government, and Talaat received reports on the numbers of deportees and their locations. On October 9 and 10, 1915, some 11,000 Armenians who had been transported from other places to Konia were sent south. Between October 13 and 16, 9,600 more followed. During the following five days 9,850 more Armenians were sent from Konia. When Ottoman military needs interrupted the rail deportations, the people were marched along the railway tracks. Still, in the month of October 1915 alone, more than 30,000 Armenians were packed into livestock cars to be sent to their deaths in the Der Zor Desert.[58]

As deportation by rail developed, detention camps sprang up alongside the tracks and stations. From Konia south to the desert, the whole stretch appeared as one long, concatenated detention camp. There was a large concentration camp by the railway station at Konia; by the end of October there were about 40,000 at Katma, a town on the deportation route north of Aleppo; the camp near Osmaniye, less than a hundred miles east of Adana, may have held as many as 70,000. In the camps the Armenians were attacked by the killing squads; women were abducted and raped; and thousands died of disease and starvation.[59]

Because of the proximity of the railway to the death camps and ultimately to the desert, the German railway engineers and employees were able to report the atrocities. At Ras-ul-Ain, a horrific refugee camp southeast of Urfa on the railway line to Mosul, two engineers reported seeing in one day three to four hundred women arriving completely naked. Hasenfratz—an employee who worked for the railway at Aleppo—reported that massacres took place beside the railway track between Tell Abiad and Ras-ul-Ain. "The bodies," he wrote, "without exception, were entirely naked and the wounds that had been inflicted showed that the victims had been killed, after having been subjected to unspeakable brutalities."[60]

As the railway and its immediate environs became a zone in which mass murder and rape were perpetually happening, the railway officials were constant witnesses to the atrocities. An engineer named Spieker reported from Ras-ul-Ain that he continually saw the arrival of remnants of the death marches; only women and children were left because all the men and boys over twelve had been killed. In his detailed reports on the systematic mass slaughter of women and children, he noted that a Turkish inspector informed him that nine out of ten Armenians had been killed on the marches. The engineer also described how Muslim railway officials and Ottoman officers raped women and sold children and women into the slave trade. One Sergeant Nuri, the overseer of the camp at Ras-ul-Ain, actually bragged about raping children. Some of the Muslim employees of the railway left their jobs in order to take part in the killing.[61]

With nearly nine hundred skilled Armenian workers and many more Armenian laborers on the construction sites in the Taurus and Amanus Mountains and in northern Syria, the Armenian presence in the railway company was significant. Because the war made the railway even more crucial for the transportation of supplies, the Armenian employees were kept on their jobs.[62] What ensued was a poignant drama in which various Germans in respectable positions tried to intervene with their own government and the Ottoman government to save the Armenians working for the railway. Günther, the railway project director from the Deutsche Bank, who worked hard to protect the Armenian staff, "estimated that already 25 percent of the 2 million Armenians in the empire had been killed," and he was certain that the government's policy would mean the extermination of the entire Armenian population.[63] Winkler, the head railway construction engineer in Adana, who likewise tried to protect his workers, was stymied by the *vali*, who told him that nothing could be done, as the deportation orders had come directly from Talaat and Enver.[64] In the end the Armenian laborers were deported, and finally so were the Armenian staff employees of the railway. In order to cover up the massacres, the Ottoman government demanded that the railway cease its bookkeeping in German and use only Turkish. The Armenian staff was to be replaced by Muslims only.[65]

All through the summer of 1915, American consul Jesse B. Jackson in Aleppo recorded the deportation of Armenians by train. On September 29 he wrote to Ambassador Morgenthau:

> SIR: The deportation of Armenians from their homes by the Turkish Government has continued with a persistence and perfection of plan that it is impossible to conceive in those directly carrying it out, as indicated by the accompanying tables of "Movement by Railway," showing the number arriving by rail from interior stations up to and including August 31 last to be 32,751. In addition thereto it is estimated that at least 100,000 others have arrived afoot.

Of the more than thirty-two thousand deported by rail, more than nine thousand were children. In this same dispatch Jackson noted that the treatment of the deportees was "so severe" that "careful estimates place the number of survivors at only 15 per cent. of those originally deported. On this basis the number of those surviving even this far being less than 150,000 up to September 21, there seems to have been about 1,000,000 persons lost up to this date."[66] Signing off to Morgenthau, he noted that he had forwarded the report in "sextuplicate, that copies thereof may be forwarded to the Governments of Great Britain, France, Russia, and Italy, respectively, if found convenient, the interests of which in this district have been entrusted to this Consulate. Copy is also being sent to the Department of State."[67]

James Bryce collected eyewitness accounts of railway deportations from the cities and towns north of Konia, where the railway was known as the Anatolian Railway. Bryce described deportations that began in June and July, when thousands of Armenians were packed into cattle cars, transported, unloaded, and left for "interminable periods" without food or shelter until they were repacked into cattle cars and sent on to the next stage in the death process.[68]

An American, Mrs. Anna Harlowe Birge, who was traveling from Smyrna to Constantinople, wrote in November 1915:

> At every station where we stopped, we came side by side with one of these trains. It was made up of cattle-trucks, and the faces of little children were looking out from behind the tiny barred windows of each truck. The side doors were wide open, and one could plainly see old men and old women, young mothers with tiny babies, men, women, and children, all huddled together like so many sheep or pigs—human beings treated worse than cattle are treated.[69]

When the American traveler protested to a German officer that this "was the most brutal thing that had ever happened," and asked him if the Germans were involved in the deportation, he answered simply: "You can't object to exiling a race; it's only the way the Turks are doing it which is bad." Having just come from the interior, the officer confessed that he too was appalled at what he called "the most terrible sights" he had ever seen: "Hundreds of people being deported over the mountains," and "old women and little children too feeble to walk were strapped to the sides of donkeys. Babies lying dead in the road. Human life thrown away. everywhere." And the trains, the American wrote, just kept coming: "The last thing we saw late at night and the first thing early in the morning was one train after another carrying its freight of human lives to destruction."[70]

An account from a traveler going through the city of Afyon Karahisar, in October 1915, read:

> The 16,000 deported Armenians who were living in the tents have been sent to Konia, in cattle-trucks. At night, while thousands of these unfortunate people, without food or shelter, shiver

with cold, those brutes who are supposed to be their guardians attack them with clubs and push them towards the station. Women, children and old men are packed together in the trucks. The men have to climb on to the top of the trucks, in spite of the dreadful cold. Their cries are heart-breaking, but all is in vain. Hunger, cold and fatigue, together with the Government's deeds of violence, will soon achieve the extermination of this last remnant of the Armenian people.[71]

In order to extort as much money as possible from the Armenians, the Turkish authorities often forced them to pay first-class fare before they put them into the cattle cars that would most likely take them to their deaths. On September 8, 1915, Dr. William S. Dodd wrote: "The exiles were compelled to pay the full fare and then packed forty or fifty together in box-trucks, cattle-trucks, or even open flat trucks. The Railway seems to be as conscienceless in wringing the money out of them as the Government or the Turks."[72]

Similarly, Dr. Wilfred M. Post, writing on September 3, 1915, testified to the coordination between the railway deportations and the killing squads:

Much that I might add is as nothing, however, to what the railway employees report as going on at the end of the line, where the people leave the railway and set out on foot, only to be set upon by brigands, who rob, outrage and kill all the way from Bozanti to Adana and beyond. . . . Whether these unfortunate people are sent on towards the east or whether they remain where they are along the road, their future is very dark, and it means annihilation for the whole race.[73]

In the end between a half and two-thirds of the more than two million Armenians living on their historic homeland in the Ottoman Empire were annihilated. While the number of dead continues to be debated, as is the case with most episodes of mass killing (the U.S. Holocaust Museum, for example, places the number of Jewish dead in the Holocaust at 5.1 to 5.4 million, while other estimates go to 6 million), scholars of genocide, including the largest body of genocide scholars—the

Association of Genocide Scholars of North America—conservatively assess that more than a million Armenians were killed, and probably somewhere between 1.2 and 1.3 million. Some historians put the figure at about 1.5 million, which spans the period from 1915 to 1922, when the last waves of killing took place.[74]

VAN, SPRING 1915

In the evolution of events that led to the extermination of the Armenians, the act of Armenian resistance to massacre in the city of Van in April and May 1915 played an important role. Regions at crossroads are often trigger points, zones of vulnerability and sometimes of suspicion. Perhaps no Armenian city was more of a trigger point than Van, situated in eastern Turkey near the Russian border. On the edge of two empires, it was a geopolitical terrain fraught with tension. The ancient region of Armenian civilization, Van (Vaspurakan in Armenian) emerged out of Urartian civilization sometime between the seventh and fifth century B.C. Having survived invasions and conquests by the Persians, Romans, and Arabs, civilization in Van evolved into a golden age in the tenth and eleventh centuries until the raids of the Seljuk Turks. During this medieval period, advanced architecture as well as achievements in music, poetry, and the visual arts defined Van's Armenian culture.[1]

By the nineteenth century Van's Armenian population was greater than its Turkish and Kurdish populations combined, and, with a sizable Armenian population across the border in Russia, the geopolitics of the region were further intensified. Relatively affluent and urban, the Armenians of Van dressed like Europeans, standing out against the Turkish and Kurdish population.[2]

At the end of the nineteenth century Van was also a place of political activism. The Armenakan Party was founded there in 1885, and shortly thereafter the Hunchak and Dashnak Parties had branches there. Progressive Russian Armenians often brought political ideas across the border. Because Russo-Turkish relations were forever fraught with tension over land and Russia's desire to protect the Christian Armenians, Van was seen as a danger spot by the Ottoman government. In the Russo-Turkish War of 1877 the Russians had captured the district of Kars, just north of Van, and in the ensuing decades there was constant population volatility as thousands of Muslims fled over the new border into Turkey, and Armenians from Turkey into Russia.

The sultan had noted that Russian Armenians in the czar's army fought valiantly against the Turks in 1877, and he was forever enraged that the European powers used the Armenian Question to force concessions after the war.[3] In 1895–96, the Armenians of Van had resisted massacre for a short time before the Turks slaughtered more than twenty thousand of them. So it is not surprising that in the spring of 1915 Van became a trouble spot again. Before May was over, the Ottoman government would once again label as sedition what was essentially resistance to massacre. The Armenian resistance at Van was seen as a provocation—in short, an excuse to proceed with the plan of extermination that had already begun.

Back in July 1914, as the Ottoman Empire was about to enter World War I, a Turkish delegation approached the Dashnak leaders, who were convened at their eighth party congress in Erzurum, the capital of historic Armenia. Lead by Dr. Shakir, who was fast assuming a major role in the plan to exterminate the Armenians, the delegation asked the Dashnaks if they would coax the Armenians over the Russian border to rise against the czar so that when war began the Ottoman army would be able to invade the Caucasus more easily. In return the Turkish delegates promised that the Young Turk government would reward the Armenians with a semiautonomous Armenia, which might include parts of both Turkish and Russian Armenia. Having experienced nothing but massacre and betrayed promises from the Turks over the past decades (the memory and the effects of the massacres in Van in 1895 and again in 1903 were still deeply felt by the Armenians of the region), the Dashnaks found the plan both unrealistic and dangerous; they declined.[4] And they urged the Young Turk leaders to remain neutral instead of joining the war.

Not surprisingly the Ottoman entrance into the war in November was accompanied by a broadcasting of its hatred of its traditional enemy, Russia. "The ideal of our nation and people leads us towards the destruction of our Muscovite enemy, in order to obtain thereby a natural frontier to our empire, which should include and unite all branches of our race."[5] The party sloganeer, Ziya Gökalp, expressed the sentiment in a poem: "The land of the enemy shall be devastated. / Turkey shall be enlarged and become Turan,"[6] and in order for this to happen, parts of Russia would have to be conquered and that included Russian Armenia.

While Armenian reaction to the war was mixed, the overwhelming fact was that Armenians, empire-wide, were loyal to the Ottoman government. Armenians had fought hard for Turkey in the recent Balkan war and now made pledges of loyalty throughout the empire—to such an extent that prayer vigils and victory services were held in Armenian churches.[7]

There was, of course, a small minority that openly opposed the Ottoman government. Outside the empire, at their annual meeting in Romania, some members of the Hunchak Party in 1913 had voiced opposition to the Turkish war effort, resulting in the hanging of twenty Hunchak leaders in Constantinople in June 1915.[8] When Turkey entered the war, some Armenians living in the borderland region left Turkey to join an Armenian volunteer unit in Russia. And one Armenian—the same Armen Garo of the 1896 Ottoman Bank incident—who was at the time an Armenian deputy from Erzurum in the Ottoman parliament, also joined a volunteer unit in Russia; to top it off he even sent a photo of himself and a few of his friends as "Armenian revolutionaries" to the *Daily Graphic* in London.

This kind of naive romanticism enraged the Turks and was despised by many Armenian leaders as well. The priest Krikoris Balakian, who would be arrested with about 250 Armenian leaders on April 24, denounced Garo and his friends as fools who didn't know what they were doing. "This kind of foolish act further provoked the Turkish officials and the general public," Balakian wrote, "who already despised the Armenians—unarmed and confused as they were."[9] In his memoir, *Armenian Golgotha,* Balakian underscored that "in these fateful days," as he put it, "there was no nationalistic Armenian policy or plan." While a few Armenians like Garo behaved irresponsibly, most didn't, and in the end "the innocent Armenian population living inside the Turkish borders would pay with the price of their own blood."[10]

As the first chapter of the war opened for the Ottoman Empire, Minister of War Enver Pasha decided to invade Russia. Driven by his pan-Turkist zeal, he took control of the Ottoman Third Army in the winter of 1914 with a plan to take the Russian military outpost of Sarikamish, near Kars, and then push through the Caucasus to Baku, where he hoped to incite the Muslim population to rise against the czar.[11] To Marshal Liman von Sanders, the head of the German Military Mission to Turkey, he confided that he hoped to march, like Genghis Khan in reverse direction, on to Afghanistan and then to India.[12]

On Christmas Day 1914, Enver Pasha did what Napoleon had done in 1812 and what Hitler would do in 1941—he invaded Russia in winter. As it had been for Napoleon and would be for Hitler, so too it proved disastrous for Enver. In two weeks Enver lost 75,000 of his 95,000 men. They were killed in battle or froze to death in the blizzards of the Turnagel Woods. Within weeks of having left the capital, he returned to Constantinople humiliated and was never to take personal command of an army offensive again. In the wake of Enver's loss on the Caucasian front, the Turks became more insecure about their land on the Russian border, and the Armenians were pointed to as the "cause of trouble" in the region. Thus the Armenians of Van became even more vulnerable.

Enver's disaster in the Caucasus was followed by more failure for the Turks. The Ottoman army's attempt to take northwestern Persia failed. This time it was Enver's brother-in-law Jevdet Bey, whose forces were driven out of Tabriz. In the aftermath of the Russian and Persian setbacks, Talaat appointed Jevdet Bey governor of Van Province in February 1915. It was a calculated move, because Talaat wished to replace the more tolerant and politic governor Hassan Tahsin.

Jevdet Bey was openly racist about Armenians, and he had a history of persecuting them. As a *kaymakam* of Saray and later *mutassarrif* (district governor) of Bashkale in Van Province, he was known for making constant searches and seizures of so-called militant Armenians in the region. He was reviled and feared for his practices of torture, which included using cats to claw and bite incarcerated victims. He also seems to have perfected the practice of nailing horseshoes to the feet of Armenians, thus earning him the name "the horse-shoe master of Bashkale."[13] In short, he made a name for himself and advanced his career through his anti-Armenian zeal. Duplicitous, aggressive, and prone to violent behavior, the new governor began his job in Van in the winter of 1915, in the wake of his lost Persian campaign, eager to make a scapegoat of the Armenian population of Van.[14]

Dr. Clarence D. Ussher wrote the most detailed account in English of what happened in that city and province in the spring of 1915. A religious man and a physician, Ussher had studied at the theological seminary in Philadelphia, earned his M.D. at the Medical College of Kansas City, and left a thriving practice in Kansas City to answer missionary leader James L. Barton's call to do missionary work in Turkey in 1898. From the start his life in Turkey was defined by the persecution of the Armenians. It was Ussher who recorded his shock on entering Turkey when customs officials confiscated his dictionary because it contained the words "liberty" and "revolution," which were considered "pernicious" by the government; they then cut the maps out of his Bible because the word "Armenia" appeared on them.[15]

After a year of relief work in Harput, Ussher left when Dr. George C. Raynolds, the missionary physician in Van, was in dire need of assistance. Approaching Van with his wife after weeks of arduous travel on horseback, he described the "sapphire-blue waters of Lake Van." A lake of myth and beauty, the Roman writer Pliny claimed it was so heavy with borax that the inflowing river waters stayed on the surface. Seventy miles long and forty-five miles wide, the lake and its surrounding rivers created the fertile land of the Van Plain. A hundred and ten villages and two extinct volcanoes dotted its shores. Perched on a great plateau some 5,500 feet above sea level, both city and lake sat beneath mountains twelve to fourteen thousand feet high in the near distance.

On this dramatic highland Ussher found Van, an ancient walled city crowded with houses, mosques, minarets, churches, and bazaars. History was everywhere. On the summit of a great rock rising three hundred feet above the city, Ussher gazed at "the towers and battlements of an ancient castle," and on "the lakeward side was carved in cuneiform characters a trilingual inscription by Xerxes." The capital of the Vannic Kingdom of the Assyrian period, "Armenian historians call it Shamiramagerd, or City of Semiramis," Ussher wrote. He was also impressed by the suburb of Aikesdan. With a large Armenian population, Aikesdan was an exotic garden city of poplars, willows, and water courses, with "orchards and vineyards stretching greenly eastward from the old walled city for four miles."[16]

Everywhere he looked he saw the destruction of the 1895 massacres in ruined houses and traumatized people. He found Dr. and Mrs. Raynolds managing an orphanage of four hundred children. "The burden of the orphanage," Ussher wrote, was so great that all three relief organizations—the British Friends of Armenia; the German Committee, led by Herr Roessler and later Pauline Patrunky; and the Swiss Committee, directed by Mr. Favre—were all working day and night.[17] Van was teeming with missionary groups from Europe as well as American men and women, many of them from New England colleges, who were operating orphanages and hospitals, heading schools and kindergartens for boys and girls, and even running a YMCA, YWCA, and a Boy Scout organization for Armenians.

Throughout the winter of 1915, Jevdet Bey conducted a ruthless campaign in the Armenian villages of the surrounding countryside, purportedly to ferret out weapons from Armenian households. His troops arrested thousands of Armenians, torturing and killing them. By early spring he had initiated a reign of terror in the region. As the war effort sped up, the governor pressed down on the Armenian population by demanding four thousand Armenian men for the Ottoman army's labor battalions. The city's leaders were horrified by the demand, knowing full well that Armenian men in the Ottoman army labor battalions were being massacred en masse all over the empire. When they asked for combat duty instead, the Armenians were turned down. The Armenians then conferred again and told the authorities that they would allow four hundred Armenians to join labor battalions, but reminded the Turks that the rest were legally exempt by the payment of a tax. Still Jevdet Bey kept insisting on the four thousand men even though the exemption fee was legal.

At the time, Ussher and his fellow missionaries didn't know that the subgovernor had already been ordered to begin massacring the Armenian intellectuals and cultural leaders in the region. However, the case of an Armenian school teacher in the town of Shadakh, south of Van, had become news. The teacher was scheduled to be hanged, and in response Armenians picketed the government building all night, informing the mayor and his gendarmes that they would not let them exit until the teacher was freed.

Seizing the opportunity Jevdet Bey proceeded to invite four prominent Armenians to Shadakh to serve on a so-called peace commission with an equal number of prominent Turks, in order to reach a solution. Jevdet Bey ordered "a guard of honor" to accompany the Armenians from Van; on their way they stopped at a village, supposedly for a feast in their honor, where the four Armenians were murdered.

The next morning, Saturday, April 17, Jevdet Bey summoned four more leaders to help pursue the ostensible mediation attempt, among them Arshag Vramian, a member of the Ottoman parliament. When they departed, the anxiety in the city was so great that Ussher went to see Jevdet Bey in his office to try to help allay some of the tension. While he was there, the colonel of Jevdet Bey's regiment entered his office. His regiment, made up mostly of freed convicts, was nicknamed the *Kasab Taburu*, or Butcher Regiment. Ussher describes the following conversation. "You sent for me," the colonel said. "Yes," Jevdet Bey replied, "go to Shadakh and wipe out its people." Then Jevdet Bey turned to Ussher and said coldly, "I won't leave one, not one so high," and he leveled his hand below his knee.[18] In the ensuing days the Butcher Regiment went on a murdering and burning spree, destroying six villages and massacring all the inhabitants. So horrifying were the mutilated bodies brought to him at the American hospital that Ussher refused to describe them.[19]

Just as Vramian's group was about to persuade the Armenians of Van to give up their four thousand men, the news of these massacres reached the people. Giving up the men would mean their murder, but refusing would mean more general massacre. Once again Ussher and his missionary colleague E. A. Yarrow went to see Jevdet Bey, and this time the *vali* demanded permission to put fifty soldiers in the missionary compound, which was situated on a hill within the Armenian quarter. The *vali* insisted that he needed to protect the Americans from the Armenians. Angry over the *vali*'s manipulative plan to get Turkish soldiers into the Armenian quarter, Ussher appealed to the Italian consul, Sbordoni, and together they explained to Jevdet Bey that with the news of the new massacres the Armenians were terrified, and that putting Turkish soldiers in the Armenian quarter would only lead to more killing.

By the end of Sunday, April 18, the *vali* threatened Ussher that if he didn't consent to the demand, the American mission would be subject to the same violence that might befall the Armenians. Ussher then consented, but warned Jevdet Bey: "Our premises are a part of America, extraterritorial by right, and neutral. If anyone," he declared, "fires a shot from our enclosure without our permission, I will shoot him myself."[20]

On Monday morning, April 19, Consul Sbordoni protested again to Jevdet Bey that what he was doing would not allay tension but create more problems. The *vali's* mood seemed more subdued, and he urged the Armenians to return to their work in the marketplace. Little did the Americans or Armenians in the city know that, "at that very hour," as Ussher later put it, "thousands of defenseless men, women, and children were being slaughtered with the utmost brutality." Already instructions had gone out throughout the province that read: "The Armenians must be exterminated. If any Moslem protect a Christian, first, his house shall be burned, then the Christian killed before his eyes, and then his [the Moslem's] family and himself."[21]

Two American nurses, Grisell M. McLaren and Myrtle O. Shane, who later wrote meticulous eyewitness accounts of the destruction of Van and Bitlis, recorded that on "April 19, 1915, a general massacre of [the] Armenian subjects" was planned. "On that day soldiers and Kurds, in some instances taking cannon with them, attacked the smaller towns and the villages of the province, and met with little or no resistance because most of the able-bodied men had been drafted into the Sultan's army and those who were left had very little ammunition. Fifty-five thousand men, women and children were slaughtered."[22]

The next day, Tuesday, April 20, Turkish soldiers were lined up in trenches around the Armenian quarter. The tense situation was ignited when the soldiers seized two young Armenian women. Two Armenian men who tried to rescue them were killed instantly. The incident took place in front of the German missionary orphanage, and as the orphanage director Herr Sporri reported, the gunfire sparked a signal for "a general fusillade by the Turks on all sides, and almost immediately Jevdet Bey opened artillery fire on the Armenian quarter in Aikesdan and also on the Armenian quarter in the walled city."[23]

Although Jevdet Bey was calling the Armenians rebels, all the American and European eyewitnesses agree that the troubles at Van were initiated by the Turks. "Although the vali calls it rebellion," Mrs. Ussher recorded in her diary, "it is really an effort to protect the lives and the homes of the Armenians," and in the villages, she went on, "it is nothing but systematic and wholesale massacre."[24] Fearing massacre again, the Armenians were prepared to fight back. What followed was one of the most remarkable acts of self-defense in the face of genocide that has ever been recorded. Three hundred men with rifles, and another thousand men and boys with pistols and antiquated weapons, defended thirty thousand Armenians in an area of more than a square mile in the Armenian quarter of Aikesdan, and an area of less than a square mile in the walled city of Van.[25]

Outside the walled city the Turks burned down almost every Armenian house, while inside the city, the Armenians came together and fought shrewdly and tenaciously. Tinsmiths, coppersmiths, blacksmiths, and jewelers turned out some two thousand cartridges and bullets a day. An Armenian professor made smokeless gunpowder. Women made uniforms for the men and cooked around the clock. The normal-school band played military marches, and a Boy Scout troop, which had been started by Ussher's thirteen-year-old nephew a year before, acted as a fire patrol and sanitary unit, and dug thousands of Turkish bullets out of the ground so the artisans could melt them down and recast them.[26]

At night the Armenians built walls around their houses in order to protect them from Turkish shells and bombs. They were able to get the Turks to waste their ammunition by sending a dog or a horse down a street at night with a lantern around its neck and then firing some shots; the Turks, thinking it was a messenger in the Armenian unit, opened fire, while Turks on the other side of the city, hearing the fire, also opened fire, believing the Russians had come. In another act of thrift, the Armenians sent a man or woman to extinguish bomb fuses before they went off; they extracted the gunpowder to reload their own cartridges.[27] Ussher recalled that the slogan "better ten days' liberty than to die the slaves we've been" circulated through the Armenian quarter.[28] (Among the young boys helping the men on the front lines was the Armenian American painter Arshile Gorky [born Vostanig Adoian], then an eight-year-old living with his mother and sister.)

As the siege of the city continued, the Armenians in the dozens and

dozens of villages of the province were being slaughtered; thousands more
took to the mountains and hid in caves.[29] And Jevdet Bey called more of his
soldiers from the villages to the city. By the second week, village refugees
were making their way to the city, and the Armenian quarter became a
scene of chaos, death, and disease. Dr. and Mrs. Ussher and their staff now
worked day and night tending the sick and dying refugees. Working almost
without sleep for days at a time, they grew desperate, and by the end of the
month Ussher and Yarrow found a dozen messengers to carry the following SOS message over the Russian and Persian borders.

Van, April 27, 1915

To Americans, or any Foreign Consul.
    Internal troubles in Van. Government threatens to bombard
American premises. Inform American Government American
lives in danger.

(Signed) C. D. USSHER
E. A. YARROW

Reward messenger.[30]

By the fourth week Ussher wrote: "How could they possibly hold
out much longer against Djevdet Bey's greatly superior forces?" From
their window he and his wife could see the town of Shushantz on fire on
the mountainside, and the Varak Monastery, "with its priceless store of
ancient manuscripts, going up in smoke."[31] Turkish firing on the city
grew more intense, with poisoned and explosive bullets and an all-out
bombing of the walled city. By Sunday, May 16, bombs were falling on
the American compound. Ussher's house was bombed to ruins, as was
the hospital he had worked so hard to build. Miraculously no one was
injured, and in an almost surreal moment, Ussher describes hurrying
"out into the street in my operating-gown," to find men asking him "in
an agony of fear for the women and children: 'What shall we do now?
They are firing on the American flag and it can no longer protect us.
What will become of us all?' "[32] With the American compound ablaze,
the news came that the Turks had retreated and were gone. Bewildered
and fearing a military trick, the next morning the Armenians slowly
made their way into the Turkish quarter. They found the wells filled

with mutilated Armenian bodies, and piles of men and women with their throats slit.

However, one of Ussher's SOS messages had made it across the Persian border into the hands of a Russian consul, who in turn had sent word to Moscow. Within days the news of the siege at Van appeared in the Russian and American press. On Tuesday, May 18, a Russian-Armenian regiment preceded the Russian army into Van, and by May 20 the keys of the city were handed over to General Nikolaieff. The Russians occupying the city and outlying region reported that the villages were filled with corpses and the rivers choked with dead bodies. "We have absolute proof," Ussher wrote in the wake of the Russian reports, that "fifty-five thousand" Armenians had been massacred.[33]

As summer approached, the medical efforts among sick and wounded refugees grew more overwhelming, and typhus broke out. Having worked tirelessly for months, Ussher and his wife both became ill. In the middle of July, Elizabeth Ussher died. Ussher, himself in a coma with typhus, didn't know of his loss for weeks.[34]

Having overestimated the Ottoman Third Army, General Nicolaieff's regiment, which had occupied Van and Bitlis for ten weeks, decided to retreat in late July. Nicolaieff informed the Armenians that the Russians were about to evacuate and urged them to leave immediately. During the retreat thousands of Armenians were killed by Turks and Kurds, and others died of starvation. Ussher's description of more than a quarter of a million Armenians pouring over the border into Russia in the middle of August is rendered in almost biblical imagery. The Yerevan Plain, he wrote, "filled with a shifting multitude overflowing the horizon, wandering aimlessly hither and thither; strangers in a strange land, footsore, weary, starving, wailing like lost and hungry children."[35]

The testimony of Turkey's military and diplomatic allies confirms what Americans like Ussher, Grace Knapp, McClaren, and Shane lived through and witnessed. According to Vice–Field Marshal Joseph Pomiankowski, an Austrian, the Van resistance was an act of "desperation [*Verzweiflung*] on the part of the Armenians who saw that the general slaughter had begun."[36] Scheubner-Richter, the German vice-consul in Erzurum, noted that the disaster at Van was the result of a chain of Turkish provocations:

the attempts to force the Armenians to give up men to the labor battalions, the arrest of notables, and the trapping and murder of Deputy
Vramian and other political leaders.[37]

Some of the most fascinating and perceptive testimony comes from a
Turkish-speaking Venezuelan mercenary, Rafael de Nogales, an officer in
the Turkish army at Van, where he directed artillery fire for four weeks
against about six hundred Armenians fighting from behind their home-
made barricades. At the start his Turkish aides claimed that the Armenians were the aggressors, so he was astonished to discover that "the
aggressors had not been the Armenians, after all, but the authorities
themselves!" He was also astounded when the mayor told him "that he
was doing nothing more than carry[ing] out an unequivocal order ema-
nating from the Governor-General of the province . . . *to exterminate all
Armenian males of twelve years of age and over.*"[38]

De Nogales turned out to be full of praise for the Armenians: "The
resistance of the Armenians was terrific and their valor worthy of all
praise."[39] However, he faulted the Armenians for not being aggressive
enough in their strategy, and felt that they might have beaten the Turkish
forces back to Bitlis and thus "have saved the lives of thousands of their
own brethren who were perishing daily in neighboring towns and
throughout the vilayet of Van."[40]

De Nogales's assessments substantiated the reports of the other witnesses who maintained that the Armenian posture at Van was defensive and
an act of resistance to massacre. The murder of Vramian, he noted, was an
act of aggression, and the sadistic violence ordered by Jevdet Bey against the
Armenians all spring he called "a bacchanal of barbarity," with its practice of
splitting the heads of the victims with a *yataghan* (sword), or leaving murdered bodies on the ground with slit throats.[41] As an army officer, he knew
that the Armenian resistance increased Jevdet Bey's rage, and that what
resulted was a further order to massacre all the remaining Armenians in the
surrounding villages. Even "the very Kurds were appalled," he wrote, by
the butchering of innocent women and children.[42] The now familiar pattern
of Turkish denial followed immediately at Van. Dr. Ussher wrote explicitly
that it was the "Turkish government, not the Turkish people, that has done
all this." And the government, he went on, "tried to deceive its
Mohammedan subjects and arouse their hatred against the Christians." The
governor issued a statement of total fabrication, telling his people that "the

fifty-five thousand slaughtered Armenians" were "fifty-five thousand Mohammedans massacred by Christians."[43] Astonishing as it might seem, it continued the pattern of denial that Sultan Abdul Hamid began in the 1890s, when he claimed that nothing bad had happened to the Armenians.

For all the fabricated claims the Turkish government made then—and has made since—about the Armenians at Van being in rebellion and therefore deserving of what transpired, the bystanders at Van in 1915—American, German, Swiss, and Italian missionaries and diplomats—agreed that the Armenians were desperate and heroic in protecting themselves from total annihilation. As the political scientist Robert Melson explains, the Armenians were neither attempting to destroy the Turks or the Ottoman Empire nor attempting to secede or join Russia.[44] The historian Roderick Davison also notes that the affluent and upper "classes of Ottoman Armenians wished rather for a regenerated and orderly Turkey,"[45] and as for the politically activist Dashnaks, they were neither rebelling against the Ottoman state nor seeking secession. "Their program was essentially one of reform within the Ottoman Empire." In short, they believed that "a complete separation of Armenia from Turkey was ethnographically and geographically impossible."[46]

Because the events at Van have been so important to Turkish claims that Armenians were seeking to destroy the Ottoman state, it must be underscored that a stateless, discriminated-against minority population, without any military organization, who are also under siege cannot engage in civil war, nor can they cause the downfall of a state. As the German ambassador, Wolff-Metternich, explained, the local uprisings at Van and in several other towns in the spring of 1915 were "defensive acts" to avert being massacred.[47]

In assessing Turkish claims that Armenians provoked their fate because they were a threat to national security, Robert Melson has put it well: "If the Armenians had behaved differently, if they had acted less threateningly, the Committee of Union and Progress would not have decided on genocide in 1915. If there had been fewer Jewish communists, or bankers or department store owners, or journalists, or beggars, there would have been no Holocaust."[48]

APRIL 24

In exterminating the Armenians of Turkey, the CUP sought to wipe out the Armenian cultural leadership as early as possible. By killing the cultural and community leaders, the Young Turks hoped to silence Armenia's most accomplished and potent civic voices. The plan was to eliminate all Armenian writers, political activists, artists, teachers, and church and civic leaders. The able-bodied men were being massacred in the labor battalions of the Ottoman infantry as early as the winter of 1915, and if the cultural leadership could be silenced in the spring and summer, the CUP hoped to render the Armenians totally helpless and vulnerable.

What happened on the night of April 24, 1915, in Constantinople was a seminal event in the Armenian Genocide, and it was part of a pattern that would be established all over Turkey as the genocide progressed. In cities, towns, and villages everywhere, Armenian cultural leaders were arrested, tortured, and killed as quickly as possible. Some who survived, like the distinguished composer and musicologist Gomidas Vartabed, went insane. In the end thousands of Armenian cultural leaders were killed, and the core of Armenia's intellectual life was destroyed. In Van, Dr. Ussher recorded the roundup and arrests of Armenian professors and cultural leaders in late April and May 1915, and in Harput, American consul Leslie Davis reported that in June and July, Armenian intellectuals and professors were among the first to be imprisoned and murdered.

What happened in Constantinople was dramatic. Since the mid–nineteenth century the capital had been home to the richest and most influential Armenian community in the empire, and the center of Armenian intellectual and cultural life.[1] This made it the obvious target for the CUP to begin its formal eradication of Armenian cultural leaders. On the night of April 24 and into the following day, about 250 cultural leaders were seized in a first round of arrests, and in the coming weeks another several hundred from the city and its vicinity would be arrested.

"On the night of Saturday, April 24, 1915," the priest Krikoris Balakian wrote, "the Armenians in the capital were snoring in a calm sleep—exhausted from their Easter celebrations, there on the heights of Stambul near Hagia Sophia—while in the central police station a secret project was in motion."[2] Weeks earlier SO member and Constantinople chief of police Petri had sent letters to all police officers containing the list of Armenians to be arrested—a list that had been compiled with the help of Armenian spies, most notably one Artin Mugerditchian.[3]

Krikoris Balakian wrote the most detailed and reliable account of the April 24 arrests in Constantinople. One of the 250 arrested on that night, he was sent to prison in the interior, escaped, and spent the next four years outwitting CUP officials. His memoir, *Armenian Golgotha,* is a vivid account of those four years and was written immediately after his escape from Turkey to Manchester, England, where he served for a while as pastor of the Armenian church there. A man of considerable learning, Balakian was an ordained priest and had done graduate study in architecture in Germany. He wrote several books on Armenian architecture, religion, and culture, and after several years in Manchester, went to France, where he became a bishop of the Armenian church, spending most of his remaining years in Marseilles.

On the evening of April 24, Armenian leaders were arrested all over the city and found themselves in large red military buses headed first to the military barracks at Selimiye, a town on Constantinople's Asiatic side, and then by a steamboat "to the rocky shores of Sirkedji," on the European side, where they were taken to the central prison. There, behind "gigantic fences and iron bolted gates," they were led to a wooden shack in the center of the prison grounds, in which they sat stunned under the light of a lantern.[4]

Balakian describes the iron gates of the prison creaking open and shut all night, and watching as the familiar faces of friends and colleagues kept being shoved inside the shack. They were political leaders, public servants, and nonpartisan intellectuals. "Like some dream," Balakian wrote, "it seemed as if on one night, all the prominent Armenians of the capital—assemblymen, representatives, progressive thinkers, reporters, teachers, doctors, pharmacists, dentists, merchants, and bankers—had made an appointment in those dim cells of the prison. More than a few people were still wearing their pajamas, robes, and slippers."[5]

Another survivor of the Constantinople group of leaders, Dr. Khachig Boghosian, a physician, recalls being taken to that same central prison, where he too sat in disbelief.[6] "So, here we were, the majority of the Armenian intellectuals and public figures of Constantinople." Balakian recorded, "on the Sunday after Easter 1915, sitting in the central prison, scared and waiting for any news of help from anywhere. And we kept asking each other: why is this happening?"[7]

It wasn't until the next evening that the warden checked off their names and they were marched by a troop of military police to the administration office. There they were searched, and the police confiscated "everything from us—money, small insignificant pieces of paper, pocket knives, pencils, diaries, even our umbrellas and canes, and always they pretended that they would be returning them to us later."[8] The military police then put them on buses in groups of twenty—with about a dozen soldiers in each bus—and a caravan of military buses, led by the general police chief in his own car, proceeded from Hagia Sophia Boulevard toward Sirkedji.

Balakian described "the terror of death" that hung in the air of the bus, especially as they passed the rocky coast where in previous decades the sultan's military police had thrown to their deaths hundreds of Armenian and Turkish intellectuals and political activists. The group was then put on a steamship that normally held about 65 people, but was now loaded down with about 250 Armenians and dozens of military police—young soldiers, commissars, army spies, and police officials of various ranks.[9]

They sailed out on the rough waters of the Sea of Marmara and finally landed at Haydar Pasha's wharf, where they were marched out of the steamship in pairs to a huge embarkation station. As the ornate process continued, the Armenian leaders were then taken to a special train, which was, as Balakian put it, "waiting and ready to take us to the depths of Asia Minor, where, except for a few rare cases, we would all meet our deaths.

"With the lights out," Balakian wrote, "the doors of the cars shut, and with police and police soldiers posted everywhere, the train started. And so we began to move further and further away from the places of our lives, each of us leaving behind grieving and unprotected mothers, sisters, wives, children, possessions, wealth, and everything else. We headed out to a region unnamed and unfamiliar. To be buried forever."[10]

Sometime past midnight an official on the train, who happened to be Armenian, whispered in Balakian's ear: "Reverend Father, please write down the names of your arrested friends on this piece of paper and give it back to me." The man then "slid a piece of paper and a pencil into my hand, and leaving the lamp by me, he went off to the busy policemen who were in charge of us . . . my heart was pounding and in haste I wrote, in the flickering dim light, the names I could remember, and slid the list back to the Armenian official."[11] It was at this point that Balakian began to bear witness in a more formal way, and perhaps the writing down of the names was part of the process that led him to write his memoir.

The train proceeded south along the coastline of the Sea of Marmara and by dawn they were passing through Nicomedia (Izmit) and Bardizag. At dusk they came to the town of Eskishehir, where the Ankara and Konia railway lines separate, and then, after some delay and much apprehension among the prisoners, the train veered off toward Ankara. Around midday on Tuesday they arrived at the Sinjan Koy railroad station, near Ankara. At the station Ibrahim, the chief of the central prison, who had been with them since Constantinople, stood up and began to read off the list of names: "Silvio Ricci, Agnuni, Zartarian, Khazhag, Shahrigian, Jihangiulian, Dr. Daghavarian, Sarkis Minasian," the names were shouted out. They were all progressive intellectuals, nonpolitical party people, conservatives, Balakian recalled, "some seventy-five in all. We were riveted on each name as it was called," he wrote, "and then we kissed those who were leaving us. In that instant, we began to weep, and as one person wept, others began to weep too, and we had this feeling that we were being separated from each other forever."[12]

The first group was taken to Ayash, northwest of Ankara, while Balakian's group would be taken to Chankiri, to the northeast of Ankara. In both places the men were imprisoned, tortured, and most of them killed in the subsequent few months in the desolate countryside of the region.[13] Balakian describes many of their deaths, among them the murders of the famous poet Daniel Varoujan and the novelist and Ottoman parliament member Krikor Zohrab. Varoujan and four colleagues had been with Balakian in prison in Chankiri, and on Thursday August 12, Jemal Oguz, the CUP responsible secretary, telegraphed the police guard office on the Chankiri-Kaylajek road to inform them of the coming of the deportees. When the carriages carrying Varoujan and his colleagues reached the Chankiri-Kalayjek road, they were ambushed by four Kurdish *chetes*. "The whole thing," Balakian wrote, "had been arranged in advance, and in secret."[14]

The *chetes* then took the five Armenians to a nearby creek, undressed them, and folded up their clothing for themselves. Then "they began to stab them to death, slashing their arms and legs and genitals, and ripping apart their bodies." Only the thirty-three-year-old Daniel Varoujan tried to defend himself, and this provoked the killers further; they not only "tore out his entrails, but dug out the eyes of this great Armenian poet."[15] The killers then divided the pillage among themselves, taking more than 450 Ottoman gold pieces that were sewn into the clothing of Dr. Chillingerian and Onnig Maghazadjian. They paid off the police, and after dividing up the belongings, left in the carriages.[16]

Balakian learned the details of the killings from one of the Turkish carriage drivers—the twenty-year-old son of the local bathhouse keeper—who returned to Chankiri depressed and shaken. Sobbing as he spoke, he said to the Armenian priest, "I don't want to be in this trade anymore. I'm going to sell my horse and carriage and get out of this town. I don't want this kind of profit." When the carriages returned to Chankiri without Varoujan and the others on Friday, the news of their murders spread terror among the deportees and the Armenian families of the town. The interim governor, who had guaranteed that the men would reach Ankara safely, went immediately to Tuney (the town where they were killed) with the chief of police from Kastamouni and an investigative team. There, they "found the five dead men in unrecognizable condition in the creek."[17]

Dr. Boghosian described similar scenes. His group of deportees was led out of the Chankiri prison, he recorded, on Assumption Sunday in August 1915. Marched out of town, tied to each other by ropes, and joined with a group of several hundred more men, they were sent out into the "bright moonlit night," with three carts filled with "spades, hoes, pick-axes, and shovels." Along the way more than two dozen of them were killed by the gendarmes, who bludgeoned them to death with their rifles. They were spared for the moment when a Turkish captain redirected their caravan south to Kayseri. Along that route more than 200 died of starvation and dysentery—familiar ways of dying in the extermination process.[18] Most of them would die in the coming months, but Dr. Boghosian, like Krikoris Balakian, was among the lucky survivors.

What happened to these deported Armenian cultural leaders happened to Armenian intellectuals all over Turkey. In this calculated way the CUP destroyed a vital part of Armenia's cultural infrastructure, and succeeded in practically silencing a whole generation of Armenian writers. The death toll shows that at least eighty-two writers are known to have been murdered, in addition to the thousands of teachers and cultural and religious leaders. It was an apocalypse for Armenian literature, which was in its own moment of a modernist flowering. Daniel Varoujan, Siamanto (Adam Yarjanian), Krikor Zohrab, Levon Shant, Gomidas (Soghomon Soghomonian), and many others had taken Armenian poetry, fiction, drama, and music into a new era. Fortunately many of the poems, novels, plays, and essays survived and are an important part of the Armenian literary tradition today.[19] But it may nevertheless be that the Young Turk government's extermination of Armenian intellectuals in 1915 was the most extensive episode of its kind in the twentieth century. In many ways it became a paradigm for the silencing of writers by totalitarian governments in the ensuing decades of the century. After April 24 it would be easier to carry out the genocide program, for many of the most gifted voices of resistance were gone.

Part III

AMERICAN WITNESS

THE AMBASSADOR

AT THE CROSSROADS

N o single American has become more profoundly associated with the Armenian Genocide than Henry Morgenthau, who was appointed by the newly elected President Woodrow Wilson in 1913 as U.S. ambassador to the Ottoman Empire. Looking back at this period of his life in 1918, two years after leaving his post, Henry Morgenthau wrote: "It was certainly an amazing fate that landed me in this great headquarters of intrigue at the very moment when the plans of the Kaiser for controlling Turkey, which he had carefully pursued for a quarter of a century, were about to achieve their final success."[1] Given Morgenthau's moral fiber and personal education, it is not surprising that he worked as he did—with courage and persistence—to try to save the Armenians from annihilation.

Henry Morgenthau came to the United States at the age of nine in 1868 with his parents, Lazarus and Babette Morgenthau, affluent Jews from Mannheim, Germany. One of twelve children, he emerged as the family prodigy in his early adolescence and developed a strong sense of discipline that was anchored by faith. His father had espoused radical Reform Judaism from his days in Mannheim, and in Manhattan, when the family joined Congregation Adas Jeshurun, Lazarus Morgenthau became close friends with the liberal rabbi David Einhorn.[2]

Reading William Penn's *No Cross, No Crown* as an adolescent, Henry was also deeply affected by Quakerism. Like Ben Franklin, he made lists of virtues to practice each day. He felt he needed to do "what my conscience prompts me, not what my pride dictates."[3] Quakerism, Rabbi Einhorn's liberal Judaism, and the secularized Judaism of Felix Adler, the founder of the Society for Ethical Culture, would inspire in Henry a call to conscience and social action that would give the young Morgenthau his ethical foundation. "His true religion" became "service to democracy" as his grandson Henry III put it, which was part and parcel of Adler's Ethical Culture.[4]

It was through Rabbi Stephen Wise that Morgenthau first entered the arena of public service. When Wise returned from California in 1906 to found the Free Synagogue in Manhattan, he asked Morgenthau, then a successful lawyer and businessman, to become its first president. Both men shared commitments to political reform and social service, and the Free Synagogue embodied a liberal Jewish ethos. "Pewless and dueless," as it was known, the Free Synagogue held services at Carnegie Hall, and it soon became the alternative to the mainstream Temple Emanu-El.

Morgenthau's friendship with Rabbi Wise led to a network of personal relationships in the American Jewish community that would become important for him. As a young man in his twenties, the charismatic Wise had been the rabbi of Temple Beth Israel in Portland, Oregon, where Solomon Hirsch, a Republican businessman and politician, was the congregation's president. During the administration of President Benjamin Harrison, Hirsch had become the first American Jew to hold ministerial rank by becoming minister to Turkey. It was from Hirsch that Wise, already a committed Zionist, came to believe in the importance of having a Jew head the Turkish mission, for the Ottoman Empire included a large Jewish population, including those in Palestine.

In 1911 Morgenthau and Wise invited Woodrow Wilson, the governor of New Jersey, to a celebration of the Free Synagogue's fourth anniversary. At dinner Morgenthau sat with Wilson; the two seem to have bonded, and Morgenthau offered Wilson his "unreserved moral and financial support." That evening seems to have been the turning point in Morgenthau's political career.[5]

The second decade of the twentieth century was a propitious time for Jews to enter the political world, for the ruling Protestant elite exercised a slightly weaker grip on power. Having made a small fortune as an attorney and a real estate investor, Morgenthau now felt himself "released from the toils of materialism" and believed it was his duty to "pay back in the form of public service, the overdraft which I had been permitted to make upon the opportunities of this country."[6]

In sizing up Wilson as a dark-horse candidate for the presidency in the upcoming election, Morgenthau seized the moment to leave the world of business for the world of politics. His involvement in public service had begun with his presidency of the Free Synagogue and directorship of Mt. Sinai Hospital. But in 1911, when he succeeded Henry L. Stimson (future secretary of state) as the president of New York City's Committee of Safety, a citizens' group that formed in response to the disastrous Triangle Shirtwaist Factory fire in downtown Manhattan, he took on a new public persona. With this prominent post, Morgenthau entered the world of public service as a liberal Democrat to whom Wilson's progressivism greatly appealed.[7]

Prior to the Democratic convention in the summer of 1912, Morgenthau was giving five thousand dollars a month to the campaign, and continued to give generously throughout the fall. Only some of Wilson's wealthy Princeton classmates, such as Cleveland H. Dodge, gave more. After Wilson was nominated on the twenty-sixth ballot at a dramatic convention, Morgenthau felt let down when he wasn't made chairman of the campaign finance committee. Still, the day after Wilson was elected, Morgenthau was among a select group who sat down for an early lunch at Wilson's home on Cleveland Lane in Princeton.

In the weeks following the election Stephen Wise complained to Morgenthau that thus far "no Jew has been appointed to a single place of importance. It seems an almost deliberate slight. Have you led him to feel that you would accept nothing?"[8] Morgenthau at once resented being categorized as a Jew but felt he deserved the appropriate recognition as one of "Our People," as he put it. When Wilson offered him the ambassadorship to the Ottoman Empire, Morgenthau refused. "The Jews of this country," he replied, "have become very sensitive and I think properly so over the impression which has been created by successive Jewish appointments to Turkey, that that is the only diplomatic post to which a Jew can aspire." Many of Morgenthau's Jewish friends urged him to decline the post, and Oscar Straus, he told Wilson, had been criticized by some of the Jewish community "for accepting a second and even a third appointment to Constantinople."⁹ Wilson replied angrily that Constantinople "was the point at which the interest of American Jews in the welfare of the Jews of Palestine is focused, and it is almost indispensable that I have a Jew at that post."¹⁰ Morgenthau answered: "Would prominent Methodists or Baptists be told here is a position, find one of your faith to fill it?"¹¹

Having turned Wilson down, Morgenthau and his family left for a summer vacation in Europe. However, in southern France, he met up with the U.S. ambassador to France, Myron T. Herrick. A wealthy industrialist and former governor of Ohio, Herrick extolled diplomatic service as the chance of a lifetime and told Morgenthau it would benefit his family for generations to come. This inspired Morgenthau to rethink his decision just at a moment when he was meeting with Stephen Wise, who was passing through France on his way back from the Holy Land.¹²

Over dinner in Lyons, Wise told Morgenthau how his trip to the Holy Land had brought him to the dramatic realization of "how completely Palestine was a suzerainty of the Turkish Empire," and how he had experienced anti-Semitic indignities at the hands of the Turkish authorities even though he was armed with a letter of introduction "of warm friendliness from President Wilson."¹³ The rabbi made it clear to Morgenthau that a Jew in the Turkish post would be crucial in helping to oversee the well-being of the Jews of Palestine and could help foster a Zionist future. Although Morgenthau wasn't a Zionist, he was deeply concerned about Turkish anti-Semitism, and this cemented his decision. He cabled Wilson: HAVE RECONSIDERED. WILL ACCEPT. WILL BE AT THE REGINAPALAST, MUNICH MONDAY, WARM REGARDS, HENRY MORGENTHAU. By the time he arrived at the hotel, a telegram was waiting for him: GLAD YOU ARE WILLING TO ACCEPT. WILL BEGIN ARRANGEMENTS AT ONCE. WOODROW WILSON.¹⁴

Like Clara Barton, Morgenthau was a self-reliant American with a strong sense of moral purpose, who found himself in "the dazzling, decadent capital of the Ottoman Empire."¹⁵ He was an outsider to the world of diplomatic intrigue and maneuvering, in lieu of which he brought to his new post his straitlaced, no-nonsense personality and his businessman's practical ethos. He was energetic, direct, and open. His selection of an Armenian, Arshag K. Schmavonian, as his *dragoman* was a good example of his judgment; Schmavonian had been a longtime legal adviser to the embassy, and the ambassador sized him up as intelligent and trustworthy, someone "who possessed knowledge of every American interest in Turkey."

Morgenthau was such a fish out of water in the diplomatic world of Constantinople that when he arrived without his wife, who happened to be on her way, the Turkish officials began pumping Schmavonian to find out who was the ambassador's mistress. "The ambassador doesn't have a mistress," Schmavonian answered firmly. "Impossible. We must have this information for the police records," the officials persisted. Weeks later a Turkish official said again to Schmavonian, "That ambassador of yours is really very clever. You know we still haven't been able to discover who his mistress is." Schmavonian reported all this to Morgenthau, who from then on told the story with great relish.[16]

Early in his ambassadorship he confessed that while he was concerned about the problems surrounding the American missionary activities, "whose ramifications reached into all parts of Turkey," and Ottoman policies of anti-Semitism in Palestine, the problem that preoccupied him most deeply was the Armenian Question.[17] "To both Morgenthau and the German ambassador, Wagenheim," the ambassador's grandson Henry Morgenthau III wrote, "the Armenian presence in both of these opposing empires [Ottoman and Russian] appeared to have many parallels with the Jewish presence, among the opposing nations of Eastern Europe. As alien minorities, essentially powerless in themselves, both the Jews and the Armenians were always being accused of traitorous collaboration by the governments that ruled them."[18]

When Morgenthau first settled into his new post in Constantinople, he was alarmed by the recent accession to power of the CUP triumvirate—Enver, Talaat, and Jemal. Morgenthau called the new Committee of Union and Progress "an irresponsible party, a kind of secret society" that ruled by "intrigue, intimidation, and assassination."[19]

Then, as the Ottoman Empire joined Germany in World War I in November 1914, Morgenthau witnessed the Ottoman declaration of war that was issued simultaneously with a declaration of *jihad* sent throughout the empire. That November, even as Enver was trying to convince Morgenthau over tea at the American embassy that no harm would come to Americans as the result of the declaration of *jihad*, Morgenthau believed that the call for *jihad* had "started passions" that would fuel the extermination program against the Armenians.[20] By the spring of 1915,

Morganthau began receiving detailed dispatches and telegrams about the deportations and massacres of the Armenians from his consular staff in the interior of Turkey. Those reports would soon be heard around the world, and they would become essential to Morgenthau's new sense of conscience and responsibility.

THE NEWS FROM THE AMERICAN

CONSUL IN HARPUT

A s the eyewitness accounts from American foreign service officers stationed in the Ottoman Empire began to accumulate in Ambassador Morgenthau's office and at the State Department in Washington, they were becoming the first body of U.S. diplomatic litera- ture about a major international human rights tragedy. Written by profes- sional, educated men, the narratives are often eloquent in their clean language and clinical images. They provide a certain detachment and per- spective on events that might otherwise seem to surpass description. Americans who had been raised in peace and prosperity at home now found themselves face to face with a kind of horror for which they could not have been prepared. In their consistency the narratives also corrobo- rate one another as they disclose the plan and process of a final solution for the Armenians by the Young Turk government.

Harput was an ancient city and region on the central plateau, where Armenians had been a flourishing presence since the eleventh century. At the time of the Genocide, the Armenian community was a prosperous force in education, the professions, business, and commerce. Leslie Davis had come to Harput to be the U.S. consul on May 31, 1914. Davis, a thirty- eight-year-old former attorney, had been born and raised in the rural

seaport village of Port Jefferson on the north shore of Long Island. After
graduating from Cornell University in 1898 and studying law at George
Washington University and New York Law School, Davis also worked
part-time as a journalist, and his facility as a writer was no doubt nurtured
then. After two years as an attorney, he grew restless and applied for a job
in the foreign service of the State Department. It appears that he was rea-
sonably well connected, because his candidacy was endorsed by five con-
gressmen, three senators, the president of George Washington University,
and President Wilson himself.

He landed his first appointment in 1912, at the consulate in the Russian city of Batum, on the Black Sea. For his love of horseback riding and
the rustic life, he stood out among his superiors, and for this he was
thought of as lacking in urbanity and sophistication. When he used
his first vacation to take a riding and hiking tour of Uzbekistan and the
Caucasus—where he climbed Mount Ararat (then in Russia)—his colleagues suggested that he would do better in a more remote place; accordingly the State Department sent him to Harput.[1]

Davis called Harput "one of the most inaccessible places in the entire
world."[2] It had taken him three weeks to get there from Constantinople
on horseback. Even for an outdoorsman like Davis, the trip was arduous.
The *khans,* or way stations, were so filthy and swarming with vermin that
he found it safer to sleep on the rooftops in the open air, even in the cold-
est of weather. Arriving in late April, Davis found himself looking out
at the dramatic valley that descended from a four-thousand-foot-high
plateau, where the city of Harput was perched. It was early spring, the valley beneath the plateau was turning green, and this great wheat region of
central Anatolia was coming to life.

With a population of thirty thousand, Harput was the largest city in
the province, but the actual seat of government, where the consulate was
located, was its twin city—Mezre, or Mamouret-ul-Aziz—in the valley
about ten miles south. Of the 500,000 people living in the province, about
150,000 were Armenians. The American Board of Foreign Missions had
founded a college there in 1876, first called Armenian College, later
changed under Turkish pressure to Euphrates College, and so Davis
found himself in the midst of an Armenian cultural life that included an
impressive corps of Armenian students and professors. Not long after his
arrival, Davis recorded in his diary how peacefully the Armenians and

Turks were getting along. But not long after, he would write: "Who could have then foreseen, amid these peaceful surroundings, that the following year there was to be enacted in this region what is probably the most terrible tragedy that has ever befallen any people in the history of the world?"[3]

On the eve of the Armenian deportations, Davis began noticing changes. When the Capitulations, which had always protected foreigners in Turkey, were abrogated in the fall of 1914, the recently appointed *vali,* Sabit Bey, turned increasingly arrogant and told Davis that he would be out of work soon. Davis described Sabit Bey as "shrewd," "cunning," "rude," and "ignorant," and noted something sociopathic about his behavior: "I have seen the tears roll down the cheeks of the Vali at the imaginary sufferings of a young man who was playing the part of a wounded soldier in an amateur theatrical performance given for the benefit of the Turkish Red Crescent Society. Yet, a hundred thousand people were made homeless and most of them perished from violence" as the result of his orders.[4]

Shortly after the abrogation of the Capitulations, the expulsion of European Christians from the region began. French Capuchin monks and Franciscan sisters in Harput and in the surrounding cities of Malatia, Diyarbekir, and Mardin were harassed and terrorized. In Harput the Catholics soon fled their building, which was then converted into a Turkish hospital. By March 1915 the American schools in Harput had been ordered closed, and a process of framing the Armenians as seditious was under way. Davis noted that their supposed search for bombs and weapons often led the Turkish gendarmes to bury bombs in the backyards of the accused, in order "to manufacture evidence against the Armenians."

He described the process in detail. First the gendarmes would surround a town to prevent anyone from leaving, and then more gendarmes would go house by house demanding that the occupants surrender their weapons, when often there were no weapons to be found. "I have seen many houses," Davis wrote, "where the gendarmes had dug up the floors and torn away the walls in their efforts to find weapons which they thought were concealed there." The situation became so absurd that some terrified Armenians actually went out and bought weapons from the police, spending "large sums of money for some old gun or revolver," which they believed they could surrender to appease the gendarmes and avoid arrest. But this, of course, had the opposite effect.[5]

Armenian survivors described similar scenes all over Anatolia. Farther west in Kayseri, where Armenians constituted a significant part of the commerce and business of the city, Virginia Meghrouni wrote that "continually, day and night, officers searched for weapons in Armenian homes . . . even small kitchen knives were confiscated; so were historical materials and books listing names of Armenian leaders." She described the shock that went through the community when

> deportation notices were posted in Kayseri on June 15. All over the city Armenian shops and businesses were ordered closed immediately, and Armenians were informed that they must be prepared for a deportation; in doing so they were instructed to leave their goods and belongings behind and their money in the bank, and that all would be safeguarded. Shortly thereafter, twenty prominent Armenian men were hanged in the town square.[6]

In Sivas, where the Armenian population comprised nearly 40 percent of that large city, Kerop Bedoukian, the son of a grocer, recalled that the "town crier walked back and forth in our street notifying the inhabitants that they had to leave three days hence. . . . Every day," he remembered, "streets were being emptied of Armenians, especially in the new and wealthy district called the Upper Field."[7] In the city of Marash, in the rocky highlands just south of Zeitun, the pastor Abraham Hartunian described the Armenian quarter as being "surrounded by a chain of soldiers . . . the houses of notables were put under special guard," he noted (his own among them), "and the gendarmes entered monster-like and ordered us to remain where we were standing."[8] Marash had a significant Armenian presence, and on the eve of the deportation, it was teeming with Armenian and American missionary culture. Overnight Rev. Hartunian watched his world—with its magnificent church, spacious campus where six hundred Armenians attended school, a YMCA, a Ladies' Aid Society, a Girls' Christian Endeavor, and a prosperous commercial life— expunged.[9]

Davis also recorded news he received from an American missionary, Dr. Floyd O. Smith in Diyarbekir, about a hundred miles southeast, who telegraphed Henry Riggs in Harput, describing what he called "the worst state of terror he had ever seen." Not an Armenian man dared appear on the streets, he informed his colleagues in Harput. Most of the men of the city had been arrested and imprisoned, and many had already been killed. Turkish "soldiers were stationed on the roofs of the houses ready to shoot at sight any Armenian who ventured to show his face even in his own dooryard."[10]

In a legal claim against the Ottoman government filed through the U.S. State Department in 1920, after her arrival in the United States, one genocide survivor from Diyarbekir, Nafina Chilinguirian (née Shekerlemedjian, later Aroosian), wrote in clear detached words about her arrest and deportation. In answering the questions on the U.S. State Department's claim form—"Application for the Support of Claims Against Foreign Governments"—Chilinguirian described the "state of terror" Dr. Smith was reporting to Leslie Davis:

> At 1 August 1915, our parish in Diyarbekir was besieged by the gendarmes under the command of the vali of Diyarbekir. The same day with the menace of death they removed us, the Armenians. We could take [with] us only our ready money, if it was easy to take, our birth and marriage certificates; my husband Hagop Chilinguirian's Naturalization Paper and Passport; all our other goods were left behind. The Turk officers of the Turkish Government, and by their allowance the Turk people, plundered and captured our goods left behind. The deporter gendarmes separated the men from the women and binding them to each other, they carried all of us to an unknown direction. After three days journey, they killed one by one the man deportees of whom only a few were saved. So were killed mercilessly my brothers and sisters, and other relatives mentioned in the Answer 55. My husband in spite of that he was a citizen of U.S.A. was forced to be deported with us, his Naturalization paper and Passport being taken of him by the gendarmes.

After her husband died on the deportation march, Chilinguirian, a twenty-five-year-old mother of two small daughters (Zivart, age two, and Arshalois, an infant), was robbed and beaten by "Turks and the gendarmes." She continued:

So for thirty-two days we were obliged to wander through mountains and valleys. Fatigue and hunger enforced by the whip of the
cruel gendarmes diminished the number of the deportees. After
many dangers whose description would take much time, a few
women and children, included I myself, arrived at Aleppo, Syria
in the beginning of September 1915.[11]

Events in Diyarbekir mirrored what Davis was calling a "reign of terror" in Harput. As June arrived, many of the Armenian men who had been
arrested earlier in spring and released "were now rearrested together with
hundreds of others . . . and thrown into prison." Most were "brutally tortured."[12] The Armenian professors at Euphrates College were among the
main targets. Alice Muggerditchian Shipley, whose father worked for the
British consulate and was smuggled out of the city, lived next door to one of
the college teachers, Professor Donabed Lulejian. She recalled that one professor, Mr. Vosperian, had lost his mind because he was forced to watch his
colleagues tortured to death by having their fingernails and toenails pulled
out, their hair and beards plucked out, and finally their eyes gouged out.[13]

Shipley recalled how the Turks dropped Vosperian naked on his
doorstep one night. For several weeks thereafter, this once distinguished
man ran up and down the streets at night naked and screaming like a mad-
man, until one day they found him dead. It was "a nightmarish scenario,"
she wrote, "that horrified the neighborhood."[14] What happened to the
Armenian cultural leaders in Harput was happening everywhere, and torture was used everywhere. In his memoir Ambassador Morgenthau
described the practices of Turkish torture:

A common practice was to place the prisoner in a room, with
two Turks stationed at each end and each side . . . [and] then
begin with the bastinado . . . a form of torture . . . [which] con-
sists of beating the soles of the feet with a thin rod . . . [until] the
feet swell and burst, and not infrequently . . . they have to be
amputated. The gendarmes would bastinado their Armenian
victim until he fainted; they would then revive him by sprinkling
water on his face and begin again. If this did not succeed in bringing their victims to terms, they had numerous other methods of
persuasion. They would pull out his eyebrows and beard almost

hair by hair; they would extract his finger nails and toe nails; they would apply red-hot irons to his breast, tear off his flesh with red-hot pincers, and then pour boiled butter into the wounds. In some cases the gendarmes would nail hands and feet to pieces of wood—evidently in imitation of the Crucifixion, and then while the sufferer writhed in his agony, they would cry: "Now let your Christ come and help you!"

One day I was discussing these proceedings with a responsible Turkish official, who was describing the tortures inflicted. He made no secret of the fact that the Government had instigated them and, like all Turks of the official classes, he enthusiastically approved this treatment of the detested race. This official told me that all these details were matters of nightly discussion at the headquarters of the Union and Progress Committee. . . . He told me that they even delved into the records of the Spanish Inquisition and other historic institutions of torture and adopted all the suggestions found there.[15]

Professor Lulejian, who had been educated at Yale and taught biology at Euphrates College, testified to such practices of torture. After escaping from prison after being tortured himself by the *kaymakam,* he hid in the consulate for several weeks and described to Leslie Davis the extent of the torture he and the others received in prison. Davis reported. Lulejian's experience: "Some were bastinadoed, some were beaten on their bare backs, some had their finger nails torn out."[16] According to Alice Shipley, others had their "nails and toenails pulled out," and then "they hanged them upside down in the outhouse until their heads were in the filth. Then they sliced the bottoms of their feet and poured salt on them."[17]

Then, on the night of June 23, a group of distinguished Armenian prisoners—including the bishop of the church, most of the professors at Euphrates College, and many of the leading merchants and professional men—were taken from the prison by oxcart and sent, like the Constantinople leaders, into the wilderness to be killed. On Saturday afternoon, June 26, Davis and his colleagues were startled, as Davis put it, "by the announcement that the Turkish Government had ordered the deportation of every Armenian, man, woman, and child (there were not many men left), in Mamouret-ul-Aziz, Harput and the adjacent villages."[18]

In his dispatch of June 30, 1915, Consul Davis wrote to Ambassador Morgenthau:

> Sir: I have the honor to report to the Embassy about one of the severest measures ever taken by a government and one of the greatest tragedies in all history. . . .
>
> Another method was found to destroy the Armenian race. This is no less than the deportation of the entire Armenian population, not only from this Vilayet, but I understand, from all six Vilayets comprising Armenia. . . .
>
> The full meaning of such an order can scarcely be imagined by those who are not familiar with the peculiar conditions of this isolated region. A massacre, however horrible the word may sound, would be humane in comparison with it. In a massacre many escape but a wholesale deportation of this kind in this country means a longer and perhaps even more dreadful death for nearly everyone. I do not believe it possible for one in a hundred to survive, perhaps not one in a thousand.[19]

What the American consul described was happening at that very moment to Armenians all over Turkey. It started in Harput and Mezre as it did in most places—with an announcement "by the town crier Mahmoud Chavoosh," Davis noted, "who went around the streets, accompanied by a small boy beating a drum, and called out the terrible proclamation in a stentorian voice." He gave the orders that "all those living in one part of Mamouret-ul-Aziz were to leave on Thursday, July 1st," and ordered the rest of the Armenians in the city to leave on Saturday, July 3; "those in Harput were to go on Monday, July 5th, and those in the neighboring villages of Huseinik, Keserik, and Yegheki a few days later."[20] Alice Shipley recalled how she and her sisters looked—"between the cracks of our curtains" from the second-story windows of their house with its European furniture and paintings—as the gendarmes emerged from the side streets into the square between the college and their house.[21]

The missionaries begged the Turkish officials to be allowed to go with the Armenians to help them in case of sickness and to assist in caring for the children. When they were told they couldn't, Davis grew furious. The *vali* adamantly refused, assuring the consul that every one would be "taken good care of," a phrase that Davis later understood to be a mockery.[22]

In every city, town, and village a significant part of the Armenian population was financially stable, or even wealthy, and this caused great resentment and envy among their Muslim neighbors. A disproportionate number of Armenians were successful in small business, trade, and commerce; they were artisans, craftsmen, and farmers as well as teachers, clergy, and physicians. Armenian culture was steeped in what later came to be called the Protestant work ethic. With the coming of the missionaries, a new class of educated and intellectual Armenians had emerged as an academic elite throughout the empire. By 1914 there were 1,996 schools and 451 monasteries stretching from Constantinople to Van.[23]

Armenian homes, whether modest or affluent, were often furnished with art, artifacts, carpets, and European furniture; and it was known by their Turkish and Kurdish neighbors that Armenians had their savings and often gold and valuable jewelry stored in their houses. Armenian churches—and there were some 2,530 of them across Turkey[24]—were not only places of worship but civic places where Armenian culture was collected and presented as part of the artistic and historic life of the community. Like small museums, Armenian churches housed rare scriptures and books as well as paintings, frescoes, gold-and-jewel-studded chandeliers, and other precious objects. Of the desecration of Armenian churches, Morgenthau later wrote:

> I do not believe that the darkest ages ever presented scenes more
> horrible than those which now took place all over Turkey. Nothing was sacred to the Turkish gendarmes; under the plea of
> searching for hidden arms, they ransacked churches, treated the
> altars and sacred utensils with the utmost indignity, and even held
> mock ceremonies in imitation of the Christian sacraments. They
> would beat the priests into insensibility, under the pretense that
> they were the centres of sedition. When they could discover no
> weapons in the churches, they would sometimes arm the bishops
> and priests with guns, pistols, and swords, then try them before
> courts-martial for possessing weapons against the law, and march

them in this condition through the streets, merely to arouse the fanatical wrath of the mobs.[25]

In 1915 the material wealth of Armenian culture was an open house for plunder. As the local Turkish and Kurdish community began pillaging Armenian homes, Davis looked on in horror:

> The scenes of that week were heartrending. The people were preparing to leave their homes and to abandon their houses, their lands, their property of all kinds. They were trying to dispose of their furniture and household effects, their provisions and even much of their clothing, as they would be able to carry but little with them. They were selling their possessions for whatever they could get. The streets were full of Turkish women, as well as men, who were seeking bargains on this occasion, buying organs, sewing machines, furniture, rugs, and other articles of value for almost nothing. I know one woman who sold a two hundred dollar organ to a Turkish neighbor for about five dollars. Sewing machines which had cost twenty-five dollars were sold for fifty cents. Valuable rugs were sold for less than a dollar. Many articles were given away, as their owners were unable to sell them and were obliged to leave them behind. The scene reminded me of vultures swooping down on their prey. It was a veritable Turkish holiday and all the Turks went out in their gala attire to feast and to make merry over the misfortunes of others.[26]

Henry Riggs was also astonished by what he saw. In the public square, there were "mountains of bedding, furniture and utensils . . . sold at auction . . . [for] one fifth of their value, and often far less." For many of the Muslims, it was "the opportunity of a life time to get-rich-quick." Some Turks and Kurds attacked the homes of defenseless women, raping them and taking their possessions. Some Turks, Riggs reported, especially those of "the better class looked with genuine horror at the treatment accorded to the Armenians, and when it came to enriching themselves as a result of the sufferings of the poor victims, they would not do it." Such booty they believed was *haram* (forbidden), and would put a curse on them and their legacies.[27]

It became clear to Davis that the Temporary Law of Deportation and Confiscation and its new Emval-i Metruke (abandoned goods) commission was a charade. The commission was ostensibly set up to guard the property of the deported Armenians and, after supposedly paying out of it any debts of the owners, was to send the money to them in their new homes. Most of the Armenians were killed, as was undoubtedly intended by the government, and as Davis put it, "none who survived ever received any money from the Committee."[28] As he tried to help Armenians claim their money, he realized that it was, as Consul Jackson later put it, "a gigantic plundering scheme."[29] After the commission had "gotten possession of hundreds of thousands of dollars," Davis noted, "it conveniently lost its books and explained that, as all the money received had been used up for expenses and there were no funds on hand, there was no necessity anyway of rendering any account!"[30] Deutsche Bank Director, Arthur von Gwinner, and the Ottoman parliamentary senator Ahmed Riza all reached similar conclusions.

Armenian businessmen were forced to abandon their businesses, their shops, their merchandise, their lifetime accumulations. Kerop Bedoukian watched in horror as the gendarmes took over his father's grocery store, and then "systematically," he writes, "the contents of the stores" everywhere were all being confiscated and "loaded onto ox-drawn carts" and supposedly "taken to government storage depots."[31] Farther west in Ovajik, near Ismit, not far from Constantinople, Serpouhi Tavoukdjian also watched as the Turkish gendarmes took "bolts of rich silks and cloth" from her father's store and then pillaged her brother Lazarus's toy store.[32] Antranig Vartanian, a fifteen-year-old boy whose family were livestock farmers on the Moush plain, described being forced by the Turkish gendarmes to go into a barn, where hundreds of Armenians had been burned alive, and take from the corpses jewelry and valuables. "I saw the corpse of a woman propped up by some barn beams," he recalled vividly. "She had been strangled to death outside of the barn, and the remains of a beautiful embroidered apron were still on her body. I saw gold bracelets and necklaces and other jewels on her body and I took them back to the gendarmes." The gendarmes were so delighted with the jewels that they spared Vartanian's life.[33]

Those who took their money with them were robbed of it immediately; others left it in the bank, and others deposited money and valuables with German or American missionaries. Realizing that the consulate was the safest place to leave money and valuables, still others deposited it with Leslie Davis, and his quarters soon became what he called "a safe deposit vault" for the Armenians. It was "pathetic," Davis recalled, "to see the people bringing their money, their jewels, their valuable documents, and articles of all kinds to the Consulate and to the missionaries, asking us to keep them."[34] With more than two hundred thousand dollars in gold hidden at the consulate, Davis worried about being raided by the Turkish authorities, and found it more than ironic that when the *vali* came over for evening tea and card games, the safe with the Armenian gold stood there in the same room. By the fall of 1915 Davis was receiving orders from the *vali* demanding that he turn over to the government all the money and property the Armenians had been leaving in his care. When he refused to comply, he found himself drawn deeper into the crisis.[35]

Davis was also horrified by the economic significance of killing off the Armenians; as he put it: "It was literally a case of killing the goose that laid the golden egg, for there would be no one left to till the soil and the authorities might have foreseen the famine which actually did visit the land the following year." Davis noted that "Nearly all the merchants, bankers, doctors, dentists, lawyers, teachers, carpenters, brick-layers, tile-makers, tinsmiths, bakers, tailors, shoe-makers, and other artisans so essential to the life of the people were Armenians. . . . By one stroke," Davis wrote, "the country was to be set back a century."[36]

By July 4 the town was in chaos, and Davis felt "stranded" amid "the terrible scenes" in "this uncivilized part of the world." So acute was his sense of crisis that he felt as if "the world were coming to an end." As the deportations continued, diplomatic life broke down, and Davis cancelled the customary ritual of holding a Fourth of July reception at the consulate, noting that "the Turkish officials were too busy in carrying out their plans to get rid of the Armenians" even to notice.[37] On July 1 the first group of deportees was sent to the desert south of Urfa, and on July 3 the second party was sent on a different road "to prevent the ones who left last from learning the fate of those who had preceded them." Several thousand Armenian soldiers had already been sent away from the government building (the Red Konak), and it was soon discovered that they were all

Sultan Abdul Hamid II in military dress. He ruled the Ottoman Empire from 1876 to 1908 and was responsible for the massacres and deaths of about 200,000 Armenians in 1894–96. Prime Minister Gladstone dubbed him the "great assassin," and the press referred to him as "the bloody sultan." *(From the collection of Mark A. Momjian)*

"The Trench Dug for the Bodies of the Victims" in Erzurum, October 1895, from *The Graphic* (London), December 7, 1895. The original caption reads, "This photograph shows the horrible spectacle presented to the visitors to the Armenian cemetery two days after the massacre. Two rows of dead, thirty-five deep, had already been laid down and partially covered . . . [in] a huge grave fifty-three feet square for the reception of the slaughtered Armenians." *The Graphic* covered the massacres with riveting images throughout the 1890s.

Boston's Faneuil Hall, a meeting place for political activists since the American Revolution and the site of the first meeting of the American movement on behalf of the Armenians, November 1894. *(Courtesy of Boston Athenaeum)*

Alice Stone Blackwell, daughter of the pioneering feminist Lucy Stone, was editor of the *Woman's Journal* and for nearly four decades a leader of the U.S. movement to save the Armenians. *(Painted by K. Skserjian; courtesy of the Library of Congress)*

Clara Barton, founder of the American Red Cross and leader of its first international mission—to aid Armenian survivors of massacres in 1896. *(Courtesy of the Library of Congress)*

Julia Ward Howe—abolitionist, suffragist, and, in her seventies, impassioned speaker against the Turkish massacres of the Armenians. Massachusetts Governor Frederick Greenhalge called her speech at the Faneuil Hall rally "a prose Battle Hymn." *(Courtesy of the Library of Congress)*

"The Troubles in Armenia—Retreating Villagers Pursued By Kurds," *Harper's Weekly,* March 14, 1896. *Harper's Weekly* covered the Armenian massacres throughout the 1890s with in-depth articles and vivid illustrations.

This cartoon from *Punch,* 1909, shows Europe appealing to the new Young Turk regime to stop massacring Armenians.

PUNCH, OR THE LONDON CHARIVARI.—May 5, 1909.

A FIRST DUTY.

Europa (*to the new Sultan*). "AS YOU 'RE A YOUNG TURK, SIR, I COUNT ON YOU TO MAKE A CLEAN SWEEP OF THE OLD METHODS."

The Adana massacres, April 1909: the razed Armenian quarter,
from Ernst Jäckh, *The Rising Halfmoon*. Berlin-Schöneberg, 1911.
(Courtesy of Informations-und Dokumentationszentrun Armenien, Berlin)

Adana massacres, April 1909: "Armenian children whose flesh was ripped
off with cotton-chopping tools and whose knee tendons were severed,"
from Ernst Jäckh, *The Rising Halfmoon*. Berlin-Schöneberg, 1911.
(Courtesy of Informations-und Dokumentationszentrun Armenien, Berlin)

The sheikh-ul-Islam, the spiritual leader of all Sunni Muslims, announcing on November 14, 1914, before the Fathi Mosque in Constantinople the *jihad* against "infidels and enemies of the faith." From *The History of the First World War* (Berlin, Union Deutsche Verlagsgesellschaft, n.d.). *(Courtesy of Informations-und Dokumentationszentrun Armenien, Berlin)*

Talaat Pasha, the Ottoman Empire's Minister of the Interior in 1915, who was chief director of the genocide of the Armenians. *(From Ambassador Morgenthau's Story by Henry Morgenthau)*

Enver Pasha, Minister of War in 1915 and a leading force in the plan to exterminate the Armenians. *(From the collection of Mark A. Momjian)*

Armenians were drafted into *amele taburlari*—labor battalions—of the
Ottoman army. Stripped of weapons, they were massacred while on
their labor assignments. *(Courtesy of Informations-und
Dokumentationszentrun Armenien, Berlin)*

Armenians being marched out of Harput under armed guard, May
1915. A German businessman took this photograph from his window.
(Photograph courtesy of an anonymous donor to Project SAVE)

Armin T. Wegner photographs. Armin T. Wegner was a second-lieutenant in the German Army, stationed in the Ottoman Empire. In 1915, Wegner defied orders and investigated the massacres of the Armenians, taking photographs of Armenian deportation camps in the Syrian desert. He was able to get some of his materials to Germany and the U.S. but was eventually arrested. In the 1930s he wrote Hitler imploring him to cease his treatment of the Jews. *(Armenian National Institute, Inc., Washington, D.C.; photos by Armin T. Wegner, courtesy of Sybil Stevens)*

Execution of Armenians in a public square.

1915: Armenian deportees walking.

Armenian deportees in a concentration camp in the Syrian desert.

Starved Armenian woman and two small children.

858, July 16, 1 p m.

~~Confidential.~~ Have you received my
841? / Deportation of and excesses against
peaceful Armenians is increasing and from harrowing reports of eye witnesses it appears that
a campaign of race extermination is in progress
under a pretext of reprisal against rebellion.
        Protests as well as threats are una-
vailing and probably incite the Ottoman government to more drastic measures as they are determined to disclaim responsibility for their
absolute disregard of capitulations and I believe nothing short of actual force which obviously United States are not in a position to
exert would adequately meet the situation./ Sug-
gest you inform belligerent nations and mission
boards of this.

                    AMERICAN AMBASSADOR,
                            Constantinople

Telegram from Ambassador Henry
Morgenthau to the Secretary of State, July
16, 1915, warning of "a campaign of race
extermination" against the Armenians.
(From the National Archives, State Department
Record Group 59. 867.4016/76)

Henry Morgenthau, U.S. Ambassador to
Turkey 1913–16. He worked tirelessly to
save the Armenians and bring the Genocide
to the world's attention. (From the collection
of Mark Momjian)

The New York Times

New York Times headlines of 1915. In 1915 alone, the *New York Times* published 145 articles on the Armenian Genocide. The coverage stressed that what was happening to the Armenians was "government planned," "systematic" "race extermination." (*Left to right:* October 4, October 7, and December 15, 1915.)

800,000 ARMENIANS COUNTED DESTROYED

Viscount Bryce Tells House of Lords That Is the Probable Number of Turks' Victims.

TELL OF HORRORS DONE IN ARMENIA

Report of Eminent Americans Says They Are Unequaled in a Thousand Years.

TURKISH RECORD OUTDONE

A Policy of Extermination Put in Effect Against a Helpless People.

ENTIRE VILLAGES SCATTERED

Men and Boys Massacred, Women and Girls Sold as Slaves and Distributed Among Moslems.

10,000 DROWNED AT ONCE

Peers Are Told How Entire Christian Population of Trebizond Was Wiped Out.

MILLION ARMENIANS KILLED OR IN EXILE

American Committee on Relief Says Victims of Turks Are Steadily Increasing.

POLICY OF EXTERMINATION

More Atrocities Detailed In Support of Charge That Turkey Is Acting Deliberately.

Armenian relief poster
by Douglas Volk, 1918.
*(Courtesy of Near East
Foundation, New York)*

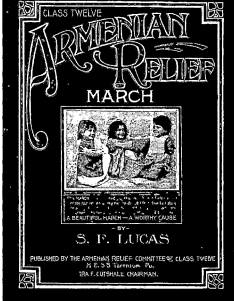

Sheet music sold to benefit
Armenian Relief, 1920.
*(From the collection of
Harry S. Cherken Jr.)*

Theodore Roosevelt called the Armenian massacres "the greatest crime of the war" and advocated U.S. intervention to save the Armenians. *(Courtesy of Harvard College Library, Theodore Roosevelt Collection)*

President Woodrow Wilson proposed a U.S. mandate for Armenia. He drew the boundaries for an independent Armenia in 1920, but the Wilson Award to Armenia and the Treaty of Sèvres were quashed by the Kemalist revolution in Turkey. *(From the Woodrow Wilson House)*

Starving Armenian refugees.
(James Barton, The Story of Near East Relief, *Macmillan, 1930)*

Orphans in Armenia, ca 1917–19
(Courtesy of Armenian National Institute, John Elder Photo Collection)

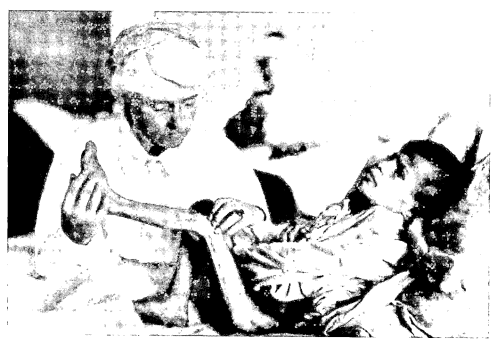

A Near East Relief nurse examines an Armenian child.
(*James Barton*, The Story of Near East Relief, *Macmillan*, *1930*)

"Children waiting in the snow for admission into the 'Orphan City,'
a daily spectacle from the early morning until late at night." The
Orphan City in Alexandropol, Armenia, was run by Near East Relief.
(*James Barton*, The Story of Near East Relief, *Macmillan*, *1930*)

Armenian orphans spell out "America We Thank You."
*(From the papers of Kate Clough and William Eagle Rambo,
with permission of Barbara Rambo Hoshiko)*

Sunday school children in the U.S. were recruited to raise money for relief of the "starving Armenians." *(From the U.S. National Archives and Records Administration)*

shot to death by the gendarmes. A band of deportees from Erzurum, mostly women, arrived in Harput and told Davis that all the men of their party "had been butchered" and that some of them had been left "absolutely naked," and the rest "robbed of everything."[38]

The experience of deportation was a shock to Armenians, who had been living peacefully in their domestic worlds and businesses and farms and then, in a matter of days, found themselves marching on foot under armed guard into the wilderness. The deportations quickly became either scenes of mass killing for the men, or death marches for the women, children, and elderly who were whipped, raped, tortured, and shot in an ongoing procession. Kerop Bedoukian's memoir, *Some of Us Survived*, depicts a ten-year-old boy's astonished and candid view of being on a march. "The caravan stretched out for miles," he writes, "wagon wheels squeaking, guards on horseback galloping back and forth, whipping anyone who straggled behind. I ran along the caravan to lift my spirits."[39] He reports the inner details of life on a death march. A gendarme wrestles a donkey away from a young woman with a baby, then "the Turk's scimitar descended on her wrist and the hand fell off." The boy feels guilt for watching this and being able to do nothing.[40]

As life on the deportation broke down and people were reduced to living like animals, young Bedoukian watches "a woman relieve herself in public." He stares in amazement as she yells, "They don't even let you shit in peace." Not long after, he noticed Turks coming around with "short sticks in their hands . . . tearing apart every pile of shit," in order to find gold coins they believed Armenians may have swallowed to hide from the officials.[41] As the caravan moved south from Sivas, Bedoukian saw rivers and brooks filled with "swollen" and "worm-eaten" corpses.[42]

In Harput the summer wore on, and Davis found himself working harder and harder to save Armenians, a people for whom at the start, he confessed, he had no particular affinity. But as events enveloped him, he followed his conscience and, day by day, became the diplomat as rescuer—an early version of Raoul Wallenberg, the Swedish diplomat who risked his life to save a hundred thousand Hungarian Jews. Davis found himself walking a tightrope with the Turkish officials against whom he was covertly working.[43] As the second week of July unfolded and "the town crier announced that on Tuesday July 13th, every Armenian *without exception* must go,"[44] Davis took further risks by housing Armenians at the consulate.

It was perhaps easier for Davis, psychologically and professionally, to start his rescue project by housing Armenians who were American citizens or had relatives in the United States. He later noted how great his satisfaction was when he returned home in 1918 and could tell those Armenian American families face-to-face that their loved ones back in Harput "had been saved." Making good use of the spacious, three-story consulate, Davis housed as many Armenians as he could inside and then began putting them in the garden. The garden was large, with high walls and mulberry trees that provided good cover for the refugees. All that summer about forty Armenians slept outside in that garden. And each night everyone at the consulate could hear the Turks in the square in front of the building holding prayer meetings. "We could all hear them piously calling upon Allah to bless them in their efforts to kill the hated Christians," Davis recorded. "Night after night this same chant went up to heaven and day after day these Turks carried on their bloody work."[45] During the day Davis made time to provide food as well, but he was so understaffed and now had so many people to feed that he decided it was best to go to the market himself each day to buy as much bread as possible, but always with great discretion "in order not to attract attention."[46]

Leslie Davis worked hard to save Armenians in his region, but he also believed he could make a difference by sending telegrams and dispatches to Ambassador Morgenthau with the hope that the reports they contained would help mobilize relief efforts back home. "Telegram after telegram and dispatch after dispatch" he wrote, "went out from the Consulate . . . to convey to the Embassy and the Department [of State] news of the terrible tragedy which was taking place around us." He hoped his dispatches would lead to what he called "some effective protest or some action taken to stop it," and hoped that "the civilized world might learn of the needs of the survivors."[47] Some of the telegrams did make it through, but many were intercepted by the CUP officials. Davis was not alone in his efforts; he worked carefully with other Americans and Europeans who also were risking their lives to rescue Armenians.

When the deportation orders were announced, Davis and six others went to see the *vali*, Sabit Bey. Four American missionaries—Dr. Henry Atkinson, Mr. Pierce, Henry Riggs, and his brother Ernest W. Riggs, the current president of the college—along with the German Protestant missionary Johannes Ehmann, and Mr. Picciotto, Austrian assistant director of the Ottoman Bank, were "received in sullen silence," Henry Riggs wrote. When the group asked the *vali* to halt the order for the deportation, they were told it was impossible, as "the order had been sent from Constantinople." As they adamantly requested provisions and safety for the Armenians on the deportation, Sabit Bey answered, "I am going to furnish them with guards who will see to it that no one harms them." He then assured them that "no one's nose shall bleed on the journey." The statements were so absurd, Riggs wrote, that it made them all the more anxious.[48]

One encounter with the Turkish authorities tested Davis's mettle and disclosed a new facet of the government's operation. At the end of the summer of 1915, a new police chief (*mudir*), Reshid Bey, was assigned to the district. A native of the region, he had been recalled by Talaat from his post in Baghdad because he knew the lay of the land so well. A fat, boyish young man with a smooth face, he played, as Davis put it, "one of the bloodiest roles of all in the tragedy enacted that summer." A ruthless fanatic, he was intent on one thing: wiping the region clean of Armenians. To Davis he was sociable and friendly, even though he disliked the consul's concern for the Armenians.[49]

On the occasion of one of the principal Turkish holidays that summer, Davis appealed to the *vali* to stop the deportations. The *vali* asked Davis to put his request in a formal letter and told him that the police chief would see him about it that evening. When Reshid Bey showed up at the consulate that night, he told Davis he had come to collect the letter that the *vali* had asked him to write earlier (asking for a reprieve for the remaining Armenians in Harput)—but he now demanded at the *vali's* request that Davis state in the letter "that all the Armenians who were guilty of plotting against the Government had been deported or otherwise punished and that none of those who remained were implicated in any plots or guilty of any offense against the Government." Davis was astonished by the request and understood immediately the motivation behind it. The *vali* and the police chief wanted to exploit his humane gesture "to make it appear," as Davis put it, "that all the Armenians who had been deported or otherwise punished were guilty of some offense against the Government." Furthermore, Davis was convinced "that the Turkish Government would have had it published in this form throughout the civilized world as a full justification by the American Consul at Harput."

As Davis entertained the chief of police, he was nervously aware of the more than forty Armenians sleeping in the garden or hidden away in parts of the consulate. Obsessed with obtaining this written statement from Davis, the police chief stayed till about two o'clock in the morning. Holding firm, Davis told him that he had no objection to putting his request to stop the deportations into writing, but he could not make any further statements about things he did not believe.

Still refusing to take no for an answer, Reshid Bey then offered to stop the deportations at once if Davis would just blame the Armenians for their fate. Continuing to bait Davis, Reshid Bey now claimed to have "just received new orders instructing him to take more severe measures than ever against the Armenians." If Davis "would only make the desired statement," he said, "it would save many lives." Revolted by these tactics, Davis called his bluff and refused to budge. "I had to take the responsibility," he later wrote "of refusing to give him the statement he sought and I am sure the result is no worse than it would have been if I had done as he asked."[50] The consul was correct in his assessment. The episode taught him something profound about the Turkish determination to exterminate the Armenians while simultaneously trying to cover up the crime.

LAND OF DEAD

A fter the summer had passed with ongoing deportations from the twin cities of Harput and Mezre, Krikor Maghakian, an Armenian whom Leslie Davis had taken in and made *cavass* (assistant), asked the consul if he would ride with him out to his native village of Bozmashen to see what was left of it. Davis agreed and also brought along Dr. Atkinson, the missionary physician at the American hospital in Harput.

On an early autumn day, the sky high and blue on Turkey's eastern plateau, Leslie Davis and his companions rode toward Lake Göeljük, through a region where thousands of Armenians lived in dozens of villages and towns. *Harput* (the Armenian name of both the city and the *vilayet*) means "stone fortress," is rugged highland, sliced by ridges, ravines, and valleys. Davis and his friends rode past fig and pomegranate orchards and through the broom and thyme flanking the dirt roads. The calls of hoopoes and larks, or a black hyena rustling the brush, broke the silence now and then. They pushed on under that seemingly endless pure blue sky until night, when they chose to sleep on the rooftop of the *khan* because they so feared the typhus-carrying lice in the rooms below.

In his journey south from the consulate in Mezre on that day in September 1915, Davis witnessed a panorama of what had become the century's first genocide. His skill as a writer, no doubt enhanced by his brief career as a journalist, enabled him to record what he saw in clean, stark images, without embellishment or emotional intrusion. In fact, his narrative of atrocity is remarkably contemporary.

Almost immediately upon leaving, on the road out of Mezre, they encountered scenes of death. They saw a man digging near a spring under a clump of trees by the road. As they got closer they realized he was "a gendarme digging two shallow graves in the sand." Alongside him they saw "the body of a dead woman," and "a few feet away was another corpse." By the nearby spring there was a dying woman with a child, and when Maghakian tried to give her some bread, she "cried out that she wanted to die." Whenever Davis rode by that spot in the coming months, he saw their skulls rotting in the sand.[1]

When they reached Bozmashen they found it in ruins. In what had once been a completely Armenian village of about three hundred houses, only two families now remained, and they had been spared "because they worked on the farm of one of the gendarmes who had charge of deporting the inhabitants of that village." The houses were in shambles—doors and windows smashed and the walls crumbling into the streets. They saw "no other living creature in this once prosperous village" except, Davis noted, "a few hungry looking cats . . . prowling around." When they reached Krikor's own house, which was "one of the largest and best," they found it "occupied by gendarmes stationed there by the Government." They went inside, talked with them for a while, and started back home.[2]

On the way back they decided to visit the neighboring village of Hoolakeuy, a village the size of Bozmashen, which also had been inhabited wholly by Armenians. They found a ghost town, the streets strewn with the remains of destroyed houses, everything in ruins except for half a dozen people wandering around aimlessly. In the weeks that followed, Davis, now astounded by the total destruction that had consumed the region, visited dozens of Armenian villages. Among them: Huseinik, Morenik, Harput Serai, Upper Mezre, Mezre, Kessrik, Yegheki, Sursury, Sursury Monastery, Tadem, Hooyloo, Shentelle, Garmeri, Keghvenk, Kayloo, Vartatil, Perchendj, Yertmenik, Morey, Komk, Hoghe, Haboosi, Hintzor, Hinakrak, Tcherkeny, Visian, Korpe, Hagop, Dzaroug, Harsek, and Pertag. "All of the purely Armenian villages were in ruins and deserted," Davis noted, and in those with mixed populations, "the Armenian homes were empty."[3]

"Everywhere it was a scene of desolation and destruction," Davis went on. "The houses were crumbling to pieces and even the Christian churches, which had been erected at great expense and with much sacrifice, had been pulled down." In their "fanaticism," Davis wrote, the Turks and Kurds "seemed determined not only to exterminate the Christian population but to remove all traces of their religion and even to destroy the products of civilization."[4]

One day not long after these excursions, a Turk confided to Davis that he had seen thousands of bodies around Lake Göeljük, some five hours to the southeast by horseback, and offered to take him there. Davis agreed, and they started out at about four o'clock in the morning on the Diyarbekir road in order to get away without being seen. Within miles they saw dead bodies alongside the road: "They had been covered with a few shovelfuls of dirt," Davis recalled, "as the gendarmes found it easier to do this than to dig holes for them. The result was that in almost every case one could see the arms or legs or even the heads sticking out of the ground. Most of them had been partially eaten by dogs."[5]

At the village of Mollahkeuy they moved on to the plain where they found several hundred dead bodies scattered over the dry ground, nearly all of them women and children. Later, a survivor described the massacre to Davis. "She had been brought there with the other inhabitants of her village and saw most of them killed." She had been left for dead among the corpses and escaped in the night; Davis gave her enough money to escape to Russia. Now, as they surveyed the landscape, they saw that some of the bodies had been burned. "I thought at first this had been done as a sanitary measure," Davis wrote, but his Turkish friend explained that the gendarmes and the Kurds would burn the bodies in search of gold pieces the Armenians often swallowed for safekeeping.[6]

They climbed a steep mountain and then descended into a valley that led to Lake Göeljük below—a spot that Davis recalled having been a favorite summer camping ground for the American missionaries and foreign service officers. A large and beautiful lake, Göeljük—a source of the Tigris River—was the only significant body of water in the region; its name, meaning "little lake," was a Turkish translation of the Armenian *Dzovuk*.[7] The banks of the lake were high and steep, with deep ravines. They rode around the lake, looking down at "hundreds of bodies and many bones in the water below." It was rumored that the Armenians had been pushed over the cliffs by the gendarmes—a rumor that "was fully confirmed," Davis wrote, "by what we saw. In some of the valleys there were only a few bodies," he wrote, "but in others there were more than a thousand."⁸ Davis perceptively realized how cleverly the Turks exploited the severe chasms in the rocky and remote topography in order to carry out the mass killing. Around Lake Göeljük, Davis noted that the ravines were "triangular in shape and shut in on two sides by high precipitous banks which the people when attacked were not able to climb. Two or three gendarmes stationed on each side could prevent a multitude from escaping that way." At the bottom, of course, there was nothing but water, and as Davis put it, a "row of fifteen or twenty gendarmes" could keep the Armenians from escaping into the water or along the narrow paths around the lake. "Thus the victims," he wrote, "were literally penned in and butchered in cold blood."⁹

The consul's descriptions bring us close-up in a way that witnessing with precise language can:

> One of the first corpses that we saw was that of an old man with a white beard, whose skull had been crushed in by a large stone which still remained in it. A little farther along we saw the ashes of six or eight persons, only a few fragments of bones and clothing remaining unburned. One red fez was conspicuous. There were also some skull bones, as they are the strongest and are always the last to be destroyed. These ashes were about twenty feet from a tree under which there was a large red spot. This upon closer examination proved to be blood, which appeared to have been there for two or three weeks. The tree had a number of bullet holes in it, indicating that the men whose ashes we saw had probably been stood up against it and shot.¹⁰

The ghoulish images seemed endless. As they approached the next ravine, they saw "a row of twenty or thirty heads sticking out of the sand at the edge of the water." Just the heads, Davis wrote, because "the gendarmes with characteristic Turkish negligence had buried the bodies in the sand at the edge of the lake because it was easier to dig and the sand had washed off and been blown away, leaving the heads exposed." Everywhere he looked there were corpses: corpses piled up on the rocks at the foot of the cliffs; corpses in the water and on the sand around the lake;

corpses filling up the huge ravines. As they passed a clump of trees covered with vines and bushes in the middle of a ravine, Davis's Turkish guide told him to look in, and he saw "about fifteen or twenty bodies under the trees, some of them sitting upright as they had died."[11] In one ravine Davis estimated that there were about a thousand corpses, in another about fifteen hundred. "The stench from them was so great" that Davis rode as high up on the ravine as he could, but he couldn't escape it.[12]

Davis learned that because the Muslims considered "the clothes taken from a dead body to be defiled," all the Armenians were forced to strip before being killed, and Davis describes "gaping bayonet wounds on most of the bodies." Because bullets were so precious, it was "cheaper to kill with bayonets and knives." Davis was also shocked to find that, as he put it, "nearly all of the women lay flat on their backs and showed signs of barbarous mutilation by bayonets of the gendarmes, these wounds having been inflicted in many cases probably after the women were dead." The bodies, they learned, were of Armenians who had been marched there from distant places.[13] In other parts of Turkey, the same methods of massacre by butchery were occurring because the Turks didn't want to waste ammunition. In Ankara and its surroundings, only a couple of hundred miles east of Constantinople, the killing was done with "axes, cleavers, shovels, and pitchforks," Krikoris Balakian wrote. It was like a slaughterhouse; Armenians were hacked to pieces, and the killing squads mixed with townspeople "dashed infants on the rocks" before the eyes of their mothers. The carnage around Ankara was so horrible that Talaat Pasha ordered more than forty thousand corpses to be quickly buried in mass graves, but the stench of death and the mounds of bodies overwhelmed the landscape.[14]

South of Harput, Davis and his companion left the lake, traveling through the village of Keghvenk, and again the stench of rotting corpses overwhelmed them. "We could smell the dead bodies," Davis wrote, but "as it was getting late and we had already seen so many, we did not feel like going even that distance out of our way to see any more." But as they rode from Keghvenk back to Mezre, they saw thousands of corpses half buried, and later Davis learned that many of them were the men who had been imprisoned before the deportation. Within ten miles of Mezre they saw the remains of Armenian camps where thousands had been held before they were massacred. Arriving home at about nine o'clock in the evening, Davis wrote: "I felt that I understood better than ever what the 'deportation' of the Armenians really meant. I felt also that I had not been wrong in speaking of Mamouret-ul-Aziz . . . as the 'Slaughter-house Vilayet' of Turkey."[15]

A few weeks later Davis made another trip to Lake Göeljük. This time he and Dr. Atkinson went by themselves. Leaving at about three o'clock in the morning one day in late October, Davis was eager to see the other side of the lake and get a fuller picture of the area. On the east side of the lake, they found many bodies of Armenians who had recently been killed, most likely the inhabitants of the village of Göeljük, which they found "absolutely deserted, except for a few hungry cats which were prowling around among the ruins of the houses."[16]

Again the scenes of death were everywhere. In one of the most remote places along the lake, Davis and Atkinson saw hundreds of bodies piled on top of one another on the beach. They lay "within a space not more than two or three hundred feet in length and hardly a quarter that distance in width." It was at the outlet of a steep small ravine leading to the lake, and as they rode down the hill they were shocked at how people could be brought to such a place. Then they saw that almost all of them were women and children who had been recently killed. "We noticed bayonet wounds on many of them. . . . One woman," Davis observed, "on the edge of the pile lay flat on her breast with the head of her little baby protruding from under her body. All of the bodies were naked," he went on, "and many of them showed signs of the brutal mutilation which the gendarmes inflicted upon so many of the women and girls whom they killed."[17] They turned away and clambered back up the bank. Feeling the exhaustion of their long day, they found the Kazim *khan* at the northern end of the lake on the Diyarbekir road and went to sleep on the roof in the bitter cold, wrapped in their blankets.

The next morning they woke feeling "stiff and lame," and continued their journey around the lake, finding "bodies and skeletons and bones everywhere." Many of the bones, Davis reported "were bleached and dry, showing that they had been there since early summer." After two hours they arrived at a large valley where they saw "more dead bodies than I had seen in any other place on either trip. We estimated," Davis wrote, "that there were not less than two thousand in that one valley." Davis's reportage was both close-up and panoramic. He noticed the body of a dead woman and "right alongside of her head was the body of a tiny infant that could not have been more than a few days old." Then he backed up and looked at what was the largest valley around the lake and saw it "strewn all over" with partially buried bodies. Everyone had been stripped naked, and nothing of value could be found anywhere.[18]

The actual process of deportation and massacre also became more apparent as Davis noticed the remains of deportee campfires with "a few broken jugs, a few earthen bowls, some wooden spoons, and quite a number of passports." The passports showed that the people were from Erzurum, among other places, and Davis referred to the valley, which covered several acres, as "one large burying ground."[19]

"We estimated," Davis wrote, "that in the course of our ride around the lake, and actually within the space of twenty-four hours, we had seen the remains of not less than ten thousand Armenians who had been killed around Lake Goeljik." And in later rides in the direction of the lake, which he made right up until the time he left his post in 1917, Davis wrote, "I nearly always discovered skeletons and bones in great numbers in the new places that I visited, even as recently as a few weeks before I left Harput."[20]

"That which took place around beautiful Lake Goeljik in the summer of 1915 is almost inconceivable," Davis wrote. "Thousands and thousands of Armenians, mostly innocent and helpless women and children, were butchered on its shores and barbarously mutilated." Having made two trips around the lake in the fall of 1915, Davis realized that remote, difficult-to-navigate places like Lake Göeljük were perfectly suited to what he termed "the fiendish purposes of the Turks in their plan to exterminate the Armenian population." This was part of the plan and process, and Davis now suspected that other such spots all over Turkey were being used for the same purposes.

They arrived home safely that evening, and as far as Davis knew, none of the Turkish officials were aware of his excursions.[21]

The slaughter of the Armenians throughout Harput was recorded and reported by many other neutral eyewitnesses, including American missionaries Tacy Riggs Atkinson and her husband, Dr. Henry Atkinson, both of whom kept diaries (Ms. Atkinson's has been published). The American missionary Henry Riggs, who had been President of Euphrates College, left behind one of the most detailed accounts of the Armenian Genocide in Harput in a riveting memoir, *Days of Tragedy in Armenia*. The Danish educator Marie Jacobsen also recorded her experiences, later published as *Diaries of a Danish Missionary—Harpoot 1907–1919: Eyewitness Account of the Armenian Genocide*. The German Protestant missionary Johannes Ehmann recorded his testimony, and some of it is included in the telegrams he sent his government imploring it to intercede. Alice Muggerditchian Shipley's *We Walked Then Ran* gives a detailed account of the arrest, deportation, and massacre in Harput, and Donabed Lulejian's memoir of his time in prison, *Those Black Days*, presents a vivid record of the torture and murder of the Armenian intellectuals and leaders of the Harput *vilayet*.

After being hidden in the consulate by Leslie Davis, Professor Lulejian escaped through the Dersim to Russia, where he stayed briefly. Shortly before his death in 1918 of typhus in Erzurum, where he had just started an orphanage for Armenian survivors, Lulejian wrote what might be called a prayer-prose-poem called "A Handful of Earth." His brother Levon recalled how, after passing through a ruined village littered with the corpses of men, women, and children, Donabed found a "piece of thick window-paper" in a stable and began writing.

> At least a handful of earth for these slain bodies, for these whitened bones! A handful of earth, at least, for these unclaimed dead. . . .
>
> We dislike to fancy the bodies of our dear ones worm-ridden; their eyes, their lovely eyes, filled with worms; their cheeks, their kiss-deserving cheeks, mildewed; their pomegranate-like lips food for reptiles.
>
> But here they are in the mountains, unburied and forlorn, attacked by worms and scorpions, the eyes bare, the faces horrible amid a loathsome stench, like the odor of the slaughterhouse. . . .
>
> There are our women with breasts uncovered and limbs bare. A handful of earth to shield their honor! There are our boys, naked and torn, with bullets in their hearts and in their heads: a handful of earth to cover them! There are our brides, disembow-

eled, hacked to pieces, with babies yet unborn: a handful of earth, only, to screen from our eyes this sorrowful scene! There are our boys with feet cut away and heads battered against the stone. . . .

Let the Armenian become a fossil. Let him be the disgrace of the civilization which tore him to pieces. . . . Let him be the curse of the religion which abandoned him and left him without succor. Give, God, the handful of earth requested of Thee![22]

What Leslie Davis testified to in his reports, Donabed Lulejian also testified to—although neither of them saw each other after the summer of 1915, months before Davis made his trip to Lake Göeljük. Lulejian transformed his witness into a benediction, into a prayer for the dead, reminding us that if language can't bring back the dead, it can insist on the sacredness of life, the civility of burial, and the dignity of memory.

as a place teeming with Armenian survivors, most of whom were sick or dying of dysentery and crammed into makeshift hospitals.[1] Hundreds of thousands of Armenians passed through Aleppo on their way to the Deir el-Zor desert about a hundred miles southeast, where they died of starvation, torture, and massacre. Today on that ground stands the Martyrs' Church, a Genocide memorial site, and the nearby area of Margadeh, still strewn with bones, is a frequented spot of pilgrimage.

With the new Ottoman government's wartime restrictions on diplomatic correspondence, all official dispatches to Constantinople had to be mailed unsealed, and inspected by a censor. Even though Jackson had close personal relations with Enver Pasha and Jemal Pasha, he found it impossible to "induce them to lift the restrictions" on his correspondence with the embassy in Constantinople.[2] Determined to circumvent the censorship and get his messages to Ambassador Morgenthau, he used a private courier and also communicated with a foreshortened code.

"It was in February, 1915," Jackson wrote, "that the Turkish Government decided to disarm the Armenians in Zeitun, a town situated about five days travel North of Aleppo, an action that was rightly judged to be the forerunner of further and more disastrous events in which the Armenian race was to be the main sufferer."[3] In the following weeks and months, the Armenians in the region just north and west of Aleppo—in Aintab, Alexandretta, Marash, Urfa, Biridjik, and many smaller towns and villages—were disarmed. In Marash, for example, Abraham Hartunian noted that as they were being deported they saw the corpses of the massacred Armenians from Zeitun "piled all over the outskirts of their city." It was clear from the start that the gendarmes were ordered to go into the most remote mountain towns—like Zeitun, Fundejak, and Dereköy. In Fundejak, for example, the Armenian men tried to hold off some three thousand Turkish military and killing squads, and the remaining Armenians—mostly women and children—were "annihilated."[4]

In Aleppo Province in the summer, Talaat Pasha installed the leadership he needed to carry out the genocide program. First he removed Jelal Bey and then Bekir Sami Bey as governors of Aleppo because they were too lenient with the Armenians. Finally Talaat brought in one of his protégés, Mustafa Abdullah Bey, who made sure the CUP plan would be put in place in Aleppo Province. By the summer, news of deportations from all over the empire reached Jackson: from Sivas, Erzinjan, Harput, Trebizond, Samsoun, Erzurum, Moush, Bitlis, Diyarbekir, Mardin, Malatia, Kayseri, Talas, Konia, Ankara, Broussa, Adana, Mersin, Hadjin, and hundreds of other towns and villages of Turkey.[5]

In late July 1915, Jackson reported that as the temperature ran somewhere between 105 and 115 degrees, "a group of more than 1,000 women and children from Harput was being conducted southward near Veren Chiher [Veran Shehir], East of Diyarbekir." The women and children were then turned over to a band of Kurdish *chetes* who abducted "the best looking women, girls and children, killing those who put up the most resistance," and beat and stripped the rest of the women, Jackson went on, "thereby forcing them to continue the rest of the journey in a nude condition." About three hundred of these women arrived in Aleppo days later "entirely naked, their hair flowing in the air like wild beasts," having traveled "afoot in the burning sun." Some of these women came to the consulate, and Jackson recorded that their bodies were "burned to the color of a green olive, the skin peeling off in great blotches, and many of them carrying gashes on the head and wounds on the body as a result of the terrible beatings."[6]

These scenes kept passing before Jackson's eyes, and only weeks later he described what he called "one of the most terrible sights ever seen in Aleppo," the arrival of "some 5,000 terribly emaciated, dirty, ragged and sick women and children, 3,000 on one day and 2,000 the following day." They were the only survivors, Jackson reported, of what he termed "the thrifty and well to do Armenian population of the province of Sivas," where the Armenian population had been "over 300,000 souls." They told Jackson that they had traveled about a thousand miles on foot since before Easter, and hundreds of the women had been carried off into harems, or raped, robbed, and left naked.[7]

What Jackson saw was the remnant of women who survived the kind of sexual violence that Aurora Mardiganian described in her survivor narrative, *Ravished Armenia*. Mardiganian, from a wealthy banking family in Chemeshgezek, a town north of Harput, was one of thousands of young Armenian girls raped and thrown into harems. Her descriptions of sexual violence confirm and go even beyond what Jackson saw and heard. Having been in a house full of Armenian girls who were raped and then killed by Turkish soldiers, she escaped and before long found herself with about four hundred young men and women who agreed to convert to Islam to save their lives. After they had converted, the gendarmes robbed them all, stripped the women and raped them in front of their husbands, who were tied up and forced to watch before they were killed. Then, the surviving women were marched to Malatia, south of Mezre near the Euphrates. Approaching the city of Malatia, they found the wells stuffed with the corpses of dead women, and as they entered the city, they saw sixteen girls crucified on wooden crosses, vultures eating their corpses. "Each girl had been nailed alive upon her cross, spikes through her feet and hands," Mardiganian wrote, "only their hair blown by the wind, covered their bodies."[8]

In Aleppo too, the city was becoming overwhelmed by corpses and famine-ravaged refugees. By the fall a typhus epidemic had broken out in the city and the surrounding towns and villages, and the entire place resembled something from the Black Plague. "The number that succumbed in the city was so great," Jackson wrote, "that the sanitary authorities could not cope with the situation, and the military authorities provided huge ox-carts into which the dead bodies were thrown, 10 or 12 in each cart, and the procession of 7 or 8 carts would proceed to the nearby cemetery with their gruesome loads of ghastly uncovered corpses, usually nude, with the heads, legs and arms dangling from the sides and ends of the open carts." At the cemetery, the gendarmes dumped the bodies into trenches that had been dug for the purpose. For months the procession of death carts passed in front of the consulate. Several of Jackson's closest friends and members of his consular staff died in the epidemic, and, as he wrote, his own survival seemed "almost a miracle."[9]

Because of his strategic location on the line of the deportation marches, Jackson quickly became a receiving station for reports on the atrocities in the region, and he informed Morgenthau that reigns of terror had begun in Diyarbekir and Urfa, and that the gendarmerie was now "searching the houses of the Armenians for weapons, and not finding any." In Urfa (the site of massacre and the burning of the cathedral in 1895–96), the gendarmes told the bishop of the city that unless weapons were produced, "the entire Armenian population" of Urfa would suffer the fate of Zeitun, where everybody had been massacred or deported in early April. What Jackson emphasized to Morgenthau was that "the people here [Urfa] have always been loyal to the Government and have never resisted; not even when they were butchered like sheep. Why the local Government persists in persecuting a population that has always had a good record for loyalty is very strange."[10]

In the terrible heat of August, writing again to Morgenthau (who was at his summer quarters on the Bosporus), Jackson enclosed a letter he had just received from the Reverend F. H. Leslie.[11] In the chaos of the deportations and massacres in the Urfa region, Reverend Leslie had just been made the American consular agent for the entire district of Urfa.

> My dear Consul Jackson:
>   . . . For six weeks we have witnessed the most terrible cruelties inflicted upon the thousands of Christian exiles who have been daily passing through our city from the northern cities. All tell the same story and bear the same scars: their men were all killed on the first days march from their cities, after which the women and girls were constantly robbed of their money, bedding, clothing, and beaten, criminally abused and abducted. . . . Their guards forced them to pay even for drinking from the springs along the way and were their worst abusers but also allowed the baser element in every village through which they passed to abduct the girls and women and abuse them. We not only were told these things but the same things occurred right here in our own city before our very eyes and openly on the streets. The poor weak women and children died by thousands along the roads and in the *khan* where they were confined here. There must be not less than five hundred abducted now in the homes of the Moslems of this city and as many more have been sexually abused and turned out on the streets again.[12]

Desperate and fearing total annihilation for the Armenians, Reverend Leslie begged Jackson to send him his own vice-consul, Samuel Edelman, to help. "I cannot handle this work nor remain here much longer,"[13] Leslie pleaded. Not long after, the American pastor was imprisoned for aiding the Armenians. Already mentally broken from what he had witnessed, he was now tortured in prison, and he committed suicide there. Later Jackson was able to get Leslie's wife and child out of the country.[14]

With reports like these coming to him, Jackson informed Morgenthau on August 19 about the fate of the Armenians in Aintab, about fifty miles north. A historic Armenian city on the eastern edge of Cilician Armenia, "the city of Aintab," Jackson wrote, "is being rapidly depopulated of Armenians, several thousands have already passed through Aleppo on their way to the South." Jackson also noted that as one of the wealthiest Armenian communities in the empire, the Aintab Armenians offered "a splendid opportunity for pillage." All their household belongings were plundered, and the stores of the Armenian merchants, who upheld the economy of the city, were stolen. Even that early, it became clear to Jackson that the plan to exterminate the Armenians was, as he put it: "a gigantic plundering scheme as well as a final blow to extinguish the race."[15]

Jackson described in detail the arrival of trains deporting Armenians from the north. "Since August 1, the German Baghdad railway has brought nine trains each of fifteen carloads," he wrote; each car was stuffed with thirty-five to forty people, so that already five thousand had arrived by train, making a total of twenty thousand who had already arrived. "They all relate harrowing tales of hardships, abuse, robbery and atrocities committed en route." In the twenty-five-mile span between Urfa and Arab Pournar, "the beaten paths are lined with corpses of the victims."[16] In a dispatch of September 29, Jackson would send Morgenthau charts and tables enumerating the railway deportations by city, town, and Armenian religious sect (Armenian Apostolic, Armenian Protestant, Armenian Catholic), and giving the numbers of children and adults. "The deportation of Armenians from their homes by the Turkish government," he concluded, "has continued with a persistence and perfection of plan."[17]

Thirteen-year-old Virginia Meghrouni and her mother found themselves on one of those cattle cars sent east to Ras ul-Ain. Full of survivors suffering from dysentery—"glued together in a car without windows," as she put it—the car stank of excrement, and when they reached Ras-ul-Ain, the guards shoved them out into the desert, calling them "infidel dogs," and telling them, "You're on your way to slaughter valley."[18]

From his vantage place in Aleppo, Jackson continued to watch the sweeping uprooting of the Christians from all over the empire. "From Mardin the Government deported great numbers of Syrians, Catholics, Caldeans, and Protestants," he wrote to the ambassador in Constantinople, "and it is feared all Christians may later be included in the order and possibly even the Jews." By August 19 Jackson reported that practically all the Armenians from the provinces of "Van, Erzerum, Bitlis, Diarbekir, Mamouret ul-Aziz, Angora and Sivas . . . have already been practically exterminated."[19] Conservative estimates, Jackson noted, had already placed the death toll by August 15 at well over five hundred thousand,[20] but a month later, Jackson informed Morgenthau that the survival rate of the deportation marches was about 15 percent, which put the toll of vanished Armenians at about a million.[21]

As the summer unfolded, Jackson, much like Leslie Davis in Harput, became more and more involved in rescuing Armenians. The Armenians in Aleppo, and nearby Meskene, Rakka, and Deir el-Zor were dying by the thousands daily, Jackson wrote Morgenthau. In Aleppo the consul was "furnishing funds" through the churches to about nine thousand Armenians. But, he told the ambassador, "I am trying to keep those in the outside towns alive, also, but it is a terrible task, as many persons have been beaten to death, and some hung or shot for having distributed relief funds." He underscored to the State Department that it was "a veritable reign of terror." "You cannot make it too black," he went on. "The sides of the roads are strewn with the bones or decaying bodies."[22]

As deportee encampments cropped up along the railroad tracks on the southwest side of the city, Jackson visited each of them once or twice a week to distribute bread or funds. While some were able to get shelter under ragtag tents, most of the Armenians were left out in blistering heat and sun. The deportation trail and the encampments continued south of Aleppo along the muddy, corpse-filled Euphrates as it moved past the towns of Meskene, Hamam, Rakka, Sebha, Abu-Harari, and finally to Deir el-Zor. At Ras ul-Ain, a station on the German Baghdad railway about 200 miles east of Aleppo, and about 180 miles east of the Euphrates River, Jackson reported that "careful estimates" placed the number dead at three hundred thousand.[23]

When Virginia Meghrouni and her mother were thrown out into the desert at Ras ul-Ain, they were stunned to find miles of large black tents in which thousands of people were dead or barely breathing. They went into a tent and saw people "stretched out on the bare ground, side by side," she writes, "some were dead and the ones still alive looked like cadavers, barely breathing." Flies, insects, and birds were eating corpses, and the stench was unbearable. Virginia remembers being frightened at the sight of the women who had escaped harems or slavery and bore the insignias of their captivity—severe tattoo marks on their bodies.

> They wore long, blue, sleeveless caftans with several, very long strips of cloth, swinging from the shoulders, to shield their faces against the desert winds. Some covered their heads with turbans; some toted cushions on their heads carrying heavy loads; some had babies suspended in cloth bags on their backs; some displayed rings in their nostrils. And all flaunted garish, dark blue tatoo marks—on their faces, bosoms, hands, arms, ankles, even knee caps.[24]

Armin T. Wegner, the German nurse and second lieutenant in Field Marshal von der Goltz's retinue, spent time, against orders, in the Armenian refugee camps at Ras ul-Ain (as well as Rakka, Meskene, Aleppo, and Deir el-Zor). From Ras ul-Ain in November 1915 he wrote:

> I have just returned, this very moment, from a round of inspection of the camp: hunger, death, disease, desperation on all sides. You would smell the odour of feces and decay. From a tent came the laments of a dying woman. A mother identifying the dark violet badges on my uniform as those of the Sanitary Corps, came towards me with outstretched hands.
>
> Taking me for a doctor, she clung on to me with all her might, I who had neither medicines, nor bandages, for it was forbidden to help her. But all this is nothing compared to the frightful sight of the swarms of orphans which increase daily. At the sides of the camp, a row of holes in the ground covered with rags, had been prepared for them. Girls and boys of all ages were sitting in these holes, heads together, abandoned and reduced to animals, starved, without food or bread, deprived of the most basic human aid, packed tightly one against the other and trembling from the night cold, holding pieces of still smoldering wood to try to get warm.[25]

Defying Turkish and German orders, Wegner took hundreds of photographs (which today comprise the core of the witness images of the

Genocide), made notes, wrote letters, and even carried letters from deported Armenians to Constantinople, where he gave them to Ambassador Morgenthau to send back to the United States. When a letter to his mother describing the Armenian atrocities was intercepted, he was kicked out of the Armenian camp zone and forced to work in the cholera wards, where he fell seriously ill and was sent back to Constantinople, and then to Germany. Risking his life, he hid in his belt the negatives of the photographs he and other German officers had taken.[26]

As things grew increasingly desperate in Aleppo and hundreds were dying daily of typhus and other diseases, of bayonet wounds, or starvation, and as dogs fought over the dead bodies of children, Jackson appealed to Morgenthau for funds from the American Committee for Armenian and Syrian Relief. Knowing that the ambassador was a bridge to the committee, he begged for $150,000 a month, "which would hardly furnish bread," he wrote, "to say nothing of clothing, shelter, medical treatment."[27] By October 1915 the relief process was under way back in the United States, and by late fall the money began to come from the committee in New York City, and Jackson started to feed and clothe as many survivors as possible.[28]

Like Davis in Harput, Jackson found himself in the midst of chaos, and soon the U.S. consulate in Aleppo became, as he called it, "the Mecca for the deported Armenians that were lucky enough" to survive. As the hungry, sick, and dying arrived in Aleppo daily begging for aid, Jackson urgently appealed to Morgenthau to raise more money back home in the United States for Armenian relief.[29] Although the Ottoman authorities had "issued strict orders" against giving aid to the Armenians, Jackson asserted, "I never paid the slightest attention to them." And, as thousands of refugees began arriving at the consulate by the day, Jackson found that distribution of relief became "most burdensome, and it was necessary to set apart the afternoons for this work."[30]

Not only did Jackson work in the camps along the Euphrates, but he supported the heroic work of Beatrice Rhöner, a Swiss missionary who had been working in Marash, and of Norah Altounyan, the daughter of a prominent Armenian doctor of Aleppo and an Irish missionary. Each of these women opened up several orphanages. Beatrice Rhöner was later killed for her relief work, but the orphanages continued to operate even after Jackson left Aleppo in 1917, when another brave Swiss resident of Aleppo, Emil Zollinger, took over the operation.[31]

The consulate was busy night and day helping Armenians escape further redeportation. Daily the Turkish officials came "fanatically," as Jackson put it, looking for Armenians who were sheltered at the consulate. At night the consular staff sneaked the refugees out to "secret friends among the townspeople" and "even to the friendly Bedouin Arabs adjacent to the city."[32]

Between Aleppo and the surrounding towns and villages, there were about two hundred thousand Armenian refugees needing relief as Jackson began to correspond and work closely with the American Committee for Armenian and Syrian Relief at "No. 1, Madison Avenue, New York City," as he recorded. As in Harput, many Armenians in Aleppo left their money and valuables at the consulate, all of which Jackson was able to protect and return until he was forced to leave in 1917, when he turned the remaining valuables over to the Dutch consul for protection.

Jackson began to receive hundreds of letters and telegrams from Armenian Americans in the United States inquiring about their families who had been deported to Aleppo and vicinity. Vice-Consul George W. Young spent most of his time tracking down refugees and replying to the anxious relatives overseas. These messages and much other valuable information, "including copies of military and political reports, and details of massacres and racial disturbances," Jackson burned at the instructions of the State Department before leaving Aleppo. He was forced to destroy twelve years' worth of what he considered valuable historical information. But he felt there was no alternative, especially in light of what had happened to the French consul general at Beirut, who in failing to destroy his records found them seized by the Turks. As a result "more than sixty estimable men of Syria were exposed and hanged, and some 5,000 more were deported and all had their property confiscated by the Turkish Government."[33]

As Jackson struggled to rescue Armenians and as he watched their property and wealth being confiscated, Morgenthau was dealing with Talaat Pasha back in Constantinople. He continued to try to reason with the minister of the interior, telling him that after the war he would have to meet with "public opinion everywhere, especially in the United States. Our people," he said, "will never forget these massacres. . . . You are defying all ideas of justice." Not only was Talaat unreachable, but at one point, he changed the subject and made an astonishing request. Knowing that many Armenians with American ties had life insurance policies with the

New York Life Insurance Company and the Equitable Life of New York, Talaat said to the ambassador: "I wish that you would get the American life insurance companies to send us a complete list of their Armenian policy holders. They are practically all dead now and have left no heirs to collect the money. It of course all escheats to the State. The Government is the beneficiary now. Will you do so?"

Outraged by this, Morgenthau lost his temper, told Talaat he would never get such a list from him, and stormed away.[34]

As the summer of 1916 arrived, Jackson was still working hard, trying to outsmart the Turks and bring relief to the Armenians of the outlying regions. In August he sent one of his part-time employees, German businessman Auguste Bernau, to the towns of Meskene, Rakka, and Sebka, southeast of Aleppo and close to the death zone of the Deir el-Zor. When Bernau's report of his mission was forwarded by Jackson to the Chargé d'Affaires Hoffman Philip at the American Embassy in Constantinople, it was sent on to Secretary of State Robert Lansing in Washington, marked "Very confidential." The Bernau report arrived safely at the State Department in late September 1916, and the markings on it indicate that Secretary of State Lansing and President Wilson both read it.[35]

Bernau left Aleppo on August 24, 1916, and arrived in Meskene six days later. As an agent for the Vacuum Oil Company, Bernau was hoping that his business trip to the region might disguise his covert mission to help the Armenians. But when Jemal Pasha learned of Bernau's relief mission he was furious and threatened to have Bernau arrested. Jackson ignored the governor's threat, and as he wrote to Hoffman Philip back at the embassy, "I can see no other way than to continue, even in the face of disastrous results to myself."[36] So with three million Turkish lira, under Jackson's auspices, Bernau went to those areas along the Euphrates that were clotted with concentration and refugee camps.[37]

"It is impossible to give an account of the impression of horror which my journey across the Armenian encampments scattered all along the Euphrates has given me," Bernau wrote Jackson. "Brutally dragged out of their native land," naked, starving, robbed of everything, he found them "penned up in the open like cattle." A few of the survivors had made makeshift tents out of cloth and had bought watermelons or a sick goat for food, but everywhere, he reported, "you see emaciated and wan faces, wandering skeletons, lurking for all kinds of diseases and victims moreover to hunger."³⁸ And, "The young girls, often even very young ones, have become the booty of the Musulmans." If they weren't killed, he noted, they were raped and sold into slavery or harems.³⁹

But even Bernau had not seen what Aurora Mardiganian experienced north of Aleppo in Diyarbekir, where the killing squads played "the game of swords" with Armenian girls. Having planted their swords in the ground, blade up, in a row, at several-yard intervals, the men on horseback each grabbed a girl. At the signal, given by a shout, they rode their horses at a controlled gallop, throwing the girl with the intent of killing her by impaling her on a sword. "If the killer missed," Mardiganian writes, "and the girl was only injured, she would be scooped up again until she was impaled on the protruding blade. It was a game, a contest," the traumatized survivor wrote in her memoir, and after the girls were dead, the Turks forced the Jews of the city to gather up the bodies in oxcarts and throw them in the Tigris River.⁴⁰

"As on the gates of 'Hell' of Dante," Bernau wrote, "the following should be written at the entrance of these accursed encampments: 'You who enter, leave all hopes.' " Feeling that what he had "seen and heard surpasses all imagination," he underscored: "I thought I was passing through a part of hell. . . . everywhere it is the same Governmental barbarism which aims at the systematic annihilation through starvation of the survivors of the Armenian nation in Turkey, everywhere the same bestial inhumanity on the part of these executioners and the same tortures undergone by these victims all along the Euphrates from Meskene to Der-i-Zor."⁴¹

In Meskene alone, Bernau reported, there were sixty thousand Armenians buried, and "as far as the eye can reach mounds are seen containing 200 to 300 corpses." Bernau saw men, women, and especially children eating "herbs, earth and even their excrement," and every day dozens were dying of typhus and dysentery. As he watched a group of women who were searching for barley seeds in some horse dung, he gave them bread and they "threw themselves on it like dogs dying of hunger, took it voraciously into their mouths with hiccups and epileptical tremblings." Within minutes another 250 women, children, and old people who hadn't eaten for a week "precipitated themselves towards me from the hill," Bernau wrote, "extending their emaciated arms, imploring with tears and cries a piece of bread."[42]

Bernau also noted what had become a pattern around the empire. When a government official was discovered to be lenient toward the Armenians, Talaat saw to it that he was immediately replaced. The governor at Deir el-Zor, Ali Souad Bey, had placed under his protection a thousand orphans and "was looking after their subsistence." He was quickly removed from his post and replaced with the fanatically anti-Armenian Zekki Bey, who ran a new reign of terror with tortures, public hangings, and mass killings.[43]

Bernau begged Jackson to keep some flow of money coming, even though the Ottoman authorities were trying to halt any and all aid. If funds were not sent, Bernau wrote with urgency, "these unfortunate people are doomed; if, on the contrary the funds are fairly substantial, it is believed that many among them can survive" until the war is ended and their fated decided. "I think, Mr. Consul, I have said enough regarding this forsaken wreck of humanity," Bernau signed off, "so that immediate measures be taken for the purpose of giving them assistance, and under the impression that my weak voice will be heard and bring results I close my report and beg you to accept the assurance of my most distinguished sentiments."[44]

———⬤⬤⬤———

"SAME FATE":

REPORTS FROM ALL OVER TURKEY

A s Armenian relief was being mobilized back in the United States, consular dispatches from all corners of Turkey affirmed what Leslie Davis and Jesse Jackson were reporting from their outposts. Oscar Heizer in Trebizond and W. Peter at Samsoun, both on the Black Sea coast, Charles E. Allen from as far west as Adrianople in Thrace, Edward I. Nathan in Adana and Mersin, and George Horton in Smyrna were all communicating with Ambassador Morgenthau. These reports also were crucial to Morgenthau's assessement of the bigger picture, and this chain of communication from the remotest outposts in the interior of Turkey through the ambassador in Constantinople to the United States was essential for the mobilization of the Armenian relief efforts that would have a large impact on wartime and postwar American culture.

Writing from the historic Greek city of Trebizond, where much of the indigenous Greek population would soon be wiped out as well,[1] the American consul Oscar Heizer told Morgenthau in July of 1915 that he was having a difficult time maintaining cordial relations with the Turks, who were "very hostile to all outside suggestion and interference in their internal affairs." Nevertheless he felt it urgent to explain to Morgenthau what was going on—"I desire to write to you confidentially in regard to the events which have taken place here recently."[2]

"On Saturday, June 26th," he wrote, "the proclamation regarding the deportation of all Armenians was posted in the streets." By Thursday, July 1, "all the streets were guarded by gendarmes with fixed bayonets, and the work of driving the Armenians from their homes began." From the consulate, Heizer watched "groups of men, women and children with loads and bundles on their backs" being driven past, headed to "the road toward Gumushhane [sic] and Erzingan in the heat and dust." A whole society was marched past him: "clergymen, merchants, bankers, lawyers, mechanics, tailors and men from every walk of life," and, as he put it, the "whole Mohammedan population knew these people were to be their prey from the beginning and they were treated as criminals." What he found even more unfathomable was the brutalization of the women and children.[3]

Leon Surmelian, the son of a prosperous pharmacist in Trebizond, remembers the shock of waking up one morning in June 1915 to find "a Turkish soldier with fixed bayonet at our door," and in the distance dozens of Turkish soldiers guarding the roads, with their "bayonets flashing in the early morning sun." The gendarmes searched their house for weapons and found none. A week later the town crier posted notices on the streets from the governor, ordering the Armenians to be ready to be deported "for the duration of the war." Any Muslim who protected or hid an Armenian would be punished by hanging, the order read.[4]

As soon as the deportees became weak and fell behind, they were "bayoneted," Heizer reported, "and thrown into the river and their bodies floated down past Trebizond to the sea, or else lodged in the shallow river on rocks," and so the stink of putrefaction was everywhere. Various eyewitnesses reported to Heizer that two weeks later, bodies were still rotting "on snags in the river" and that "the smell was something terrible."[5]

"By July 6," Heizer wrote to Morgenthau, "all the Armenian houses in Trebizond, about 1000, had been emptied of inhabitants," and the people put on forced marches. "There was no inquiry," Heizer underscored, "as to who were guilty or who were innocent of any movement against the government. If a person was an Armenian that was sufficient reason for being treated as a criminal and deported."[6] Although the Vatican was protesting the massacres and seeking special protection for the Catholic Armenians, Pope Benedict XV's letter to the sultan requesting this didn't arrive until September, and by then the Catholic Armenians had been sent to their deaths along with the rest.[7] As occasional survivors returned from near drowning, Heizer learned that the Turks were now filling boats with Armenian men and taking them out to the Black Sea and drowning them, and he watched with horror as the boats came back empty each day. In the end it is estimated that thousands were drowned in the Black Sea.[8]

As he watched from his office day by day, Heizer was shocked at what Jesse Jackson had referred to as the Ottoman government's "gigantic plundering scheme." Again, to Morgenthau, he described how the Armenian houses in Trebizond were "being emptied of furniture by the police one after the other. The furniture, bedding and everything of value is being stored in large buildings about the city," he reported. Since there was no attempt at labeling or properly storing any of these objects, Heizer reported, the idea that the government had any plan to return anything to the Armenians was "simply ridiculous."[9] Like Henry Riggs, who described Turkish women plundering Armenian goods in Harput, Heizer also watched a "crowd of Turkish women and children follow the police about like a lot of vultures and seize anything they can lay their hands on." As soon as the more valuable things were taken out of a house by the police, the women and children would rush in and take the rest, leaving every house stripped clean. "I see this performance every day with my own eyes," Heizer wrote the ambassador; "I suppose it will take several weeks to empty all the houses and then the Armenian shops and stores will be cleared out." And the government's commission, which was supposed to be overseeing all this, had no intention of returning any of the goods to the Armenians.[10]

Leon Surmelian watched his family life and his comfortable home with its Parisian furnishings and carpets and piano disappear overnight. The young boy also watched in despair as the Turks confiscated his father's pharmacy: "We almost wept when we saw the shutters of our pharmacy drawn in broad daylight. . . . Poor father, they had taken his pharmacy away from him," and everywhere "the city was dead, the stores closed, the streets deserted."[11] When Surmelian escaped from captivity a year or so later, he sneaked back to his family's house, only to discover that it had been picked clean of every item. As he walked the empty rooms he was haunted by the absence of what had once been his childhood home. "Even the linoleum had been stripped off the floor," he exclaimed. He soon discovered that every Armenian house in the region had been plundered and walls and floors torn up in the search for hidden treasures.[12]

Every day Heizer received testimony, and some of it directly from the perpetrators. One day, for example, Heizer spoke with a young man who had been doing his military service in the construction or labor battalion (*inshaat tabouri*), building a road out toward the town of Gümüshane. "He told me," Heizer wrote, "that fifteen days ago all the Armenians, about 180, were separated from the other workmen and marched off some distance from the camp and shot." He heard the gunfire, and shortly after, he and some others were "sent to bury the bodies which he stated were all naked having been stripped of clothing."[13] The bodies of women and children kept being "thrown up by the sea upon the sandy beach below the walls of the Italian Monastery," and Heizer watched as Greek women buried them in the sand. Another Turkish man, who held a high position in the Trebizond government, came to the consulate and spoke to the vice-consul with great emotion about what he termed the "inhuman treatment" to which the Armenians of Trebizond were being subjected.[14]

Writing on July 10, 1915, from the American consulate at Samsoun, about two hundred miles west of Trebizond on the Black Sea, Consul W. Peter explained to Morgenthau that the process of forced conversion to Islam was another method the Turks were using to expunge the Armenians and their culture. Peter reported, "Until now about 150 families have been converted to Islamism and the rest [have] been sent to the Interior."[15] Leon Surmelian, whose experience was representative of what many Armenians went through, described how he and a group of other Armenian boys were put up on an auction block outside of Trebizond to be bought by Muslim families and thus forcibly converted. In Surmelian's case, it proved to be a way to gain time, as he lived with a Muslim family for a while and then escaped.[16] Even though the Armenians had converted, Peter explained to Morgenthau, the *mutassarrif* had made it clear that even the Islamicized Armenians would still have to leave.

Peter went on to explain that the men had already been massacred by the local peasants, and that the women and children would soon die of "hunger, thirst and despair." Again the material wealth was confiscated, and Peter noted that "the private houses of Armenians as well as their stores and depots have been sealed by the Government, but they have already begun to fill a good number of these dwellings" with displaced

Muslims from the Balkans, *muhajirs*, local Turks, and emigrants from elsewhere in the region "who will surely steal everything in them."[17]

In late August, Peter wrote to Morgenthau describing the network of deportation and massacre that spanned out from the major cities south of Samsoun, Amasia, Tokat, and Sivas and east to Arabkir, Malatia, Harput, and Erzinjan. An Ottoman official, Arditti, who was an inspector of public debt, "gave me," he wrote, "confidentially the following details":

> 1) Samsoun, Amassia, Merzifoun people, all arrived to Amassia. Then all men were taken, bound and some of them killed between Amassia, Tokat and Turchal. All those who arrived to Tokat were directed toward Tchiflik or Gishgischa and murdered. Women and children were taken in ox-carts to Scharkysschla then they were sent to Malatia and finally thrown in the Kyrk Gos or Euphrates.
>
> 2) Tokat. The same thing as above with the difference that all pretty women and all children were taken in the Turkish houses.
>
> 3) Erbaa, Nixar, Messoudieh. The men were bound during the night and then thrown in part in the river Kelkit. The others were murdered near Tokat. Women and children, via Scharkyshla, Malatia same fate as No. 1.
>
> 4) Scharkyshla, Gemereck, Azizieh, Gorun, Derendeh, all sent on foot to Malatia, same fate.
>
> 5) Sivas, Divrik, Kangal in ox-carts to Kangal, then all on foot to Malatia, men murdered en route, same fate.
>
> 6) Egin, Arabkir, Keban, Kharpout, Malatia, same fate.
>
> 7) Karahissar, Souchehri, Zahra, Chavik, all murdered.
>
> 8) Erzinguian, Kamch part murdered, the rest thrown in the Euphrates.[18]

Peter underscored that "all Armenians have been killed, according to the Inspector. . . . Not one Armenian is to be seen."[19]

As far west as Adrianople, in Thrace, in March 1916, Consular Agent Charles E. Allen described his view of the process of Turkification and general ethnic cleansing. Once again the Turks employed forced conversion to Islam and installed *muhajirs* in the homes of deported Armenians, but in this case the Greeks, who were the largest Christian population there, were the worst hit. The authorities are working toward "the Turki-fication of Thrace," Allen wrote Morgenthau. "They are simply expelling" the Greeks and seizing their property, and "installing" Muslims in their houses. About half the Greek population of Thrace had already been deported back to Greece, and the few remaining Armenians had con-verted to Islam to avoid death, and would "be required to intermarry with the Turks." Allen conjectured that "this method of securing the disap-pearance of the Armenian race" might have been promoted by the Ger-mans in order to prevent more killing, as "the Turks would probably have preferred a quicker and more effective method."[20]

Not far from Adrianople, in Ovajik, just west of Constantinople, ten-year-old Serouphi Tvoukdjian woke to find the town crier ordering all Armenian families to prepare to be deported in four days. They were "herded into side-entrance box cars," taken by rail to Konia and Adana, and then released and forcibly marched into the Syrian desert.[21] Farther west in the great port city of Smyrna, the American consul, George Hor-ton, documented a similar Turkification frenzy in a report to Secretary of State William Jennings Bryan in February 1915. "I have the honor to inform you," he wrote, "that lawless Turkish bands are appearing in increasing numbers in this district and are spreading a reign of terror among the Christians of all races." Horton closes his letter to Bryan with the refrain of a song Turkish students in Smyrna were singing:

> Revenge! Revenge! Revenge!
> Let us kill, let us cut to pieces,
> Let us swim in blood up to our knees,
> Revenge! Revenge! Revenge!
> Let us wipe the stain from our clothes.[22]

Farther south along the Mediterranean coast, in Adana Province, which still bore the scars of the 1909 massacre, Consul Edward Nathan reported the same pattern of massacre and deportation that was in motion in all other areas of Turkey. Writing to Ambassador Morgenthau on July 26, 1915, Nathan informed him that "deportation measures on a large scale" are to be carried out "against Armenians in the cities of Adana, Tarsus and Mersina."[23]

So rapid and massive was the deportation from Adana and its *vilayet* that in Katma, at the eastern edge of Cilicia, Shukru Aghzarian and some of the other surviving deportees "found about 200,000 Armenian deportees living in tents without food or water." Hundreds were dying by the day, and to make this worse, the "local Turks," Aghzarian writes, "threw offal into the wells" and "often cut the ropes" on the water buckets.[24]

Nathan emphasized that the Ottoman government had sent a "member of the Special Commission on Deportations . . . to superintend the matter." The deportees were forced to give all their real estate titles to the authorities, and the rest of their immovable wealth, he noted, was "taken possession of by the Government."[25] The entire region, Nathan explained, was being stripped of its "best commercial element." Because the Armenians were the chief employees of foreign businesses such as the Singer Manufacturing Company, the German agricultural machine companies, and the various petroleum companies, the impact on the region would be disastrous.[26]

Again, the pillaging of Armenian wealth happened simultaneously with the deportations. North of Tarsus and Mersin in the city of Marash, Abraham Hartunian described his disbelief: "The gendarmes swarmed through the Armenian quarter and drove the dwellers out with their whips. There was no sparing the old, the children, the women." By official order the Armenians were driven "out of their houses," leaving "behind their palatial mansions, fertile fields, fruitful gardens, vineyards, and fabulous riches, and they passed through the streets with only the clothes on their backs."[27] Donik Yessaian received a letter in Detroit, where he was then living, from his adopted Turkish brother Hashim, ten miles east of Kayseri in the town of Efkereh. Hashim reported on the deportation in their town and how "the soldiers swarmed into the houses like hungry locusts and demanded that the Armenians give up all their jewelry, money, rugs, and other valuables." In return they gave the women "government receipts."[28]

Nafina Chilinguirian's account of the government's confiscation and pillaging of her family's wealth provides a unique close-up view. In her suit against the Ottoman government, filed under the auspices of the U.S. State Department's "Claims Against Foreign Governments," Chilinguirian was asked to make an itemized list of goods stolen from her family, and she recorded the following. From her husband's shop in Diyarbekir: "1000 kg. of sugar; 500 kgs of coffee; 2000 kgs. of hemp-cords; 1000 parcels of sacks;

1000 curry combs; 25,000 kg. of rice; 6000 kgs of gall-nuts." Similarly, at her brother Harutiun Shekerlemedjian's shop in the village of Karadja Hagh, 150 tons of rice were confiscated by the government, along with his entire stock of clothes and textiles: calicoes, clothes, silks, and leather. Jewels and available money, she goes on to list, were stolen from her brothers and sisters. So thorough was the pillaging that Mrs. Chilinguirian wrote that the Turks stole the "jewels and money . . . that were kept in the ground in a box" at her family's house.[29]

She then listed the murdered members of her family, all of whom had been living peacefully in their homes when they were seized and killed during the first days of August 1915:

My father Hagop Shekerlemedjian, 75 years old, killed by Turks
My mother Lucia Shekerlemedjian, 50 years old, killed by Turks

" brother Dikran	"	35	"	"	"	"	"
His son Karnig	"	7	"	"	"	"	"
My brother Harutiun	"	30	"	"	"	"	"
His son Levon	"	2	"	"	"	"	"
" daughter Azniv	"	5	"	"	"	"	"
My sister Hadji Anna Der Hovsepian 28	"	"	"	"	"		
" " Arusyag Berberian	25	"	"	"	"	"	
" aunt Gadar Keshishian	55	"	"	"	"	"[30]	

In Adana *vilayet,* Consul Nathan noted how effective the CUP infrastructure was and how the arrival of Ali Munif Bey, *musteshar* of the Foreign Office, and the local CUP club had helped to deport more than six thousand Armenians in a short time.[31] In early September, writing from Mersin, Nathan informed Morgenthau that "thousands of additional Armenians from the north have arrived here and been transported to the Aleppo region."[32] In October, Nathan's report to Morgenthau opened with the words: "I have the honor to inform Your Excellency that the stream of deported Armenians from the North continues unabated." Nathan underscored that the "Police and other officials also forbid them [the Armenians] to be aided, which makes it evident that slow death is the ultimate fate of the majority." Like Jesse Jackson, Leslie Davis, Oscar Heizer, Henry Riggs, and others, Nathan too witnessed the endless plundering. "The new law concerning the real estate and personal property of deported persons is being carried out in a manner which I fear will leave little if anything for the Armenians," he reported. As in many parts of Turkey, the Armenian houses were being taken over by *muhajirs* and Ottoman officials. And, in a manner now familiar in towns and cities all over the country, "the goods of deported merchants," Nathan told Morgenthau, "are being taken possession of by Commissions designated for this purpose and abuses of all kinds are reported."[33]

By November 1915 Nathan was writing to Morgenthau with further "distressing" details of starvation and disease. Nathan hoped that Morgenthau's appeal to the Ottoman government would be heeded, and expressed frustration at European inaction. He reminded Morgenthau of what happened in Adana *vilayet* in 1909, when neither the British nor other European governments with their warships in the harbor at Mersin did a thing to prevent thousands of Armenians from being massacred. Now he feared history would repeat itself, and worse.[34] In that same month Armin T. Wegner wrote about traveling through the same region. "The roads are lined," he wrote in a letter, "with famished and suffering Armenian refugees, like a weeping hedge that begs and screams, and from which rise a thousand pleading hands; we go by, our hearts full of shame. . . . This flood of outcasts, hundreds of thousands of refugees, drags itself along through the Taurus and Amanus passes."[35]

While Armenians were being decimated in Adana Province, other unique methods of massacre were being employed farther east on the Moush Plain. A vital farming region of wheat, barley, millet, tobacco, as well as livestock, it was a place where Armenians had flourished for nearly a thousand years. Of the more than seventy thousand Armenians living in the Moush region, almost none survived. After the gendarmes and the killing squads (made up mostly of the Kurds of the region) had wiped out the Armenian men, who fought back valiantly in resistance, the women, children, and elderly were forced into haylofts and barns that were then set on fire. By this method much of the Armenian life in region was wiped out. Fifteen-year-old Antranig Vartanian was one of the few who eventually escaped. Vartanian recalled how the gendarmes marched them out of his village, Haskouy, and after three days the starving deportees found themselves in the town of Ereshter, where at evening they were brought to a barn and told they would stay there for the night. Then the gendarmes "pushed hundreds of us into the barn," Vartanian remembers. "We were jammed in like sardines in a can, and I found myself against the barn wall where there was an air vent." Seeing that the air vent was big enough, Vartanian squeezed himself through the hole and escaped. Outside he found a small pond and hid in the water. Peering up from the surface of the water, he watched as the gendarmes surrounded the barn, and poured kerosene on it. "From the ditch I watched the fire engulf the barn and heard the horrible cries of my friends and townspeople being burned alive. The smell of burning flesh and hair was horrendous."[36]

As the evidence became overwhelming, Ambassador Morgenthau—in his quintessentially direct way—repeatedly confronted Talaat Pasha about his government's treatment of the Armenians. "Why are you so interested in the Armenians?" Talaat angrily asked Morgenthau. "You are a Jew; these people are Christians. . . . Why can't you let us do with these Christians as we please?" Indignant, Morgenthau answered,

> You don't seem to realize that I am not here as a Jew but as American Ambassador. My country contains something more than 97,000,000 Christians and something less than 3,000,000 Jews. So, at least in my ambassadorial capacity, I am 97 per cent Christian. But after all, that is not the point. I do not appeal to you in the name of any race or any religion, but merely as a human being. . . . The way you are treating the Armenians . . . puts you in the class of backward, reactionary peoples.

"We treat the Americans all right," Talaat answered. "I don't see why you should complain."

"But Americans are outraged by your persecutions of the Armenians."

"It is no use for you to argue," Talaat answered on another occasion; "we have already disposed of three quarters of the Armenians; there are none at all left in Bitlis, Van, and Erzerum. The hatred between the Turks and the Armenians is now so intense that we have got to finish with them. If we don't, they will plan their revenge." Morgenthau then tried to persuade Talaat by reminding him of the economic consequences of wiping out the Armenian population. "These people are your business men. They control many of your industries. They are very large tax-payers."

"We care nothing about the commercial loss," replied Talaat. "We have figured all that out and we know that it will not exceed five million pounds."

"You are making a terrible mistake," Morgenthau answered, and repeated the statement three times.

"'Yes, we may make mistakes,' he replied, 'but'—and he firmly closed his lips and shook his head—'we never regret.'" Not long after, Talaat boasted to the ambassador, "I have accomplished more toward solving the Armenian problem in three months than Abdul Hamid accomplished in thirty years!"[37]

AMERICA'S GOLDEN RULE: WORKING

FOR ARMENIA AGAIN

Honest men may differ as to practically every point . . . but in the case of Armenia, it is impossible to admit that there can be honest difference of opinion [about] the termination of the insane regime of Turkish brutality.
—*New Republic*, 1919

E arly on, Ambassador Morgenthau was informed by the Turkish authorities that the "treatment of Turkish subjects by the Turkish Government was purely a domestic affair; unless it directly affected American lives and American interests, it was outside the concern of the American government." But Morgenthau refused to accept what he called the "cold-blooded legalities of the situation," and by the summer of 1915 he was urging President Wilson and his administration to appeal to Turkey to put a stop to the annihilation of the Armenians and to immediately grant Americans "every facility" to administer relief and financial assistance to the survivors of the deportations. He also asked Wilson to appeal to the German government to "insist" that Turkey stop "this annihilation of a Christian race."

The Armenian relief project during the time of the Genocide was spawned by urgent pleas from Ambassador Morgenthau, the U.S. State Department consuls, and American missionaries in Turkey. When the deportations began, the Ottoman government cut the lines of communication from the Armenian provinces. As early as April 1915, Morgenthau wrote, "I was suddenly deprived of the privilege of using the cipher for communicating with American consuls." When the letters began to be censored, Morgenthau assumed correctly that events were unfolding that the Ottoman government was trying to conceal.[1]

But letters and dispatches, of course, did make it through to Morgenthau, and some of them arrived by hand from American missionaries who
against great obstacles succeeded in getting through to the embassy in
Constantinople. The ambassador recalled that "for hours they [the mis-
sionaries] would sit in my office with tears streaming down their faces,"
reporting the atrocities they had witnessed. Many of them were "broken
in health" by what they had seen, and the letters they brought Morgenthau from the American consuls confirmed their most dreadful stories
and more. The missionaries and the consuls kept sending the ambassador
the same message: Only "the moral power of the United States" could
save the Armenians from annihilation.[2]

So, when on September 3, 1915, Ambassador Morgenthau telegraphed the State Department to convey that "destruction of the Armenian race in Turkey is progressing rapidly,"[3] he urged Americans to create
a formal Armenian relief organization. The ambassador gave assurances
"that hundreds of thousands of starving and rag-clad survivors were
within reach of relief measures and could be saved if sufficient funds were
available in America and immediately transmitted to the volunteer committees of resident Americans overseas."[4]

Unlike the 1890s Armenian relief movement, this one emerged from
a large wartime American culture of relief movements. From its initial
position of neutrality, the United States spawned numerous relief efforts
shortly after World War I broke out. As German atrocities against the Bel-
gians became sensational news near the outbreak of the war, Belgian relief
committees cropped up all over the United States. Organizations as
diverse as the DAR, *Ladies' Home Journal*, the Rockefeller Foundation, and
the Rocky Mountain Club sent tons of food to ravaged Belgium in 1914.
Soon Michigan, Ohio, New Jersey, New York, and Pennsylvania all had
Belgian relief organizations, and by the end of the war, Belgian relief
totaled about six million dollars' worth.[5]

Propelled by an extraordinary organization of women, the American
Women's Hospitals established dispensaries and hospitals in various allied
countries, while the National Surgical Dressings Committee sent eighteen
million dollars' worth of surgical dressings abroad. Committees sprang up
for various countries: Serbian Relief Committee, Russian War Relief Committee, Polish Victims Relief Fund Committee. In Paris, Gertrude Stein
and Alice B. Toklas were among the Americans who worked for the

American Fund for French Wounded. Jacob Schiff, who had been a leader in the Armenian relief movement of the 1890s, was now instrumental in various Jewish relief efforts, and was heeding Ambassador Morgenthau's reports to send money for the Jews in Palestine who were also suffering at the hands of the Turks. The Jewish Joint Distribution Committee focused in particular on the plight of the Jews, Armenians, Greeks, and Syrians who were in peril in the Ottoman Empire.[6]

Not surprisingly, the news of Morgenthau's September 3 telegram reached James L. Barton—the foreign secretary of the American Board of Commissioners for Foreign Missions in Boston—who immediately wrote his friend and colleague Cleveland Dodge in New York urging him to call a meeting. "The situation is certainly critical," and "there is no better place than your office," he wrote, for "the Armenians have no one to speak for them." Only days later a group of men met at Cleveland Dodge's Madison Avenue office.[7]

A benefactor of education at home and in the Near East, Dodge was chairman of the board of trustees of Robert College in Constantinople, the oldest American college in the Near East; he had helped to build the American University in Beirut. As a trustee of Princeton University (where he and Woodrow Wilson began a close personal friendship as students), Dodge was the primary benefactor of the preceptorial system, Wilson's brainchild when he was the university's president. By 1915 Dodge was a distinguished American philanthropist in the old mugwump tradition of civic-minded entrepreneurs like Spencer Trask and Henry Morgenthau.

At this September meeting at Dodge's office, the Committee on Armenian Atrocities was formed and its officers selected. James Barton was voted director; Charles R. Crane, treasurer; and Samuel T. Dutton, secretary. Crane, a businessman and a friend of President Wilson, was president of the board of trustees of the Constantinople College for Women and he knew Turkey well. Dutton, a professor at Columbia Teacher's College, was the treasurer of Constantinople College for Women and secretary of the World Peace Foundation, and had been a member of the Balkan Commission in 1913.

Other founding board members who were present that day included leading Zionist spokesman Rabbi Stephen Wise, who was also chairman of a Jewish Emergency Relief Commission; the publisher George A.

Plimpton; Oscar S. Straus, former ambassador to Turkey; as well as the distinguished journalist Talcott Williams, Bishop David H. Greer, and financier and civic leader Isaac N. Seligman. (In order to maintain its sense of nonpartisan neutrality, the committee decided it would not allow Armenians to join its ranks.) As the committee broke up that afternoon, the members decided that Samuel Dutton's offices at 70 Fifth Avenue would be the organization's future home. Dodge's generosity was such that he agreed to meet all the organizational expenses, and he went on to make large monthly contributions for years.[8]

Even though the United States and the Ottoman Empire had a diplomatically neutral relationship, the Young Turk government was censoring all communications having to do with the Armenians. James Barton recalled that "knowledge of the actual conditions was delayed several months in reaching America, owing to the rigid censorship and the purpose of the Turkish authorities to keep the world in ignorance of the horrible facts."[9] But by early fall of 1915 Barton and his colleagues in New York City had received the message clearly from American diplomats. One dispatch of early September from an American consul conveyed the ultimate reality: The "authorities" make no "secret of the fact that their main object is the extermination of the whole Armenian race. . . . The vali admitted quite frankly: 'We are determined to get rid, once and for all, of this cancer in our country.'"[10]

At that first meeting one hundred thousand dollars were raised, half of the amount offered on the spot. Although it was a small sum given the need, none who met that day could have imagined that out of that ad hoc committee would emerge one of the most remarkable international philanthropic agencies in American history.[11] From that beginning until its termination in July 1929, the Committee on Armenian Atrocities, which later became Near East Relief and was incorporated by Congress in 1919, raised in money and kind more than $116,000,000—a sum that would be more than a billion dollars in contemporary terms. As President Wilson put it: "The fate of Armenia has always been of special interest to the American people."[12] Albert Shaw, the editor of the *American Review of Reviews*, claimed in 1930 that not since the Civil War had Americans come together in this way: "The special appeal of the Near East Relief transcended anything in the way of a nationalizing movement of charity and brotherhood that we have ever known."[13]

Looking back at this phenomenon, President Calvin Coolidge described the relief effort as a nationwide passion that encompassed "all classes of our people, religious bodies of all creeds, fraternal organizations of whatever name and purpose, schools, colleges and individuals, with a single spirit and purpose. . . . No private enterprise," he went on, "ever undertaken by Americans and in the name of America has accomplished more to arouse, in the minds and hearts of all the peoples of the countries in which this organization has carried on its operations, a sincere regard and even affection for America." Sounding a bit like Woodrow Wilson, Coolidge declared that Near East Relief "represented the true spirit of our country" in its demonstration of brotherhood, "sacrifice," and "service." "Its creed was the Golden Rule and its ritual the devotion of life and treasure to the healing of wounds."[14]

The Committee on Armenian Atrocities was shaped by the modern era's new penchant for bureaucracy and specialists, and by the new "Social Gospel" movement with its commitment to bringing together Christianity with social engagement. For the most part, the more self-styled activists and philanthropists such as Julia Ward Howe, Alice Stone Blackwell, and Spencer Trask, who worked for the Armenian relief movement in the 1890s, were now increasingly replaced by bureaucrats who assumed managerial positions and specialized in fund-raising and public relations.[15] Business executives now joined and took over the missionary organizations that were working thousands of miles away in the Anatolian wilderness.

All that fall of 1915, James Barton and Samuel Dutton, the new businessmen-philanthropists, scrupulously gathered all the available data in Washington and "carefully sifted the evidence and evaluated the witnesses," as Barton put it, convinced more than ever that "they could save a remnant of a whole race if immediate funds could be made available." The State Department files, with reports by the "American consular and diplomatic agents," Barton noted, had made them realize that they had "greatly underestimated the extent of the disaster that had befallen the Armenians."[16]

As the Committee on Armenian Atrocities began to disseminate its findings, the media had a new corpus of knowledge to write about. Given its overwhelming coverage of the unraveling devastation of World War I in Europe, press coverage of the Armenian atrocities was quite extraordinary.

The *New York Times,* for example, published 145 articles on the Armenian massacres in 1915 alone (an article about every two and a half days). Notwithstanding the cautious, conservative philosophy of the *Times,* and its desire to present balanced views of current events, the articles on the Armenian massacres carry a special kind of authority.[17]

Although the Armenian Genocide was covered in newspapers all over the nation, the coverage in the *New York Times* was at the pulse of the Committee on Armenian Atrocities, and thus at the center of America's relief effort. Articles on the massacres, announced with front-page headlines, created a significant, unfolding narrative of what was evolving into the century's first genocide. By the end of 1915 the word "Armenia" and its familiar contiguities like "atrocities," "massacre," "deportation," "outrage," "race extermination," and "Turk,"[18] had assumed a cultural, political, and linguistic density that would mark a place in the popular imagination, so that as President Hoover would say, looking back at 1919, the "name Armenia was in the front of the American mind . . . known to the American schoolchild only a little less than England."[19] Given the different legacies of the Holocaust and the Armenian Genocide in the realms of international justice and current popular consciousness, it is ironic to recall how poorly reported the extermination of the Jews was in the American press. Even as late as 1942, Holocaust historian Deborah Lipstadt notes, "there was still no mention of a systematic extermination program" against the Jews.[20] From the start, however, the Armenian massacres were described clearly as race extermination. Week after week from 1915 on, the *New York Times* used terms describing what would later be defined as genocide: "systematic," "deliberate," "authorized," "organized by government," "systematic race extermination."[21] The *Times* coverage makes it clear that the reports by American and European diplomats and missionaries, neutral bystanders, and massacre survivors all corroborated that the slaughter and deportation of the Armenians was a well-organized, government-planned operation, aimed at exterminating a race of people. An article of August 18, 1915, for example, quoted British MP Aneurin Williams, noting that reliable sources confirm that "it is a plan to exterminate the whole Armenian people."[22]

The national media coverage of the atrocities furthered the momentum of the newly formed Committee on Armenian Atrocities and helped to publicize its presence in the wartime American landscape. Less than three weeks after the Committee on Armenian Atrocities was formed, a front-page story in the *New York Times* read: TELL OF HORRORS DONE IN ARMENIA: REPORT OF EMINENT AMERICANS SAYS THEY ARE UNEQUALED IN A THOUSAND YEARS: A POLICY OF EXTERMINATION PUT INTO EFFECT AGAINST A HELPLESS PEOPLE. The article helped to launch the Committee on Armenian Atrocities by underscoring that a "systematic" "policy of race extermination is in progress," that "torture, pillage, rape, murder, wholesale expulsion and deportation and massacre [in] all parts of the empire" is being "directed from Constantinople."[23]

Only days later, on October 7, a *Times* headline read: 800,000 ARMENIANS COUNTED DESTROYED: VISCOUNT BRYCE TELLS HOUSE OF LORDS. Lord Bryce "gave a heart-piercing account of the circumstances under which the Armenian people are being exterminated as a result of an absolutely premeditated policy elaborately pursued by the gang now in control of Turkey." "Even the atrocities of Abdul Hamid pale" next to these atrocities, Bryce emphasized: "There is not a case in history since the days of Tamerlane where a crime so hideous and on so gigantic a scale has been recorded."[24]

Even before the dramatic coverage of October 1915, the *New York Times* had been covering Ambassador Morgenthau's struggle with the Young Turk government over the Armenian atrocities. In April when the massacres began more publicly, a *Times* article (APPEAL TO TURKEY TO STOP MASSACRES) reported that Ambassador Morgenthau, with Secretary of State Bryan's backing, had appealed to Turkish authorities to cease the massacres. A day later a headline read MORGENTHAU INTERCEDES, and went on to explain that the ambassador had confronted the Ottoman authorities about "the treatment of the Armenians." Blunt and outspoken, Morgenthau had never played the game of diplomatic niceties, and he had repeatedly tried to impress upon Enver and Talaat that the president of the United States was a close friend of the missionaries whose lives and work were entwined with the Armenians. "I told him [Enver Pasha] that Mr. Cleveland H. Dodge, President of the trustees of Robert College, and Mr. Charles R. Crane, President of the trustees of the Women's College, were intimate friends of President Wilson." "These," he explained to the Minister of War, "represent what is best in America and the fine altruistic spirit which in our country accumulates wealth and then uses it to found colleges and schools."[25]

In September 1915 Morgenthau had gone so far as to announce an idealistic plan to bring more than a half-million Armenian massacre survivors to the United States, and the headline in the *New York Times* read: WOULD SEND HERE 550,000 ARMENIANS: MORGENTHAU URGES SCHEME TO SAVE THEM FROM TURKS. "I should like to see each of the Western States raise a fund to equip a ship to bring the number of settlers it wants," Morgenthau stated. "The Armenians," he went on, "are a moral, hard-working race, and would make good citizens to settle the less thickly populated parts of the Western States." The article closed by reporting a rare moment of Turkish candor: "Turks admit that the Armenian persecution is the first step in a plan to get rid of Christians, and that Greeks will come next. Jews also are marked for slaughter or expulsion. American missionaries must also be driven out, for Turkey henceforth is to be for Turks alone."[26] In the evolving Morgenthau–Young Turk drama the *Times* reported on September 16, ANSWER MORGENTHAU BY HANGING ARMENIANS, that Morgenthau's protests of "the extermination now in progress," was met by Turkish anger as twenty leading Armenians were hanged in Constantinople. The article went on to estimate that already between eight hundred thousand and one million Armenians had been killed.[27]

As World War I spiraled out of control into unforeseen realms of horror and carnage, Americans debated the pros and cons of entry into the war, and the press coverage of Germany intensified. Not only was the Hun lambasted for the sinking of the *Lusitania* and for Germany's murderous campaign in Belgium, but now Germany's role as Turkey's ally was scrutinized by the State Department, the Committee on Armenian Atrocities, and the press. As Barton and the committee read the reports of German educators who were working in the interior of Turkey, they realized that the German military was in command of Ottoman troops and was involved in the Armenian deportations and massacres. Some German diplomats recorded what was happening or spoke out against their ally, however. German Consul Scheubner-Richter in Erzurum wrote in August 1915 that "by July 15 almost all of the Armenians had been expelled from Erserum." A German Protestant petition to the imperial chancellor in Berlin protested that "since the end of May, the deportation of the entire Armenian population from all the Anatolian Vilayets and Cilicia in the Arabian steppes south of the Baghdad-Berlin railway has been ordered."[28]

Because some Germans were speaking out like this, the American Committee on Armenian Atrocities and the American press found the stance of the German ambassador in Constantinople, baron von Wagenheim, and the German ambassador to the United States, count von Bernstorff, shocking. Wagenheim declared: "I do not blame the Turks for what they are doing to the Armenians. . . . They are entirely justified."[29] As the German-Turkish alliance was reported in the press, the *Times* of August 6, 1915, referred to the Germans as "masters of the Central Ottoman Administration, [who] have to their everlasting shame not only permitted, but rather encouraged these horrors." Several weeks later Ambassador von Bernstorff was quoted in a *Times* headline of September 28 as saying that Armenian atrocities were PURE INVENTIONS.[30] The next day Ambassador von Bernstorff's denial was a front-page headline: ARMENIANS' OWN FAULT, BERNSTORFF NOW SAYS, followed by a description of Bernstorff's statement to the State Department asserting that the Armenian atrocities were "greatly exaggerated" and had been provoked by the victims. Two pages later the *Times* countered with ARMENIAN WOMEN PUT UP AT AUCTION: VON BERNSTORFF ANSWERED; and the article carried Samuel Dutton's warning that Germany would also be held responsible for the Armenian massacres.[31]

All that fall, the words "Morgenthau," "Von Bernstorff," "Bryce," "Armenian," "Atrocities," "Germany," "Turks," "Horrors," "Refugees" made up the *New York Times* headlines. And those words were supplemented by numbers. What did it mean to a popular audience in 1915 to read the numbers of Armenian dead? The numbers brought home to Americans the urgency of the need to practice the Golden Rule. NINE THOUSAND ARMENIANS MASSACRED AND THROWN INTO TIGRIS (August 4, 1915); 600,000 STARVING ON ROAD (August 27, 1915); 1,500,000 ARMENIANS STARVE (September 5, 1915); 500,000 ARMENIANS SAID TO HAVE PERISHED (September 24, 1915); 800,000 ARMENIANS COUNTED DESTROYED; 10,000 DROWNED AT ONCE (October 7, 1915). Such death tolls for the mass killing of innocent people were without precedent in the history of the print media.

In that sense, too, there is something apocalyptic and "modern" about the 1915 genocide of the Armenians. While the death tolls in the trenches of Western Europe were close to 2 million by the summer of

1915, the extermination of innocent civilians in Turkey (the Armenians, but also Syrian and Assyrian Christians and large portions of the Greek population, especially the Greeks of the Pontus, or Black Sea region) was pushing toward 1 million. The casualties of World War I inaugurated the modern age in a way that would haunt the century. By the end of World War I, about 10 million would be dead. By the end of World War II, about 6 million Jews would be murdered in Hitler's genocide, and some 50 million people would die in the war. In the 1970s, the Cambodian dictator Pol Pot would kill about 1.8 million of his own people. The Hutu would kill eight hundred thousand Tutsi in the Rwandan genocide of 1994. Seen from the beginning of the twenty-first century, the reportage of the Armenian Genocide remains a seminal event: It was the first time Americans were confronted with unfathomable numbers of the murder of innocent, unarmed civilians.

Days after the formation of the Committee on Armenian Atrocities, James Barton went to Washington to meet with Assistant Secretary of State Alvey Adee, who was in charge of the State Department's files, and "the entire files" of the State Department were placed at the committee's disposal. When Barton arrived in Adee's office on September 21, he was whisked off to a private room, and a clerk was assigned to his service.[32] He worked all day making copies of dispatches and telegrams, careful not to copy out the cipher codes lest he imperil security. After reading Morgenthau's reports and telegrams, as well as reports from American, Canadian, and German consuls and missionaries, Barton was deeply affected. "The revelations of the situation in Turkey surpassed all expectations," he wrote, for the "mass of material laid before me that day was found to contain the most overwhelming indictment of the Turkish government backed by German endorsement."[33]

Arriving back in New York City at midnight, Barton went to his room at the Hotel Roosevelt and stayed up until the early hours of the morning preparing for the press what he had copied at the State Department. He was overwhelmed by what he called "this vast collection of authentic material from Turkey concerning the regimented and designedly inhuman deportations of an entire race of men, women and children," and felt the news had to reach the American public immediately.[34]

In the ensuing days the committee worked hard at getting the news out. Melville Stone of the Associated Press agreed to become a counselor on press relations, and the AP soon became a channel of news from overseas to the United States.[35] Within a week a *New York Times* article (COMMITTEE ON ATROCITIES SAYS 500,000 VICTIMS HAVE SUFFERED ALREADY) reported that the newly formed Committee on Armenian Atrocities had made public the first results of its "investigation of the terrible conditions existing among the Armenians," and that "massacre and torture of the Armenians are confirmed."[36] By Thursday, October 7, as fund-raising became a national issue, the *New York Times* headline read: ROCKEFELLER FOUNDATION LEADS DONATIONS TO AMERICAN COMMITTEE WITH $30,000.[37]

From the start the Rockefeller Foundation expressed its sense of moral urgency over the atrocities by giving generously to the committee. In 1896 John D. Rockefeller Sr. had supported Armenian relief more than once. Lady Henry Somerset had even cabled him for money in a moment of crisis in March 1896, when she was working with Armenian refugees in Marseilles. Now, as the whole process started up again, the recently formed Rockefeller Foundation, which had been set up in 1913 under the leadership of John D. junior "to promote the well-being of mankind throughout the world," took a vigorous role in trying to save the Armenians.

As early as August 1915 the Rockefeller Foundation was receiving detailed reports from its own War Relief Commission about the plight of the Armenians, and it relied on these to guide its philanthropic policy. In an extensive war relief report of 1915–16, Eliot Wadsworth and Jeremiah Smith Jr. of the foundation noted that the Ottoman government was hostile to foreigners investigating civilian conditions in their country and that government censorship was severe and communication was difficult. To the horror of Wadsworth and Smith, the few Turkish officials they met tried to cajole them into giving Rockefeller Foundation money to the Ottoman government instead of to the dying Armenians.

What Wadsworth and Smith reported about the devastation of the Armenians corroborated the U.S. and European consular reports and the missionary, survivor, and other eyewitness accounts: The Armenians were being subjected to "torture" and a "policy" of "massacre" and "wholesale deportation," and forced conversion to Islam. The report called the "situation of the Armenians . . . a desperate one," and noted that "there is perhaps as much necessity for relief at the present time as in 1895 and 1909 when large relief funds . . . were raised by friends of Armenians in both England and the United States."[38] Before the war was over Ambassador Abram Elkus, who replaced Henry Morgenthau in 1916, sent his own message to the Rockefeller Foundation about the need for Armenian and Syrian relief. This was met by receptive ears, as one of the foundation's investigators, Edward Stoever, deemed that there was "a definite government policy toward the [Armenian] race as a whole."[39] Before the first year of fund-raising for Armenian relief was over, the Rockefeller Foundation had given $290,000. By the end of 1917 the foundation had poured about $610,000 into Armenian and Syrian relief.[40]

In mid-October the Committee on Armenian Atrocities cabled its first $100,000 to Ambassador Morgenthau, and the funds were then distributed to the sites of massacre where American diplomats, physicians, nurses, and missionaries used them for relief, food, and medical supplies. Within weeks the committee had become a phenomenon, and by the third Sunday of October, at a New York meeting reminiscent of the Boston Faneuil Hall gathering in 1894, thousands packed the Century Theater at Sixty-second Street and Central Park West to protest the Armenian massacres. At the Century Theater that Sunday, James L. Barton, Rabbi Stephen Wise, and the Catholic scholar and editor Jesuit priest John J. Wynne were among those who took the podium. Before the afternoon was over a passionate crowd had adopted a resolution—the text of which was printed in the *Times* the following Monday—that underscored American public sentiment of the past months.

"Whereas the civilized world has been shocked" by the Armenian Massacres in the Turkish Empire, and "Whereas, these crimes and outrages committed upon an industrious, thrifty and peace-loving people find no justification in the light of law or humanity" and "resolved that as American citizens, we make our solemn protest against . . . the Turkish Empire to put an end to these wrongs and to render every aid to the American Ambassador and others who would rescue and repatriate a people, who, by their history and achievements have been a credit to the empire." And, "Resolved . . . that the slaughter of noncombatant men, the tortures, mutilations, and outrages committed upon women and children wherever committed have given to the fairest places upon the earth the semblance of hell . . . we call upon the nations at war to cease these crimes against civilization and morality."[41]

By November the Committee on Armenian Atrocities was meeting regularly and creating a larger network for fund-raising and national education. In their drive to educate the public, the committee prepared pamphlets about the history of the Christians in Turkey and about the eradication of the Christians in the Ottoman Empire. The wartime organization for the relief of women and children, the Committee of Mercy, headed by former Harvard president Charles W. Eliot, former secretary of state Elihu Root, and New York City mayor John Mitchel, had joined forces with Barton's committee. By early 1916 there were dozens of local committees for Armenian and Syrian relief in sixteen states, with the leading banks in the communities serving as the depositories for funds. "From platform to pulpit," speakers from the national and local committees addressed mass meetings, and money began to pour in.[42] As Howard M. Sachar has put it, "Rarely in history did an appeal for voluntary contributions evoke so instantaneous and heartfelt an outpouring of public generosity." Along with the Rockefeller Foundation, the Guggenheim Fund gave $30,000. Fund-raising rallies "packed New York's Amsterdam Opera House, the Philadelphia Stadium, Detroit's Billy Sunday Tabernacle"; a rally at the New York Hippodrome raised $75,000, even "the entire proceeds of the Harvard-Yale football game of 1916" were donated to the fund. By the end of 1916, an astounding $20 million had been raised.[43]

In May 1916 Alvey Adee at the State Department conveyed to the committee Ambassador Morgenthau's pleas for more money. Mr. W. W. Peet, who was leading the relief drive in Constantinople, wrote, "So insufficient are the funds that many exiles in the destitute places have only grass to eat and they are dying of starvation by the hundreds. One thousand Turkish pounds are required each week for the Aleppo center."[44] Aleppo had become a center for emaciated, disease-ravaged death march survivors, many of them women and children who had been raped and sexually assaulted. "I think there must be some Fifty Thousand [survivors] hidden in the families in Aleppo," Consul Jesse Jackson wrote to Morgenthau, "about nine thousand of which are on the relief lists of the Churches to whom I am furnishing funds. I am trying to keep those in the outside towns alive, also, but it is a terrible task, as many persons have been beaten to death, and some hung or shot for having distributed relief funds. . . . It is a veritable reign of terror."[45] For a telegram like this to get past the formidable Turkish censorship was not easy, because the Turks intercepted telegrams at both the sending and receiving ends.

Talaat even flaunted this. One day as Morgenthau was meeting with the minister of the interior, Talaat pulled out of his drawer "a handful of yellow cablegrams" wiring money for relief. With a grin Talaat asked Morgenthau to give "this money to us." When Morgenthau expressed confusion, Talaat answered: "Here is a cablegram for you from America, sending you a lot of money for the Armenians. You ought not to use it that way; give it to us, we need it as badly as they do." When Morgenthau replied that he had not received any such cablegram, Talaat answered, "You will. I always get all your cablegrams first."[46]

But Jackson, like the other consuls, coded his telegrams and dispatches and sent them by hand to Constantinople, where they reached Morgenthau. He then got them to the State Department, and then they traveled to the Committee on Armenian Atrocities in New York City. It was this nexus of communication that helped bring the news to the media and acted as a catalyst for the relief project around the nation.

Notwithstanding Talaat's pilfering the ambassador's mail, Morgenthau still received the cabled money, and communication continued. The chain of information often involved datelines and telegrams from Europe, and one in particular from Lord Bryce—who was now compiling his famous Parliamentary Blue Book—reached James Barton in June 1916. Bryce, who had earned headlines in the *Times* the previous fall, now made a special appeal to Barton from London, urging him to enlist the U.S. State Department:

> The mass of refugees round Aleppo and in Northern Arabia . . .
> must now be in sore distress. We of course, cannot reach them,
> and there is of course the danger that anything sent would not
> reach those in distress but would be seized by the Turks. . . .
> Would it be possible to get your government to make any appeal
> to the Turks, to let supplies go through? . . . otherwise, these
> poor people will perish.[47]

Lord Bryce's appeal prompted Barton to contact Adee at the State Department, where he arranged through the navy for the U.S. collier *Caesar* to take relief supplies to the Aleppo region. For the US *Caesar* to pass through the wartime blockade off the Syrian coast, Secretary of State Lansing secured permission through the French ambassador to the United States, Jules J. Jusserand. The whole process of U.S. Naval relief was a brave and extraordinary act revealing the success of the chain of communication that traveled from Lord Bryce in London to the Committee in New York City, to the State Department, the navy, the French ambassador in Washington, D.C., the French navy in the Mediterranean, and then on to the Armenian refugees.[48]

As the movement for Armenian relief spread across the nation, by July 1916 Congress passed a resolution asking President Wilson to designate a special day for Americans to express their sympathy for the Armenians and to contribute to the relief effort. The next month a presidential proclamation declared that "Saturday October 21 and Sunday October 22" would be "joint days for Americans to make contributions for the Armenians and Syrians."[49] In the weeks that followed Barton and the Committee were so overwhelmed by the request for literature on the Armenian atrocities that they "were running the presses day and night. . . . It surpasses anything I have ever seen before," Barton wrote.[50]

As 1917 arrived, the grass-roots drive for "the starving Armenians" continued in intensity. All across the United States, churches and synagogues, Lions, Kiwanis, Rotary Clubs, and women's organizations held fund-raisers. Children learned about Armenia and the relief movement in their Sunday school classes and got involved in weekly fund-raising projects. The phrase "starving Armenians," which seems to have been coined by Clara Barton in 1895 when she was being recruited for her mission to Armenia, became an epithet through which the news of the massacres was transmitted, in particular to children, who were told endlessly by their parents that, considering the starving Armenians who were dying at the hands of the Turks, it was a sin to waste food by not cleaning their plates.

Human rights activist Louise Franklin-Ramirez recalled working for the "starving Armenians" in 1917 when she was twelve. "Thousands of American children all across the nation that year," she recalled, "sold lemonade, ice cream, and apple pies with their Sunday school or civic group." She

and her mother set up a stand in their neighborhood in the Rock Creek section of Washington, D.C., and sold thousands of strawberries—a penny for
a strawberry dipped in sugar, and a nickel for strawberry ice cream or strawberry shortcake—to help the cause. "It hit us hard. . . . It was shocking to
learn that other children in the world were without food," she recalls.[51]
"The Armenian Genocide was a turning point in my life," Mrs. Franklin-
Ramirez remarked, "because it awakened me to human rights."[52]

Ruth Hartshorne, living in Cleveland, Ohio, remembers her mother
saying regularly, "Eat up your Grape-Nuts, remember the starving Armenians." Hartshorn recalls that during those years "I vividly imagined a
steamship piled high with Grape-Nuts setting out to sea for the Armenians."[53] During the teens and the twenties, millions of children had heard
the phrase "starving Armenians," and thousands of them were working
for Armenian and Syrian relief, contributing to the more than ten million
dollars that was raised during wartime.

As the world war entered its second year, the Armenian Genocide became
for Americans not only an international human rights crisis but an issue
that was entangled in the controversial issue of U.S. entry into the war.
Intellectuals and politicians were expressing strong opinions. Ezra Pound,
the new "genius" of literary modernism, wrote in New Age in October
1915 that the United States could no longer maintain its neutrality
because the "broader interests of humanity" were at stake—interests that
lay at the heart of American history from its Enlightenment foundations
to the abolition of slavery. "Tyranny in the modern world is most visible,"
he wrote, "in German militarism and the Armenian massacres."[54] The literary critic Walter Kalaidjian has noted, as well, that Pound's protégé,
T. S. Eliot, appropriated the deportation of the Armenians in a haunting
image in "The Wasteland." The image of "hooded hordes swarming/
Swarming over endless plains, stumbling in cracked earth/Ringed by the
flat horizon only" is apocalyptic, Kalaidjian remarks, suggestive of both
the horror of World War I and the deportations of the Armenians carried
out on the eastern front.[55]

H. L. Mencken, perhaps the most famous wit and journalist of the
era, expressed in his inimitable way his reaction to the Armenian situation: "The same Armenians who were being exterminated in 1896 are

being exterminated again. The only difference is that in the present case the accommodating Secretary Lansing has given the atrocity-mongers a life by addressing a moral note to the Turkish Government." If Mencken treated the liberal philanthropists with a touch of irony, he was also acerbic about hollow, bureaucratic gestures from government officials, and he continued, "The circulation of such notes now constitutes one of the chief duties of the State Department."[56]

The war gave a sense of political realism to the Armenian massacres that peacetime had not accorded to Abdul Hamid's massacres in the 1890s. Although Congress and the Senate passed a resolution in 1896 calling for President Cleveland to denounce the sultan's massacres, and some senators, like Wilkinson Call of Florida, had asked for immediate intervention and even an independent Armenia, there was no urgent political circumstance drawing the United States into Turkish affairs in the 1890s. World War I changed that, and now with Turkey as Germany's ally, the call for U.S. involvement became more pressing each month as the intransigent trench war continued. Wilson's policy of neutrality grew increasingly controversial, and the debate over American entry into the war preoccupied the country. Soon, President Wilson would have to confront the issue of the Armenian massacres in a new, direct way.

Theodore Roosevelt had shifted from his earlier ambivalence about entry into the world war and by 1915 had become a passionate advocate. For him the Armenian massacres, which he called "the greatest crime of the war," became an ongoing part of this thinking about the American character, foreign policy, and international ethics. The former president refused an invitation to a meeting with the Committee on Armenian Atrocities that fall of 1915 because he disapproved of what he considered to be the missionaries' too-passive response to the Armenian massacres. In responding to Samuel Dutton he expounded on the massacres and the problem of American neutrality, as well as on some of his lifetime convictions about American culture:

> My Dear Mr. Dutton:
>   Even to nerves dulled and jaded by the heaped-up horrors of the past year and a half, the news of the terrible fate that has befallen the Armenians must give a fresh shock of sympathy and indignation. Let me emphatically point out that the sympathy is

useless unless it is accompanied with indignation, and that the indignation is useless if it exhausts itself in words instead of taking shape in deeds.

If this [American] people through its government had not shirked its duty . . . in connection with the world war for the last sixteen months, we would now be able to take effective action on behalf of Armenia. Mass meetings on behalf of the Armenians amount to nothing whatever if they are mere methods of giving a sentimental but ineffective and safe outlet to the emotion of those engaged in them. Indeed they amount to less than nothing. . . . Until we put honor and duty first, and are willing to risk something in order to achieve righteousness both for ourselves and for others, we shall accomplish nothing; and we shall earn and deserve the contempt of the strong nations of mankind.[57]

For Roosevelt honor and duty meant to "speak softly and carry a big stick," and in this case that meant going to war. Roosevelt was enraged by pacifist sentiment, which he believed was holding sway over Wilson's policy, and his passion for entry into the war was equal to his dislike of Wilson, whom he called an "abject coward" and the "worst President since Buchanan."[58]

Roosevelt went on in his letter to Dutton:

All of the terrible iniquities of the past year and a half, including this crowning iniquity of the wholesale slaughter of the Armenians, can be traced directly to the initial wrong committed on Belgium by her invasion and subjugation; and the criminal responsibility of Germany must be shared by the neutral powers, headed by the United States, for their failure to protest when this initial wrong was committed.[59]

Thinking about justice for Armenia was not new for Roosevelt. As president during the first decade of the century, he corresponded regularly with prominent Americans such as Andrew Carnegie, Jacob Schiff, Oscar Straus, Progressivist clergyman Lyman Abbott, and others, registering his concern about the plight of the Armenians under Ottoman rule. For the most part he concluded that there were no opportune political conditions for United States intervention at that time. Writing in 1907 to his friend Lyman Abbott, he said, "I put righteousness above peace, and should be entirely satisfied to head a crusade for the Armenians," but "it would be simple nonsense to start such a crusade unless the country were prepared to back it up; and the country has not the remotest intention of fighting on such an issue."[60]

In a 1906 letter to Andrew Carnegie about the upcoming Hague Conference on International Peace, he wrote that he was skeptical about a plan for international disarmament, because he believed that "it would only be safe to do so if there were some system of international police; but there is now no such system, if there were, Turkey for instance would be abolished forthwith unless it showed itself capable of working real reform." While Roosevelt saw certain colonial arrangements such as Russia in Turkestan, France in Algeria, and England in Egypt as positive for the peace and order they created, he told Carnegie that, conversely, "it would be an advantage to justice if we were able to effectively interfere for the Armenians in Turkey, and for the Jews in Russia . . . and in the Congo Free State."[61]

It is ironic but indicative of the breadth of the response to the Armenian Genocide that the British philosopher and social critic Bertrand Russell—one of those pacifists Roosevelt detested—spoke out as vigorously against his country's policy on the Armenians as Roosevelt spoke out against Wilson's. Having taught at Harvard in 1914, Russell was no stranger to the new wave of American pacifism, but his perspective on the Armenian Question went back to the 1890s, when Gladstone had come out so dramatically against the sultan. For Russell his government's inability to sustain a moral stance against the Armenian massacres was an important issue in the evolution of British foreign policy. He even attributed the erosion of democratic dissent in his country's foreign policy to Gladstone's successor, Lord Rosebery, who "dramatically dropped the agitation against the Armenian massacres."[62] In doing so, Russell contended, Lord Rosebery commenced a new drive for consensus in British foreign policy, one that represented a further "closing of the ranks among the governing classes against their common enemy, the people."[63]

In assessing the power of empires and their abuse of small cultures and nations, Russell criticized what he called the "unbelievable barbarities of the Turks. . . . The fact that the Turks," he wrote, "had for ages displayed a supremacy in cruelty and barbarism by torturing and degrading the Christians under their rule was no reason why Germany should not, like England in former times, support their tottering despotism by military and financial assistance. All considerations of humanity and liberty were subordinated to the great game."[64]

The impact of the Armenian Genocide forced Americans to look more deeply at themselves in other ways. An editorial in *The Nation* in October 1915 called to task the "hollow" argument that is made when nations or states (as in the case of the American South) claim "that a people's internal acts are its own affair." Lynching African Americans, the editorial noted, could no more be substantiated by this kind of reasoning than Turkey's "defense of the extermination of a nation."[65] These were both issues of universal human rights.

In the end the Armenian Genocide tested certain humanitarian ideals that Americans of the late Victorian and early Progressive eras held dear. The revitalized effort to save Armenians and rescue survivors in 1915–18 was made more complex by President Wilson's refusal to declare war on the Ottoman Empire—for after the Armistice, the United States would have less leverage in Turkey. In the postwar period, the popular support of a just settlement for Armenia would be led by the American Committee for the Independence of Armenia (ACIA), and that movement would test the relationship between popular appeals for aid and justice and the limits of what the federal government would and would not do for a foreign people.

Part IV

THE FAILED MISSION

WILSON'S QUANDARY

Armenia is to be redeemed . . .

> —Woodrow Wilson,
> September 1919

Merciful God! It's all true! Nobody has ever told the whole truth!
Nobody could!

> —Eleanor Franklin Egan, *Saturday*
> *Evening Post,* December 1919

L ess than a month after the Armistice in 1918, Woodrow Wilson
became the first president to cross the Atlantic while in office.
When he left New York aboard the SS *George Washington* on
December 4, thousands of people jammed the city's streets to send him
off on the voyage he called his "highest duty"—to make good on the sacrifice American soldiers had made to make the world safer for democracy.[1]
Ships on the Hudson River blew their whistles, navy fliers circled low over
his ship, and confetti rained down all over Manhattan. When he arrived in
Paris ten days later, two million Frenchmen and women lined the streets
shouting, *"Vive le Président Wilson!"* and *"Wilson le juste!"* Wilson rode in an
open carriage, waving his top hat to deafening cheers, as the parade proceeded down the Champs-Elysées.

As Herbert Hoover put it, Wilson's eloquent plan for peace, with its
goals of "independence of peoples," "self-determination," "justice," "new
order," and a "lasting peace," had stirred hope among the masses everywhere in the world.[2] Wilson had unveiled his famous Fourteen Points the
previous January (1918), when the war still seemed unstoppable. Five of
these points pertained broadly to open diplomacy: the end of secret
treaties, free use of the high seas during times of peace and war, the reduc-
tion of armaments, the removal of barriers to free trade, and an impartial
adjustment of colonial claims. Eight points dealt with the goals of national

self-determination, including the German evacuation of Russian territory, the restoration of Belgian independence, the return of Alsace-Lorraine to France, the creation of an independent Poland, and the autonomous development of each of the peoples of the Austro-Hungarian and Ottoman Empires. The fourteenth point—for which Wilson would fight to the death with his own Senate—was his League of Nations—"a general assembly of nations" to foster "the mutual guarantees of political independence and territorial integrity."

In the twelfth point Wilson specified that "the other nationalities which are now under Turkish rule should be assured an undoubted security of life and an absolutely unmolested opportunity of autonomous development." While a group of top advisers urged him to spell out autonomy for Armenia and sent Wilson this memorandum—"It is necessary to free the subject races of the Turkish Empire from oppression and misrule. This implies at the very least autonomy for Armenia"—Wilson's chief adviser, Col. Edward House, steered him away from mentioning that detail.[3]

Wilson's commitment to the idea of national sovereignty was part of his vision of world democracy. A president who had been a prominent scholar of American government, Wilson arrived at the Paris Peace Conference with deep convictions about democracy. He believed that morality should guide relations between nations, and that in the coming age all nations would be judged by ethical standards.[4] For him World War I was "a war of emancipation," a war fought, in part, for the smaller peoples of the world so that they could have, as he put it, the "right to determine their own fortunes, [and] to insist upon justice."[5] The Armenians were a classic case of such "smaller peoples."

Realizing that emerging nations like Armenia would need a transitional period of mentoring, Wilson advocated that they be protected by a "League of Nations," and by a "mandate" system that would further protect them from being overtaken due to the imperial designs of larger countries.[6] Under the mandate system, the League of Nations would authorize an established nation to be a protector and an administrator over a newly formed nation; the idea was to help emerging nations reach a point of stability before they stood on their own. In Wilson's mind this was a rational and peaceful way to ensure political change.

Given his high hopes for a new democratic world order, it is perhaps not surprising that Wilson found himself embattled with his European allies, whom he saw as driven by imperialistic designs on the spoils of war. When the issue of mandates came up, Wilson urged the universal application of a mandatory system for all former German and Turkish colonies.[7] When conversation turned to Armenia, there was concern and uncertainty. British prime minister David Lloyd George affirmed that Armenia was one place that would do well with mandated status, since it had lost a large portion of its population—having been "massacred, outraged, and pillaged for a generation"—and would thus need guidance and protection. But Britain, France, and Italy were all reluctant to accept the responsibility of an Armenian mandate, arguing, in Lloyd George's words, that "they were already overburdened with the mandates they were prepared to accept in Mesopotamia, Palestine, other parts of Anatolia, Syria, and Africa."[8]

With the Europeans backing away from the Armenian mandatory, the United States emerged as the only country acceptable to all, given its wartime neutrality toward the Ottoman Empire. By 1919 Wilson seemed more inclined to act for Armenia than he had been previously, and realizing that a just settlement for Armenia would embody many of the ideals of self-determination and justice of his Fourteen Points, he appeared openly optimistic about an American mandate for Armenia. "I think there is a very promising beginning in regard to countries like Armenia," he wrote.[9]

But the Paris Peace Conference did not go smoothly for Wilson and his team. As one of the Big Four—with French president Clemenceau, British prime minister Lloyd George, and Italian president Vittorio Orlando—Wilson struggled for months to forge agreements and compromises over the terms of the peace. When Wilson returned from Paris on July 8, he was exhausted both physically and mentally, but he was about to face his biggest challenge. When he presented the treaty—"one of the greatest documents in human history," as he called it—to the Senate on July 10, with its provision for a League of Nations, he was met with opposition and, in some quarters, hostility. Henry Cabot Lodge, the chairman of the Senate Foreign Relations Committee—a fierce Republican isolationist, who had become a bitter enemy of Wilson and his League—led the opposition. In the weeks of hearings before the Foreign Relations Committee,

. Lodge and his colleagues dragged Wilson through a relentless process of compromises and amendments, and by the middle of August, Lodge was now hoping he could have the entire treaty defeated.[10]

Angry and physically frail, having suffered a stroke in mid-July, Wilson was still passionately committed to the treaty and his dream of making the world safer for democracy through a League of Nations. In late August he told his physician, Dr. Cary T. Grayson, that he was planning a grass-roots campaign and major tour of the West in order to bring the League of Nations and his vision of a new world order directly to the American people for their approval. "I cannot put my personal safety, my health in the balance against my duty," he told Grayson. "I must go."[11] Traveling in a private train from Washington on September 3 with his close advisers Joseph Tumulty and Dr. Grayson and his wife, Edith Galt Wilson, Wilson was weak and often trembling as the result of yet another stroke. In three weeks of September he made thirty-seven speeches to huge crowds often as large as thirty thousand, and almost always without a loudspeaker to help prevent the strain on his voice. From Kansas City to Salt Lake City, with speech after speech, he was paraded through the town or city and ran endless gauntlets of hand-shaking and crowd greeting.

On that Western trip Wilson addressed the issue of Armenia with the kind of moral fervor that defined his grass-roots campaign. In part he knew that the issue of an American mandate for Armenia might help to promote his treaty, because it had been a cause dear to the hearts of the nation for so long. To an overflowing, flag-waving crowd of more than fifteen thousand in Kansas City's Convention Hall, Wilson appealed to America's sense of responsibility to protect the Armenians, who, as he put it, had been exterminated from their homeland.[12] The treaty, Wilson told the crowd, would protect vulnerable people, and, citing the "example of Armenia," Wilson exclaimed that they were "helpless, at the mercy of a Turkish government which thought it the service of God to destroy them." In some way, consciously or unconsciously, Wilson may even have been acknowledging his own administration's failure to act against Turkey during the war. "When I think of words piled upon words, of debate following debate, when these unspeakable things are happening in these pitiful parts of the world, I wonder that men do not wake up to the moral responsibility of what they are doing."[13]

At the Mormon Tabernacle in Salt Lake City, on September 23, Wilson, once again before a full house, raised the issue of America's political responsibility to Armenia. He lambasted the Turkish government for its crimes against Armenia, which were now, he noted, compounded by Turkey's denial of responsibility, as that government claimed "that it was unable to restrain the horrible massacres which have made that country a graveyard." But Armenia, Wilson told his audience, would no longer suffer because it "is one of the regions that is to be under trust of the League of Nations. Armenia is to be redeemed," the president stated, "so that at last this great people, struggling through night after night of terror, knowing not when they would see their land stained with blood, are now given a promise of safety, a promise of justice, a possibility that they may come out into a time when they can enjoy their rights as free people that they never dreamed they would be able to exercise."[14]

Two days later, on September 25, after stirring speeches to huge crowds in Pueblo and Denver, Colorado, Wilson collapsed. At four o'clock in the morning, Dr. Grayson found him fully dressed, sitting in his drawing room car, in a stupor, the left side of his face sagging and the left side of his body paralyzed. He had had another stroke. When he noticed that it was Grayson in the car, he mumbled, "I am not in condition to go on. . . . I just feel as if I am going to pieces." As he stared through the train window into the dark Colorado morning, tears rolled down his cheeks. Again he strained to speak, telling Grayson that he had to go on—otherwise Lodge would think him a quitter. Immediately Mrs. Wilson and Dr. Grayson canceled the rest of the president's engagements and ordered the train back to Washington. Only days after his return, Wilson suffered another and more debilitating stroke, which further impaired his speech, so that by October 6, Dr. Grayson was forced to inform the cabinet that the president had suffered a "nervous breakdown."[15] For the remainder of his term, Wilson would have to fight his battles for the treaty, the League of Nations, and the mandate for Armenia in rapidly declining health.

While the campaign for Armenia was part of Wilson's final struggle for his vision of international justice, the Armenian massacres had been a complex and unresolved issue for the president. He had been sympathetic to the plight of the Armenians from the time the massacres had been confirmed by Ambassador Morgenthau. As early as the fall of 1915, Colonel

House suggested to him that the U.S. government make an official "protest over the Armenian massacres."[16] In December 1915 Wilson wrote to a former Princeton classmate, who was a missionary in Turkey, that "the situation with regard to the Armenians is indeed nothing less than appalling. You may be sure that we have been doing everything that is diplomatically possible to check the terrible business."[17] In the summer of 1916 Wilson had issued proclamations for Armenian and Syrian relief, and he had spoken out on Armenia during his reelection campaign that same year. But the deeper struggle over America's commitment to Armenia was wrapped up in the thorny issue of America's entry into World War I, and specifically Wilson's quandary over whether to declare war on Turkey.[18]

The president had resisted entry into the European war with a strong stance of neutrality throughout the last half of his first term in office, but had found it increasingly difficult to defend his position as acts of German aggression began to encroach on his parameters of neutrality. The sinking of the *Lusitania* in April 1915, which took twelve hundred lives—a hundred of them American—and German violations of Wilson's neutrality policies on the high seas, especially involving German submarines, continued to stir the bellicose forces at home. After the famous Zimmermann telegram was intercepted, revealing Germany's hope of getting Mexico and Japan to join the war on the side of Germany, Wilson's efforts to keep the United States neutral eroded, and he came to the difficult conclusion that war was inevitable. After Congress overwhelmingly declared war on Germany and the Austro-Hungarian Empire in April 1917, the president faced the issue of war in the east.

Not only was Wilson reluctant to expand the war effort, but he found himself facing antiwar pressure—ironically, from American missionaries. As Alexis de Tocqueville once noted, when one meets a missionary one is often "surprised to meet a politician where you expected to find a priest."[19] Given the relatively young diplomatic relationship the United States had with the Ottoman Empire, the missionaries had accrued a good deal of political power in the course of their long involvement in the region. In 1915 the missionaries had more power than ever because of their personal friendships with President Wilson, which would put them in opposition to what might have been one way to help and perhaps save the Armenians.

Wilson's moral idealism, rooted in his Christian faith, had brought the president and many leading missionary figures together as lifetime friends. At the center of the missionary influence surrounding Wilson was Cleveland Dodge, whose family was one of the primary benefactors of the missionary movement in the Ottoman Empire. His daughter Elizabeth was married to George H. Huntington, a professor at Robert College in Constantinople; his son Bayard was the son-in-law of Howard Bliss, the president of the Syrian Protestant College. By 1915 Cleveland Dodge had become the chief benefactor of the Committee on Armenian Atrocities, and later a primary force behind Near East Relief.

Wilson was also good friends with other missionaries, such as his Princeton classmate William N. Chambers, who had been a key rescuer during the Adana massacres in 1909, and the writer and editor Albert Shaw, an influential member of Near East Relief. Even Colonel House was a friend of Dr. George Washburn, the son of the former president of Robert College.[20] Clearly the president's world was tied in with missionary politics in an unprecedented way.

With more than two decades of American anger against the Turks for their treatment of the Armenians, public opinion favored war with the Ottoman Empire. As Walter Lippmann of the *New Republic* put it, Americans wouldn't fight for other countries' imperial interests, but "they will fight for justice, whether it is in Macedonia, or in Turkey."[21]

On the other side of the fence, the American Board of Commissioners for Foreign Missions (ABCFM) realized early on that war with Turkey would be disastrous for its interests. Although some of ABCFM's property in Turkey had been confiscated and destroyed during the massacres, a formal declaration of war would mean the complete seizure of missionary properties and perhaps expulsion from the Ottoman Empire—in effect the destruction of nearly a century of their work. One missionary stationed in Mardin summed up the missionary perspective in a letter to James Barton; having to leave, he wrote, "would be out of the question . . . so long as America keeps her finger out of this muss, and from this stand point, on top of the Mardin mountain, we see no reason for America's having anything to do with it [war]."[22] Barton, who had been so instrumental in the Armenian relief movement of 1915, now became a powerful missionary voice against war with Turkey.[23]

The missionaries also made the point—again not without self-interest involved—that if they were expelled from the Armenian provinces, there would be no humanitarian relief for the Armenians, and the Armenians would be totally annihilated. Realizing that the ABCFM was now in "danger of becoming the victim" of their own Armenian relief campaign, Barton went on a public relations campaign in the Western states to promote neutrality with Turkey. In short, he embraced what Theodore Roosevelt called the pure hypocrisy of keeping the United States out of war with Turkey, in part, to protect the missionary interests in the Ottoman Empire, especially their vast real estate holdings, which were then worth about $123 million.[24]

Even Clarence Ussher, who only three years earlier had lost his wife and nearly his own life fighting to protect the Armenians during the siege of Van, declared that war against Turkey would make it impossible to continue the rescue of the "remnant of the Christian races of Turkey," and would play into the hands of Germany, which desired, he believed, to see the United States at war with the Turks.[25] A professor at the Syrian Protestant College, Maynard Owen Williams, inflated the missionary stance further by asserting in an article in The Independent that the real enemies were the Germans and the best way to fight them was to keep the missionaries firmly entrenched in the Ottoman Empire, where they could be moral beacons in a land of chaos.[26]

As the missionaries became increasingly defensive and self-interested, the quandary over war with Turkey took on increasing moral proportions. They had formidable opponents, including Rabbi Stephen Wise, who was also a member of Near East Relief. Wise believed that France, England, and the United States would be in a far better position to help the Jews and the Christians of the Ottoman Empire if the United States declared war on the Turks. Angry with Barton over the issue, Wise wrote, "I confess to you that I am greatly concerned about the Armenian problem," fearing that without proper intervention in Turkey, "the entire liberation of Armenia" would not be possible.[27]

Not yet the staunch isolationist he would become after the war, Henry Cabot Lodge agreed. The powerful Republican chair of the Senate Foreign Relations Committee, who had a lifelong dislike of the Ottoman Empire because of its violent, despotic system, endorsed war with Turkey as early as December 1917, believing that intervention could make a difference in the Armenian crisis.[28] Lodge called Turkey "a disgrace to the world, [which] has never been so bad as under the control of Germany," and he went on, "I should not like to see the United States, when the time for peace comes, in the miserable attitude of being at peace with Turkey." He referred to Turkey as "a plague spot" and "a breeder of wars," and he insisted that the "massacres must not under any pretense be condoned nor her iniquities rewarded. . . . The Syrians and the Armenians must be made safe."[29]

No one, however, articulated his disgust with missionary hypocrisy more forcefully than former president Theodore Roosevelt, who had sounded off to Cleveland Dodge and his fellow missionaries in 1915 when the Committee on Armenian Atrocities was first formed. Then he had lambasted the missionaries for being too passive about confronting the Armenian atrocities. He had berated Wilson's "cowardly" neutrality and his refusal "to take effective action on behalf of Armenia." Now, in 1918, he felt the pang of Wilson's failure to declare war on Turkey with even greater rage.

In a letter to Cleveland Dodge in May 1918, more than a year after the United States entered the war, and only about six months before the Armistice, Roosevelt made what is perhaps his most eloquent summation of the failure of American policy toward Turkey in the wake of the Armenian Genocide. Disappointed with Cleve Dodge for putting the missionaries' self-interest ahead of the call to duty, Roosevelt scolded his old friend: "In Turkey public opinion is nil and the people always obey any effective executive force, and obey nothing else." Roosevelt rebutted Dodge's contention that there were decent Turks who were not in favor of the massacres, asserting, "The perpetuation of Turkish rule is the perpetuation of infamy, and to perpetuate it on the theory that there are large numbers of Turks who have fine feelings but who never make those feelings in any way manifest, is an absurdity." The missionary colleges must not be used "as props for the Turkish infamy," Roosevelt insisted, or the good they had done in the past would become a mockery. The former president was then as blunt as ever:

> Moreover, I feel that we are guilty of a peculiarly odious form of hypocrisy when we profess friendship for Armenia and the downtrodden races of Turkey, but don't go to war with Turkey. To allow the Turks to massacre the [Armenians] and then solicit permission to help the survivors, and then to allege the fact that we are helping the survivors as a reason why we should not follow the only policy that will permanently put a stop to such massacres is both foolish and odious.

In concluding, Roosevelt noted that not going to war against Turkey was similar to America's refusal to go to war with Germany and Austria—only worse because it condoned the crime against Armenia. "The Armenian massacre," Roosevelt asserted, "was the greatest crime of the war, and failure to act against Turkey is to condone it; because the failure to deal radically with the Turkish horror means that all talk of guaranteeing the future peace of the world is mischievous nonsense; and because when we now refuse to war with Turkey we show that our announcement that we meant 'to make the world safe for democracy' was insincere claptrap."[30]

The Armistice came, and the United States had remained neutral toward Turkey. The anger and disappointment about America's failure to declare war on the Ottoman Empire was felt as keenly by the Armenian American community as it was by Roosevelt. They understood that Wilson's failure to declare war on Turkey would limit U.S. power in settling peace with the Ottoman Empire after the war. Mihran Sivasly, a prominent Armenian American in Boston, spoke for other Armenian Americans when he underscored that declaring war on Turkey would have put the United States in a better position to assure that Armenia would be treated justly after the war. James Barton was particularly alarmed that "some of these people," as he then referred to Armenian Americans, believed that because the missionaries opposed war with Turkey, they were defending Turkey.[31] And yet, when asked by the editors of New Armenia to declare in their pages his position on the future of the Ottoman Empire after the war, and in particular the future of Armenia, Barton declined, fearing that such a statement would make him persona non grata in Turkey and "turn the Turkish officials against the missionaries." Yet Barton confessed privately that "after the war the Turkish government should not rule over any part of Armenia, Syria or wherever Greek populations predominated," and only under limited conditions should the Turks rule themselves.[32] In the coming years Barton's position on Armenia would continue to change with the political winds.

As Wilson was dealing with the Allies at the Peace Conference in Paris, an extraordinary movement for Armenian independence was evolving back home in the United States. The year 1919 was one of social violence and political turmoil in the United States. Inflation had risen 77 percent from the prewar years, and labor strife led steel workers, coal miners, and even the Boston police force into the streets on strike. A revitalization of the Ku Klux Klan, which had gained a hundred thousand new members, led to the worst race riots in American history, and before the year was over, twenty-five race riots around the country had claimed hundreds of lives and resulted in millions of dollars' worth of damage.

Labor strife and fear of Bolshevism fueled more nativist hysteria. What soon became known as the Red Scare escalated when some radicals and anarchists sent bombs through the mail, setting off a bomb in front of the home of Attorney General A. Mitchell Palmer. The attorney general responded with a slew of arrests and raids nationwide. By the end of that year some six thousand Americans who were not even Communists were dragged into prisons, and Congress passed laws creating restrictive immigration quotas. In this xenophobic social climate, it may seem astonishing that the Armenian cause in the United States could evolve and reinvent itself with vigor.

In the fall of 1918 a distinguished group of Americans led the formation of the American Committee for the Independence of Armenia (ACIA). While powerful Americans had pioneered the Armenian National Relief Committee in 1896 and the Committee for Armenian and Syrian Relief in 1915, they were primarily business elites, clergy, and missionary leaders. But in 1918 the ACIA was led by a group of politicians and high-ranking government officials, and, for the first time, several Armenian Americans. James W. Gerard, former U.S. ambassador to Germany, chaired the ACIA executive committee, which included Charles Evans Hughes (Republican candidate for president in 1916), Elihu Root, Henry Cabot Lodge, Charles W. Eliot, and Cleveland Dodge. The ACIA general committee boasted William Jennings Bryan, Charles J. Bonaparte, Rabbi Stephen Wise, Samuel Gompers, Oscar Straus, Lyman Abbott, and Alice Stone Blackwell, among other philanthropists, industrialists, and clergy. The governors of nineteen states were represented, among them Al Smith of New York and James Cox of Ohio, both of whom would be presidential candidates in the coming decade.

One Armenian American in particular was a catalyst for the ACIA. Vahan Cardashian, a talented and fiery attorney, born in Caseria (Kayseri), Turkey, in 1883, had come to the United States in 1902. Having graduated from Yale Law School in 1908, he married a wealthy New York socialite, Cornelia Holub, an activist in the women's movement. Fluent in Turkish, Cardashian became an attorney for the Turkish embassy in Washington and for the Turkish consulate in New York City, and in 1913, as the Balkan Wars were being settled, he was hired by the Chester Group, an American business alliance that was eager to set up business in Turkey.[33]

As an attorney in diplomatic circles, Cardashian met and corresponded with Theodore Roosevelt and former ambassadors Andrew White, Joseph Choate, and Horace Porter, as well as university presidents Nicholas Murray Butler and Charles W. Eliot. Behind the scenes, he networked for support for Armenia. When the news of the massacres broke in the American press, and he learned that his mother and sister had been killed by Turkish gendarmes, Cardashian was stunned and enraged. Storming into the office of the Turkish ambassador, he cursed the ambassador and quit. From then on, his work for Armenia took on a new tone.[34] In 1918, having left the Armenian National Union, an early activist and fundraising organization (the other being the Armenian General Benevolent Union), he began working on the formation of ACIA and soon teamed up with James Gerard.

By December 1918, Henry Cabot Lodge had proposed a resolution in the Senate (Res. 378, December 19, 1918) calling for an independent Armenia that would stretch from the Mediterranean to the Black Sea—an idea embraced by many of the surviving Armenians in Turkey, who wished to see their full historic homelands returned to them.[35] As 1919 arrived, the ACIA and the American Committee for Armenian and Syrian Relief, which would soon become Near East Relief (affirmed by an act of Congress in 1919), were working hard together for the future of a new Armenia.

The two organizations planned their debut with a gala benefit. On February 8, 1919, a clear, cold breezy night in Manhattan, more than four hundred Americans filled the Grand Ballroom at the Plaza Hotel. Social and political figures, writers, actors, scientists, clergy, educators, and other leading cultural figures turned out for Armenia. In a banquet room with huge American flags draping the walls, the cast of characters that night represented extraordinary solidarity by American elites with an American minority culture—an ethnic group that in 1919 had a population of a mere one hundred thousand. The turnout underscored the support Armenia had accrued in American popular culture over the past three decades.

The success of the evening had already been foreshadowed by the telegrams of acceptance that had been arriving throughout January. Thomas Edison telegrammed ACIA organizers Harutun Azadian and George Koolakian in Syracuse: THEY SERVE BUSINESS WITH ENTERPRISING DISTINCTION AND RESOURCE. . . . ACTS OF BARBARISM SHOULD BE CONDEMNED, and he asked to have his name put to any proclamation for THE DEMOCRATIC LIBERATION of Armenia. From Paris, Koolakian and Azadian received a telegram from President Wilson expressing zeal for the future of Armenia:

> INDUSTRIOUS THE ARMENIANS HAVE DEMONSTRATED UNFAILING APTITUDE FOR FREEDOM AND DESERVE LONG WANTED DEMOCRACY MUCH IS PLANNED FOR FREE ARMENIA   STABILITY IS NEEDED IN THE NEAR EAST   INCLUDING ARMENIA IN OUR FOURTEEN POINTS WILL INSURE ACHIEVEMENT OF THIS IMPORTANT GOAL   AN EXAMPLE FOR ALL PEOPLES WE NEED TO PUT TO REST FOREVER THE INJUSTICES AND SUFFERINGS OF YOUR NATION FOR ALL OF HUMANKIND LEST THEY BE REPEATED . . . I AM CONFIDENT THE AMERICAN DELEGATION WILL VOTE ON THIS RESOLUTION TOMORROW . . . CONGRATULATIONS . . . YOUR WORK IS WELL DONE
> ADMIRABLY WOODROW WILSON

Roosevelt and Wilson now seemed to be sounding the same note, and from his Oyster Bay home at 7 P.M. on January 5, Theodore Roosevelt sent a telegram accepting his invitation to the gala:

> ROOSEVELT FAMILY WILL ATTEND   NUMBER UNCONFIRMED   ONE OF THE EARLIEST NATIONS AND THE FIRST CHRISTIANS ARMENIA HAS BEEN A PROUD BULWARK OF WESTERN CIVILIZATION DEMONSTRATING LONG AGO HER INALIENABLE RIGHT TO DEMOCRATIC SELF GOVERNMENT   HER AWAITED HOUR OF LIBERATION IS UPON US   IT IS OUR REQUITED DUTY TO SEE THAT JUSTICE AND FREEDOM BE OPPORTUNED TO ALL WHO SEEK ITS HALLOWED GROUND NONE ARE MORE DESERVING THAN THE ARMENIANS   THEODORE ROOSEVELT, SAGAMORE—[36]

For Roosevelt, who was often a virulent Anglo-Saxon supremacist, the pull of Armenia as a "bulwark of Western civilization" was congruent with the way many Americans continued to think of Armenia—an educated, entrepreneurial Christian culture, shaped, in part, by a century of Protestant-American influence. In an age of American xenophobia, this appeared to be an anomaly.

Having sent the telegram, Roosevelt went to bed and never woke up, dying of a heart attack in his sleep. But it was fitting that one of the last things he wrote was his testimony about an issue that had aroused his anger since the era of the sultan's massacres in the 1890s.

The gala at the Plaza on February 8 was a culmination of three decades of working for Armenia. The black-tie event drew the political elite: Joseph Tumulty, Wilson's White House secretary, standing in for the president, who was in Paris; the powerful head of the Senate Foreign Relations Committee, Henry Cabot Lodge; Charles Evans Hughes; William Jennings Bryan; Bernard Baruch, then Chairman of the U.S. War Industries Board; and Andrew W. Mellon. Table by table, uncanny groups of people were gathered. Notwithstanding Theodore Roosevelt's death a month earlier, his daughters Alice Roosevelt Longworth and Ethel Roosevelt and his sister, Corrine Roosevelt Robinson, were there. Aurora Mardiganian was a featured guest; this Armenian massacre survivor's account had been made into a film, *Ravished Armenia,* which had been screened the night before.

William Howard Taft, Warren G. Harding, Colonel House, and former attorney general Charles J. Bonaparte surrounded Edith Galt Wilson at another table. J. Pierpont Morgan, Calvin Coolidge, and U.S. Navy Secretary Josephus Daniels joined influential Armenian Americans Harutun and Akabi Azadian and George G. Koolakian. New York governor Al Smith joined Alice Stone Blackwell, Rabbi Stephen Wise, industrialist George Eastman, the feminist Lucia Ames Mead, and Columbia University president Nicholas Murray Butler. At other tables champagne glasses were clinked by Ambassador Henry Morgenthau, Adolph S. Ochs of the *New York Times,* Fiorello H. La Guardia, and Mrs. Thomas A. Edison.[37]

The evening opened with the singing of the song *Armenia,* and then ACIA Executive Chair James W. Gerard, the toastmaster, paid tribute to the memories of Theodore Roosevelt and Julia Ward Howe for their support of the Armenian cause over the decades. William Jennings Bryan spoke about the new democracy he believed Armenia would be and the

American ally it was natural to become. Charles Evans Hughes took the floor and spoke at length in praise of the Armenian people for their "industry, their intellectual achievement, their aptitude for education," and the other familiar qualities that were now associated with the Armenians. "Now," said Hughes—who had narrowly lost to Wilson in the 1916 election and would soon turn his back on Armenia for the sake of oil interests—"we rejoice that the hour of liberation has come." The Armenians, he went on, have demonstrated "a capacity to survive incredible misfortunes"; "they have rare intelligence," and "it would be unthinkable that Armenia should be left longer under Turkish control."[38] The evening closed with a pageant depicting scenes from Armenia's 2,500-year history, and then the singing of the *Battle Hymn of the Republic*—a fitting American anthem and a tribute to the woman who had stood up for Armenia a quarter century earlier.[39]

But the gala had really begun the night before at the Plaza with the screening of a sensational silent film called *Ravished Armenia*. Mrs. Oliver Harriman and Mrs. George W. Vanderbilt, whose families had been big supporters of Near East Relief, hosted the evening. A passionate believer in the new age of cinema, Mrs. Harriman exhorted the crowd that the world must visualize what happened to Armenia, and "the screen" was the best "medium" to reach the millions of people who must be reached.[40]

Ravished Armenia was based on the survivor account of an Armenian girl, Arshalois (meaning "morning light") Mardigian, who in the United States had changed her name to Aurora Mardiganian. Aurora had arrived at Ellis Island in November 1917, a sixteen-year-old with one surviving brother, for whom she was searching in the United States. In New York City she was taken in by an Armenian family who placed ads in the papers to help her search. The advertisements caught the eye of several journalists at the *New York Sun* and the *New York Tribune*, who interviewed Aurora and published her story.

When Harvey Gates, a twenty-four-year-old screenwriter who would become know for *If I Had a Million* (1932), *The Werewolf of London* (1935), and *The Courageous Dr. Christian* (1939)—read about Aurora, he was both deeply moved and saw a unique opportunity.[41] He and his wife, Eleanor, persuaded Nora Waln, Aurora's guardian, that the girl should abandon her plans to work in a dress factory and pursue a career in the movies. They soon became Aurora's legal guardians and transcribed her story, which was published as *Ravished Armenia* in the United States in 1918 (and as *Auction of Souls* in England in 1919). The book came with a preface and testimony by H. L. Gates, the president of Robert College in Constantinople, and Nora Waln, who verified the truth of Aurora's story. While the book sold well, its more sensational venue would be the big screen.

Ravished Armenia was an epic story and a first in film history, bringing genocide to the screen. Aurora's story begins in April 1915 in the city of Tchemesh-Gedzak (Chemeshgadzak), a town just north of the twin cities of Harput and Mezre in what Leslie Davis had recently called "the slaughterhouse province" of Harput. From her comfortable, affluent home (her father was a banker), Aurora is arrested and then abducted by Turkish gendarmes and thrust into a ghoulish world of massacre and violence. As she describes the death marches across Anatolia, *Ravished Armenia* depicts the story of what Ambassador Morgenthau had already called "the murder of a nation."

Col. William N. Selig, a pioneering producer from the 1890s, bought the film rights to Aurora's story, and Oscar Apfel, who had recently directed *The Squaw Man* with Cecil B. DeMille, was signed on as director. Irving Cummings and Anna Q. Nilsson, well-known movie actors of their day, were signed to leading roles.[42] Just as President Wilson was heading to Paris for the Peace Conference, Gates was bringing Aurora Mardiganian to Los Angeles to act in her own story at $15 a week. "They said $15 was a lot of money," and "I was naive," Aurora said, looking back at her life. At the Selig studios in Santa Monica, *Ravished Armenia* was made in less than a month, with death march scenes filmed on the beach near Santa Monica and Mt. Baldy standing in for Mt. Ararat.

Aurora barely spoke English and knew nothing about the world of cinema. On the set, when she saw actors in red fezzes, she fell into terror. "I thought they were going to give me to the Turks to finish my life," she said, breaking down in the middle of the scene. It took Eleanor Gates's consoling and explanations to assure Aurora that the actors were not Turks but Americans playing their roles, and that they would not harm her.[43] Today we would call Aurora's response post-traumatic shock.

Having experienced the deaths of her mother, father, brother, and sisters at the hands of the Turks, she was left alone to endure and witness torture, mass rapes, the crucifixion of women, the sale of women into slavery and harems, and the notorious "game of swords" in which girls and women were thrown by *chetes* and gendarmes from horses and impaled on swords that were set blade-up in the ground. As film critic Anthony Slide put it, no matter how hard both the book and the film tried to portray the violence Aurora experienced and witnessed, they were both "relatively sanitized versions of what [she] actually suffered and witnessed."[44]

When Aurora saw Apfel's version of the Armenian women being crucified on large, well-constructed crosses with their long hair covering their nude bodies, she told the director, "The Turks didn't make their crosses like that. The Turks made little pointed crosses. They took the clothes off the girls. They made them bend down. And after raping them, they made them sit on the pointed wood, through the vagina. That's the way they killed—the Turks. Americans have made it a more civilized way. They can't show such terrible things." Aurora then told Apfel and the others how her pregnant aunt, who was trying to protect her two-year-old son, was killed. "The Turks, they took a knife and cut open her abdomen. They said, this is how we are going to end all you people. They pulled out a fetus from her. Put it on a stone. They took the end of the gun that they had, which was heavy, and started to pound and pound and pound her baby."[45]

Ravished Armenia opened to mostly positive reviews. "Nothing could be more affecting than this vivid picture of the greatest tragedy of the world," wrote Hanford C. Judson in *Moving Picture World*, May 31, 1919. A critic in the *Los Angeles Evening Express* saw the film as transcending the more conventional Orientalisms of the time: "Now the producers have broken with tradition and in stage setting, costume, and action have reproduced not a conventional *Arabian Nights* slave market and harem scene, but have taken as their models these places as they actually exist today or did exist before the British entered Constantinople." In *Variety* the editor Sime Silverman said the movie was "superbly produced" but should not be taken as "a truthful representation" of the Turks' much more "fiendish and ghoulish torture" of the Armenians. Still, he wrote, "if *Ravished Armenia* in time may be given credit for the removal of Turkey from the map of the world, it will have helped in part to avenge Armenia and to have been of immeasurable benefit to civilization." Other critics called the film "cheap sensationalism."[46]

Yet the film was controversial enough to be banned in Pennsylvania, until the Court of Common Pleas in Philadelphia interceded. The British Foreign Office tried to censor the twice-daily screenings of *Auction of Souls*, as the film was titled in the UK, at London's Royal Albert Hall. Although the film was being sponsored by the newly created League of Nations, the Foreign Office was concerned that it would arouse anti-Turkish sentiment in England at a time when Great Britain was in peace negotiations with Turkey; the Foreign Office was also afraid that it might arouse anti-British sentiment throughout the Muslim world. Even though Scotland Yard threatened prosecution if the film was screened, protests from the League of Nations and intervention by the Home Office salvaged the show, but not without compromise. The screening was approved only under the condition that all references to Christians in the subtitles be removed, and that the scene of the Armenian women being crucified be deleted.

Although she was traumatized and exploited, underpaid by Gates and Selig, and forced to act with a broken ankle, the result of an accident on set, Aurora Mardiganian was introduced to the American public in Los Angeles in January 1919 as a kind of sensation, or perhaps an exotic freak. The film had catapulted her into strange stardom with a full-page color portrait on the cover of the January 12, 1919, issue of *American Weekly*. As her new American "mothers," Mrs. Harriman and Mrs. Vanderbilt, paraded her around the country for screenings among the elite of American society, she found herself lonely and angry; and the more she was portrayed as the "Joan of Arc of Armenia," the more morose she became. In the middle of May 1920, after grueling weeks of media appearances, Aurora broke down and threatened suicide. Gates, refusing to stop the show, sent her to a convent school and hired Aurora look-alikes. Later she sued Gates for the seven thousand dollars he owed her. Traumatized by the sexual violence she had endured on the death marches, she had nothing to do with men until she finally married an Armenian American in 1929 and moved to Los Angeles, where she lived until her death in 1994.[47]

As Gates, Apfel, and Selig were making *Ravished Armenia* in November 1918, Henry Morgenthau's memoir of his years as ambassador to Turkey was published by Doubleday and Doran. Compelled by the extraordinary episode of history he had just lived through, and aware that he was bearing witness to something, as psychiatrist and historian Robert Jay Lifton has put it, "for which there was as yet no name," Morgenthau used terms such as "organized attempt to wipe out a whole nation," "the murder of a nation," and "the massacre of a nation."[48] At the moment of the Armistice and in the weeks following, as President Wilson was preparing to leave for Paris, *Ambassador Morgenthau's Story* was met by wide critical acclaim.[49] Coming after the years of press coverage of the Armenian massacres and the humanitarian aid movement, *Ambassador Morgenthau's Story* brought to the American public a more coherent narrative of the massacres and a context in which to understand the Young Turk nationalism that made possible the extermination of the Armenians.

With the Armistice, the Committee on Armenian and Syrian Relief began a new era of activism and fund-raising to aid the Armenians. In addition to working with magazines and newspapers for coverage of the disaster that surrounded the Armenians, the Syrians, Greeks, and other Christians stranded in and on the fringes of the now-defeated Ottoman Empire, the committee began a poster campaign to spread the news to Americans with compelling images and catchy slogans. The focus was on relief to the orphans and refugees all over the Near East, and the phrase "starving Armenians" came into the popular culture with a new force. Posters were plastered in storefront windows, in subway cars and streetcars, and on highway billboards around the country. The American Railways Express went so far as to donate poster space on all of its trains, as did nearly all the streetcar systems around the nation.[50] The posters appealed to Americans to send money to the orphans and refugees of the Armenian Genocide and to the other uprooted and devastated Christians of the Ottoman Empire. The posters featured dramatic images with slogans such as: "Hunger Knows No Armistice," "Has This Little Girl a Home in Your Heart?" "They Shall Not Perish."

Like Mrs. Harriman and the ACIA, the Near East Relief organization also realized the power of cinema. They commissioned documentary footage of the orphanages and the relief work in progress, and showed them in schools, churches, and movie houses around the country. The aftermath of genocide came in newsreels titled "Alice in Hungerland," "Stand by Them a Little Longer," "Uncle America's Golden Rule Children." On the Sunday before Wilson left for the Paris Peace Conference, "Four Minute" speeches, as they were called—short exhortations about the crisis of the starving Christians in the Near East—were given by seventy-five thousand speakers to Sunday schools across the nation.[51]

In the midst of the outpouring for Armenia in February 1919, a voice from Germany also reached out to President Wilson. The indefatigable Armin T. Wegner, who had smuggled out eyewitness photographs of the Genocide and published a collection of his letters from Turkey in Berlin (*The Way of No Return: A Martyrdom in Letters*) now addressed Woodrow Wilson in an open letter published in *Tageblatt* in Berlin. As one of the few European "eye-witnesses of the dreadful destruction of the Armenian people," Wegner wrote, "I appeal to you" for a just settlement for an independent Armenia. "No people in the world," Wegner went on, "has suffered such wrongs as the Armenian Nation. . . . The Armenian Question," he exclaimed, "is a question . . . for the whole human race." Wegner told Wilson that he was writing to him as "a German," from a nation that was Turkey's ally, and he begged Wilson not to allow Armenia to be ignored or betrayed once again by European "selfishness" and "neglect," as it had been at the time of the Treaty of Berlin in 1878. As an international peace advocate, however, Wegner underscored that he was not making an "accusation against Islam," as "the spirit of every great religion is noble."

The Armenians, he reminded Wilson, were "a highly civilized nation with a great and glorious past, which has made unforgettable contributions to art, literature, and science," and had suffered as no nation had. "It would be an irremediable mistake," he wrote, "if the Armenian districts of Russia were not joined with the Armenian provinces of Anatolia and Cilicia to form one common country entirely liberated from Turkish rule."[52] The letter came at a moment when hope for Armenia was in the air.*

By the winter of 1919 Wilson's stance on Armenia was more affirmative than it had been during the war, when the missionaries helped sway him from declaring war on Turkey. Having made public proclamations for Armenia and its independence, Wilson now found himself facing a hostile political climate in Washington. In Europe, Great Britain, France, and Italy were moving slowly on a settlement for Armenia, but in eastern Turkey and Transcaucasia, an emerging Republic of Armenia faced new disasters.

---

* Years later, in the mid-1930s, Wegner wrote to Adolf Hitler protesting his anti-Semitic legislation, for which Wegner was imprisoned and exiled.

THE RISE OF A NEW TURKISH NATIONALISM AND THE CAMPAIGN AGAINST ARMENIA

As newsreels across the United States were showing images of Armenian refugees, and Near East Relief was raising unprecedented amounts of money through churches, synagogues, billboards, and editorials, the conditions for what remained of Armenia grew worse. With the bulk of the genocidal killing done, Turkey was still not finished with Armenia. In the spring of 1918 and then in the fall of 1920, first the Ottoman army, and then the new Kemalist army invaded the new Republic of Armenia. How this situation arose is part of a complex series of events that followed the collapse of the Russian Empire. Unexpected and sometimes bizarre political and military events unraveled the fate of what had become a fledgling republic.

As World War I evolved on the Turkish-Russian border in the spring. of 1916, the czar's army took back parts of the Turkish-Armenian *vilayets* that Russia had been awarded at the Treaty of San Stefano, following the Russo-Turkish War of 1877. By February 1916 the Russian army had occupied Erzurum; by April, Erzinjan; and by July the Russians had taken Van and the surrounding region.[1] The arriving Russians encountered an eerie scene, for once densely populated Armenian villages and towns were now desolate, with only the remains of massacred corpses and ruins of houses and businesses.

By March 1917 the first phase of the Bolshevik revolution in Russia turned the political situation upside down. As Czar Nicholas II abdicated his throne and was later imprisoned, a provisional government was established and immediately began to disengage Russia from the war. In the spring of 1917, Russian troops were pulled out of the occupied areas of Turkish Armenia (Van, Bitlis, Erzurum, and Trebizond) and the Armenians were urged (as were other ethnic groups under Russian rule, such as the Finns and Ukrainians) to seek independence and self-government. It was a fine idea but something that the Armenians were hardly capable of doing, having no adequate military or governmental power to sustain them in a geopolitical region where they were under constant attack by the Turks.[2]

The impact on the Armenians would be terrible. For in that brief interim when the Russians had control of northeast Turkey, they put the Armenians in administrative positions in Van, Erzurum, Bitlis, and Trebizond. But, as the Russians evacuated the Turkish-Armenian *vilayets*, they abandoned those Armenian territories that would have stayed in Russian hands had the Russians stayed in the war.[3] With the retreat of the Russian army and the collapse of the czar's empire, the Turks quickly recaptured the Armenian *vilayets*, and not long after that the three Russian Transcaucasian states—Armenia, Azerbaijan, and Georgia—formed a provisional Transcaucasian Federation. In January 1918, when the Ottoman general Vehib marched his troops into Transcaucasia, he found a ragtag Russian army made up of Russian Armenians, a few Russian soldiers who had stayed on, and some Armenian volunteer and irregular units that were seeking vengeance. This was an army fighting without a solidified state behind it, in a time of political chaos, disorganization, and uncertainty about the future of Russia.[4]

It was on the Transcaucasian-Turkish front during World War I in 1917–18 that the Turks invaded Transcaucasian Armenian areas once again, massacring Armenian civilians, including women and children, and laying waste to towns and villages. And, reciprocally, Armenians attacked civilian populations in Turkish towns and villages, massacring civilians and doing as much damage as they could. Having survived genocide, some of the Armenian irregulars were attempting to avenge the atrocities of 1915.[5] Today, the Turkish government, in its efforts to deny the Armenian Genocide, points primarily to these 1918 killings as evidence that Ottoman Armenians did equal damage to the Turks, and thus deserved to be exterminated as an entire race in 1915. It is an equation, of course, that makes no sense—either historically, politically, or morally—and is part of the Turkish attempt to deny historical truth.

Then, as if out of nowhere, Armenia was set back more dramatically by the Brest-Litovsk Treaty between the new Soviet Union and the Central Powers. Signed on March 3, 1918, the treaty allowed the new Bolsheviks to get out of the war, which they opposed ideologically for its imperialist goals and which they could not financially afford. In return the Soviet Union had to give up Poland, the Baltic States, and part of Byelorussia to Germany and Austria-Hungary, and cede to Turkey three heavily Armenian districts—Kars, Batum, and Ardahan. Overnight the Armenians awoke to the nightmare of being under Turkish rule. In Transcaucasia the Armenians were now caught between the chaos of the collapsed Russian empire, a hostile Turkey, and the unstable confederation of Transcaucasia, which would soon collapse.[6]

By March 1918 the Turks had taken Erzurum, and before the spring was over they had reconquered the rest of the Turkish Armenian territory that had been occupied in 1916. Crossing the 1914 border, the Turkish offensive advanced into the Transcaucasian Armenian heartland. On May 15 Third Army Commander Gen. Vehib Pasha's forces invaded Alexandropol, where the Armenians fought fiercely so as to allow the inhabitants to flee to Tiflis and Yerevan. Now thousands of refugees fled into the shrinking Armenian territory that was still free of Turkish troops. Within days the Ottoman Third Army's fifth, ninth, eleventh, and thirty-sixth divisions captured Hamamalu (now Spitak), and then advanced to Sardarabad, just seventy-five miles from Yerevan.[7] In that dry Transcaucasian town, as well as in the towns of Bash-Abaran and Karakilisia, the Armenians made a desperate last stand on May 22. With an army made up of genocide survivors and soldiers of a famine-ravaged world, outnumbered two to one by the Turks, the Armenians, led by Gen. M. P. Silikian and Gen. Drastamad Dro, drove the Turks back to Hamamalu.[8] Had the Armenians not made this stand at that crucial moment, it is likely that Armenia would have been completely wiped out and its name expunged from the map.

On May 30, 1918, with the Transcaucasian Federation collapsing, and no help coming from Russia or any Allied country, Armenia was forced to declare its independence. It was not a happy occasion, and the Armenian National Council made its declaration in a somber statement noting that "certain grave circumstances" necessitated the formation of "national government" in order "to pilot the political and administrative helm of the Armenian provinces."[9] For Armenia it was a time of fear and doubt. All that was left was a small landlocked area of eleven thousand kilometers. Kars and Alexandropol had been captured, and the population of the new republic included three hundred thousand Armenians of the region and another three hundred thousand starving refugees. Amid war, chaos, famine, and relentless Turkish assault, Armenia declared its self-rule for the first time since 1375, when the French king Levon VI ruled Cilician Armenia.

For all its precariousness Armenia emerged out of chaos as a democratic republic with a parliamentary system and a legislative body with popular representation and political parties.[10] With its penchant for democracy, and its brave effort to commence a new country, the new Armenia was still unable to halt the complex flow of events that continued to shape its future.

Even after the Turks surrendered to the Allies in the armistice at Mudros near Gallipoli on October 30, 1918, they were allowed to keep their troops in territory beyond the 1914 Russian border. But as they withdrew from areas such as Alexandropol and Kars, they displayed continued cruelty toward the defeated Armenians. An American officer named Arrol, who was stationed near Alexandropol with a small U.S. relief effort, noted in late December 1918 that as they were leaving the Armenian areas, the Turkish soldiers stole large quantities of humanitarian supplies, sabotaging the efforts to save Armenians who were dying of starvation. Arrol reported the theft of some 112,000 tons of wheat, 3,000 tons of cotton, and household goods from the trains and stockpiles. What they couldn't carry they left along the way to rot. Arrol also noted that numerous children had been raped and beaten, and the corpses of dozens of Armenian women littered the road.[11]

As circumstances continued to backfire for Armenia, another improbable turn of political fate occurred. In 1919 Russia and Turkey, bitter longtime enemies, made an alliance. In their mutual disdain for the Entente at the Peace Conference, the Bolsheviks and the new Kemalists found themselves with a similar political stance toward Europe. The Bolsheviks had cut themselves free of the imperialist agendas of England, France, and Italy, and the Kemalists, who were rapidly taking over Turkey, were preparing to fight the European plan to dismantle the Ottoman Empire in order to secure peace. As Lord Curzon had put it, to the anger of the Kemalists—Turkey had been for centuries "a source of distraction, intrigue and corruption . . . of unmitigated evil to everybody concerned."[12]

For the new Armenian Republic, timing was crucial. At the peace conference in Paris, the Allies seemed to be engaged in a slow chess game. Back in the United States, Woodrow Wilson was stalled by failing health and a hostile Republican-dominated Congress. The Allies' inability to formulate the Turkish part of the postwar treaty helped give more time to the new nationalist movement that was forming around the leadership of Mustafa Kemal and Kiazim Karabekir, who had been second in command to Kemal and a hero in eastern Anatolia in part because of his opposition to any plans for an autonomous Armenia.[13]

Mustafa Kemal had first become a hero in 1915, when his division played a decisive role in defeating the British at Gallipoli. Shortly thereafter he gained fame for fighting back the Russians in the Armenian *vilayets* of Bitlis and Moush in 1916.[14] From then on he was deeply involved in defending eastern Anatolia from any plans for an autonomous Armenia. By 1919 he was key in organizing the Association for the Defense of the Rights of Eastern Anatolia.[15] Kemal was outraged at Grand Vizier Damad Ferid's acceptance of "the principle of Armenian autonomy,"[16] and the Kemalists then passed a resolution forbidding the return of the Armenian refugees to the eastern *vilayets* without permission of their association.[17] Because of this phobia about Armenia, the very word "America" also had become hated in the eastern region of Turkey, due to its association with a free Armenia.[18] Yet, when he was confronted by U.S. general James G. Harbord in Sivas in 1919, and questioned about the Armenian massacres, Mustafa Kemal lied to him, claiming that he was committed to "fair and just treatment of all races and religions," including the Christians.[19]

It wasn't only opposition to the Armenians that galvanized the Kemalists. Even more dramatically, the Kemalists had found further popular support among the Turks after the arrival of Greek troops in Smyrna in May 1919. After some debate and disagreement among France, Britain, and the United States, the Greeks had been given permission to occupy Smyrna and its district.[20] Greece had both ethnic and historic claims to Smyrna—the famous port on the west coast of Asia Minor had been a center of Greek civilization for two millennia, the birthplace of Homer, and on the eve of World War I, the Greeks had still constituted the vast majority of the city's population.[21] In giving Greek president Eleuthérios Venizélos permission to send his troops to Smyrna, the rest of the Allies were also fending off Italy's designs on western Turkey.[22]

The Greek landing at Smyrna quickly engulfed Greece and Turkey in war, which turned out to be a disaster for all the Christians left in Anatolia. As the Smyrna crisis helped to fuel Kemal's new nationalism, its impact on the Armenian struggle for a homeland would be decidedly negative. General Harbord said most prophetically that "the events at Smyrna have undoubtedly cheapened every Christian life in Turkey" and would no doubt result in further aggression.[23] Tens of thousands of raw recruits now joined the Kemalist forces poised to fight the Greeks at Smyrna. Civil war then broke out in Turkey as the Kemalists bitterly opposed the Ottoman government. Mustafa Kemal lashed out at Grand Vizier Damad Ferid as "weak," "cowardly," and "subservient."[24] Ferid's government, he believed, had caved in to the British demand for a war crimes tribunal, as well as to the postwar demands the Allies were now making on the empire. At the Grand National Assembly in Ankara, the Kemalists went so far as to denounce Damad Ferid as a "traitor."[25]

By the fall of 1919, as the Kemalists were taking on the Greeks, Damad Ferid's government fell, and the Kemalists accrued more influence in government in Constantinople and throughout the country.[26] In the coming years there were three Greco-Turkish battles, and in September 1922 the Turks would burn Smyrna to the ground after killing tens of thousands of Greeks and Armenians and expelling the Greeks and remaining Armenians from the city and the region.[27]

As Kemalist nationalism found its footing and assumed unofficial political leadership, the nationalist stance against Armenia became increasingly virulent. Procrastination by the Entente in Paris gave the Turks the time they needed to invade Armenia. But before that happened, politics at the peace conference and in the United States made Armenia's situation tenser and even more complex. In April 1920 the Allies asked President Wilson to draw a boundary line for the western part of Armenia; but in May the United States rejected a proposed American mandate for Armenia.

And on August 10, 1920, the Allies brought Damad Ferid Pasha and his government to the conference table with a treaty they had been preparing for months. Like the Greek occupation of Smyrna, the Treaty of Sèvres came as an affront to the Turks and especially to the Kemalists. Because the Ottoman Empire had been a multicultural empire comprising numerous ethnic groups, many of which were living on their historic lands, the Treaty of Sèvres in some ways was aimed at decolonizing the empire.

Section VI, articles 88–93, of the treaty dealt exclusively with Armenia: (1) Turkey was to recognize Armenia as a free and independent state; (2) the president of the United States would determine the boundary between Armenia and Turkey, a boundary that would pass through the provinces of Erzurum, Trebizond, Van, and Bitlis; (3) the boundary was to include an outlet for Armenia on the Black Sea; (4) Turkey must renounce any claim to the ceded land; (5) although Armenia had been crippled by massacre and deportation, the European powers were asking Armenia to assume financial obligations for the former Turkish territory that was awarded to it; (6) Armenia would agree to protect the interests of minorities in its new state.[28] The treaty was at least a fair settlement for Armenia, but by the time it was signed, the politics in Turkey and the military advances against Armenia had made it almost obsolete. Now the Kemalists were determined to revoke the Treaty of Sèvres with its awards of territory not only to Armenia, but to Kurdistan and Greece.

The "National Pact" the Kemalists had drawn up in 1919 demanded all of Turkish Armenia, including areas that had been in Russia (Kars and Ardahan) that were now part of the Armenian Republic.[29] The Armenians desperately clung to the promises of the Europeans at Versailles and in the Treaty of Sèvres, but the tide was turning. The Kemalists were solidifying Turkey, and no foreign power was willing to accept a mandate for Armenia, even though the Europeans were agreeing to ask the League of Nations to consider the idea. In the West the commitment to Armenia, in the wake of postwar fatigue, was dying fast.

By the fall of 1920 the Kemalist army was acting on its commitment to destroy Armenia, now a precarious, isolated country of genocide

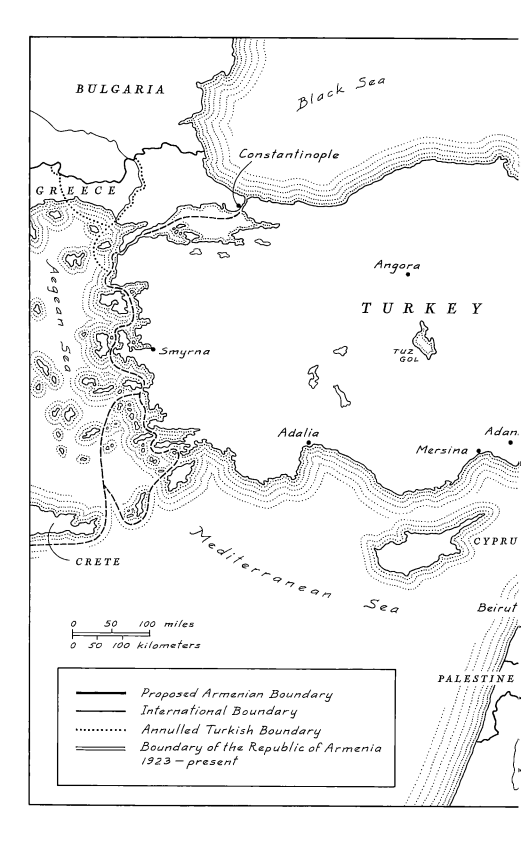

BULGARIA

Black Sea

Constantinople

GREECE

Angora

TURKEY

Aegean Sea

Smyrna

TUZ
GOL

Adana

Adalia

Mersina

CRETE

Mediterranean

Sea

CYPRUS

Beirut

0   50   100 miles
0   50 100 kilometers

PALESTINE

_____ Proposed Armenian Boundary
_____ International Boundary
.... Annulled Turkish Boundary
========= Boundary of the Republic of Armenia
           1923 — present

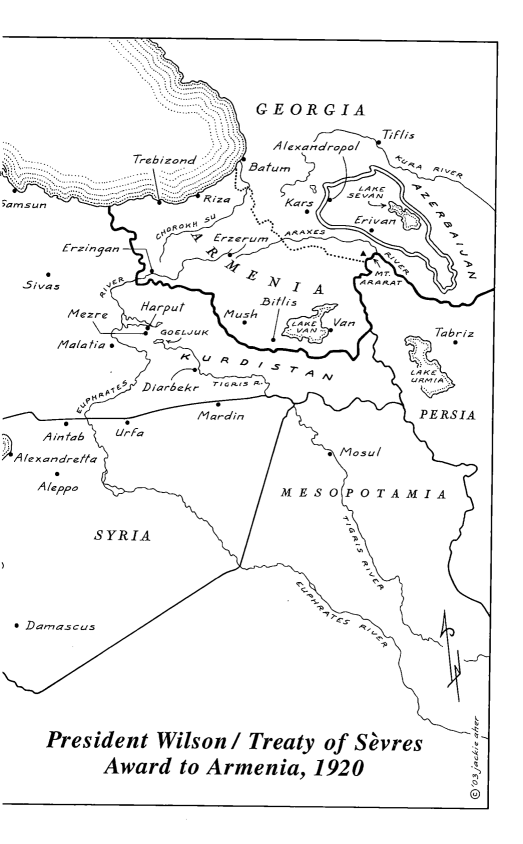

President Wilson / Treaty of Sèvres
Award to Armenia, 1920

refugees ravaged by disease and famine. Once again Armenia found itself in a situation beyond its control. In the summer of 1920, the Soviets were pressing Armenia to join the Soviet Union, and war actually broke out between Armenia and the Soviet Union in July. From the other side of the world—so it seemed—the West was urging Armenia not to join the Soviets, which in the end would cost Armenia even more territory.[30]

In this tense period a draft of a treaty between Soviet Russia and Kemalist Turkey remained unratified in Ankara because the Soviets now asked that some of Turkish Armenia be awarded to the present Armenian Republic. The Soviets also asked that the peoples of Turkish Armenia (the term used by the Soviets) and Batum, eastern Thrace, and the regions inhabited jointly by Turks and Arabs should be given the right to decide their own fate. Refugees living in Soviet Russia, and those who had been made homeless by war and massacre, were to be allowed to return to their homes and participate in a referendum.[31]

The Turkish response to the Soviet requests is revealing. Kiazim Karabekir's answer is an early and quintessential statement of Turkish denial of the Armenian Genocide. He retorted: "In Turkey there has been neither an Armenia nor territory inhabited by Armenians. . . . Those [Armenians] living in Turkey committed murder and massacres, and have escaped to Iran, America, Europe, and some of them to Armenia. How is it possible to call back these murderers and give them the right to vote?"[32] When Soviet foreign commissar Grigori Chicherin put the same proposal to the Turkish delegation in Moscow, he was told the same thing: "No Armenian provinces have ever existed in Turkey."[33] In this way, the Kemalists were continuing the work of the Young Turks in their effort to erase Armenia in fact and idea from the map it had inhabited.

Notwithstanding the Soviet concern for Armenia, Kemal launched an offensive against the Armenian Republic in September 1920.[34] In a top-secret cipher telegram the Ankara government under Mustafa Kemal communicated the following to Kiazim Karabekir: "It is indispensable that Armenia be annihilated politically and physically."[35] In September, Karabekir led his army across the 1914 border into Armenia, and within weeks the Turks had occupied the towns of Karaurgan, Bardiz, Kaghizman, and finally, at the end of the month, Sarikamish. The underequipped Armenian army, with no foreign support, fought valiantly but could not stop the Turks from marching on to the crucial

Armenian fortress and stronghold at Kars, about fifty miles south of Alexandropol.

What happened at Kars in October 1920 was tragic, somewhat surrealistic, and another instance of unexpected circumstance. The Armenians of Kars saw an army approaching the city, but due to communications failures, political infighting, and propaganda, they were led to believe that it was a Turkish Bolshevik army coming to help them. As the army entered the city the Armenians, who had woefully inadequate arms, quickly realized that the invading army was the enemy—the Kemalist army. The Armenians were stunned and unprepared, and what ensued was another Turkish massacre of innocent Armenian civilians, women, and children, and then the pillaging, looting, and raping. In the end six thousand Armenians were killed. With the fall of Kars, the future of the Armenian Republic seemed dimmer than ever.[36]

On November 22, as the Armenians were in desperate need of assistance from Soviet Russia, President Wilson finally drew his boundary line for Armenia. Six months earlier what became known as the Wilson award might have made a big difference, but now it seemed like a mockery. The Wilson award fine-tuned the terms of the Treaty of Sèvres, awarding Armenia a significant piece of territory: 42,000 square kilometers, including areas of Turkish Armenia and Russian Armenia, and including 400 kilometers of coastline on the Black Sea and the historic Armenian cities of Erzinjan, Moush, Bitlis, and Van. It was, as historian Christopher Walker has put it, "a fair and just award."[37]

Despite the Wilson award the Turks continued their rampage. From Kars they went on to Alexandropol, and took control of the railway line and continued massacring Armenians. With the Turks this deep in the Armenian heartland, the Soviets intervened and worked quickly to bring Armenia in to the Soviet Union.

In this moment, the Turks and the Soviets both offered Armenia their peace settlements. In the treaty offered at Alexandropol, the Turks demanded that Armenia relinquish the Wilson award, and give up Kars and Surmalu; Nakhichevan and Zangezur were then to go as protectorates to the Turkic republic of Azerbaijain to the east. This would reduce Armenia to 27,000 square kilometers. Hoping to render Armenia impotent, the Turks demanded that Armenia be allowed to have an army of only twelve hundred troops with a maximum of twenty machine guns and eight cannons. And to top it off the Turks proposed that Armenia become a protectorate under Turkish rule, reserving the right to temporary military action inside the "country."[38]

At the same time the Soviets were meeting with the Armenians in Yerevan, where new negotiations were under way. The Armenians hoped that the Soviets would negate some of the outrageous demands and bitter losses embedded in the Treaty of Alexandropol. Although the Soviets also demanded that the Armenians give up any claims to the Wilson award and the Treaty of Sèvres, unlike the Turks they recognized a larger Armenian territory that would include Yerevan Province, part of Kars Province, Zangezur, and parts of Kazakh and Tiflis districts.[39] In accord with the Yerevan negotiations, the Armenians prepared to become part of the USSR. Having resisted the Soviets until what seemed like the bitter end, in part because of Western pressure to avoid an alliance with the USSR, the Armenians now, in the latter part of 1920, realized that it was better to join the Soviet Union than to be decimated for good by the Turks.

Thus the boundaries of the Armenian Soviet Socialist Republic were shaped by the Treaty of Moscow (March 16, 1921) and the Treaty of Kars (October 13, 1921), which emerged in the wake of Soviet-Turkish negotiations. The Armenians were spared some of the crushing conditions of the Treaty of Alexandropol, but the template of the Turkish demands at Alexandropol shaped the basic terms of the new Armenian Soviet republic. Under the new treaties of Kars and Moscow, Armenia was forced to cede Kars and the surrounding areas the Turks had invaded in September 1920. The border was redrawn along the Araxes River, a border that remains today. Finally—and tragically—Armenia was asked to declare the Treaty of Sèvres null and void.

Turkey's demands at these treaty conferences, and the invasions of 1918 and 1920, make clear the extent to which Turkey was pushing for Armenia's extinction. But there would be one more chance for the question of Armenia to be heard—and that would be at the Lausanne Conference in Switzerland in 1922.

———∞∞∞———

TURKISH CONFESSIONS: THE

OTTOMAN COURTS-MARTIAL,

CONSTANTINOPLE, 1919–1920

To be in Constantinople after World War I. To see the once great capital through Armenian eyes. Gosdan Zarian—one of the eminent Armenian writers of his generation, and one of the few to survive—described Constantinople after the Armenian Genocide: "Multi-colored stones, splendid ornaments, all mixed with bloodied rags, rubbish dumps, open wounds."[1] Scutari, the once teeming Armenian section of Constantinople, Zarian now called "a state of mind." "Orphans, refugees," he wrote; "there is horrible misery on the shores of the Bosphorus." Alone in the city, he was haunted by the murder of his fellow writers: "How did Siamanto die?—he who was so afraid of death and so much in love with life. And Varoujan, Artashes Haroutiunian, Kegham Parseghian . . ."[2]

Shortly before Zarian recorded his impressions, the Turks had begun a series of courts-martial in Constantinople, aimed at bringing the perpetrators of the Armenian Genocide to justice. The trials represent a milestone in the history of war-crimes tribunals. Although they were truncated in the end by political pressures, and directed by Turkey's domestic laws rather than an international tribunal, the Constantinople trials were an antecedent to the Nuremberg Trials following World War II.

Never having declared war on the Ottoman Empire, the United States found itself without any postwar political clout with the Turks, but the victorious European Allies, especially the British, were in a position to push the Ottoman Empire to create a tribunal to punish its own leadership for committing crimes against humanity, notably the atrocities committed against the Armenians and its brutal treatment of prisoners of war. British anger toward the Turks had escalated after the war, when British soldiers returned with horror stories of the torture and cruelty they had endured in Turkish prisons.[3]

In Germany the Allies had already set up a tribunal at Leipzig, where the German political and military leadership were being tried for war crimes. But the trials in Constantinople were propelled by Great Britain, where strong pro-Armenia organizations had been at work since the 1890s when Gladstone and Bryce made such powerful statements. By 1915 the influential British Armenia Committee added new momentum to the older committees of the 1890s, and Arnold Toynbee, Aneurin Williams, Noel Buxton, and Arthur G. Symonds joined the now elder statesman Lord Bryce as leaders in the Armenia movement.[4] The landmark statement by the Allies, who were warning Turkey about crimes against Armenia, was made in London in May 1915, when the phrase "crimes against humanity" was coined.[5]

As the massacres were being reported in 1915, the House of Lords accused the Ottoman Empire of making "government by massacre part of their political system," and of "systematically exterminat[ing] a whole race out of their domain."[6] Prime Minister Lloyd George had proposed sending troops to Turkey "to prevent the Armenians from being massacred."[7] "[T]here was not a British statesman of any party who did not have it in mind," Lloyd George wrote, "that if we succeeded in defeating this inhuman Empire, one essential condition of the peace we should impose was the redemption of the Armenian valleys for ever from the bloody misrule with which they had been stained by the infamies of the Turk," which reduced the Armenian population "by well over a million."[8]

In 1918 Foreign Minister Arthur Balfour called for the Young Turk triumvirate—Talaat, Enver, and Jemal—to be criminally tried along with Wilhelm II. His successor, Lord Curzon, did the same, declaring that the Young Turk leaders "had massacred hundreds of thousands of their own subjects . . . [and] deserved any fate which was inflicted upon them."[9] At that moment the mood everywhere seemed to be in favor of justice for the Armenians, and even the Ottoman grand vizier, Damad Ferid, while avoiding mentioning the word "Armenian," made a stab at a confession at the Paris Peace Conference when he said:

> In the war nearly the whole civilised world was shocked by the recital of the crimes alleged to have been committed by the Turks. It is far from my thought to cast a veil over these misdeeds, which are such as to make the conscience of mankind shudder with horror for ever; still less will I endeavour to minimise the degree of guilt of the actors in the great drama. The aim which I have set myself is that of showing to the world with proofs in my hand, who are the truly responsible authors of these terrible crimes.[10]

With almost a million British and British colonial soldiers stationed throughout the Ottoman Empire after the Armistice, and the British navy along the Turkish coast, British pressure for a war crimes tribunal was bolstered. Thus, after the Armistice in November 1918, the Fifth Committee of the Ottoman parliament, and what was known as the administration's Mazhar Inquiry Commission, had begun collecting evidence and holding hearings about the Armenian massacres and corruption in the military in order to determine whether there was proper evidence for holding criminal trials. By January 1919, Somerset Calthorpe, Britain's high commissioner in Constantinople, was pushing the Turks to start rounding up those accused of mistreating British prisoners of war and those responsible for the Armenian atrocities.[11]

TURKISH TESTIMONY

The sultan, Mohammed VI, assured the British Crown that he was ready to punish the perpetrators of the Armenian massacres, and Ahmed Reshid, the Ottoman foreign minister, told Calthorpe that "with regard to the Armenian massacres, it was not merely the intention but the firm decision of the Government to punish the guilty."[12] By late January, Ahmed Reshid had made a list of sixty people in Constantinople who were responsible for the massacres, and he assured Calthorpe that they would soon be arrested. The prospects for a trial seemed bright, and Calthorpe seemed vigilant, even demanding the arrests of Talaat and Enver, who had fled Turkey two days after the Armistice and were hiding, with the sanction of the German government, in Germany.[13] By March 10 the Ottoman authorities had arrested about fifty prominent CUP leaders, and Grand Vizier Damad Ferid announced that "from today onwards all tyranny, injustice, atrocities, deportation, and massacres are banished from this country."[14] Gary Bass, a scholar of war crimes tribunals, has called it a "remarkable catch . . . comparable only to Nuremberg and Tokyo."[15] Those arrested included Said Halim Pasha (grand vizier, 1913–17), numerous government ministers, a slew of provincial administrators, and a number of former provincial governors from Smyrna, Boghazlyan, Mosul, Brusa, and Diyarbekir. By April more important CUP leaders had been arrested, and at least 107 were in jail.[16]

As the arrests were taking place, testimony was being given, evidence collected, and four major trials were set up to deal with (1) the massacres at Yozgat; (2) the massacres at Trebizond; (3) the lower-level CUP leaders involved in the Special Organization charged with killing the Armenians; (4) and a trial of wartime Turkish cabinet members. There were lesser trials dealing with the Armenian massacres in Harput, Mosul, Baiburt, and Erzinjan. Still more trials for Armenian atrocities in Adana, Aleppo, Bitlis, Diyarbekir, Erzurum, Marash, and Van were planned but never held.[17]

THE TRIALS

The tribunal prepared more than two hundred files to indict those in the military, in the CUP, and those at the top levels of the government. The accused were tried on the basis of municipal law and the Ottoman penal code, thus legitimizing the trials in a national legal context. The tribunal substantiated the key·charge of premeditated mass murder organized by the central committee of the Ittihad Party and carried out by the Special Organization (*Teskilât-i Mahsusa*) largely made up of criminals released from prisons who constituted the killing squads.[18]

In light of Turkish government denial today, it is particularly noteworthy that the records of all of these trials are to be found in *Takvim-i Vekayi*, the official gazette of the Ottoman parliament, which meticulously covered the most important aspects of the trials, such as the Key Indictment, the Key Verdict, and all the ancillary indictments and verdicts.[19]

The Yozgat trials, dealing with the massacres of the Armenians of Ankara Province, took place between February 5 and April 7, 1919. (Yozgat was a city a hundred miles east of Ankara, where tens of thousands of Armenians had been killed). Nearly all the defendants were subjected to pretrial interrogations, both written and oral, during which they made some significant confessions.[20] The trials document a microcosm of the Genocide, as Vahakn Dadrian has put it. The killing there was a paradigm of the broader process of Armenian extermination throughout Turkey. The Armenians of Ankara Province were well removed from any war zone; a fifth of them practiced Armenian Catholicism, not the more despised Armenian Apostolicism, and gave their allegiance to the pope; moreover, they spoke primarily Turkish.[21]

Hasan Mazhar, former governor-general of Ankara Province and a career civil servant, headed the commission of inquiry, known as the Mazhar Commission, and subpoenaed forty-two official documents from the postwar district governor of Yozgat, each of which was authenticated by Interior Ministry officials.[22] Mazhar was one of those Ottoman bureaucrats who could be called a righteous Turk, because he had refused Talaat Pasha's orders to deport and massacre the Armenians; consequently he was dismissed from his job. When Talaat's special emissary, Atif, relayed the order to the effect that "the Armenians be massacred and destroyed during the deportations," Mazhar had replied: "I cannot do what you are asking me to do."[23]

Dozens of authenticated ciphers were introduced at the Yozgat trials. Time and again they revealed that the word "deport" in fact meant "to massacre." For example, a secret telegram of July 17/18, 1915, from Lieutenant Hulusi, the gendarmerie chief of Boghazlyan, in the Yozgat district, informed his superiors that the Armenians of the region were to be "deported, that is, destroyed." In a telegram of July 22, 1915, Colonel Rejayi, the deputy commander of Ankara Fifth Army Corps, was informed that the Armenian deportees from Boghazlyan were "sent on to their destination"; when he wired back to ask what was meant by "destination," the reply came that "they were killed."[24] In his written testimony the *kaymakam* of Kilis quoted Abdulahad Nuri, who had received orders from Talaat explaining that "the salvation of the country requires the elimination of the Armenians," and Nuri added that he had "personally received the order of annihilation."[25]

In a dramatic courtroom episode, Col. Halil Rejayi testified that he had received from one Colonel Sahabeddin cipher telegrams that made it clear that "deportation" in fact meant "massacre." When the judge showed Sahabeddin the deciphered telegrams bearing his name, he fainted and was carried out of the courtroom. When he recovered and resumed testimony at the next sitting, he confessed: "I can confirm that the Armenian population was massacred in and around Boghazlyan."[26]

Other testimony revealed that Maj. Tevfik Bey, commander of the Yozgat gendarmerie, had almost completely wiped out the Armenian population of Yozgat, slaughtering the males between ages fifteen and seventy-five at Tash Punar village with "hatchets and axes as the victims kept screaming like birds." The screams and the deaths that followed were so horrible that some of the Muslim population from the neighboring villages appealed to Maj. Tevfik to have mercy on the women and children—in the name of the *shari'a*.[27] An affidavit from Maj. Mehmet Salim, the military commandant of Yozgat, made it clear that the deportations were part of a "policy of extermination," and that in order to render the Armenians defenseless they were marched off in twos or fours "with arms and hands tied up" and later killed with "axes, spades, swords, knives, hatchets."[28]

Perhaps the most dramatic event of the Yozgat trials was the testimony against District Governor Mehmed Kemal. Kemal had ordered the deaths of tens of thousands of Armenians in Yozgat and throughout Ankara Province. At the session of February 11, 1919, Kemal was described as having been "angry at the ineptness of the Turkish villagers rounded up to help his five hundred mounted brigands massacre a convoy of several thousand deportees. Shouting furiously at them, 'You don't seem to know how to slaughter,'" he then demonstrated that it would be more effective if they slashed their victims' throats diagonally instead of horizontally. The testimony on February 10 noted that, outside of the village of Guller, where thousands of Armenians were being butchered, Kemal was "observed smoking a water-pipe amidst the moans, groans, and shrieks of the people in mortal agony."[29] At the verdict Kemal defended himself by asserting that he had strengthened the Ottoman state by obeying orders.[30]

In response to the testimony against District Governor Kemal and Maj. Tevfik Bey, the court ruled that the two men had acted "against humanity and civilization," having ordered deportations and massacres and "practiced all methods of murder."[31] The court sentenced Maj. Tevfik Bey to fifteen years of hard labor, and Kemal Bey to death by hanging. When these verdicts were announced, there were angry protests, especially among the new nationalists of Mustafa Kemal's movement. The tribunal officials were so anxious about the Kemalist response that they scheduled the hanging for the afternoon rather than the morning, as was customary. Kemal Bey was hanged on April 10, and the funeral that followed created mayhem as hundreds of CUP members with wreaths reading "to the innocent victim of the nation," and the *softas* rallied vowing to destroy the English. British intelligence grew furious at the inability of the Ottoman government to control the execution of a low-level bureaucrat who had been convicted as a criminal.[32] One British diplomat complained, "Not one Turk in a thousand will think that any other Turk deserves to be hanged for massacring Christians."[33] Nevertheless it was a historic event, as Gary Bass put it, the "first instance of condign punishment for participation in massacres."[34] But the response to the trial foreshadowed the increasingly tenuous ground on which the pursuit of justice would proceed.

In the chapter "The Confessions of a Slayer Captain," about the Yozgat massacres, in his memoir *Armenian Golgotha*, Krikoris Balakian echoes and corroborates what was confessed at the Yozgat hearings. About a year after his arrest on April 24, 1915, in Constantinople, Balakian found himself on a deportation trail that had taken him from the prison at Chankiri, east to Chorum, and then south to Yozgat. On the road to Yozgat, Balakian became friendly with a Turkish captain named Shükri, with whom he rode for a couple of hours on horseback. Shükri, feeling certain that Balakian would soon be killed, answered the priest's questions candidly and even with a bit of braggadocio.

When Balakian asked Captain Shükri where "all these human bones along this road of ours" had come from, the captain replied: "These are the bones of the Armenians who were massacred" during August and September 1915. He went on to explain that Talaat Pasha ordered the bodies to be gathered and buried immediately, but that winter floods had washed up the corpses from their shallow graves and scattered them everywhere. When the priest asked him if the remains were of the local Armenian population or of Armenians from far away, Shükri told him that they were all from the local region.[35]

He went on to say that "this order was carried out most severely by district governor Kemal."[36] Balakian kept bantering with the Turkish captain, pretending to be an opponent of Armenian "extremists" and a Turcophile, and in this way kept the conversation going.

When Balakian asked Captain Shükri if the women were also massacred (because he thought the young ones might be spared and sent to harems), he was told that Kemal (the *kaymakam* of Boghazlyan) had the women and children massacred, including infants. Kemal even told the captain that he had "made a vow on the honor of the prophet: I shall not leave a single Armenian alive in the *sanjak* of Yozgat,"[37] a statement that was confirmed at the fifth sitting of the trial on February 12 by Maj. Memhet Salim, the military commandant of Yozgat.[38]

Shükri went on to tell Balakian how he and District Governor Kemal lured the Armenian women, children, and elderly onto the death march by having the town crier announce that they would be going to meet their husbands in Aleppo and ordering them to bring as much of their valuables and possessions as possible. The naive women even made baklavas and coffee cakes to celebrate the reunion with their husbands. About sixty-four hundred women and children were sent out on foot or in carriages or oxcarts and taken on a five-hour journey to a place known as Three Mills, where they were fleeced of all their valuables by a group of Turkish women, who were sent in to find all the gold and jewels they had hid on and in their bodies. The women were then massacred with "axes, hatchets, scythes, sickles, clubs, pickaxes, and shovels," Captain Shükri admitted, "in the name of holy *jihad*" and by "order of the government."[39]

As a priest Balakian was particularly interested in the role of religion in the massacres and asked Captain Shükri how a religious Muslim could order the murder of innocent women and not be accountable to God and his conscience. The Turkish captain told him that "a *jihad* was proclaimed . . . the Sheikh-ul-Islam had issued a *fatwa* to annihilate the Armenians as traitors to our state, and the Caliph ratified the *fatwa*." When the Armenian priest continued by asking him how he would "atone for his sins" in the "other world," the captain answered: "I have already atoned for them as I've always done after such killings. . . . I spread out my prayer rug and pray, giving glory to Allah and the Prophet who made me worthy of personally participating in the holy *jihad* in these days of my old age."[40] The captain's confessions not only corroborate the testimony given at the Yozgat trials, but also disclose something profound about how deeply the ideology of Islamic *jihad* was part of the psychology of the Turkish extermination program for the Armenians, as well as for the Greeks, Assyrians, and other Christians in the empire.

In the end the Yozgat trials documented that 61,000 of the 63,605 Armenians of Ankara Province (about 96 percent) had been deported and most of them killed.

Although the uproar after District Governor Kemal's hanging on April 10 created a new atmosphere of tension around the trials, the Ottoman government continued the trials in full force. On April 27, 1919, the court admitted that "the disaster visiting the Armenians was not a local or isolated event. It was the result of a premeditated decision taken by a central body [the Secret Organization of the CUP] . . . and the immolations and excesses which took place were based on oral and written orders issued by that central body."[41]

But in May 1919 the political climate changed further with the Greek occupation in and around the historic Greek city of Smyrna. The occupation became a further cause for the new Turkish nationalists, who saw both it and the military tribunal as evidence of continued Turkish resignation to defeat at the hands of the Allies. In this political climate the trial concerning the massacres in Trebizond Province along the Black Sea reflected a waning commitment to prosecution and justice.[42]

Among the charges made were that Turkish physicians had killed children by injecting them with morphine and then drowning them in the Black Sea. Dr. Ziya Fuad testified in writing that Dr. Ali Saib had "caused the death of untold numbers of Armenian children who were injected with morphine." But Ali Saib was acquitted, in part because Damad Ferid's government fell during the summer of 1919, and a pro-Kemalist government that was less sympathetic to the tribunal let Saib go on the grounds that they would have to retrieve the corpses of the children to determine if morphine had been used.[43]

Maj. Manastirli Tevfik, commander of the Trebizond gendarmerie regiment, was found guilty in May 1919 of conducting nightly mass drownings of Armenians in the Black Sea. The wartime adjutant and interpreter of the German officer Colonel Stange, a commander of a Special Organization force, testified to the drowning operations in the Black Sea and the poisoning of Armenian children at the Red Crescent Hospital. He too was acquitted.[44]

The main verdict of the Trebizond trials was delivered on May 22, 1919, and it corroborated the essential findings of the Yozgat trials. The verdict asserted that Jemal Azmi, the governor-general, and Yenibahcheli Nail Bey, the CUP Responsible Secretary, issued the orders to deport and massacre the Armenians. Again, it was made clear that "deportation" meant "massacre." After leaving the city, the deportee convoys were driven out of the city; the verdict read:

> The men were separated from the women in the convoy of the Armenians, who were deprived of the means of protection. The brigands, deployed . . . first robbed [the deportees] of their goods and possessions and then [proceeded to] kill and destroy [the men]. . . . Under the pretext of transporting them by the sea route to another place, the male and female infants were taken in split groups on board of barges and caiques to the high seas and, hidden from sight, were thrown overboard to be drowned and destroyed.[45]

In the main Trebizond verdict Jemal Azmi and Yenibahcheli Nail were condemned to death in absentia. Hehmet Ali, a customs inspector, was sentenced to ten years of forced labor; and a deportation official, and the police chief, to one year in prison.[46] With the acquittals of the Turkish physicians and the light sentences, the writing was on the wall. Nevertheless the Trebizond testimony confirmed what U.S. consul Oscar Heizer had reported to Ambassador Morgenthau in 1915 and what survivors like Leon Surmelian reported: that the Armenian Genocide was planned and carried out by the central government.

The hearings proceeded into the summer of 1919 with the trials of midlevel bureaucrats—the CUP Responsible Secretaries and cabinet ministers and CUP leaders. Of the twenty-nine Responsible Secretaries indicted, only eleven appeared in court, which was indicative of the collapsing authority of the tribunal.[47] Despite this, in the reading of the Key Verdict—the document of evidence against the CUP members and cabinet ministers—the trial demonstrated that Responsible Secretaries in the interior provinces had dismissed provincial governors who refused to comply with orders to deport and massacre the Armenians. This was the case with the dismissal of Governor Jemal, who was replaced by Mehmet Kemal in the Yozgat district of Ankara Province, and the dismissal of Governor-General Reshid Pasha in Kastamonu Province.[48]

Among the most important statements in the Key Verdict was the tribunal's conclusion that all of the Responsible Secretaries were "accessories to the criminal decision-making of the Central Committee of the party," and that they had made effective use of the legislation of May 14/27, 1915—the Temporary Law of Deportation. The Key Verdict declared that the Responsible Secretaries had used this law "for personal gain" by "appropriating the riches [of the victims], and plundering of properties. The Key Verdict also noted that the Responsible Secretaries had "organized and produced through the new work of their organization branches . . . criminal gangs and mobs, specifically geared to [the goal of] massacring and annihilating the Armenians and pillaging and looting their possessions."[49]

During this time Kemalist nationalism was taking hold of the country and increasing the public's disapproval of the tribunal. Correspondingly the sentences grew weaker, as the court refrained from handing down death sentences, finding most of the defendants only "guilty of robbery, plunder, and self-enrichment at the expense of the victims."[50] In May 1919 the British were shocked to learn that twenty-six prisoners arrested for the Armenian massacres in Trebizond were released, and then in June when another fifty were released.[51]

From the later part of 1919 on, a political thicket emerged around the war crimes issue. The Turks had taken about twenty-nine British soldiers as prisoners, including Col. Alfred Rawlinson, whose brother was also a high-ranking military officer. And the British were now holding about sixty Turkish prisoners in jail on the island of Malta, most of them accused of Armenian atrocity crimes. Their hope was to have many of them (including Said Halim, Halil Menteshe, Ahmet Nesimi, and Ali Münif) appear before an International Tribunal, but that opportunity would never come.[52]

In this climate of mounting political tension, the pursuit of justice continued, and leading members of the CUP government were put on trial, and cabinet ministers, two grand viziers (Said Halim and Talaat Pasha), three Sheikhs ul-Islam, and several army commanders faced prosecution.[53] The evidence against these top CUP members was delivered in the Key Indictment. What made the Key Indictment so powerful was its inclusion of forty-two incriminating documents that had been gathered by the Mazhar Commission. These documents—telegrams, decoded telegrams, memos, telegraphic orders, statements, and depositions—highlighted the role of the Central Committee and confirmed that the campaign to exterminate the Armenians was premeditated and deliberate. The documents also revealed that the Special Organization engineered the killing squads—the majority of whom were "criminals released from prisons." Since most of the CUP's files and records disappeared after the war, these forty-two documents spoke loudly.[54]

The published version of the Key Indictment refers to the Armenian atrocities as "massacre," "plunder of properties," and to "torching of corpses and buildings," "rape," and "torture and torment." The indictment maintained that crimes against the Armenians were committed "in a particularly organized way . . . in the capital and in the provinces," and it underscored that what happened was "the extermination of an entire people constituting a distinct community." The indictment also stated that the deportations were not dictated by military necessity, nor were they a disciplinary measure.[55]

In outlining the extermination plan, the Key Indictment noted that "the Special Organization was set up by the leaders of the CUP," and that the chief organizer of the operation was the Special Organization chief, Dr. Behaeddin Shakir, who "presided over the activities of the Organization for the success of which he put to use the Responsible Secretaries and Inspectors of the party."[56] Among the forty-two documents in the Key Indictment was a cipher telegram from Behaeddin Shakir to Resneli Nazim, in which Shakir wrote: "Are the Armenians, who are being deported from your area, being liquidated? Are the harmful people, who you say are being banished and dispersed, being destroyed or are they being merely removed and sent away?"[57]

Another central document in the Key Indictment was the statement from Third Army Commanding General Vehib, which articulated with particular verve the scope of the Armenian Genocide:

> The massacre and the annihilation of the Armenians and the loot-ing and plunder of their properties were the result of the decision of the Central Committee of Ittihad and Terakki. Behaeddin Shakir was the one who procured the butchers of human beings in the Third Army zone, who directed and used them. All the human tragedies, all the incitements and acts of depravity within the Third Army operational zone came about and manifested themselves as a result of Behaeddin Shakir's machinations. These involved the recruitment, on the one hand, of the gallowsbird kind, and on the other, gendarmes with blood on their hands and blood in their eyes.

He went on:

> In summary, here are my convictions. The Armenian deporta-tions were carried out in a manner entirely unbecoming to [the ideals of] humanity, civilization, and government. The massacre and annihilation of the Armenians, and the looting and plunder of their properties were the result of the decision of the Central Committee of Ittihad and Terakki. The butchers of human beings, who operated in the command zone of the Third Army, were procured and engaged by Dr. Behaeddin Shakir. The high ranking governmental officials did submit to his directives and orders. All the tragedies, the incitements and acts of depravity in the Third Army zone were enacted under the guidance of Behaeddin Shakir. Traveling with a special automobile, he stopped by at all major centers where he orally transmitted his instructions to the party's local bodies and to the governmental authorities.[58]

As Vahakn Dadrian has put it, the final verdict found the Committee of Union and Progress guilty of subverting the standard functions of the government, using cabinet ministers as submissive tools, and (as the Nazi government would later do) using wartime conditions as a pretext for domestic genocide. The verdict made clear that the Young Turk government's plan to liquidate the Armenians was a project that also aided their wartime ambitions against Russia.[59] The court then found the heads of government—Talaat, Enver, Jemal, and Dr. Nazim—guilty of first-degree murder and sentenced them to death in absentia.

By the end of 1919, faced with the Kemalist takeover of Turkey, Grand Vizier Damad Ferid resigned and was followed by a succession of grand viziers eager to come to terms with Kemal and his forces. The British commitment to the war crimes tribunal continued to wane due to the political climate in Turkey and British postwar fatigue in general.[60] Only 320,000 British troops remained in the Ottoman Empire, where there had been a million a year earlier. More and more, the British looked on as the Ottoman officials who were running the trials appeased the Kemalists by freeing prisoners or handing out light sentences.[61]

By 1921 Britain had abandoned the idea of war crimes trials in Turkey. After much debate and disagreement over the pursuit of justice in Turkey, the War Office, led by its new secretary, Winston Churchill, decided that it would free its Turkish prisoners, held at Malta, in exchange for the British prisoners the Turks were holding. It was a pragmatic deal of which one member of the Foreign Office noted that it destroyed Part VII (Penalties) of the Treaty of Sèvres. "The whole transaction" he called "tantamount to complete capitulation to Turkish blackmail." The fact that the newly signed treaty contained a section on the "Turkish government's" "criminal acts" and "massacres" was a galling irony. This change in British policy came at great cost to international justice. In August 1921, the British released forty-three Turkish prisoners who were accused of perpetrating the Armenian massacres.[62]

The abandonment of the Constantinople war trials was a major failure, and it helped to accelerate the amnesia in the West about the Armenian Genocide in the ensuing decades. Nevertheless the trials produced more evidence about the organized plan to exterminate the Armenians. That evidence came from Turkish officials who had themselves organized and participated in the massacres and deportations, and from a body of official government documents.[63] Although there were three hangings and many prison convictions, none of the convicted served out their prison sentences, and the majority of the perpetrators escaped punishment after the British-Turkish prisoner exchange deal.

In one sense history reveals that when justice isn't served in a legal capacity, some people will take matters into their own hands. Immediately after the war the radical wing of the Dashnak Party, like the future Jewish Nazi hunters after World War II, began hunting for the chief architects of the Armenian Genocide. In the early 1920s Armenians assassinated some of the leading CUP members. Armenian avengers killed Said Halim, the former grand vizier, in Rome in 1921 and also Behaeddin Shakir in Berlin in 1922. Jemal Pasha was killed by Armenians in Tiflis in July 1922. Enver Pasha died at Bukhara in August 1922 during a battle led by an Armenian Bolshevik officer.

Because many of the high-ranking Young Turks fled to Germany after the Armistice, where the German government seems readily to have given them asylum, Germany became the site of a dramatic assassination and subsequent trial in 1921. Talaat Pasha—who had fled to Germany and was living incognito in Berlin—was assassinated on March 14, 1921. In clear daylight, in the Charlottenburg district of Berlin, a twenty-four-year-old Armenian, Soghomon Tehlirian, walked up behind Talaat Pasha, shouted, "This is to avenge the death of my family," and pulled the trigger.[64] Tehlirian, who had witnessed the rape of his sisters, the beheading of his brother, and the murder of his parents on a death march in Erzurum in 1915, had been left for dead in a pile of corpses and subsequently escaped. When he was put on trial in Berlin, in what became a celebrated case throughout Europe, he was acquitted on grounds of what today would be termed temporary insanity, when the jury heard the account of his experience in the Armenian Genocide.[65]

At the Tehlirian trial in June, several extraordinary documents were submitted that disclosed Talaat Pasha's official orders to exterminate the Armenians. In July of 1921, *Current History*, the monthly magazine of the *New York Times*, ran an astonishing feature: "Why Talaat's Assassin Was Acquitted." The article featured facsimiles of decoded cipher telegrams in Ottoman script from Talaat Pasha and noted that "the official Turkish documents . . . proved beyond question that Talaat Pasha and other officials had ordered the wholesale extermination of the Armenians." The dispatches had been sent to Aleppo, which the article noted was the head-quarters of the Deportations Committee. A dispatch of September 16, 1915, read:

> It has been previously communicated to you that the Govern-ment by order of the Jemiet [the Young Turk Committee] has decided to destroy completely all the indicated persons living in Turkey. Those who oppose this order and decision cannot remain on the official staff of the empire. An end must be put to their existence, however tragic the measures taken may be, and no regard must be paid to either age or sex, or to conscientious scru-ples. *Minister of the Interior,* TALAAT.

Realizing that American consuls like Leslie Davis and Jesse B. Jackson were sending detailed reports of the Genocide to ambassador Morgen-thau in Constantinople, Talaat warned his committee in Aleppo in a dis-patch of November 18, 1915:

> From interventions which have been recently made by the Amer-ican Ambassador at Constantinople on behalf of his Government, it appears that the American Consuls are obtaining information by secret means. . . . For this reason it is important that, to save appearances, a show of gentle dealing shall be made for a time, and the usual measure be taken in suitable places. . . . The people who have given such information shall be arrested and handed over to the military authorities for trial by court-martial. *Minister of the Interior,* TALAAT.

In December 1915 Talaat wrote again to the Prefecture of Aleppo that journalists were obtaining photographs and letters that depicted the mas-sacres and were giving them to "the American Consul at Aleppo. Have dan-gerous persons of this kind arrested and suppressed. *Minister of the Interior,* TALAAT." On January 15, 1916, Talaat wrote to his Aleppo committee:

> We hear that certain orphanages which have been opened received also the children of the Armenians. Whether this is done through ignorance of our real purpose, or through contempt of

it, the Government will regard the feeding of such children or any
attempt to prolong their lives as an act entirely opposed to its purpose, since it considers the survival of these children as detrimen-
tal. . . . *Minister of the Interior,* TALAAT.

Although these documents reached the American public in the summer of 1921, after the political tide had turned against Armenia, they confirmed for Americans once again the massive evidence the press had
reported, that Ambassador Morgenthau had delivered in his memoir, and
that the American consuls and missionaries had already brought home to
the American public.[66]

—⊶⊷—

THE AMERICAN MANDATE

FOR ARMENIA

We literally dreamed Armenia and massacres.
                                    —Maj. Gen. James G. Harbord

While the perpetrators of the Armenian Genocide were still being tried in the spring of 1919, and the fledgling Armenian Republic was trying to survive assaults from Turkey, President Wilson was preparing to send the first of two fact-finding commissions to Turkey. His goal was to get thorough eyewitness reports on the social and political conditions in the defeated empire so that he could assess the possibilities for mandate programs there. The King-Crane Commission set out for its destination in June 1919, followed by the Harbord Mission in September.

At the peace conference the Allies, searching for solutions for dealing with the breakup of the Ottoman Empire, and determined to create an independent Armenia, planned a multilateral investigative commission. But as they continued to squabble over their claims to territory in the defeated Ottoman Empire, the French and the British soon concluded it would be best for the United States to make an investigative mission alone. Heeding that request Wilson chose Henry Churchill King and Charles R. Crane to head the first mission. King was the president of Oberlin College and a theologian, who had been chairman of the Committee on the War and Religious Outreach. He seemed an ideal choice. Charles R. Crane, the president's good friend, was former secretary of the original Committee on Armenian Atrocities in 1915, as well as president of the board of trustees of Constantinople College for Women. Clearly he understood the Armenian crisis from the inside.[1]

The King-Crane Commission arrived in Jaffa on June 10, 1919, and had among its distinguished members Professor Albert H. Lybyer of the University of Illinois, who had just finished serving in the Balkan Division of the American Commission to Negotiate Peace; Dr. George R. Montgomery, a clergyman who had spent most of his life in Turkey, studied at the University of Berlin and at Yale, and served as a special assistant to Ambassador Morgenthau; and Capt. William Yale, a civil engineer who had worked for Standard Oil in the Ottoman Empire and, during World War I, served the U.S. State Department and army in Egypt.[2] The commission's goal was to assess the possibilities for mandate programs for Syria, Mesopotamia, and the non-Arabic-speaking portions of the Ottoman Empire. The commission members conducted interviews, mainly in Constantinople, with many Turkish organizations, as well as with various Armenian delegations, including representatives of the Apostolic, Catholic, and Protestant churches. They even received communications from Mustafa Kemal, who was beginning to solidify his new nationalist movement.[3]

Although all the Turkish groups interviewed spoke for equal rights for minorities, very few were ready to accept the cession of any territory for the creation of a non-Turkish state, and especially not for Armenia. The Turkish organizations that were interviewed wanted, for the most part, to see the Armenian question disappear. One anomalous Turkish voice, Ahmed Emin Yalman, the editor of *Vakit,* advocated that the size of the Armenian state should be proportional to the prewar Armenian population.[4]

By the end of the summer the commission had heard many voices, among them the remaining American missionaries, who gave poignant testimony. In Sivas, Mary Graffam, a teacher who had risked her life to save Armenians in 1915, testified that it would "be impossible for the Turks and Armenians to live together." Without an Armenian state, Graffam said, the Armenians would be victimized again, and it would be "past human imagination."[5] From Marsovan, Dr. George E. White, president of Anatolia College, testified that unless Armenia were liberated from Turkish domination, there could be "no real security for the life of a man, the honor of a woman, the welfare of a child, the property of a citizen or the rights of a father." White felt that Turkey's "public institutions" were "hopeless," and that the whole nation should be placed "under the governance of a firm, friendly mandatory power without fail."⁶

In its final report the King-Crane Commission asserted that "the Armenians should be provided with a definite territory," taken from both Russia and Turkey, "with an outlet on the Black Sea," and organized into "a self-governing, independent state."⁷ The commission recommended that Armenia should not be given a territory too large for it to govern or one in which the Armenians would not be a majority. It emphasized that the Armenians were entitled to "an amount of land which took into account their losses" in the massacres of 1894–96, 1908–9, and 1915–16, which they estimated at about one million dead. The report recommended a large part of the four historic Armenian provinces of Trebizond, Erzurum, Bitlis, and Van be awarded to Armenia; with this, the report asserted "the Turks and Kurds could not justly complain, because this would be 'historical Armenia.' "⁸

Nor did the report mince words about the idea of justice. The "great and lasting wrongs in Turkey which must be set right" and the "incessant corruption, plunder, and bribery" that had characterized the Empire compelled the commission to call for an autonomous Armenian state. Turkey's crimes were, the report read, "black as anything in human history," and must be dealt with in seeking "a righteous solution of the Turkish problem." The King-Crane Report concluded that the Armenian massacres justified at the very least an adequate independent Armenia. There was a tone of astonishment in the report over the fact that neither the Turkish government nor the Turkish people have "recognized or repudiated the crime of the Armenian massacres."⁹ An independent Armenia was essential, the report went on, because of:

> the demonstrated unfitness of the Turks to rule over others, or
> even over themselves; because of the adoption of repeated mas-
> sacres as a deliberate policy of State; because of almost com-
> plete lack of penitence for the massacres . . . because the most
> elementary justice suggests that there must be at least some
> region in Turkey where Armenians can go and not have to live
> under Turkish rule; because nothing less than that could give
> to the Armenians any adequate guarantee of safety; because,

consequently, nothing less will satisfy the conscience of the world . . . the Armenians have surely earned the right, by their sufferings, their endurance, their loyalty to principles, their unbroken spirit and ambition, and the demonstrated industry, ability and self-reliance to look forward to a national life of their own.[10]

The report further advocated that Turkey express penance for what it had done to Armenia by "the allotment of the territory within her borders, recommended for the Armenian state," and "by encouraging repatriation of the Armenians" and making "just reparation" to the thousands of people still living who were torn from their homes and might now be returning to them.[11]

The commission submitted its report to the peace conference in Paris on August 28, 1919, just as Wilson was losing his battle with Lodge and the Senate Foreign Relations Committee over the treaty and the League of Nations. Within a week the president would embark on his Western trip with the hope of selling the idea of the League of Nations to the American people. Though Wilson was advised of the Commission's recommendations, by the time the report reached the White House, the president had returned from Utah debilitated by his recent stroke and beleaguered by his sense of losing his fight with Congress.

In Paris the report seems to have been read by French and British Foreign Office officials, but otherwise from the moment it was submitted to the delegations at the peace conference, the King-Crane Commission report was neither published nor circulated, and as one historian has said, it disappeared in a "shroud of complete silence."[12] Henry White and Harry N. Howard, both members of the commission, believed that the report was suppressed because the French and British delegates did not like its recommendations. One can only conjecture how the peace conference and the United States might have responded to the report, but its disappearance was a setback for Armenia. If the King-Crane Report was, as one newspaper editor put it, "one of the great suppressed documents of the peace-making period," then it very well might have changed the United States' isolationist attitude about its postwar responsibilities. And it might have saved the lives of millions of people who were killed in the aftermath of the war.[13]

THE HARBORD MISSION

As the King-Crane group was in the midst of its mission in the summer of 1919, James Gerard, who was still working on behalf of ACIA, cabled President Wilson imploring him to send immediate aid to the Republic of Armenia, including troops to help the Armenians hold on to the western part of their new republic, which the Turks were trying to take.[14] Even Republicans like Lodge and Hughes, who would soon turn against the American mandate for Armenia, supported this request. In July, Hoover, now the postwar head of international food relief, emphasized that aid could only be administered by rail, and that the new Georgian government was interfering with aid and trying to skim some off for itself. "It is impossible to depict the situation in Armenia," Hoover wrote, "for, until the last sixty days, the population has been eating the dead."[15]

In late July, Maj. Joseph Green, who had been sent to Armenia by Wilson to be a commissioner to the new republic, cabled the Allies in Paris to inform them that the Turks were advancing into Armenia and that military protection would be needed to avoid "disaster . . . more terrible than massacres of 1915." If Armenia were completely wiped out now, it would be, he wrote, "to [the] everlasting shame of the Allies." To make matters worse the British were scheduled to withdraw their troops from the Caucasus, and Hoover wrote Undersecretary of State Frank Polk that "we are faced with a practical extermination of the Armenians."[16]

Heeding the urgings of Hoover and Green, and the American appeal for the "starving Armenians," Wilson appointed Gen. James G. Harbord to lead an American military mission to Armenia. Harbord was a seasoned general who had commanded American troops at Soissons and Château-Thierry, and served as chief of staff under Gen. John Pershing in 1917–18, and he welcomed the assignment. In September 1919, as Wilson was heading West on his grass-roots campaign, the Harbord Commission was aboard the naval transport ship *Martha Washington*. They sailed into the Golden Horn on September 2 with a group of army officers, including two brigadier generals.[17]

With several cars on loan from the army, piles of reports by the American Mission to Negotiate Peace, a few sawed-off shotguns, several secretaries, translators, and photographers, and a good French chef who was reduced to cooking bacon and onions over campfires, the Harbord group set out a bit like Clara Barton's relief teams twenty-three years earlier, for remote highland places of ruin and postmassacre devastation.[18] Although now railway and car travel made some of the journey easier, "no group of investigators ever attacked a task with more industry," Harbord wrote. "We literally dreamed Armenia and massacres."[19]

Like the King-Crane Commission, the Harbord Commission was an investigative team, but with a military perspective. The commission was to report on political, military, geographical, administrative, economic, demographic, and other factors that would affect potential U.S. interests and responsibilities in the region. The members spoke with a broad range of groups and peoples, from the Armenian catholikos at Etchmiadzin, Armenia, to Mustafa Kemal and his Nationalist officers in Sivas, Turkey. They interviewed representatives of every government exercising sovereignty in the region, as well as numerous private individuals—Turks, Kurds, Armenians, Greeks, Tatars, Georgians, Russians, Persians, Jews, Arabs, British, French, and Americans, mostly missionaries who had lived there a long time.

As the commission traveled out of Constantinople in early September, they stopped at the American mission in Ismid, about fifty miles east of the capital, where they learned from missionaries and survivors that only "a small percentage" of the deported Armenians ever returned, and that all their property had been confiscated by the Turks, a pattern they would soon find to be true wherever Armenians had lived throughout the empire.[20] Several days later they reached Adana, which, as Harbord recalled, was the "scene of the great massacres of 1909, and where again in 1915 many thousands were deported and slain." Amid the beauty of the fields and the marketplaces teeming with tomatoes, eggplants, grapes, and figs, Harbord's team was moved by the American orphanages that dotted the city. They were shocked to see young girls all over the city with "blue tattoo marks spotting chin, brow, and cheeks"—just as Virginia Meghrouni had described the women in the refugee camps along the Euphrates—indicating that they had been captives in Muslim harems. Brutalized by their experiences, the girls could be seen working ceaselessly with lemon juice and other astringents, trying to erase "these badges of slavery," which caused them great shame.[21]

Having trouble driving their giant Ford motorcars through the crude, unpaved roads of southern Anatolia, they were often forced to get out and push their cars through the mud. The local people, who had never seen such machines, were terrified. Arriving in Aleppo, the team learned that only 150,000 Armenians had survived the deportations as far as Syria; and about half of these had not returned to their homes but were barely surviving in refugee camps.[22]

From Aleppo they then hooked back north-northwest through the heartland of Turkish Armenia. They traveled through Diyarbekir, Harput, Malatia, and on to Sivas, then back eastward to Erzurum, Kars, then across the border into Yerevan, the new capital of the Armenian Republic. In Harput, Harbord noted that the once prominent American missionary college—Euphrates College—had been emptied of its Armenian students and teachers, though American missionaries were still there, "doing splendid work." Even on the rocky highland road from Harput to Malatia, Harbord found two recent Smith College graduates, who spoke no Turkish but were running an orphanage for seven hundred Armenian children.[23]

In Sivas, a once sizable multicultural city in north-central Anatolia, and the site of the largest Armenian massacre in that part of Turkey, Harbord and his men met up with Mustafa Kemal and members of his new Nationalist Party. Harbord was alarmed that the new movement was going to revive the disastrous pan-Turkic sentiments of the Young Turks,[24] but he found Kemal a passionate patriot seeking to hold his country together and hoping, too, for the United States to assume a mandate for Turkey during an interim period. "I reminded General Kemal," Harbord wrote, that "the Turks had never shown themselves capable of consolidating in peace what they had won in war," and he confronted Kemal about Turkey's responsibility for the Armenian massacres. In answer, Harbord wrote, Kemal "deprecated the Armenian massacres" and blamed everything on "foreign intrigue."[25]

Also in Sivas they saw more orphanages, run by steadfast missionaries like Dr. E. C. Partridge and his sister-in-law, Mary Graffam, to whom the King-Crane Commission had spoken earlier in the year. The head of the Sivas Teachers College, Graffam was an Oberlin graduate whose work, Harbord noted, had "probably never been equalled by any other woman in the chronicles of missionary effort."[26] At one of Graffam's orphanages, Harbord found 150 "brides," as they were called—Armenian girls of an average age of seventeen who had been forced to marry Muslims during the deportations and had since escaped or been rescued. "Many of these," Harbord wrote, "are still no more than children, and the stories of the treatment received by these little girls of tender years would be beyond belief in any other part of the world."[27] In the midst of this chaos, Graffam had managed to lease a farm from some Germans in the hills outside Sivas and was planning to reopen her school there in the coming year. When she died unexpectedly in surgery the next year, it was a devastating blow to the Armenians and the entire missionary community in Turkey.[28]

As they continued their journey east to Erzurum, driving through ruins everywhere, Harbord recalls being overwhelmed by emotion and a sense of his commission's "impotency":

> When the final decision is made that we as a nation will take no part in solving the problems of this region which are so inextrica- bly interwoven with the motives that sent us into the World War, and are so inevitably the forerunner of future wars, if not righ- teously solved, there will be no member of our American Mili- tary Mission to Armenia who will seek the duty of explaining our attitude to a wondering world. Someone who has not seen the horror of starvation and the abomination of desolation in this war-worn region can more satisfactorily present the virtue of our adherence to the non-entangling advice of George Washington, and inquire as did Cain in this same neighborhood—"Am I my brother's keeper?"[29]

When Harbord submitted his final report to the secretary of state in October 1919, he summarized the recent history of the Armenians, which he called "a story of massacre and of broken and violated guarantees": the promises for reform for the Armenians made by the sultan and the Ottoman government from the end of the Russo-Turkish War in 1877 had never been kept; in 1880, 1895, and 1914, the Turks ignored or abrogated European demands for reform on behalf of the Armenians; and "there have been organized official massacres of the Armenians ordered every few years since Abdul Hamid ascended the throne."[30]

In its next point the report summarized the "greatest of these tragedies," when "massacres and deportations were organized in the spring of 1915" and carried out by a "definite system," whereby "the soldiers [went] from town to town," and all the Armenian men were "summoned to the government building in each village and then marched out and killed." The women, old men, and children were placed on forced marches and were "driven on foot under a fierce summer sun, robbed of their clothing and such petty articles as they carried, prodded by bayonet if they lagged; starvation, typhus, and dysentery left thousands dead."[31]

Point five made a conservative assessment of the number of Armenians killed. "The official reports of the Turkish government" showed 1.1 million Armenians to have been deported, and Harbord stated that "this wholesale attempt on the race," a premodern term for genocide, had taken about eight hundred thousand Armenian lives, although he noted that many other estimates placed the number at over a million.[32]

While the King-Crane Commission advocated a single mandate for the new Armenian Republic, the Harbord Report held that it would be feasible to unite the Armenian Republic with Turkish Armenia under a mandatory power. The report deemed Turkey "bloodthirsty, unregenerate, and revengeful," and was adamant that the Turks could never rule any part of Armenia again.[33] At that very moment, the report noted, a new surge of "organized attacks by the Turkish Army" against the new Armenian Republic justified both commissions' concern that the Turks would not stop trying to annihilate the Armenians unless a third party interceded.[34]

Having listed fourteen reasons in favor of the mandate and thirteen against, in its final point the report implored the United States to take the mandate. On the affirmative side, the commission argued that the U.S. was "morally bound to accept" these "obligations and responsibilities," as one of the "chief contributors to the formation of the League of Nations. With some of the fervor of good old American providentialism, the commission believed that the United States would "clean this hotbed of disease" and would "furnish a shining example" to the world. Alluding to American missionary involvement and humanitarian aid, the commission affirmed America's "strong sentimental interests in the region." United States rule "would definitely stop further massacres of Armenians and other Christians, give justice to the Turks, Kurds, Greeks, and other peoples." As the report noted in its point 13, "Better millions for a mandate than billions for future wars."[35]

On the "against" side, the Harbord Commission pointed to the U.S. tradition of adhering to the Monroe Doctrine and its stipulations that the United States should stay in its own sphere of influence and not get involved in the "politics of the Old World." The report pointed out that European powers could take on the mandate and hence continue their own involvement in the region. Acknowledging that an American mandate would be expensive and would put Americans at risk, it asked whether it might not be more advisable to invest American money closer to home.[36]

But point 14 underscored what Harbord had written earlier about America's responsibility to its suffering fellow humans on the planet: "Here is a man's job that the world says can be better done by America than by any other. America can afford the money; she has the men; no duty to her own people would suffer; her traditional policy of isolation did not keep her from successful participation in the Great War. Shall it be said that our country lacks the courage to take up new and difficult duties?"[37] Such words coming from a major general who served as General Pershing's chief of staff only two years earlier should have been heard clearly.

The Harbord Report was sent to President Wilson on October 16, 1919, and was read attentively at the White House. Assistant Secretary of State Polk immediately wired Secretary of State Lansing telling him that Harbord had "presented a remarkable report on the Armenian situation," urging him to give Harbord "all the time you can when he arrives."[38]

DEFEAT OF THE MANDATE

Back at home, among the American people, the movement for Armenia was in full force. In the early part of 1920, there was across the nation passionate opinion in favor of the mandate for Armenia. Pro mandate sentiment ran from the eastern establishment to the southern and western states. The New York Times and the New Republic were constant advocates of the mandate, as was the entire Protestant Church Press. Congress received a mass of petitions on behalf of the mandate, and sixteen state legislatures passed pro mandate resolutions. "It was simply the majority of the American people," as Howard M. Sachar put it, "those articulate or silent opponents of the League months earlier" who now saw a part of the international scene differently.[39]

By February 1920, the ACIA had become angry with the French and British because of their own designs on Turkish Armenia. The French were claiming Cilicia and parts of Sivas and Harput, while the British were proposing that southern Van and Bitlis go to the Kurds under a British mandate, and Erzurum and Trebizond to the Turks. That would leave only Yerevan, Kars, and northern Van to the Armenians, and as both the ACIA and the Armenian delegation at Paris rejected these boundaries, the tensions over the mandate proposals grew. In the winter and spring of 1919–20, the White House and Congress were "besieged by resolutions and appeals" on behalf of the mandate for Armenia and for aid and military intervention for the new Armenian Republic.[40] In the wake of renewed Turkish military assaults on Armenia, John Sharp Williams, Democratic senator from Mississippi, presented a resolution endorsed by Near East Relief asking for immediate relief for the estimated one hundred thousand Christian and Jewish women and girls held captive in Turkish harems.[41]

James L. Barton, now chairman of Near East Relief and himself on a fact-finding mission in the devastated Turkish-Armenian provinces, wrote to the *New York Times* in April that the Harbord Report so totally confirmed "the need for an American mandate . . . that if the President and Foreign Relations Committee turned it down, the United States would be"—as the *Times* headline read—IN PONTIUS PILATE'S CLASS.[42] The missionary politician, who had first worked tirelessly to raise money during the Armenian massacres in 1915 and then opposed war with Turkey in 1917 in order to protect missionary interests, was now an advocate of the Armenian mandate.

But the mood toward Armenia on Capitol Hill was growing cooler. Even though France, Great Britain, and Italy had recognized the Armenian Republic in late January 1920, the Senate held back on official recognition because the final Armenian borders had not yet been settled. On March 15 the frustrated ACIA held a mass rally at Carnegie Hall, headed by the prominent labor leader Samuel Gompers and the Episcopal bishop, William Manning. The rally produced yet more resolutions that were telegraphed to President Wilson. But it wasn't until April 23 that the United States agreed to recognize the Armenian Republic—a process, Vahan Cardashian wrote, that "was like trying to extract teeth from a fish."[43] Ironically, just three days later the Allies at San Remo, Italy, asked President Wilson to accept a mandate for Armenia and to assume the immediate task of defining Armenia's western border, which was to include significant parts of the Turkish Armenian provinces. The Allies had awarded

land to Armenia, and now waited for Wilson's democratic hand to draw
the official boundary.

Thus the spring of 1920 turned out to be an intense moment of conflicting
opinions and urgent action appeals. But with Mustafa Kemal and his
armies taking over what was supposed to become the western section of
the new Armenian Republic, Wilson proved incapable of drawing Armenia's western boundary. Was the president so debilitated by his failing
health that he couldn't put the fate of the Armenian Republic on his desk?
Or was his fight for the mandate distracting him from drawing the boundary line? Or was his stance a combination of pragmatic politics and inept
idealism? The fact was that Armenia needed the legitimation of its boundaries, along with some military intervention to help maintain the territory.

By early April the Harbord Report was before the Senate. In lieu of
any action on behalf of Armenia, Senator Warren G. Harding's subcommittee offered an ineffectual and somewhat demeaning resolution, which
congratulated the new Armenian Republic, expressed hope for its aspirations, and gave Wilson permission to send a battleship and some marines
to Batum to help protect the Armenians from Kemalist forces.

Henry Cabot Lodge, once a morally energetic proponent of intervention, now confessed privately that he believed that the Senate would
approve little more than "expressions of sympathy and congratulations on
the establishment of the republic."[44] He called Armenia a "poorhouse"
with nothing to offer American interests. Like most Republicans, he fell
back on the traditional notions of the Monroe Doctrine.[45] In the spring of
1920, with the upcoming presidential election in view, the gap between
the Republicans and the president hit a new note of hostility.

By early May it was clear that Wilson was going to ask the Senate to
approve the mandate for Armenia, even though it was apparent that the
overwhelming sentiment in the Senate was against it. Knowing the mandate was going to be a political failure, James Gerard and the ACIA urged
Wilson to forget about the mandate for the moment and ask the Senate
for military aid and equipment for Armenia. Gerard then begged Wilson
to use his executive powers to protect Armenia as President Taft had done
for Chile in 1912. Again, Wilson backed off, seeming to have lost confidence in his own authority.[46]

On May 29, five days before the vote on the mandate was scheduled, Wilson said to Congress, "I cannot but regard it as providential, and not as a mere coincidence, that almost at the same time I received information that the conference of statesmen now sitting at San Remo . . . had formally resolved to address a definite appeal to this Government to accept a mandate for Armenia." In his grandeloquent way, Wilson told Congress that for the United States not to accept the mandate "would do nothing less than arrest the hopeful processes of civilization."[47] An editorial in the *New York Times* three days before the vote attacked the Republican isolationists: "Our vehement patriots have managed to attach a moral stigma to anything that looks like disinterested aid to others. And they control Congress."[48] Agreeing with many of the Republicans that Armenia had little to offer but need, one Chicago paper was sure that Armenia would not find a desirable foster parent "until she discovers oil or something."[49]

The Senate debate over the mandate was predictable. Democrats like John Sharp Williams spoke for the internationalist position in support of Armenia:

> I for one do not see how my country can take itself out of the world. It is a part of it and the earth now is a very narrow place, with its aeroplanes and its wireless and all the other things which bring its peoples close together. Even if it were advisable to *be* off the earth, we cannot *get* off it, nor can we escape and shirk the burdens and responsibilities of a situation while we accept all of its advantages.[50]

Two days before the vote went to the Senate, Lodge's Foreign Relations Committee voted 11 to 4 against the proposal. Lodge seemed more than ever bent on destroying anything Wilson wanted, and with the Republican convention just around the corner on June 8, Lodge wanted this business completed before what he hoped would be the beginning of a new Republican era. The isolationist Republicans held the day, and Senators like William E. Borah of Idaho and Frank Brandegee of Connecticut exemplified the Republican stance, making use of the Monroe Doctrine and the reservations the Harbord Report had listed in its no column. The mandate for Armenia was convincingly trounced by a vote of 52 to 23. In a way that typified the isolationists, Lodge exclaimed: "Do not think I do not feel badly about Armenia. I do, but I think there is a limit to what they have a right to put off on us."[51]

Once again Wilson's behavior forces one to ask questions that have no easy answers. Was Wilson naive in believing that American sentiment was so high for Armenia that the mandate would make it through the Senate? Did he believe that American concern about and aid to Armenia over the past four decades would be consummated by an affirmative Senate vote? Or was he acting out of high-minded idealism, believing that this was a battle to fight no matter what the odds? Did he want to make good on his earlier promises? Or had the recent strokes so debilitated him that he had, indeed, lost his judgment?

Wilson even made one last stab for the mandate when he wrote a plank for the Democratic platform at the convention later that summer. He gave it to Secretary of the Treasury Carter Glass to bring to the convention. It read: "We hold it to be the Christian duty and privilege of our Government to assume responsible guardianship of Armenia which now needs only the advice and assurance of a powerful friend to establish her complete independence and to give her distracted people the opportunities for peaceful happiness which they have vainly longed for through so many dark years of hopeless suffering and hideous distress." But Glass, who had worked hard for the League of Nations with the party, admitted to Wilson that he felt the Armenian mandate idea was dead.[52] And the plank was not brought forward.

Several days later Lewis Einstein wrote about the betrayal of Armenia in *The Nation*:

> We refrained from declaring war on Turkey and left one of the greatest moral issues of all time without so much as the expression of our indignation. The reason for our failure in this has been attributed to the wish to shield American property in Turkey and to the hope that our missionaries might be able to protect the native Christian population. But the utter fallacy of the latter idea had become self-evident from the massacres, while the possible though most unlikely destruction of American property would have been far preferable to our virtual acquiescence in the crimes committed.[53]

———∞∞∞———

THE NEW U.S. OIL POLICY

IN THE MIDDLE EAST AND

THE TURNABOUT ON

THE ARMENIAN QUESTION

*Show this administration an oil well and it will show you a
foreign policy.*
> —Senator Pat Harrison
> of Mississippi

T he defeat of the mandate for Armenia was certainly a sign of the
shifting mood of U.S. foreign policy. The State Department was
naturally the center of the policy toward Armenia, and it was
inseparable from the emergence of the new Turkish Republic and the politics of oil that was to create new alliances. What happened to U.S. foreign
policy in the years following World War I would set some significant prece-
dents for the century to come. As the issue of Armenia became more politically charged after the war, American views grew more divided. Popular
opinion and popular culture continued to be overwhelmingly in favor of a
just settlement for Armenia. American philanthropy, most notably under
the auspices of Near East Relief, continued to send unprecedented amounts
of money, food, and clothes to the Armenian and many other refugees of the
postwar devastation in the Near East. But the new mania for the petroleum
markets of the Middle East that would now drive U.S. foreign policy was far
less interested in philanthropy and civil and political justice. (After World
War I, the term "Near East" was gradually replaced with "Middle East.")

The signs of the changing climate had become apparent at the
peace conference when the European Allies proposed a War Crimes
Commission—the "Commission on the Responsibility of the Authors of
the War and the Enforcement of Penalties."[1] It was a historic act aimed at

bringing to trial Kaiser Wilhelm and his military leaders and also the Ottoman government for its war crimes, notably the Armenian massacres.[2]

Popular opinion in Europe also favored the idea of punishing the Central Powers for war crimes and atrocities.[3] World War I had been a war like no other in history; more than twenty million lives had been lost. Great Britain, France, Germany, and the peoples of the Austro-Hungarian and Ottoman Empires had been nearly stripped of a generation of men. Mechanized and industrial warfare had killed and maimed human beings in unprecedented ways, with poison gas, tanks, automatic weapons, aerial bombing, and submarine torpedoes. And in the Ottoman Empire, genocide had been committed behind the screen of war, for the first time in the modern age.

The Hague conventions of 1899 and 1907, and the Geneva Conventions of 1864 and 1906, had banned destructive weapons such as poisonous gas and expanding bullets. Nations were prohibited from destroying the hospitals and merchant ships of their enemies. Guidelines for the treatment of prisoners of war, and the necessity of pursuing negotiations before resorting to war, were also codified. So when the U.S. delegation voted against the War Crimes Commission at the peace conference, it was both a regressive act and one that paved the way for the new oil diplomacy that Secretary of State Robert Lansing was so eager to propel.

It was more than ironic when Lansing was made the chairman of the War Crimes Commission, for he had no sympathy for pursuing crimes against humanity. An ardent nationalist, he saw the world through the prism of national self-interest. He had already expressed his antipathy to Wilson's small-nation sovereignty in the Fourteen Points, and as Wilson's adviser Colonel House remarked, Lansing believed "that almost any form of atrocity is permissible provided a nation's safety is involved."[4]

As the supposed chair of the War Crimes Commission, Lansing tried to halt its very formation and managed to keep the words "crimes against humanity" out of the peace treaty. However, the Allies had already gone on record in their London statement of 1915 to the Young Turks when they declared that the massacres of the Armenians would be considered "crimes against humanity." Thus, by 1919, the Armenian massacres had spawned the idea of banning and punishing "crimes against humanity," which now focused on domestic campaigns to exterminate a particular ethnic or religious group.[5]

Lansing's opposition to the idea of war crimes and international justice was also fueled by his views about international trade and commerce. Economic relations, he believed, must have top priority. Alarmed at what the Bolshevik revolution had done to Russia's economic structures, Lansing was determined to see that the postwar settlements would not cripple the capitalist system of which the United States was the emerging leader.[6] It was an outlook that would define the beginning of an era in which humanitarian concerns would take a backseat to material and military national self-interest.

Wilson's triumphal visit to Paris after the Armistice made clear that the United States had emerged as a world power. And with America's new status, American foreign policy focused more deeply on the brimming sense of economic opportunity the new world order had to offer. As the decade that would be known in the United States as the Roaring Twenties approached, a new urban, industrial America embraced the natural resource that would propel the age: oil. Henry Ford was fast making the automobile a middle-class commodity. Cars, trucks, and airplanes would soon change the terrain of the U.S. economy. Already railroads, ships, industry, and homes were turning from coal to oil. As Lord Curzon, Britain's foreign minister, wrote after the Armistice, "The Allies had floated to victory on a wave of oil."[7]

With the end of the world war and the breakup of the nineteenth-century world order in Europe and the Middle East, a whole new set of possibilities for wealth and power emerged for the victorious Allies. The defeat of the Ottoman Empire meant that most of what is today Saudi Arabia, Syria, Iraq, Lebanon, Israel, Jordan, and the oil domains of the Persian Gulf were new territories of open economic possibility to the West. The oil fields were, perhaps, the greatest pool of natural resources in the modern age. By 1920 Britain, France, the Netherlands, and the United States were competing for the new wealth, while Mustafa Kemal, once he consolidated his new Turkish Republic, would use the lure of the oil fields as political capital with the West.

In 1914, just before the war erupted, the British had bought out the remaining sectors of the Turkish Petroleum Company, including the Ottoman government's share. Thus, by 1919, the British were the domi-

nant oil power in the Middle East, controlling both the Anglo-Persian Oil
Company (now BP) and the Turkish Petroleum Company. By 1920 the
British, the French, and the Dutch were on the verge of dividing up the oil
wealth of the Middle East and trying their best to keep the United States
out of the picture. Meanwhile the Wilson administration realized that the
oil reserves in the United States were so dangerously low that Secretary of
the Interior John Payne proposed that American naval merchant ships
revert to coal. The idea horrified the secretary of the navy, Josephus
Daniels, who saw it as a sign of military weakness.[8]

The politics of oil had assumed a priority, even a fixation, with those who
were forging the new geopolitical power structure. "Oleaginous diplomacy" became an inside epithet,[9] and "dollar diplomacy" went to a new
level. It was in this climate that the Wilson administration learned that at
the Treaty of San Remo, the Allies had divided up Turkey's oil fields
among themselves (and were now asking the United States to take the
mandate for Armenia).[10]

In Constantinople the U.S. high commissioner, Adm. Mark Bristol,
would have a significant impact on the new oil diplomacy and U.S. policy
toward Turkey. Allen Dulles, who had been Bristol's chief of staff and was
now the head of the Near East desk at the State Department, appointed
his former boss to this influential post. Bristol, who was hostile to the
Armenian mandate, became in effect a public relations man for American
business in Turkey. To one of Standard Oil's executives, he complained, "I
have tried to get our businessmen to reconcile [their] differences with the
benevolent institutions" and to make the missionaries and philanthropists
see that "their interests depend very largely upon our American business
interests."[11] Excited by business prospects with the defeated Ottoman
Empire, Bristol called Turkey "a virgin field for American business and
American financial exploitation."[12]

Mark Bristol, who was hostile to the Armenian mandate and to the
Greek occupation, worked hard to bring the missionaries and the business
community together. He told C. F. Gates, the president of Robert College,
"The Turks want us, the Americans, because they believe we have no
political string tied to our operations."[13] The future, he told the missionaries, was with the Turks and not the Armenians and the Greeks.[14] Like

Herbert Hoover and the isolationist Republicans, Bristol saw Armenia as a place devoid of natural resources and seaports, and referred to the country as a "lemon."[15] Bristol's politics were also coupled with his racist attitudes. "The Armenians," he wrote, "are a race like the Jews; they have little or no national spirit and have poor moral character."[16] To his colleague Adm. William S. Sims he wrote that the Armenians and the Greeks "have many flaws and deficiencies of character that do not fit them for self-government."[17]

To Secretary of State Lansing, Allen Dulles, and Mark Bristol, the idea of spending resources and political capital on a new Armenian state while the French, British, and Dutch took over the Mesopotamian oil fields was alarming, to say the least. By the end of Wilson's presidency, Allen Dulles, along with Lansing and Bristol, was formulating what would be known as the "open door policy" for the Middle East—a policy geared to promote American business interests, in particular the pursuit of oil.

As the Wilson administration gave way to the Harding administration in 1921, oil assumed even greater importance. On the domestic front, Harding's administration would be forever marred by the Teapot Dome scandal, in which the mismanagement of domestic oil reserves led to a private deal between two oil companies and Secretary of the Interior Albert Fall, who received kickbacks and bribes for his manipulation of President Harding.

In the arena of foreign diplomacy, Harding's secretary of state, Charles Evans Hughes, who had been an attorney and first vice president of Standard Oil of New Jersey, forged a Middle East oil strategy designed to compete for oil with the Europeans—the French, British, and Dutch. With the backing of Herbert Hoover, the State Department created something called "the American group," an informal oil cartel of seven companies led by Standard Oil of New Jersey. The American group and the State Department brokered for power with the Anglo-Persian Oil Company and the British-controlled Turkish Petroleum Company, and by 1922–23 they came to an agreement that would allow American oil interests a foothold in the Middle East oil fields.[18]

For advocates of justice for Armenia, it was painful to see Charles Evans Hughes resign as an executive committee member of the American Committee for the Independence of Armenia. When he became secretary of state, it was clear to Hughes that the two positions were incompatible, and his about-face was emblematic of the whole drift of U.S. policy toward Armenia in the postwar era.

Although isolationist Republican sentiment and the growing concern about oil in the Middle East had initially closed the door on the Armenian mandate in May 1920, the Harding administration's policy solidified a dramatic shift in U.S. policy toward Turkey—and hence toward the history of the Armenian Genocide—in that it established a new power axis that would have consequences for historical memory as well.

In 1920–22 there was more popular outcry in the United States over the failed settlement for Armenia; public sentiment was fueled by new Turkish massacres of Christians, especially in Cilicia, where Armenians were killed in 1920–21 as the French pulled their troops out of a region they had once hoped to control. In Smyrna the Greco-Turkish war ended with calculated massacres of Armenians. In the Armenian Quarter of the city, Ataturk's forces went house by house, breaking down the doors of the Armenian residences and killing family by family. They then set the two-thousand-year-old city ablaze in full view of a flotilla of Allied warships, among them three U.S. destroyers that were by U.S. policy forbidden to intervene.[19] In spite of Mark Bristol's efforts to censor news from Smyrna, word of the renewed violence and cataclysm reached the American people. The young Ernest Hemingway, then a correspondent for the *Toronto Star*, was shocked by the Turkish brutality at Smyrna, and his opening vignette, "On the Quai at Smyrna," in his first book, *In Our Time*, depicts Greek women with their dead babies in numbed horror on the pier as the Allied fleets looked on.

At the Near East desk in Washington, Allen Dulles replied quite candidly to Bristol's request that the State Department exert pressure on the American press to shift their sympathetic tone toward Armenians. "Confidentially the State Department is in a bind. Our task would be simple if the reports of the atrocities could be declared untrue or even exaggerated, but the evidence is, alas, irrefutable." The secretary of state, he went on, "wants to avoid giving the impression that while the US is willing to intervene actively to protect its commercial interests, it is not willing to move on behalf of the Christian minorities." Having to deal with minority group pressure in the United States, Dulles complained to Bristol about the agitation on behalf of the Armenians,

Greeks, and Palestinian Jews. "I've been kept busy trying to ward off congressional resolutions of sympathy for these groups."[20] In the face of public sentiment for the Greeks and the Armenians, Secretary of State Charles Evans Hughes made it clear that there would be no intervention on their behalf.

Yet, with the change of political and military reality in Turkey following the Greco-Turkish war, the United States was pressured to help create a new postwar treaty that a triumphant Kemalist Turkey was now demanding. In the Alpine city of Lausanne, Switzerland, in late November 1922, the new Turkish government under the leadership of Mustafa Kemal met with the Europeans—Great Britain, France, and Italy. The Lausanne Treaty that ensued was similar to the Treaty of Berlin of 1878, in that it was a "second-chance" treaty for Turkey. In both instances the Turks had been on the losing side of a war but had managed to convince the Europeans to overturn the initial treaties that had followed the Russo-Turkish War of 1876–7 and then World War I. The Treaty of Sèvres of 1920 had been signed by Damad Ferid's government, but Kemalists, then vying for power, refused to acknowledge the treaty. Thus, when they took over the country, the Treaty of Sèvres remained unratified, and Mustafa Kemal forced a new treaty that would be far more lenient to postwar Turkey.

The Lausanne Conference and the treaty turned out to be the final blow to Armenia. While Great Britain and France were key participants at the conference, Hughes made it clear that the United States would not be an official presence. Instead he sent three observers: Richard Washburn Child, the American ambassador to Italy, headed a trio that included Joseph C. Grew, the minister to Switzerland, and the ever-present Admiral Bristol.

At the first sitting of the conference, the United States pressed for a special agreement with the Turks concerning commercial interests. The ensuing Turco-American Treaty of Amity and Commerce promised free passage for U.S. ships in the Dardanelles, an open-door policy for American business, especially oil business, and protection of the Christians in Turkey. According to Vahan Cardashian, under Secretary of State Hughes's direction "the Department of State became a concession-hunting agency for the Standard Oil Company."[21]

But the Turks had arrived at Lausanne with an adamant stance about the Armenians. The delegation's head, Ismet Inönü, made it clear that any discussion of the Armenian question would lead to the break-up of the

conference. James Barton of Near East Relief, an unofficial observer lob-
bying for the interests of the Christian minorities, reported that "The
Turks are getting anxious lest the American delegation ask for a national
home for the Armenians."[22] Ambassador Grew acknowledged that "there
is no subject upon which the Turks are more fixed in obstinacy" than the
Armenian question.[23] The Turkish delegation maintained that the Armenian exodus from Turkey had been voluntary, and when the Armenians
came to the conference to present their case, the Turks refused to attend.[24]

Not only were the Turks adamantly against the idea of any settlement
for the Armenians, they persisted in denying the existence of the Armenians and the massacres. Barton noted that the Turks were fabricating tales
of Armenian massacres of Turks. When the pope sent a message to the
conference calling for the members of the conference to take action to
save the Armenians from further deportation and death," the Turks
angrily called it "Christian propaganda."[25] Appalled at the lack of Turkish
conscience, Barton wrote: "I have not heard a word or seen a sign that the
Turk is repentant of anything that has been done in Turkey."[26] Putting it
bluntly, Barton went on: "They all know the Armenians occupied that
country a thousand years before the Turks were heard of, and that there
are not enough Turks to occupy half the entire country now, even if all the
Turks in Europe, Syria, and Arabia came home—which they will not. Yet
no one will tell the Turk 'You must designate an adequate area to which
the Armenians may go and be safe.' "[27]

In Washington, Secretary of State Hughes made it clear to Senator
Lodge that the issue of an Armenian national homeland "posed the
gravest difficulties." Nor was there any will in the State Department to
back military intervention for Armenia. Allen Dulles concurred.[28]

The Turks came to the conference table presenting themselves as a
new, victorious nation that had routed the Greeks out of Asia Minor and
toppled the sultanate and Grand Vizier Damad Ferid's government. At
Lausanne they demanded that the Capitulations, which they had so long
detested, be abolished, that the Greco-Turkish boundary be reestablished,
and that all notions of an Armenian homeland in any part of the former
Armenian *vilayets* be abolished. So tightly was the lid shut on Armenia
in the Treaty of Lausanne that the word "Armenia" was not allowed into
the text. At Lausanne, Mustafa Kemal helped to cement further what the
Turkish historian Taner Akçam has called the foundation myths of the

new Turkish Republic. As Akçam has put it, for the sake of creating a homogenous national identity, Kemal and Kemalism created historical amnesia and in conjunction with this a refusal to acknowledge that the new Turkish state had been built not from a war "against imperial powers" but by expunging "the Greek and Armenian minorities."[29] The Turkish attitude at Lausanne was similar in many ways to the Turkist nationalism of the Young Turk era. As the *New York Times Current History* of February 1923 put it, "the Armenians were virtually thrown overboard by the conference."[30]

By the time Calvin Coolidge had become president after Harding's untimely death in August 1923, the issue of the ratification of the Lausanne treaty by the Senate was stalled in debate because of continued wrangling about the Armenian massacres and U.S. policy toward Turkey. Former members of ACIA Vahan Cardashian and James Gerard mounted one last movement, this time called the American Committee to Oppose the Lausanne Treaty (ACOLT). ACOLT was led by James Gerard, Rabbi Wise, Democratic Senator William H. King of Utah, and Senator Claude Swanson, a Democrat from Virginia. Immediately an opposing lobby formed, and not surprisingly it was led by missionaries and businessmen. James Barton, who had changed his position for reasons of political expediency during the previous decade, now led the charge for ratification of the Lausanne treaty. The American Board of Commissioners for Foreign Missions, the American Manufacturers Association, and the Near East College Association were among the primary protreaty lobby groups.[31]

Both sides went public with their views. As James Gerard, Rabbi Wise, Henry Morgenthau, and Vahan Cardashian, among others, continued to speak out, many Americans came to see how clearly the State Department had sold out the Armenians over political interests and the oil fields of the Mosul. Charles Evans Hughes articulated a State Department view in favor of the treaty in a speech he made to the Council on Foreign Relations in New York, in which he argued that because of the change in political climate in Turkey, it was time to change our relationship with Turkey.[32] Responding with outrage to Hughes, James Gerard exclaimed: "We will take this case, if necessary, into the next campaign. We will carry the discussion of the Lausanne Treaty to the floor of the Senate. We will expose the scandalous intrigue to which this Government has become a party in the making of this treaty."[33]

By May 1924, with the State Department, Council on Foreign Relations, and Foreign Policy Association in favor of the treaty, the protreaty
people sounded like the Turkish government, claiming now that the
Armenian massacres had been exaggerated and that many Turks had suffered as well because of war, famine, and disease—only their sufferings
"are less well known in the United States."[34] But in June 1924 the Coolidge
administration, realizing that the State Department did not represent
either the opinion on Capitol Hill or in the nation, refused to send the
treaty to the Senate for ratification.

The Democrats felt so strongly about the issue that their party platform for the 1924 election condemned the treaty. "We condemn the Lausanne treaty," the platform asserted, because "it barters legitimate rights
and betrays Armenia for the Chester oil Concessions." The Democrats
called for the fulfillment of President Wilson's award.[35] At the convention
Senator Pat Harrison of Mississippi brought politics to a moral lens:
"When the Christian women and children were wantonly given to the
Turkish sword this administration refused to act, but the moment the oil
magnates of the land sought a concession in the oil fields of Mosul, the
administration that refused to intervene to save Christian lives went to the
front with vigor and decision. . . . Show this administration an oil well and
it will show you a foreign policy."[36]

It wasn't until January 1927 that the Coolidge administration submitted the treaty to the Senate for debate. The Democrats voted unanimously against it, and the Lausanne treaty, profoundly unpopular with
the American people, was defeated. Senator King expressed the party's
point of view and a major reason for the treaty's defeat: "Obviously it
would be unfair and unreasonable for the United States to recognize and
respect the claim and profession of Mustafa Kemal Pasha so long as he
persists in holding control and sovereignty over Wilson's Armenia—now
a 'No Man's Land'—while nearly a million Armenian refugees and exiles
are a people without a country."[37] Although the United States would never
sign the treaty, President Coolidge finally established diplomatic relations
with the Turkish Republic in 1927 when he appointed Grew as ambassador to Turkey and then accepted a Turkish ambassador to the United
States in December 1927. But this was done amid great protest from the
stalwart supporters of ACOLT,[38] and from the various sectors of the American public that remained deeply disappointed about the fate of Armenia.

EPILOGUE

Turkish Denial of the Armenian

Genocide and U.S. Complicity

If the Holocaust was a hoax, why not the Armenian catastrophe also?
If Anne Frank's diary was faked, who is to say that certain documents
signed by Talaat Pasha weren't forged as well? . . . The Turkish attack
on truth exemplifies the new governing narrative, the one in which
truth is fugitive.

> —Terrence Des Pres,
> *On Governing Narratives:*
> *The Turkish-Armenian Case*

In 1894–95 the sultan's policy was to deny the very massacres he had
committed, and this has been the policy of every successive Turkish
regime down to the present. In one quite dramatic cover-up effort, the
sultan used the American ambassador to the Ottoman Empire, A. W. Terrell, as his mouthpiece in the American press. Angry with James Bryce's
essay in *The Century* about the Armenian massacres and his call for American aid, the sultan demanded a rebuttal in the form of an interview. The
interview turned out to be an essay by Terrell that extolled the sultan with
fulsome rhetoric (Abdul Hamid II was "the ablest sovereign in Europe")
and defended the massacres as just punishment for the "revolutionary
Armenians"; the sultan then conveyed his admiration for the Armenian
workers he had once employed.[1]

The sultan's response to the Armenian massacres and the response of
successive Turkish regimes depict what Judith Herman in her book
Trauma and Recovery describes as criminal behavior. Criminal behavior,
she notes, is always defined by the perpetrator's compulsion to "promote
forgetting." "Secrecy and silence are the perpetrator's first line of
defense." If that fails "the perpetrator attacks the credibility of his victim."
And if he cannot silence his victim, "he tries to make sure that no one lis-
tens," by either blatantly denying or rationalizing his crime.[2]

Like the sultan, the Young Turks and then the Kemalists continued to deny and rationalize the Armenian Genocide. They planned the genocide and implemented it as covertly as they could, and when they were confronted by the world, they resorted to blaming the victims and rationalizing the crime, and they did everything they could to promote forgetting. In private conversations with Ambassador Morgenthau, Talaat and Enver admitted their plans to exterminate the Armenians. In the midst of the Genocide, Talaat told the Ambassador: "We have already disposed of three quarters of the Armenians; there are none at all left in Bitlis, Van, and Erzerum. The hatred between the Turks and the Armenians is now so intense that we have got to finish with them. If we don't, they will plan their revenge." When Morgenthau brought up the financial loss to the empire that would be incurred through the destruction of the Armenians, Talaat said bluntly: "We will not have the Armenians anywhere in Anatolia."[3] Assuring Ambassador Morgenthau that the CUP was firmly in control of events, Enver bragged: "We have this country absolutely under our control. I have no desire to shift the blame on to our underlings and I am entirely willing to accept the responsibility myself for everything that has taken place. The Cabinet itself has ordered the deportations."[4]

Talaat did not display the same candor in his memoirs, a segment of which was published in the *New York Times Current History.* He overtly attacked the victims: "The responsibility for these acts falls first of all upon the deported people themselves." Talaat's strategy was to scapegoat the Armenians by claiming that the Russians used the Armenians to help them invade eastern Turkey. Inventing a counterfeit reality, Talaat made the outlandish accusation that "Armenian bandits . . . killed more than 800,000 Mohammedans." Talaat admitted that innocent Armenians were killed ("I confess it," he writes) but denied the existence of the bureaucratic organization that he and his party created for the purpose of extermination. Insisting that it was not the fault of the central government but rather of the local officials, he wrote, "I am innocent of ordering any massacres."[5] Talaat Pasha's early example of denying the Armenian Genocide created a counterfeit version of history that would be used by successive Turkish regimes.

As the Kemalists came to prominence and then power in the period between 1920 and 1922, they began to solidify the denial of the Armenian Genocide in the name of a new kind of nationalism. In 1920, in response to the Soviet foreign minister, who was asking the Turks to agree to the

award of a small portion of Turkish Armenia to the new Armenian Republic, soon to be a Soviet Republic, the Turkish general Kiazim Karabekir
crystallized the new tenor of modern Turkish denial. "In Turkey," he
responded, "there has been neither an Armenia nor territory inhabited by
Armenians. . . . Those [Armenians] living in Turkey committed murder
and massacres, and have escaped to Iran, America, Europe, and some of
them to Armenia. How is it possible to call back these murderers and give
them the right to vote?"[6] When Soviet foreign commissar Chicherin put
the same proposal to the Turkish delegation that had come to Moscow for
peace talks, the Turks replied: "No Armenian provinces have ever existed
in Turkey."[7]

This attempt to erase Armenia from Turkish history would soon
become part of the modern Turkish Republic's founding mythology.
Again, as Taner Akçam has put it: In their efforts to create a monolithic,
homogeneous Turkish state after the war the Kemalists created a totalis-
tic nationalism that was built on several foundation myths, or what
Akçam calls taboos. Traumatized by loss of empire and by the Europeans
whom they perceived as having threatened their territorial claims in the
Treaty of Sèvres, the new Turkish state hammered out the following
requirements for Turkish national identity: (1) Turkey is a society without
class distinctions; (2) Turkey is a society without ethnic minorities or cultures; (3) as a secular state, Turkey disavows Islam as an official cultural
arena; and (4) there was never an Armenian Genocide.[8]

The vehemence with which the new Turkish regime denied the
Armenian Genocide, evident at the Lausanne Conference in 1922, also
marked a turning point in the banishing of Armenia from official Turkish
consciousness. And this dovetailed with the dramatic shift in American
policy toward Turkey and the Middle East, as the United States pursued
an open door policy for the oil of Mesopotamia and a new dollar diplomacy. In the early twenties American opinion on the Armenian Genocide
also changed. The Treaty of Lausanne proved to be a litmus test; political
and missionary leaders quickly changed their views. George A. Plimpton,
an original member of the American Committee on Armenian Atrocities
in 1915, now went along with the Kemalist position: "We believe in America for the Americans, why not Turkey for the Turks?"[9] and published his
view in a tract of statements promoting the ratification of the Lausanne
treaty—*The Treaty with Turkey.*

Secretary of State Charles Evans Hughes, Secretary of Commerce Herbert Hoover, Adm. Mark Bristol, and Richard Washburn Child all contributed to *The Treaty with Turkey*, and they all agreed that Turkey's treatment of its minorities was now less important than American business interests and the vast real estate holdings of the American missionaries. Secretary of State Hughes, playing on the climate of the Red Scare, argued that "Turkey is not endeavoring to undermine our institutions, to penetrate our labor organizations by pernicious propaganda, and to foment disorder and conspiracies against our domestic peace in the interest of a world revolution."[10] Sounding what would become a familiar anticommunist note, Hughes's view of Turkey anticipated the Cold War alliance with Turkey, when Turkey would assume a role as defender of NATO on the Soviet border. Similarly James Barton, who had come to the Lausanne Conference as a supporter of Armenia, now jumped to the pro-Turkish side, arguing that the missionary influence was more important than ever in Turkey to keep the Turks looking west and away from the communist threat.[11]

So enveloped in oil mania were some Americans, like retired admiral Colby Chester, that they enthusiastically assisted the Turkish government's cover-up. Admiral Chester had become friends with Sultan Abdul Hamid in 1897 when he was sent to the Sublime Porte as an emissary for American missionary interests, only to leave Turkey having made an oil deal with the sultan. By 1922 Chester, hoping to see his promised oil rights come to fruition, wrote in the *New York Times Current History:* "The Armenians were moved from the inhospitable regions where they were not welcome and could not actually prosper but to the most delightful and fertile parts of Syria . . . where the climate is as benign as in Florida and California whither New York millionaires journey each year for health and recreation. . . . And all this was done at great expense of money and effort."[12] By the early 1920s Armenian Genocide denial was finding a home amid the new Turcophile climate in the United States.

The Turkish fixation on suppressing knowledge and memory of the Armenian Genocide took another turn in 1934, when the Turkish ambassador to the United States, Munir Ertegun, protested to the State Department about the purchase by MGM of the film rights to Franz Werfel's best-selling novel, *The Forty Days of Musa Dagh.* Werfel's novel, published in Germany in 1932, was based on a true story about the Armenians of Musa Dagh, who had heroically resisted the Turkish invasion of their mountain town in 1915. (Werfel, a Jew, was forced to flee Germany for his life in 1938, three years after the Nazis agreed to the Turkish government's request to ban *The Forty Days of Musa Dagh*.) Ambassador Ertegun threatened that if the film were released, Turkey would consider it a hostile act that would damage relations between the two countries and result in a Turkish boycott of American films. After a series of exchanges between the two governments, the State Department yielded to Turkey's demand and got MGM to drop the project. Ambassador Ertegun was ingratiating in his thanks to the State Department, telling them that the decision "has created an excellent impression in my country."[13]

It is difficult to imagine a foreign government censoring artistic expression in the United States—that crucial part of constitutional freedoms delineated in the Bill of Rights—but in 1935 the State Department decided that relations with Turkey were more important than freedom of expression. Four years later, in August 1939, Hitler, too, invoked the erosion of memory when he said to his military advisers, eight days before the Nazis invaded Poland—"Who today, after all, speaks of the annihilation of the Armenians?"[14]

After *The Forty Days of Musa Dagh* film project was in effect censored by the Turkish government, the Armenian Genocide disappeared into the black hole of historical amnesia in the United States. With the Republic of Armenia locked inside the Soviet Union during the deep freeze of the Cold War, Armenian American genocide survivors and the next generation were without a social and political environment in which to create a public discourse for the memory of 1915. The Armenian Genocide was a narrative lost to the public.

In this void Turkey continued to relegate the Armenian Genocide to irrelevance. A 1959 statement by the press attaché of the Turkish embassy in Washington posited that what the Turks did to the Armenians was "what might have been the American response, had the German-Americans of Minnesota and Wisconsin revolted on behalf of Hitler during World War II." Today, the Turkish spokesman asserted, the Armenians harbor no ill feeling toward Turkey.[15]

Then, in 1965, something unexpected happened. Armenians within Soviet Armenia and around the world—from Moscow to Beirut to the United Nations, and in cities large and small across the United States—publicly commemorated the fiftieth anniversary of the Armenian Genocide—

and by then the word "genocide" was in full use. The Lebanese parliament passed a resolution demanding reparations for the Armenians. In
Montevideo, Uruguay, the Chamber of Deputies passed an Armenian Martyrs Day Resolution; in Moscow, Armenian students marched on the Turkish embassy; on the floor of the UN, Cypriot foreign minister Spyros
Kyprianou spoke of the mass murder of a million and a half Armenians in the
century's first genocide. In Boston, New York City, Hartford, Syracuse, Los
Angeles, Cleveland, Chicago, Winston-Salem, and Detroit, Armenians came
out en masse to remember and to the educate the world. They issued pamphlets and proclamations. Governors John H. Reed of Maine and John A.
Volpe of Massachusetts issued Armenian Genocide proclamations, and on
the floor of the U.S. Senate commemorative speeches were made. A Republican representative from Michigan, future president Gerald Ford, spoke
forthrightly to Congress in a statement in which the words "genocide,"
"Armenian," and "Turkish" all appeared in the correct context: "We mark the
50th anniversary of the Turkish genocide of the Armenian people."[16]

In the Armenian American press, headlines such as OUT OF THE SMOL-
DERING ASHES, and BEFORE THE MEMORY OF OUR MARTYRS OF THE TURK
GENOCIDE OF 1915 embodied some of the intensity of the moment. It was
as if the pent-up anguish and the repressed and suppressed memories of
five decades were being released. An Armenian diasporan civic voice was
hatched, and a full-blown discourse was not far behind.[17]

The 1965 moment emerged in a new, fertile cultural environment—
without which political movements cannot take hold. A context for global
human rights had had time to settle. The Nuremberg Trials had taken
place, and the 1948 UN Genocide Convention had already codified a definition of genocide, a word that Raphael Lemkin had coined in 1944 using
the Armenian massacres as a primary example of what he meant.[18] With
the legal and moral basis of a human rights culture in place, there was an
unprecedented space for thinking about what had been termed in 1915
"crimes against humanity."

The fertile cultural environment for an actualized beginning of Armenian Genocide memory was created, I believe, by the temper of the
1960s—the African American civil rights movement, the anti–Vietnam
War movement with its focus on human rights, the women's movement,
and a rising, vibrant literature about the Holocaust. Furthermore the pop-
ularization of psychotherapy, and a new focus on trauma in the lives of

Vietnam War veterans, had an impact on survivors and their communities by affirming the value of confronting one's personal and collective past. And as Armenian Americans—now the children and grandchildren of survivors—found themselves more Americanized and established in American life, they were at home with the cultural and political mechanisms that enabled them to have a civic voice.

It was not until 1966 that an article in a leading publication appeared on the Armenian Genocide. Marjorie Housepian's "The Unremembered Genocide," in *Commentary* (February 1966), was a signal light for the new age of this reborn discourse. Then, as scholarship on the Armenian Genocide began to grow and press coverage of the Armenian Genocide followed, the Turkish government's response became increasingly hostile. Ankara began to develop an official policy of denial, hiring public relations firms to propel its campaign. More than fifty years after the Genocide, it appeared that the Turkish government was acting out a dynamic of denial that Judith Herman describes so well. "After every atrocity one can expect to hear the same predictable apologies; it never happened; the victim lies; the victim exaggerates; the victim brought it upon herself; and in any case it is time to forget the past and move on. The more powerful the perpetrator, the greater is his prerogative to name and define reality, and the more completely his arguments prevail."[19]

By the 1970s Turkey's official policy of denial had become unique in its intensity and its attempts at manipulating public opinion. The Turkish government pressured and lobbied the press to not use the word "genocide," and demanded as well that "the Turkish side" be accorded equal time whenever the Armenian Genocide was discussed in the press or on the air. Using diffuse, evasive rhetoric aimed at subverting the truth, the Turkish government used the phrase "the alleged Armenian Genocide," and referred to it as "civil war" or the Orwellian doublespeak: "intercommunal warfare." There were continued efforts to minimize the Armenian death toll. In 1919 the Turkish minister of the interior had openly declared that eight hundred thousand Armenians died in the massacres and deportations, not counting tens of thousands of Armenians killed in the labor battalions of the military.[20] But recent Turkish government claims ranged from six hundred thousand to as low as three hundred thousand, with the latter figure now seemingly in vogue in Ankara.

To make matters worse this virulent campaign of Turkish denial provoked some angry Armenians to violence. In 1973 an Armenian survivor, Gourgen Yanikian, assassinated two Turkish consular diplomats in Santa Barbara, California. Over the next several years there were several dozen such killings. These misguided efforts to vent rage and bring the unpunished crime of the Armenian Genocide to world attention only widened the chasm between Turks and Armenians and underscored the trauma that can stem from perpetrator denial.

Terrence Des Pres in his essay "On Governing Narratives: The Turkish-Armenian Case," has analyzed the Turkish denial of the Armenian Genocide as an issue of power attempting to dismantle truth. "Knowledge," he writes, "is no longer honored for its utopian promise, but valued for the services it furnishes." In the Cold War power grid, Des Pres saw that Turkey— a NATO ally of the United States, with a strategic location for missile bases on the Soviet border—was able to impose its state propaganda on the United States. Des Pres noted that in its effort to deny the Armenian Genocide of 1915, Turkey had asked the United States to ignore its own official archives, which "are thick with first-hand evidence," and had coerced the United States and the media into hearing the Turkish government's rebuttal. "This," Des Pres asserted, "is turning intellectual debate into a gimmick for the use of the powerful."[21]

As the rhetoric out of Ankara grew more irrational and desperate in the 1970s, Richard Falk, professor of international law at Princeton, felt compelled to note that the Turkish campaign of denial is "sinister" and perhaps singular in the annals of history. It is, he wrote, "a major, proactive, deliberate government effort to use every possible instrument of persuasion at its disposal to keep the truth about the Armenian genocide from general acknowledgment, especially by elites in the United States and Western Europe."[22]

Turkish organizations working in conjunction with the Turkish government were now distributing pamphlets and brochures, such as one titled *Setting the Record Straight: On Armenian Propaganda Against Turkey,* which was published by the Assembly of Turkish American Associations, Washington, D.C. The pamphlet was passed out during an Armenian Genocide commemoration held at Times Square in New York City; it read:

> In recent years claims have been made by some Armenians in
> Europe, America, and elsewhere that the Armenians suffered terri-

ble misrule in the Ottoman Empire. Such claims are absurd. Armenians were deported because they were a security threat and were
massacring Muslims but great care was taken by the Ottoman government to prevent the Armenians from being harmed during
these deportations. Thus orders were issued that: "when Armenians are transferred to their places of settlement and are on the road,
their comfort is assured and their lives and property protected; that
after their arrival . . . their food should be paid for out of Refugees
Appropriations; that property and land should be distributed to
them in accordance with their previous financial situation."

The Turkish publication continued by attacking the Armenian
survivors:

Carefully coached by their Armenian nationalist interviewers,
these aged Armenians relate tales of horror which supposedly
took place some 66 years ago in such detail as to astonish the
imagination, considering that most of them already are aged
eighty or more. Subjected to years of Armenian nationalist propaganda as well as the coaching of their interviewers, there is little doubt that their statements are of no use whatever for
historical research.

"There was no genocide committed against the Armenians in the
Ottoman Empire before or during World War I," the pamphlet asserted.
"No genocide was planned or ordered by the Ottoman government and
no genocide was carried out."[23]

While these efforts were crude and "obscene," to use Holocaust film-
maker Claude Lanzman's phrase, more sophisticated efforts at denying
the Armenian Genocide were put forth. Historians at several American
universities reportedly received funding from the Turkish government to
support the supposed "other side of the story." If scholars could be funded
by "governments to shore up the official claims of nation-states," Des Pres
noted, then knowledge was "no longer the mind's ground of judgment
but a commodity for hire."[24] Indeed, there has recently been exposed a
paper trail in academe that involved Turkey's attempt to cover up the
Armenian Genocide.

In 1962 Bernard Lewis, professor at Princeton University, in his book *The Emergence of Modern Turkey*, characterized what happened in 1916 as "the terrible holocaust . . . when a million and a half Armenians perished."[25] But sometime after that, Lewis's attitude about the fate of the Armenians in Turkey became hostile. His colleague in Near Eastern studies at Princeton, Norman Itzkowitz, also began to write and speak with hostility about the "alleged" genocide of the Armenians, and to refer to the Armenians as embittered "losers."[26] That such views were coming out of Princeton University was doubly ironic because—perhaps along with Mount Holyoke—no institution of higher learning sent more graduates to Turkey to work with and for the Armenians.

Stanford J. Shaw, who taught at UCLA, and his Turkish wife, Ezel Kural Shaw, in their history of *The Ottoman Empire and Modern Turkey* (1970) reduce the Armenian Genocide to a nonevent. They depict the Armenians as perpetrators and aggressors, calling them "the victimizers rather than the victims, the privileged rather than the oppressed, and the fabricators of unfounded tales of massacre."[27] The Shaws, in the name of scholarship, tell the reader that the Young Turk government was kind and decent to the Armenians, deporting only those near the border districts of the country, and making sure all the deportees had food and water and medical attention while they were being relocated to new homes. The Shaws put forth the following description of the death marches:

> Specific instructions were issued for the army to protect the Armenians against nomadic attacks and to provide them with sufficient food and other supplies to meet their needs during the march and after they were settled. . . . The Armenians were to be protected and cared for until they returned to their homes after the war. A supplementary law established a special commission to record the revenues being held in trust until their return. Muslims wishing to occupy abandoned buildings could do so only as renters, with the revenues paid to the trust funds, and with the understanding that they would have to leave when the original owners returned. The deportees and their possessions were to be guarded by the army while in transit as well as in Iraq and Syria, and the government would provide for their return once the crisis was over.[28]

One gets a deeper sense of what Deborah Lipstadt means when she writes that "denial of genocide strives to reshape history in order to demonize the victims and rehabilitate the perpetrators, and is—indeed—the final stage of genocide."[29]

The paper trail of denial continued, and in the 1990s the exposé of the case of Heath Lowry, also at Princeton, drew national attention. Lowry had a Ph.D. in Ottoman Studies and went to Turkey in the 1970s to work at a research institute in Istanbul and lecture at Bosphorus University. He returned to the United States in 1986 to become the director of the Institute for Turkish Studies in Washington, D.C.—a nonprofit organization set up by the Turkish government ostensibly to promote Turkish culture in the United States. Here Lowry wrote articles and op-ed columns denying the Genocide, and he lobbied in Congress to defeat successive Armenian Genocide commemorative resolutions. He went so far as to write a ninety-page booklet, published in Istanbul, that attempts to discredit Ambassador Morgenthau's memoir. Lowry seemed devoted to helping Turkey sanitize its past.

When Robert Jay Lifton's 1986 book *The Nazi Doctors* caught Lowry's attention, he was deeply disturbed that it made mention of the Armenian Genocide. Although *The Nazi Doctors* is about how physicians in the Third Reich embraced Hitler's program of mass murder, Lifton mentions the Armenian Genocide several times, and in particular the role of Turkish physicians in the killing process. After reading *The Nazi Doctors*, Lowry wrote a long memorandum to the Turkish ambassador to the United States, pointing out how dangerous was Lifton's book:

"Our problem is less with Lifton than it is with the works upon which he relies," Lowry wrote to Ambassador Nuhzet Kamdemir. "Lifton is simply the end of the chain." Lowry was upset that there was so much scholarship on the Armenian Genocide, as well as scholarship on the Holocaust that made reference to the Armenian Genocide. Sounding like an intelligence agent, Lowry writes that he has "repeatedly stressed both in writing and verbally to Ankara" that these scholars (Dadrian, Fein, Kuper, Hovannisian) must be responded to. "On the chance that you still wish to respond in writing to Lifton," Lowry closes, "I have drafted the following letter."

Ambassador Kandemir then had Lowry's ghostwritten letter typed on official stationery, signed it, and had it mailed. But when Lifton opened the envelope from the Turkish embassy, he found a surprise. It contained

not only the letter signed by the Turkish ambassador, but also inadvertently enclosed were Lowry's long memorandum to the Turkish ambassador and Lowry's draft of the letter.[30]

In the time between Lifton's receipt of the Turkish ambassador's
package and the exposé of the Lowry story, Lowry had been appointed to
an endowed chair at Princeton, the Ataturk Chair in Turkish Studies.
What added to the astonishment of many was that it was Lowry who had
orchestrated the funding for chairs in Turkish Studies at a number of
American universities. He was thus central to developing the project from
which he was now benefiting in his new chair. At Princeton the funding
came partially from the Turkish government and was matched by Ahmet
Ertegun, Atlantic Records mogul and son of former ambassador Munir
Ertegun, who had worked so hard to stop the film of *The Forty Days of
Musa Dagh* in 1935. Ahmet Ertegun was also one of Lowry's board members at the Institute for Turkish Studies. Furthermore, academics nationwide wondered how a man in his fifties, who hadn't written one scholarly
book published by a mainstream trade or university press, and who had
never held a full-time college teaching job in the United States, could be
offered a chair at Princeton.

Instead of simply sending a rebuttal to the Turkish ambassador,
Robert Jay Lifton decided to join with genocide scholars Roger Smith and
Eric Markusen to write an article called "Professional Ethics and the
Denial of the Armenian Genocide." It appeared in the *Journal of Holocaust
and Genocide Studies* in the spring of 1995, with facsimile reproductions of
the Lowry–Turkish ambassador documents, and it exposed and analyzed
the corruption of Turkey's project in American academe and the ethical
issues at stake for Princeton and other universities accepting funding from
Turkey.

Within a few months the Lowry-Princeton-Turkey story had become
national news, and was covered in the *Chronicle of Higher Education,* the
New York Times, and the *Boston Globe.* A petition, "Taking a Stand Against
the Turkish Government's Denial of the Armenian Genocide and Scholarly Corruption in the Academy," was circulated and signed by more than
a hundred scholars, writers, and public intellectuals. It was a plain-
language document that outlined the Turkish government's denial campaign, including the Lowry episode, and called for an end to that
government's tactics, especially in American institutions of higher learn-

ing, where more funding offered by the Turkish government was turning up. The petition appeared in the *Chronicle of Higher Education,* the *New York Times,* and *Washington Post.* The signatories included a wide range of voices: Anthony Appiah, Yehuda Bauer, Robert N. Bellah, David Brion Davis, Jean Bethke Elshtain, Henry Louis Gates Jr., Seamus Heaney, Raul Hilberg, Deborah Lipstadt, Arthur Miller, David Riesman, Susan Sontag, William Styron, Derek Walcott, Cornel West.

At its annual meeting in June 1998, the Association of Genocide Scholars—the definitive body of scholars of genocide—passed an Armenian Genocide Resolution. Another petition in the *New York Times* on June 9, 2000, read "126 Holocaust Scholars Affirm the Incontestable Fact of the Armenian Genocide and Urge Western Democracies to Officially Recognize It." Among the signatories were Elie Wiesel, Yehuda Bauer, Israel Charny, Ward Churchill, Saul Mendlovitz, Stephen Feinstein. By the end of the decade the world was weighing in on the Armenian Genocide. The pope, the Italian parliament, the European Parliament, the Swedish parliament all went on record acknowledging the Armenian Genocide, and, most dramatically, France had passed into law an Armenian Genocide resolution.

But in the United States the issue clearly was about power, and Turkey certainly had more of it than Armenia, which until 1991 had no nation-state. "What does it mean," Des Pres wrote, "when a client-state like Turkey can persuade a super power like the United States to abandon its earlier stance toward the genocide of 1915?"[31] The Turkish government successfully lobbied the U.S. Congress against passing a bill commemorating the seventieth and, later, the seventy-fifth anniversaries of the Armenian Genocide. It was a simple commemorative bill that had no legal ramifications and would, if nothing else, have echoed American public sentiment of the historical period of 1915.

With the Turkish denial becoming more proactive, as Turkey continued to use the power of its NATO military alliance, as well as its weapons contracts with major U.S. corporations, to pressure the United States government, the struggle over memory escalated. Armenian American lobby groups now pushed more vigorously for Armenian Genocide recognition. A Joint Resolution (HJ Res. 148), which was to designate April 24, 1975, a

"National Day of Remembrance of Man's Inhumanity to Man," passed through Congress but without any reference to Turkey. The State Department insisted that the words "in Turkey" be removed, and so the resolution read:

> The President of the United States is authorized and requested to issue a proclamation calling upon the people of the United States to observe such day as a day of remembrance for all the victims of genocide, especially those of Armenian ancestry who succumbed to the genocide perpetrated in 1915, and in whose memory this date is commemorated by all Armenians and their friends throughout the world.[32]

A day later the resolution was sent to the Senate Judiciary Committee and was shelved.[33]

The rhetoric of presidents from the mid-1970s on revealed the same problem: The U.S. government was succumbing to Turkish pressure, and the word "genocide" had become the focus of Turkish hysteria. The ironies were abundant, especially given the intense involvement of the United States for four decades during the Armenian massacres and Genocide, and the extraordinary and admirable roles of U.S. foreign service officers. The Turkish government was, in effect, conducting a campaign against American history as well; for what had been America's first, major international human rights campaign was being subverted by crude power politics.

In 1978 during a White House reception honoring Armenian Americans, President Carter avoided using the word "genocide," "Turkey," or even "Ottoman Turkish Empire." "It's generally not known in the world," he said, "that in the years preceding 1916, there was a concerted effort to eliminate all the Armenian people, probably one of the greatest tragedies that ever befell any group. And there weren't any Nuremberg trials."[34] Carter's statement was glaringly devoid of the name of the perpetrator and its crime.

As the Cold War heated up, relations with Turkey were considered ever more important, and military aid to Turkey increased from $453.8 million in 1981 to $704.1 million in 1982.[35] So it was not surprising that, although President Reagan mentioned the Armenian Genocide in a proclamation about the Holocaust in 1981 ("Like the genocide of the Armenians before it . . . the lessons of the Holocaust must never be forgotten"), he would not support any official recognition of the Armenian Genocide.[36]

In 1984, when a resolution to commemorate the Armenian Genocide came before the U.S. House and Senate, the Turkish government threatened to close down U.S. military bases in Turkey and to terminate defense contracts with U.S. firms. President Reagan, who earlier that year went to Bitburg, Germany, to pay respects to dead German S.S. officers—and in doing so conflated the elite killing corps with its victims—had no difficulty acquiescing to Turkish demands. And in 1989, when Senate minority leader Bob Dole proposed a bill to commemorate the seventy-fifth anniversary of the Armenian Genocide, Turkey enlisted Senator Robert Byrd to fight on behalf of the Turkish denial. Again intellectual debate was turned into a gimmick, and the bill lost by twelve votes. No such scenario would ever unfold against a Holocaust commemorative bill. President George H. Bush in his April 1990 statement called "April 24, 1990 a day of remembrance for more than a million people who were victims . . . of the massacres."[37] Again, no mention of Turkey or the word genocide.

By the mid-nineties, movements to commemorate historical trauma and disaster had become part of public discourse worldwide. Indeed, a culture of apology seemed to have emerged—a sign that some of the lessons of human rights disasters were registering in the moral climate of what might be called a new age. President Clinton apologized to the black families involved in the medical experiments at Tuskegee, and on a trip to Africa made efforts to apologize for slavery; the U.S. Bureau of Indian Affairs marked its 175th anniversary by apologizing to Native Americans for its history of ethnic cleansing. The Japanese government apologized and made at least token reparations to the "comfort women" of World War II; the Catholic Church of France asked God's forgiveness for its silence during the Holocaust, and the Vatican began atoning for its silence during the Holocaust; the Canadian government formally apologized to its 1.3 million indigenous people for 150 years of racism and paternalism; the Austrians began to return artworks that were pillaged by the Nazis from Jewish families; Swiss banks began negotiating settlements with Holocaust survivors and families of Holocaust victims. Boris Yeltsin's eloquent statement about the importance of addressing the past on the occasion of the funeral of Czar Nicholas II and his family in July 1998 was held up as a model of acknowledgment.

With their moral aim of opening up their records and letting the truth be known, major international corporations like General Motors, Bertelsmann, and Ford have aggressively hired Holocaust scholars to research their possible wartime collusion with the Nazis. But there was still one black hole—the Armenian Genocide.

President Clinton tried to make a decent statement for the Armenian Genocide, and on April 23, 1995, he issued the following: "On this solemn day, I join with Armenians throughout the United States, in Armenia, and around the world in remembering the 80th anniversary of the Armenians who perished, victims of massacres in the last years .of the Ottoman Empire. Their loss is our loss, their courage a testament to mankind's indomitable spirit."[38] Yet he couldn't bring himself to use the word genocide or name the perpetrators.

The deeper test for President Clinton and his administration came in the fall of 2000 when an Armenian Genocide Resolution was proposed by Congress. A simple nonbinding resolution asked the president in his annual statement of April 24 commemorating the slaughter of the Armenians to refer to the event as genocide; and the first draft of the resolution also requested that foreign service officers be educated about human rights and ethnic cleansing by being familiarized with the United States official records on the Armenian Genocide. It seemed to the House Subcommittee on International Relations and Human Rights to be a modest and rational resolution, and it was nonbinding. The House subcommittee passed it by a large majority in the face of intense Turkish government harassment.[39]

When Turkey went so far as to send some of its own parliamentary members to Washington to pressure the House Subcommittee on International Relations and Human Rights to dissuade it from passing the bill, the members of the subcommittee were so repelled by the Turkish statements of denial that Committee Chair Chris Smith, a Republican from New Jersey, was reported to have told the Turkish politicians that their behavior confirmed the very reasons why he was supporting the bill.

Several distinguished genocide and Holocaust scholars wrote to the

House Subcommittee urging them not to cave in to Turkish blackmail. Elie Wiesel wrote urging Congress to pass the resolution.[40] Deborah Lipstadt wrote to the Congressional committee:

> Denial of genocide whether that of the Turks against the Armenians, or the Nazis against the Jews is not an act of historical reinterpretation. Rather, the deniers sow confusion by appearing to be engaged in a genuine scholarly effort. . . . The deniers aim at convincing innocent third parties that there is "another side of the story." . . . Denial of genocide strives to reshape history in order to demonize the victims and rehabilitate the perpetrators. . . . I urge you to support a resolution affirming the role played by the United States on behalf of the Armenian people during the Armenian Genocide.[41]

After passing through the subcommittee the bill was going to the floor of the House, where it was expected to pass. However, within hours of the subcommittee vote, Ankara warned the United States that it would close its air bases to U.S. planes, including those near the Iraqi border, and cancel weapons contracts with the United States. In that moment, when terrorist attacks were occurring in the Middle East, the State Department issued a memo stating that Turkey had communicated that it could not guarantee the safety of American citizens in Turkey in light of unforseen violence; the implication was that H.R. 398 was part of the equation.

As the bill was going to the House with apparently enough votes to pass, Turkish hysteria seemed to reach a new level. Pressuring the State Department, Turkey told the United States that the passage of such a resolution would ruin U.S. relations with Turkey. As the violence between Israel and the Palestinians erupted that fall, and chaos seemed to envelope the Middle East, the State Department—with Israeli pressuring, at the request of Turkey—told President Clinton that the Armenian Genocide Resolution must be squashed for the sake of "national security." The president phoned House Speaker Dennis Hastert and asked that the bill be killed. Hastert unhappily followed orders. Once again the attempt to commemorate the century's first genocide had been effectively censored by a foreign government, and in this case, a foreign government with a deeply disturbing human rights record.[42]

The only silver lining in the story of H.R. 398 was that there was not any demonstrable denial on the part of American politicians; most representatives agreed that the resolution was just and fair. Because H.R. 398 included recognition of the U.S. State Department's role in rescuing survivors of the Armenian Genocide, it was doubly sad that the United States—the most powerful country in the world—could not muster the courage to acknowledge its own humanitarian history.

Soon afterward the French government demonstrated that standing firm on the memory of the Armenian Genocide could be done without great harm to international relations. In 1997 the French National Assembly began consideration of a one-sentence resolution stating that the Armenian Genocide of 1915 was a fact. The Turkish government responded with the usual threats. It denounced the French government, canceled multimillion-dollar contracts with French companies, and banned the importation of certain French products. The French government paused over the resolution before sending it on to its Senate where, if it was ratified, it would pass into law. In October 2000, shortly after the United States had caved to Turkish pressure, the French Senate passed the Armenian Genocide resolution into law. The Turkish government promptly denounced the resolution and withdrew its ambassador from Paris. Yet, for all the hysteria and threats, in about six months the Turkish government was back doing business with France and had resumed diplomatic relations with Paris.

The French had made one thing clear: ethics and international diplomacy could coexist. The governments of the world, like individuals at the scene of a crime, are bystanders with ethical roles to play, roles that make a difference. The perpetrator should not be privileged but rather ostracized until its policy changes.

When the European Parliament rejected Turkey's request in 1987 to be considered for admission to the European Community—in part because of its refusal to acknowledge the Armenian Genocide—it took a moral position on human rights. When the U.S. House of Representatives in May 1996 voted to cut aid to Turkey because of its denial of the Armenian Genocide, it made an act of moral commitment. The United States government, as well as the American press, media, and educational institutions, can no longer allow themselves to be coerced by the Turkish government. The time has come for the closing of the wound. As one brave Turkish citizen wrote on the eighty-first anniversary of the Genocide,

"History is waiting for that honest Turkish leader who will acknowledge his ancestors' biggest crime ever, who will apologize to the Armenian people, and who will do his best to indemnify them, materially and morally, in the eyes of the world."[43] Turkey's greatest modern poet, Nazim Hikmet, who spent much of his life in a Turkish prison, saw the tragedy in his country's denial of the Armenian Genocide. In his poem "Evening Walk" (1950), the poet speaks to himself:

> *The Armenian citizen has not forgiven*
> > *the slaughter of his father in the Kurdish mountains.*
> *But he loves you,*
> *because you also won't forgive*
> > *those who blackened the name of the Turkish people.*[44]

NOTES

ABBREVIATIONS:
> AA: *Auswartigen Amt* (West German Foreign Office Archives)
> ABCFM: American Board of Commissioners for Foreign Missions
> DAF: Diplomatic Archives of France
> FO: British Foreign Office
> PPC: Papers of the Paris Peace Conference

PREFACE

1. Herbert Hoover, *Memoirs—Years of Adventure* (New York: Macmillan, 1951), 385.
2. Charlotte Perkins Gilman, "International Duties," *Armenia* 1, no. 1 (1903), 10, 14.
3. Roosevelt to Dodge, May 11, 1918, *Letters of Theodore Roosevelt*, vol. 8, *Days of Armageddon* (Cambridge, Mass.: Harvard University Press, 1952), 1316–18.
4. *Central Conference of American Rabbis Yearbook XIX* (Central Conference for American Rabbis, 1909), 162.
5. Henry Morgenthau, *Ambassador Morgenthau's Story* (New York: Doubleday and Doran, 1918), 385.
6. Richard Falk, "The Armenian Genocide in Official Turkish Records," foreword, in *Journal of Political and Military Sociology* 22, no. 1 (Summer 1994), i.
7. Deborah Lipstadt, "Armenian Genocide," letter to *Princeton Alumni Weekly*, vol. 96, no. 14 (April 17, 1996); Deborah Lipstadt, *Denying the Holocaust: The Growing Assault on Truth and Memory* (New York: The Free Press, 1993), 2; Deborah Lipstadt to Hon. Chris Smith, Chair International Operations Subcommittee, September 12, 2000. Correspondence to U.S. House International Relations Committee Concerning H. Res. 398, the United States Training on and Commemorating the Armenian Genocide, 106th Congress, 2nd Session, September 14, 2000.
8. See *New York Times* coverage from 1915 in *The Armenian Genocide: News Accounts from the American Press, 1915–1922*, ed. Richard Kloian (Berkeley, Calif.: Anto Printing, 1988).

CHAPTER 1: A GATHERING AT FANEUIL HALL

1. Sir Edwin Pears, *Life of Abdul Hamid* (New York: Henry Holt & Co., 1917), 226.
2. Joan Haslip, *The Sultan: The Life of Abdul Hamid II* (London: Weidenfeld & Nicolson, 1958), 222.
3. Johannes Lepsius, *Armenia and Europe* (London: Hodder and Stoughton, 1897), see pp. 280–327 for full account of destruction of Armenian life and property; see also Vahakn N. Padrian, *The History of the Armenian Genocide* (Providence, R.I., Oxford: Berghahn Books, 1995), 155.
4. Deborah Pinkham Clifford, *Mine Eyes Have Seen the Glory: A Biography of Julia Ward Howe* (Boston: Little, Brown & Co., 1978), 257.
5. Laura E. Richard and Maud Howe Elliott, eds., *Julia Ward Howe 1819–1910* (Boston: Houghton Mifflin & Co., 1916), 189.
6. Ibid. See also *Boston Herald*, November 27, 1894.
7. Ibid., 191.
8. Ibid., 190.
9. *Boston Herald*, November 27, 1894.
10. Ibid., *Boston Globe*, November 27, 1894.
11. Mark Twain, *Innocents Abroad*, vol. 1 (New York: Harper & Brothers, 1869), 173–75.
12. Ibid., vol. 2, 185–87.
13. Clifford, *Mine Eyes Have Seen the Glory*, 52–57.
14. For a full perspective on the United Friends of Armenia, see the *Woman's Journal*, the weekly newspaper of the Boston suffrage movement, which was edited by Alice Stone Blackwell and her father after her mother, Lucy, died in 1893. The Blackwells devoted pages of their paper from 1894 through the rest of the decade to the work of the United Friends of Armenia.

CHAPTER 2: "THERE IN THE WOODS"

1. Alice Stone Blackwell, "Some Reminiscences," *New Armenia* 5, no. 2 (Feb. 1918), 20–21.
2. Isabel Barrows to Ohannes Chatschumian, Feb. 18, 1893, bMS Am 1807.1 (579), Barrows family papers, by permission of the Houghton Library, Harvard University.
3. Isabel Barrows to Ohannes Chatschumian, April 26, 1893, ibid.
4. Isabel Barrows to Ohannes Chatschumian, July 15, 1893, ibid.
5. *We the Women*, ed. Madeleine B. Stern (Lincoln, University Press of Nebraska), 179.
6. Madeleine B. Stern, *So Much in a Lifetime: The Story of Dr. Isabel Barrows* (New York: Julian Messner, Inc., 1964), 185–90.
7. Isabel and June Barrows, *The Shaybacks at Camp* (Boston: Houghton Mifflin & Co. 1887), chaps. 4–6.
8. Ibid., 56.
9. Blackwell, "Some Reminiscences," 21.
10. Ibid.
11. Ibid.
12. Alice Stone Blackwell, *Armenian Poems* (Boston: Robert Chambers, 1917).
13. Alice Stone Blackwell to Isabel Barrows, May 31, 1894, Barrows papers, Houghton Library, Harvard University.
14. Ohannes Chatschumian, Application to Divinity School, 4 October 1893, Student Folder, O. Chatschumian, UAV 328.282, Harvard University Archives.

15. Alice Stone Blackwell to Professor F. G. Peabody, September 29, 1893, Blackwell papers, Library of Congress.
16. Isabel Barrows to Professor Peabody, September 29, 1893, Barrows family papers, Library of Congress.
17. Isabel Barrows to Professor Everett, March 1, 1893 (from Leipzig), Barrows family papers, Library of Congress.
18. Ronald G. Suny, *Looking Toward Ararat: Armenia in Modern History* (Bloomington: Indiana University Press, 1993), 63–68.

CHAPTER 3: YANKEES IN ARMENIA
1. "The Haystack Prayer Meeting and Williams College," 15–16, Williamsiana Collection, Williams College, Williamstown, Mass., MCMVI.
2. Suzanne E. Moranian, *The American Missionaries and the Armenian Question, 1915–1920* (Ph.D. diss., University of Michigan, 1994), 52.
3. Frank Andrews Stone, *Academies for Anatolia* (Lanham, N.Y., and London: University Press of America, 1984), 3, 8–9.
4. Moranian, *The American Missionaries and the Armenian Question,* 55.
5. Ibid.
6. Ibid, 56; the ABCFM was the dominant missionary organization in the Ottoman Empire, but the Presbyterian Church, the Methodist Episcopal Church, and the American Baptist Union also set up stations in the nineteenth century.
7. C. H. Wheeler, *Letters from Eden: Reminiscences of Missionary Life in the East* (Boston: American Tract Society, 1868), 421.
8. Ibid., 67.
9. Ibid., 63–64.
10. Bess P. Vickery, *Mount Holyoke Courageous: A Call to the Near East* (New York: Carlton Press Corp., 1994), xxiv–xxv.
11. Ibid., 30–31.
12. Ibid., xxii.
13. Edwin M. Bliss, *Turkey and the Armenian Atrocities* (Edgewood Publishing Company, 1896), vii.
14. Moranian, *The American Missionaries and the Armenian Question,* 85.
15. George Washburn, *Fifty Years in Constantinople and Recollections of Robert College* (Boston: Houghton Mifflin & Co., 1911), 163–64.
16. Ibid., 308.
17. Christopher Walker, *Visions of Ararat* (London: I. B. Taurus, 1997), 13–16, 123.
18. Sirarpie Der Nersessian, *The Armenians* (New York: Praeger Publishers, 1970), 33–70.
19. Dickran Kouymjian, "The Destruction of Armenian Historical Monuments as a Continuation of the Turkish Policy of Genocide," in Permanent Peoples' Tribunal, *A Crime of Silence: The Armenian Genocide* (London: Zed Books, 1985), 173–85; see also Kouymjian, "Confiscation and Destruction: A Manifestation of the Genocidal Process," *Armenian Forum* 1, vol. 3 (Autumn 1998), 1–12.
20. Stepan Mnatsakanian, *Aghtamar* (New York: Alex Manoogian Cultural Fund, Erebouni Editions, 1986), 1–21.
21. Carolyn P. Collette and Vincent J. DiMarco, "The Matter of Armenia in the Age of Chaucer," *Studies in the Age of Chaucer* 23 (2001), 319.

22. Ibid., 347.
23. Ibid., 335–40.
24. Ibid., 350.
25. Christopher Walker, *Armenia: The Survival of a Nation* (New York: St. Martin's Press, 1980), 33.
26. Walt Whitman, *Leaves of Grass*, ed. S. Bradley (New York: Holt, Rinehart & Winston, 1949), 122.

CHAPTER 4: THE SULTAN AND THE ARMENIAN QUESTION
1. Lory Alder and Richard Dalby, *The Dervish of Windsor Castle: The Life of Arminius Vambery* (Bachman & Turner Ltd., 1979), 360.
2. Pears, *Life of Abdul Hamid*, 228.
3. Clarence D. Ussher, *An American Physician in Turkey* (Boston: Houghton Mifflin & Co., 1917), 5.
4. Franklin Andrews Stone, *Academies for Anatolia: A Study of the Rationale, Program and Impact of the Educational Institutions Sponsored by the American Board in Turkey: 1830–1980* (Lanham, N.Y./London: University Press of America), 173.
5. Pears, *Life of Abdul Hamid*, 6.
6. Roderick H. Davison, "Turkish Attitudes Concerning Christian-Muslim Equality in the Nineteenth Century," *American Historical Review 59* (1954), 846–47.
7. Vahakn Dadrian, "The Armenian Question and the Wartime Fate of the Armenians as Documented by the Officals of the Ottoman Empire's World War I Allies: Germany and Austria-Hungary," in *International Journal of Middle East Studies 34* (2002), 61.
8. Richard Shannon, *Gladstone and the Bulgarian Agitation* (London: Thomas Nelson & Sons, 1963), 22–23.
9. Sir Edward Hertslet, *The Map of Europe by Treaty*, vol. 4, *1875–1891* (London: Harrison and Sons, 1891), 2598–99.
10. Ibid., 2686.
11. Ibid., 2796; Walker, *Armenia: The Survival of a Nation*, 114–15.
12. Alder and Dalby, *The Life of Arminius Vambery, 359.*
13. Diplomatic Archives of Foreign Ministry of France (*Documents Diplomatiques Francais 1871–1900*), vol. 11, no. 50, 71–74, in Dadrian, "The Armenian Question," 35.
14. Walker, *Armenia: The Survival of a Nation, 87.*
15. Ibid., 86–90; Hagop Barsoumian, "The Eastern Question and the Tanzimat Era," in *The Armenian People: From Ancient to Modern Times*, vol. 2, ed. Richard Hovannisian (New York: St. Martin's Press, 1997), 182–83; Robert Melson, *Revolution and Genocide: On the Origins of the Armenian Genocide and the Holocaust* (Chicago: University of Chicago Press, 1992), 54–56.
16. Melson, *Revolution and Genocide, 54–56.*
17. Sir Edwin Pears, *Forty Years in Constantinople: The Recollections of Sir Edwin Pears, 1873–1915* (London: Herbert Jenkins, Ltd., 1915), 152.
18. *Turkey 3* (1897), doc. no. 104, October 3, 1896, 91–92.
19. William M. Ramsay, *Impressions of Turkey During Twelve Years Wanderings* (New York: 1897), 206–7.
20. Walker, *Armenia: The Survival of a Nation, 134.*
21. Richard Hovannisian, "The Armenian Question and the Ottoman Empire 1876–1914," in *The Armenian People from Ancient to Modern Times*, vol. 2, 210; Walker, *Armenia: The Survival of a Nation*, 117.

22. Prelacy of the Armenian Apostolic Church of America, *Hairig: A Celebration of His Life and Vision on the Eightieth Anniversary of His Death, 1907–1987* (New York: Prelacy of the Armenian Apostolic Church of America, 1987).

23. Louise Nalbandian, *The Armenian Revolutionary Movement: the Development of Armenian Political Parties Through the Nineteenth Century* (Berkeley and Los Angeles: University of California Press, 1963), 67, 82, see also chap. 5; Walker, *Armenia: The Survival of a Nation*, 126–30.

24. Nalbandian, *The Armenian Revolutionary Movement*, 151.

25. Walker, *Armenia: The Survival of A Nation*, 132.

26. Sir Robert W. Graves, *Storm Centres of the Near East, 1879–1929* (London: Hutchinson & Co., 1933), 132–38; see also Walker, *Armenia: The Survival of A Nation*, 135.

27. See Pears, *Life of Adbul Hamid*, 107–14; Pears, *Forty Years in Constantinople*, 144–48; Haslip, *The Sultan*, chaps. 16–20; Ernest Edmondson Ramsaur, *The Young Turks* (Princeton, N.J.: Princeton University Press, 1957), 11–13, 129–36; Paul Fesch, *Constantinople aux derniers jours d'Abdul Hamid* (Paris: 1907), 74, 58–59.

28. Pears, *Life of Abdul Hamid*, 4.

29. Ibid., 107–11; Ramsaur, *The Young Turks*, 11; Fesch, *Constantinople*, 74.

30. Pears, *Life of Abdul Hamid*, 107–11.

31. Ibid., 109.

32. Ibid., 110; Ramsaur, *The Young Turks*, 12.

33. Ibid., 110–11; Haslip, *The Sultan*, 152–53.

34. Haslip, *The Sultan*, 153.

35. Ibid., 210.

36. Ramsaur, *The Young Turks*, 11.

37. Bernard Lewis, *The Emergence of Modern Turkey*, 174.

38. Pears, *Life of Abdul Hamid*, 83.

39. Ibid., 83–85.

40. Ibid., 224.

41. Lewis, *The Emergence of Modern Turkey*, 176.

42. Ibid., 183–184; Fesch, *Constantinople*, 54.

43. Fesch, *Constantinople*, 53.

44. Robert Kaplan, *The Nothing That Is: A Natural History of Zero* (Oxford University Press, 2000), 190.

45. Fesch, *Constantinople*, 50.

46. Lewis, *The Emergence of Modern Turkey*, 184.

47. Ramsaur, *The Young Turks*, 115.

48. Ibid.

49. Ibid., 116.

50. FO 424/169, 30.

51. Walker, *Armenia: The Survival of a Nation*, 134.

CHAPTER 5: KILLING FIELDS: THE MASSACRES OF THE 1890s

1. Richard G. Hovannisian, ed., *Armenian Baghesh/Bitlis and Taron/Mush* (Costa Mesa, Calif.: Mazda Publishers, 2001), 1–2.

2. Robert H. Hewsen, *Armenia: A Historical Atlas* (University of Chicago Press, 2001), 203; Hewsen gives an excellent overview of the Armenian economy in the region.

3. Walker, *Armenia: The Survival of a Nation*, 139.

4. *Turkey* 1 (1895), 70.

5. Ibid., 70–71.

6. Ibid., 171.

7. Ibid., 114.

8. Sir Robert Windham Graves, *Storm Centres of the Near East, 1879–1929* (London: Hutchinson & Co., 1933), 144.

9. Vahakn Dadrian, *History of the Armenian Genocide*, 117.

10. *Turkey* 1 (1895), 206–7.

11. "The Armenian Crisis in Turkey," in *Woman's Journal*, Saturday, April 6, 1895, 106. For a complete account of these letters see Frederick Greene, *The Armenian Atrocities in Turkey* (New York: G.P. Putnam's Sons, 1895).

12. FO 424/178, p. 299; Graves, *Storm Centres*, p. 145–47.

13. Duke of Argyll (George John Douglas Campbell, formerly secretary of state for India and Lord Privy Seal), *Our Responsibilities for Turkey* (London: John Murray, 1896), 92.

14. Walker, *Armenia: The Survival of a Nation*, 142; Melson, *Genocide and Revolution*, 45.

15. Great Britain, House of Commons, Correspondence Relating to Asiatic Provinces of Turkey, Sessional Papers 1895, vol. 109, pt. 1c, 7894, "Events at Sassoun, and Commission of Inquiry at Moush," enclosure 2 in no. 60, Van, November 1894, quoted in Melson, *Revolution and Genocide*, 45.

16. *Turkey* 1 (1896), 94.

17. *Turkey* 2 (1896), 31.

18. Ibid., 34–35; the full text of the protest-demand is in this diplomatic dispatch—enclosure 2, no. 50—and is an important text in the history of civil and human rights.

19. Dadrian, *History of the Armenian Genocide*, 120.

20. *Turkey* 2, (1896), 31, 34–35.

21. *La Verité sur les massacres d'Armenie* (Paris, 1896), p. 28, quoted in Walker, *Armenia*, 155.

22. Pears, *Life of Abdul Hamid*, 254.

23. *Turkey* 2 (1896), 36.

24. Ibid., 37; Walker, *Armenia: The Survival of a Nation*, 156.

25. Dadrian, *History of the Armenian Genocide*, 153–54; see also Walker, *Armenia: The Survival of a Nation*, 156–162.

26. Dadrian, *History of the Armenian Genocide*, 128.

27. Ibid., 128–29.

28. *Turkey* 8 (1896), 23.

29. Ibid., 247, July 28, 1896.

30. Ibid., 205; Chargé Herbert's June 19, 1896, report to Salisbury, DAF [n.5], doc. no. 215, 240; Cambon's June 20, 1896, report to Hanotaux, quoted in Dadrian, 136.

31. Ibid., 272. William W. Howard, "Horrors of Armenia," in *Armenian Review* 18, 4 (Winter 1965), 68–72.

CHAPTER 6: HUMANITY ON TRIAL: CLARA BARTON AND AMERICA'S MISSION TO ARMENIA

1. *Congressional Record*, 54th Cong., 1st Session, 1896, vol. 28, pt. 1, 959 (January 24, 1896).

2. Richards and Elliott, *Julia Ward Howe*, 215.

3. Donald Bruce Johnson, ed., *National Party Platforms*, vol. 1, *1840–1956* (Champaign: University of Illinois Press, 1978), 108.

4. "The Armenian Crisis in Turkey"; see also Greene, *The Armenian Atrocities in Turkey.*

5. "The Women of Armenia: the Wives, Mothers, and Daughters of an Afflicted Nation," *New York Times*, August 18, 1895, 21.

6. Clara Barton, *The Red Cross in War and Peace* (Washington, D.C.: American Historical Press, 1899), 276.

7. Ibid., 277.

8. Elizabeth Brown Pryor, *Clara Barton: Professional Angel* (Philadelphia: University of Pennsylvania Press, 1987), 150.

9. Ibid., 151.

10. Ibid., 159.

11. Merle Curti, *American Philanthropy Abroad* (New Brunswick, N.J.: Rutgers University Press, 1963), 121–23.

12. Ibid., 124–26.

13. Ibid., 124.

14. Ibid., 123.

15. Ibid., 124–25.

16. Ibid., 130.

17. Ibid., 131.

18. Ibid., 131–34.

19. *Congressional Record*, 54th Cong., 1st Session, 1896, vol. 28, pt. 1, 959.

20. Ibid., 961–63.

21. Ibid., 963.

22. Curti, *American Philanthropy Abroad*, 132.

23. *Congressional Record*, 54th Cong., 1st Session, 1896, vol. 27, pt. 2, 1000–1016.

24. Curti, *American Philanthropy Abroad*, 133.

25. Ibid.

26. Ibid., 131.

27. *Woman's Journal*, January 4, 1896, front page.

28. Ibid.

29. Barton, *History of the Red Cross*, 275–76.

30. *Woman's Journal*, January 4, 1896, front page.

31. Pryor, *Clara Barton*, 213.

32. Ibid., 268.

33. Ibid., 290.

34. *New York Herald*, Wednesday, January 22, 1896, 10.

35. Ibid., January 23, 1896, 7.

36. Barton, *The Red Cross in War and Peace*, 277.

37. Ibid., 278–80.

CHAPTER 7: WALKING SKELETONS

1. Barton, *The Red Cross in War and Peace*, 334.

2. Ibid., 335.

3. J. Rendel Harris and Helen B. Harris, *Letters from the Scenes of the Recent Massacres in Armenia* (New York: Fleming H. Revell Company, 1897), 32.

4. Ibid., 33.

5. Ibid., 32.

6. Ibid., 34–37.

7. Ibid., 51–52.

8. Ibid., 87.

9. Ibid., 57.

10. Ibid., 62.

11. Ibid., 66.
12. Ibid., 86, 82–83.
13. Barton, *The Red Cross in War and Peace,* 335–36.
14. Ibid., 353.
15. Ibid., 353–54.
16. Ibid., 354–356.
17. Ibid., 337.
18. Ibid., 337–39.
19. Ibid., 339–40.
20. Ibid., 343.
21. Ibid., 343, 348.
22. Ibid., 346.
23. Ibid., 345.
24. Ibid., 345–47.
25. Elizabeth B. Theldberg, "An American Heroine in the Heart of Armenia: Dr. Grace Kimball and Her Relief Work at Van," in *Review of Reviews* 13 (April 13, 1896), 444.
26. Ibid.
27. Ibid., 446.
28. Ibid.
29. Ibid., 445.
30. Ibid., 447–49.
31. *The Graphic: An Illustrated Weekly Newspaper,* Saturday, December 14, 1895, supplement, "The Crisis in Turkey." A full-page drawing by W. Hetherell from a photograph: "Armenian Refugees Waiting for Work at the Labour Bureau of the Relief Society at Van."
32. Theldberg, "An American Heroine," 447–49.
33. John F. Kennedy, "Speech of Senator John F. Kennedy," Cow Palace, San Francisco, November 2, 1960; reprinted in *New York Times,* Thursday, November 3, 1960.

CHAPTER 8: "THE TEARS OF ARAXES": THE VOICE
OF THE *WOMAN'S JOURNAL*

1. Robert Mirak, *Torn Between Two Lands, Armenians in America 1890 to World War I* (Cambridge, Mass.: Harvard University Press, 1983), 287–92; James H. Tashjian, *The Armenians of the United States and Canada* (Boston: Armenian Youth Federation, 1947), estimates that 102,128 Armenians had entered the country by 1931, and then offers a revised estimate of his own of 190,000. My estimate splits the difference between the two figures.
2. Alice Stone Blackwell, Diary, 1895, Blackwell family papers, Library of Congress, Washington, D.C.
3. Alice Stone Blackwell, *Growing Up in Boston's Gilded Age: The Journal of Alice Stone Blackwell 1872–74,* ed. Marlene Diehl Merrill (New Haven, Conn.: Yale University Press, 1990), 28.
4. Ohannes Chatschumian to Isabel Barrows, June 8, 1894, Barrows family papers, bMS Am 1897.1 (92), by permission of the Houghton Library, Harvard University.
5. Ohannes Chatschumian to Alice Stone Blackwell, 11 April 1894, Blackwell family papers, Library of Congress, Washington, D.C.
6. Andrea Moore Kerr, *Lucy Stone* (New Brunswick, N.J.: Rutgers University Press, 1992), 1–2.

7. Ibid., 85–87.
8. Ibid., 46, 40–45.
9. Ibid., 46.
10. Ibid., 43.
11. Ibid., 125.
12. Ibid., 147–59.
13. For a full view of the coverage of the Armenian massacres, see the *Woman's Journal* from 1893 to 1896.
14. Kerr, *Lucy Stone,* see chaps. 8–9 for a detailed account.
15. Ibid., 149, 163, 194.
16. Alice Stone Blackwell to Isabel Barrows, June 1, 1894, Barrows family papers, by permission of the Houghton Library, Harvard University.
17. Isabel Barrows to Ohannes Chatschumian, December 3, 1894, Barrows family papers, bMS Am 1807.1 (579), by permission of the Houghton Library, Harvard University.
18. Alice Stone Blackwell to Bedros Keljik, March 20, 1895, Blackwell family papers, Library of Congress.
19. Alice Stone Blackwell to Bedros Keljik, March 24, 1896, Blackwell family papers, Library of Congress.
20. Alice Stone Blackwell to Bedros Keljik, March 29, 1896. Blackwell family papers, Library of Congress.
21. Ohannes Chatschumian to Isabel Barrows, April 10, 1896, Barrows family papers, bMS Am 1897.1 (92), by permission of the Houghton Library, Harvard University.
22. Alice Stone Blackwell to Isabel Barrows, June 4, 1896 (2, 12 of a 36-page letter), Barrows family papers, by permission of the Houghton Library, Harvard University.
23. Alice Stone Blackwell Papers, Reel 22, Armenia subject file, Ohannes Chatschumian folder, Library of Congress.
24. Alice Stone Blackwell to Bedros Keljik, December 16, 1895, Blackwell family papers, Library of Congress.
25. Alice Stone Blackwell, *Armenian Poems* (Boston: Atlantic Printing Co., 1896). Blackwell published a later edition of *Armenian Poems* in 1917, again to help raise funds for Armenian relief. This edition was significantly expanded and included the new early-twentieth-century poets such as Siamanto and Daniel Varoujan, who had created a great sensation and then were executed at the beginning of the Genocide.
26. Ibid., 292–93.

CHAPTER 9: THE OTTOMAN BANK INCIDENT AND THE AFTERMATH OF THE HAMIDIAN MASSACRES

1. *Daily Telegraph,* April 2, 1895; Pears, *Life of Abdul Hamid,* 240.
2. Armen Garo, *Bank Ottoman: Memoirs of Armen Garo,* trans. Haig T. Partizian, ed. Simon Vratzian (Detroit: Topouzian Pub., 1990), 1–6.
3. Mikayel Varantian, *Hai Heghopokhagan Dashnakzoutian Badmountium* (History of the Armenian Revolutionary Federation), vol. 1 (Paris: 1932), 159, quoted in Dadrian, *History of the Armenian Genocide,* 139.
4. *Turkey* 1 (1897), 13, 15.
5. Garo, *Bank Ottoman,* 108–10.
6. Ibid., 110.
7. Ibid., 112–13.

8. Ibid., 119.

9. Ibid., 129.

10. Ibid., 120–21.

11. Dadrian, *History of the Armenian Genocide*, 139–40.

12. *Turkey* 1 (1897), 15–16.

13. Varantyan, *Hai*, 168–69 [n.90], quoted in Dadrian, *History of the Armenian Genocide*, 141.

14. *Turkey* 1 (1897), 12.

15. Varantyan, *Hai*, 174 [n.90], quoted in Dadrian, *History of the Armenian Genocide*, 141–42.

16. Barton, *The Red Cross in War and Peace*, 304.

17. Ibid., 305.

18. *Turkey* 1 (1897), 18, and DAF, n. 96, in Dadrian, *History of the Armenian Genocide*, 144; Lord Kinross, *The Ottoman Centuries* (New York: William Morrow & Co., 1977), 261–62.

19. Giesl, *Zwei Jahrzehnte* 117 [n.34], in Dadrian, ibid., 145.

20. Bérard, *La politique*, 5 [n.3], 15, 17 in Dadrian, ibid.

21. Turkey 1 (1897), 9.

22. Ibid., p. 29.

23. DAF, doc. 273 [n.5]., p. 296, October 18, 1896, in Dadrian, *History of the Armenian Genocide*, 146.

24. FO 195/1944, Doc. 46, folios 253–54, September 29, 1896, in ibid., 146.

25. Ernst Jäckh, *Der Aufsteigende Halbmond*, 6th ed. (Berlin 1916), 139; P. Renouvin, E. Preclin, G. Hardy, *L'Epoque contemporaine. La paix armée et la Grande Guerre*, 2nd ed. (Paris 1947), 176, quoted in A. Beylerian, *Les Grandes Puissances, L'Empire Ottoman, et les Armeniens dans les Archives Françaises (1914–1918)*, Paris, 1983, XXIII, in Dadrian, ibid., 155.

26. Lepsius, *Armenia and Europe*, xviii, 18–19.

27. Ibid., 36; see charts and tables that present the destruction prepared by the Committee of Delegates in text under title of "Ambassadors' Report"; the tables present the destruction by place and date, pp. 280–327.

28. William M. Ramsay, *Impression of Turkey During Twelve Years' Wandering* (New York: G.P. Putnam's Sons, 1897), 211–12.

29. *Turkey* 8 (1896), enclosure 1 in Doc. No. 52, pp. 47, 48; Ambassador Currie's February 19, 1896, report.

30. Dadrian, *History of the Armenian Genocide*, 150.

31. Abraham Hartunian, *Neither to Laugh or Weep: A Memoir of the Armenian Genocide* (translated by Vartan Hartunian), 12–14.

32. FO 195/1944, doc. no. 14, folios 66–67, "confidential" report by Harput's Vice-Consul Raphael A. Fontana, May 18, 1896; Dadrian, *History of the Armenian Genocide*, 160.

33. *Turkey* 5 (1896), 12–13.

34. Ervin Staub, *The Roots of Evil: the Origins of Genocide and Other Group Violence* (Cambridge, England: University Press, 1989), 17, 66, 85.

CHAPTER 10: "OUR BOASTED CIVILIZATION": INTELLECTUALS, POPULAR CULTURE, AND THE ARMENIAN MASSACRES OF THE 1890s

1. Akaby Nassibian, *Britain and the Armenian Question, 1915–1923* (London: Croom Helm, 1984), 44–47.

2. "Professor James Bryce, M.P.," *Century Magazine*, January 1890, 470–72.

3. James Bryce, "The Armenian Question," *Century Magazine*, November, 1895, 154.

4. Ibid., 152.

5. Ibid., 153.

6. Ibid., 154.

7. A. W. Terrell, "An Interview with Sultan Abdul Hamid," *Century Magazine*, November 1897, 133–34.

8. Ibid., 134.

9. Ibid., 135.

10. H. C. J. Matthew, *Gladstone, 1875–1898* (Oxford, England: Oxford University Press, 1995), 55–56; Richard Shannon, *Gladstone and the Bulgarian Agitation* (London: Thomas Nelson and Sons, 1963), 49–88.

11. Matthew, *Gladstone*, 21.

12. Ibid., 28; Shannon, *Gladstone and the Bulgarian Agitation*.

13. William Gladstone, "Bulgarian Horrors and the Question of the East," quoted in Greene, *Armenian Massacres and Turkish Tyranny*, 126.

14. Matthew, *Gladstone*, 28; William Gladstone, *Bulgarian Horrors and Russia in Turkestan* (Leipzig: Bernhard Tauchnitz, 1876), 17.

15. Matthew, *Gladstone*, 29.

16. Gladstone, "On the Armenian Question," August 6, 1895, quoted in Greene, *Armenian Massacres*, 243–45.

17. Ibid., 245–46.

18. Ibid., 247–48.

19. Ibid., 249–51, 254.

20. Ibid., 252–253.

21. J. L. Hammond, *Gladstone and the Irish Nation* (London: Longman's, Green and Co., 1938), 696–97.

22. William and Henry James, *Selected Letters*, eds. Ignas K. Skrupskelis and Elizabeth M. Berkeley (Charlottesville: University of Virginia Press, 1997), 385, 402–03.

23. Ibid., 411–12.

24. It is interesting to note, especially in light of Princeton's harboring of Armenian Genocide deniers on its faculty in recent years, that Van Dyke was one of a number of eminent Princetonians who would, in the coming decades, either speak out against the Turkish atrocities or become engaged in Armenian relief. Already Spenser Trask (class of 1866) had headed up the National Armenian Relief Committee, and by 1915, Cleveland Dodge (class of 1879) would be heading an enormous philanthropic effort to bring relief to the survivors of the Armenian Genocide. President Wilson, professor, and later president of Princeton, would go to Congress in 1919 with a plan for an American mandate for Armenia. Van Dyke, class of 1873, also wrote the famous Princeton "Triangle Song."

25. Henry Van Dyke, *The Builders and Other Poems* (New York: Charles Scribner's Sons, 1897), 67–68.

26. Patricia O'Neill, "The Sword and the Sonnet: William Watson's Poems for Armenia 1895–1896," paper given at Texts in Time conference, University of Dublin, November 2002.

27. William Watson, *The Purple East: A Series of Sonnets on England's Desertion of Armenia* (London: John Lane, 1896); also published in Chicago by Stone & Kimball, 1896.

28. O'Neill, ibid.

29. Richard Hofstader, *The Age of Reform* (New York: Random House, 1955), 188; according to Hofstadter, in the last quarter of the nineteenth century, numbers of daily newspa-

pers went from 574 to 1,610, and to 2,600 by 1909, and daily circulation increased from about 3 million to more than 24 million.

30. Timothy Pitkins, "The Sultan, Interpreted by Recent Events," *Harper's Weekly*, February 29, 1896, 206–207.
31. Pitkins, "A Comparison of Turkish Law with Actual Conditions," *Harper's Weekly*, April 18, 1896, 395.
32. *Harper's Weekly*, January 25, 1896, 89.
33. Ibid., February 22, 1896, cover.
34. Ibid., March 14, 1896, 253.
35. Ibid., March 28, 1896, 296.
36. Ibid., April 25, 1896, cover.
37. *The Graphic: An Illustrated Weekly Newspaper*, Saturday, September 14, 1895, 310.
38. Ibid., Saturday, October 26, 1895, cover.
39. Ibid., December 7, 1895, "The Massacre at Erzerum: October 30, 1895: From Photographs Taken on the Three Following Days," 725–27.
40. Ibid., December 21, 1895, 758; see also issues of December 7, 14, and 28.
41. Henry Adams, *The Education of Henry Adams* (New York: Random House, 1931), 352.
42. Stephen Crane, *War Dispatches of Stephen Crane*, eds. Ignas K. Skrupskelis and Elizabeth M. Berkeley (Charlottesville: University of Virginia Press, 1997), 55, 57–58.
43. Gilman, "International Duties," 10–14.

CHAPTER 11: THE RISE OF THE YOUNG TURKS

1. Bernard Lewis, *The Emergence of Modern Turkey* (London: Oxford University Press, 1961), 149–50.
2. Ibid., 152.
3. Ibid., 160.
4. Ibid., 159.
5. Pears, *Life of Abdul Hamid*, 37–44.
6. Lewis, *The Emergence of Modern Turkey*, 162.
7. Ibid., 163.
8. Pears, *Life of Abdul Hamid*, 49–51.
9. Walker, *Armenia: The Survival of A Nation*, 123.
10. Ramsaur, *The Young Turks*, 11.
11. Fesch, *Constantinople*, 50–51, 74.
12. Ramsaur, *The Young Turks*, 11.
13. Ibid., 14–17; M. Sukru Hanioglu, *The Young Turks in Opposition* (Oxford University Press, 1995), 71–72.
14. Ramsaur, *The Young Turks*, 18.
15. Ibid., 19–21.
16. Ibid., 22–23; Lewis, *The Emergence of Modern Turkey*, 193–94; Haniglou, *The Young Turks in Opposition*, 74.
17. Ramsaur, *The Young Turks*, 31, Lewis, *The Emergence of Modern Turkey*, 198.
18. Ramsaur, *The Young Turks*, 32–33.
19. Mourad-Bey, *La force et la faiblesse de la Turquie: Les coupables et les innocents* (Geneva, 1897), 59, quoted in Ramsaur, *The Young Turks*, 41.
20. Lewis, *The Emergence of Modern Turkey*, 197.
21. When the Armenians and the Christian Macedonians in the Balkans advocated European intervention as stipulated in articles 23 and 61 of the Treaty of Berlin to bring

about reform, Ahmed Riza, the influential, nationalistic Young Turk, along with others, warded them off by calling their attention to the restoration of the Ottoman constitution of 1876; see Hanioglu, *The Young Turks in Opposition,* 31.

22. Fesch, *Constantinople, 356–57.*

23. Ramsaur, *The Young Turks,* 62.

24. Fesch, *Constantinople, 367–70.*

25. Ramsaur, *The Young Turks,* 70–72. The memorandum of May 11, 1895, stipulated reforms for the six *vilayets* of historic Armenia; the English found it inadequate and the Russians would not support it. See Fesch, *Constantinople,* 370–71.

26. Ibid., 95–96, 98, 100–101.

27. Ibid., 100–01, 105, 109.

28. Sir Charles Eliot, *Turkey in Europe* (London: Edward Arnold, 1908), 93.

29. Ramsaur, *The Young Turks,* 116–17.

30. Ibid., 130.

31. Ibid., 134–35.

32. Feroz Ahmad, *The Young Turks: the Committee of Union and Progress in Turkish Politics 1908–1914* (Oxford, England: Clarendon Press, 1969), 6.

33. Charles Roden Buxton, *Turkey in Revolution* (London: T. Fisher Unwin, 1909), 57; quoted in Ramsaur, *The Young Turks,* 135.

34. Lewis, *The Emergence of Modern Turkey,* 204.

35. Ramsaur, *The Young Turks,* 135–36; Lewis, *The Emergence of Modern Turkey,* 204.

36. Lewis, *The Emergence of Modern Turkey,* 204–5.

37. William Miller, *The Ottoman Empire and Its Successors, 1801–1927, with an Appendix, 1927–1936* (Cambridge, England: Cambridge University Press, 1936), 476.

38. Ibid.

CHAPTER 12: ADANA, 1909: COUNTERREVOLUTION AND MASSACRE

1. Lewis, *The Emergence of Modern Turkey,* 208.

2. Ibid., 209–10.

3. Pears, *Life of Abdul Hamid,* 311–12.

4. Ahmad, *The Young Turks,* 40–41; Pears, *Life of Abdul Hamid,* 312–13.

5. Ahmad, *The Young Turks,* 41–42.

6. Ibid., 44–45, Pears, *Life of Abdul Hamid,* 316–18.

7. Ahmad, *The Young Turks,* 48.

8. Lewis, *The Emergence of Modern Turkey,* 213.

9. Ibid., 214.

10. H. Charles Woods, *The Danger Zone of Europe* (Boston: Little, Brown & Co., 1911), 125.

11. Walker, *Armenia: The Survival of a Nation,* 183; Aram Arkun, "Les relations arméno-turques et les massares de Cilicie de 1909," in *L'actualité du génocide des Arméniens* (Paris: EDIPOL, 1999), 62.

12. Woods, *The Danger Zone,* 123.

13. Arkun, "Les relations arméno-turques . . . ," 62.

14. FO/420/219, 80.

15. Woods, *The Danger Zone,* 129.

16. Ibid.

17. FO/420/219, 80.

18. Ibid.

19. Woods, *The Danger Zone,* 130.

20. Walker, *Armenia: The Survival of a Nation,* 183.

21. Woods, *The Danger Zone,* 130.

22. Ibid., 132.

23. FO/420/219, 81.

24. Ibid.

25. Walker, *Armenia: The Survival of a Nation,* 184.

26. FO/420/219, 84.

27. Woods, *The Danger Zone,* 131.

28. Ibid., 136.

29. Arkun, "Les relations arméno-turques . . . ," 64–65.

30. Dadrian, *The History of the Armenian Genocide,* 183.

31. Ibid.

32. FO/420/219, 94–95.

33. Ibid., 137.

34. G. F. Abbott, *Turkey in Transition* (London: Edward Arnold, 1909), 305.

35. FO/420/219, 91.

36. FO/420/219, 85; Arkun, "Les relations arméro-turques . . . ," 63, fn43; 70–71.

37. Woods, *The Danger Zone,* 127–28.

38. Ibid., 137.

39. Walker, *Armenia: The Survival of a Nation,* 186–87.

40. Woods, *The Danger Zone,* 139.

41. Ibid., 143–44; Arkun, "Les relations arméno-turques . . . ," 66.

42. Y. H. Bayur, *Turk Inkilabi Taritu* (The history of the Turkish revolution), vol. 1, 225, quoted in Lewis, *The Emergence of Modern Turkey,* 207.

43. Siamanto, *Bloody News from My Friend,* trans. Peter Balakian and Nevart Yaghlian (Detroit: Wayne State University Press, 1996), 47, 37.

44. Ervin Staub, *The Roots of Evil,* 13, 85.

45. Ibid., 17–18.

46. Ibid.

47. Morgenthau, *Ambassador Morgenthau's Story,* 342.

48. Lewis, *The Emergence of Modern Turkey,* 214; Dadrian, *History of the Armenian Genocide,* 180; see also 184, fn7, for citations in Austrian, British, French foreign office records.

CHAPTER 13: THE BALKAN WARS AND WORLD WAR I:
THE ROAD TO GENOCIDE

1. A. Andonian, *Untartzag Badmountiun Balkanian Baderazmeen* (comprehensive history of the Balkan War), vol. 3 (Istanbul, 1912), 499, quoted in Dadrian, *The History of the Armenian Genocide,* 190.

2. Morgenthau, *Ambassador Morgenthau's Story,* 15.

3. Andonian, *Untartzag,* 503, quoted in Dadrian, *History of the Armenian Genocide,* 189.

4. Ibid., 499, quoted in ibid.

5. Dadrian, *History of the Armenian Genocide,* 193.

6. Ibid.

7. T. Z. Tunaya, *Turkiyede Siyasal Partiler* (the political parties in Turkey), 2nd enlarged ed., vol. 3 (Istanbul, 1984), 465, quoted in Dadrian, *History of the Armenian Genocide,* 193.

8. Ibid.

9. Dadrian, *History of the Armenian Genocide,* 196.

10. Tunaya, [n.7], 296, quoted in ibid., 196.

11. Jay Winter, "Under the Cover of War: Genocide in the Context of Total War," (paper presented at the conference "The American Response to the Armenian Genocide," Library of Congress, Washington, D.C., September 28, 2000), 4.

12. Jacob Landau, *Pan-Turkism: From Irredentism to Cooperation* (Bloomington: Indiana University Press, 1996), 37.

13. Kazim Nami Duru, *Zia Gökalp* (Istanbul: National Education Publishers, 1949), 61, quoted in Dadrian, *History of the Armenian Genocide,* 180–81.

14. Vahakn Dadrian, "The Role of Turkish Physicians in the World War I Genocide of Ottoman Armenians," in *Holocaust and Genocide Studies,* 1986, 1, no. 2, 175.

15. Ibid.; see also Haigaz K. Kazarian, "How Turkey Prepared the Ground for Massacre," *Armenian Review* 18, 4 (winter 1965), 31–32.

16. Landau, *Pan-Turkism,* 39–42; Stephan H. Astourian, "The Armenian Genocide: An Interpretation," in *History Teacher* 23, no. 2 (February 1990), 133.

17. Louis P. Lochner, *What About Germany?* (New York: Dodd, Mead & Co., 1942), 2; the Pulitzer Prize–winning AP journalist Louis P. Lochner, who had spent twenty-one years in Germany, received a transcript of this speech from his informant in the field. Finding the speech riveting and indicative of Hitler's mania to conquer the world, he published it in his book.

18. Uriel Heyd, *Foundations of Turkish Nationalism: The Life and Teachings of Ziya Gökalp* (London: Luzac, 1950), 63.

19. Ibid., 124.

20. Ibid., 132.

21. Astourian, "The Armenian Genocide," p. 135.

22. Morgenthau, *Ambassador Morgenthau's Story,* 49.

23. Ibid., 52.

24. Landau, *Pan-Turkism,* 1.

25. Ibid.

26. Ibid., 48.

27. Ibid., 49.

28. *The Great War and the Shaping of the Twentieth Century,* KCET/BBC co-production cassette 3, produced and directed by Carl Byker, Lyn Goldfarb, et al, 1996.

29. A. A. Turkei 183/39, A28584, or R14088, J no. 598, enclosure no. 1, 10 August 1915 report, quoted in Vahakn Dadrian. "The Armenian Question and the Wartime Fate of the Armenians as Documented by the Officials of the Ottoman Empire's World War I Allies: Germany and Austria-Hungary," in *International Journal of Middle East Studies* 34, February 2002, 72.

30. Dadrian, *History of the Armenian Genocide,* 410–412; in the early years of the Nazi movement, Scheubner-Richter was one of Hitler's closest advisors. The former vice consul at Erzerum called for the cleansing of alien elements in Germany, and, interestingly, had referred to the Armenians as "these Jews of the Orient, these wily businessmen." He was killed at Hitler's side in the failed putsch in Munich in November 1923, and Hitler said his loss was irreplaceable. Scheubner-Richter left a detailed record of the Armenian Genocide in the German Foreign Office; these were later compiled and edited by Johannes Lepsius, and are in his book *Germany and Armenia.*

31. Liman von Sanders, *Five Years in Turkey* (Annapolis, Md. U.S. Naval Institute, 1927), 8–9; Limon von Sanders, chief of the military operation in Turkey during World War I,

writes in detail in chapter 1 about the strong-arm tactics of the CUP, Enver's rise to power, and the deplorable conditions in the Ottoman army.

32. Morgenthau, *Ambassador Morgenthau's Story,* 61–67; Ulrich Trumpener, *Germany and the Ottoman Empire, 1914–1918* (Princeton, N.J.: Princeton University Press, 1968), 70–80.

33. Morgenthau, 41.

34. Ibid., 47.

35. Ibid., 63–64.

36. Ibid., 100.

37. Ibid., 101.

38. Ibid., 102–103.

39. Ibid., 129.

40. Trumpener, *Germany and the Ottoman Empire,* 117; Jack Zakarian, "Introduction," in Kloian, *The Armenian Genocide,* xiii.

41. Trumpener, ibid., 118.

42. Ibid., 119–20.

43. Ibid., 117–20; Morgenthau, *Ambassador Morgenthau's Story,* 161–64.

44. Morgenthau, *Ambassador Morgenthau's Story,* 169–70.

45. Jay Winter, "Under Cover of War," 8.

46. Morgenthau, *Ambassador Morgenthau's Story,* 170.

47. Landau, *Pan-Turkism,* 53.

48. Ibid.

49. Walker, *Armenia: The Survival of a Nation,* 89; Lewis, *The Emergence of Modern Turkey,* 179.

50. Trumpener, *Germany and the Ottoman Empire,* 28.

51. Ibid., 135; While the Germans tried to put off the Ottoman demand for abrogation of the capitulatory system, by 1916 it was impossible to duck the issue. By the fall of 1916, the Turks had declared null and void the Paris Straits Treaty of 1856, the London Declaration of 1871, and the Berlin Treaty of 1878. The state of war—Foreign Minister Halil told the German and Austro-Hungarian governments—had voided Turkish obligations under the treaties, and furthermore, their alliance with two European powers now put the Ottoman Empire "on a footing of perfect equality" with Europe. But Halil stressed vehemently that these treaties—especially the 1878 Berlin treaty with its article 61 stipulating Armenian reforms—were "political shackles" that had kept the Ottoman Empire under "the collective tutelage of the great powers."

52. Ibid., 114, 133.

53. Viscount J. Bryce, *The Treatment of the Armenians in the Ottoman Empire 1915–16* (London: His Majesty's Stationery Office, 1916), 636.

54. *"Kegham Ger Garaedianee Vugayutounu"* (The testimony of Kegham Der Garabedian) in G. Sassouni, *Badmoutiun Daronee Achkharee* (history of Daron) (Beirut, 1957), 838–39, quoted in Dadrian, *History of the Armenian Genocide,* 214.

55. Haigaz K. Kazarian, "How Turkey Prepared the Ground for Massacre," *Armenian Review* 18, 4 (winter 1965): 31–32.

56. Bryce, *The Treatment of the Armenians in the Ottoman Empire,* 635–36.

CHAPTER 14: GOVERNMENT-PLANNED GENOCIDE

1. Robert Fisk, "The Hidden Holocaust," Panoptic Productions, London, 1992.

2. Erik Jan Zucher, "Ottoman Labor Battalions in World War I," Turkology Update Lei-

den Project (Leiden, Netherlands: Leiden University's Dept. of Turkish Languages and Cultures, March 2002). Christians had first been conscripted into the Ottoman army in 1909 after the implementation of new constitutional reforms, and so at the outbreak of World War I, Armenian men between the ages of twenty and forty-five were drafted into the Ottoman army. It was an army with numerous problems, among them severe ethnic discrimination. Arabs, Kurds, Armenians, Greeks, Assyrians, and others were subjected to brutal treatment. Arab soldiers, for example, were often sent to the front lines, at gunpoint, shackled in chains and escorted by Turks.

3. Ibid.
4. Arnold Toynbee, *Armenian Atrocities: The Murder of a Nation* (London: Hodder and Stoughton, 1915), 81–82.
5. Bryce, *The Treatment of the Armenians in the Ottoman Empire,* 638.
6. Jay Winter, "Under Cover of War," 4.
7. Vahakn Dadrian, "The Role of the Special Organisation in the Armenian Genocide during the First World War," in *Minorities in Wartime,* ed., Panikos Panayi (Oxford, England, and Providence, R.I., Berg Publishers, 1993), 64–65; Astourian, "The Armenian Genocide," 138.
8. Bryce, *The Treatment of the Armenians,* 640.
9. Walker, *Armenia,* 206; Ussher, *An American Physician in Turkey,* 238–43.
10. Bryce, *The Treatment of the Armenians,* 638–43.
11. Richard Rubenstein, *The Cunning of History: the Holocaust and the American Future* (New York: Harper & Row Publishers, 1985), 11–12.
12. Ibid., 34.
13. Raul Hilberg, *The Destruction of the European Jews* (New York: Harper & Row), 1961, 43.
14. Morgenthau, *Ambassador Morgenthau's Story,* 333.
15. Dadrian, "The Role of the Special Organisation," 51.
16. Tarik Z. Tunaya, *Turkiyede Siyasi Pariler 1859–1952* (Political parties in Turkey) (Istanbul, 1952), 182, quoted in Dadrian, "The Role of the Special Organization," 61.
17. Jemal Kutay, *Birinci Dunya Harbinde Teskilat-Mashusa* (The Special Organization during World War II) (Istanbul, 1962), 18, 36, 78, quoted in Dadrian, "The Role of the Special Organization"; Hafiz Mehmed, deputy at Trabzon, confessed after the war that "the massacres were carried out on order from the Central Committee of Ittihad," and the Special Organization was the center of the operation, and he admitted that "until now we remained silent about this," *Ariamard,* 13 December 1918, quoted in Dadrian, "The Role of the Special Organization," 61.

    He also admitted that he had "assumed duties in missions, involving the secrets of the Armenian deportations." The Turkish historian Husamettin Erturk underscored that "the Special Organization was created by the Central Committee, for which end Enver and Talat, who in other matters were pitted against each other in a bitter struggle, joined hands. The Ittihadist Commanders of the Organization's brigands were chosen by Talat and the Central Committee; the Organization's *modus operandi* and the operational plans were determined on the basis of Enver's instructions." Mustafa Ragip Esatli, *Ittihad ve Terakki Tarihinde Esrar Perdesi* (The curtain of mystery in Ittihad's history) (Istanbul 1975), 258, quoted in ibid., 60.
18. Kutay, *Birinci,* 18, 36, quoted in ibid., 54.
19. Ahmed Refik Altinay, *Iki Komite, Iki Kital* (Two committees and two massacres) (Istanbul 1919), 40, quoted in ibid., 55.

20. Dadrian, "The Role of the Special Organisation," 64–65; Astourian, "The Armenian Genocide," 138.
21. Dadrian, "The Role of the Special Organisation," 76.
22. Ibid., 78.
23. Dadrian, *History of the Armenian Genocide*, 221; full text of this legislation can be found in Hovannissian, *Armenia on the Road to Independence, 1918*, 55.
24. Dadrian, "The Role of the Special Organisation," 78.
25. Hilberg, *The Destruction of the European Jews*, 181.
26. Arnold Toynbee, *The Western Question in Greece and Turkey* (Boston & New York: Houghton Mifflin, 1922), 280.
27. See Bat Ye'or, *The Decline of Eastern Christianity Under Islam: From Jihad to Dhimmitude*, trans. by Miriam Kochan and David Littman (London & Cranbury, N.J., Associated University Presses, 1996), 37–41; Hanioglu, *The Young Turks in Opposition*, 7–32; Dadrian, *History of the Armenian Genocide*, 1–6.
28. Krikoris Balakian, *Hai Koghkotan* (Armenian Golgotha) (Beirut: Plenetta Printing, 1977), 227–28.
29. Philip H. Stoddard, "The Ottoman Government and the Arabs, 1911–1918: A Preliminary Study of the Teskilat-I Mashusa," (Ph.D. diss., University of Michigan), 58, puts the number of men in the SO at thirty thousand. French historian E. Doumergue, in *L'Arménie, les massacres, set al question d'Orient* (Paris 1916), 24–25 also put the number at 30,000; Swiss historian S. Zrulinden, *Der Weltkrieg* (Zurich 1918), vol. 2, 657, puts the number at 34,000, quoted in Dadrian, "The Role of the Special Organization in the Armenian Genocide during the First World War," 59.
30. Stoddard, *The Ottoman Government and the Arabs*, 49, 50.
31. Altinay, *Iki Domite*, p. 23, quoted in Dadrian, "The Role of the Special Organization in the Armenian Genocide during the First World War," 57.
32. For a more comprehensive view of German Foreign Office documents on the Armenian Genocide see Wolfgang Gust, ed., "The Armenian Genocide 1915/16 from the Files of the German Foreign Office," with Sigrid Gust, Vera Draack, trans, www.armenocide.net; see also Vahakn Dadrian, "The Armenian Question and the Wartime Fate of the Armenians as Documented by the Officials of the Ottoman Empire's World War I Allies: Germany and Austria-Hungary," in *Journal of International Middle East Studies* 34 (2002), 59–85.
33. German Foreign Ministry Archives, *Botschaft Konstantinopel* K 169, no. (3876), quoted in Dadrian, "The Armenian Question," 58.
34. Ibid., no. 33 (3714), folio 62, quoted in ibid.
35. Ibid., *Turkei* 183/41, A23991, quoted in ibid.
36. Zucher, "Ottoman Labor Battalions in World War I."
37. Ibid.
38. Ibid.
39. Vahakn Dadrian, "The Determinants of the Armenian Genocide," presented at Yale Center for International and Area Studies, Working Paper Series, Yale University, February 26, 1998), 10–11.
40. *Auswärtiges Amt* (West Germany's Foreign Office Archives, Bonn, otherwise designated AA), K170, no. (4674), folio 63, quoted in Dadrian, "The Armenian Question," 12.
41. AA, *Botschaft Konstantinopel* K170, 23 August 1915, report, long entry no. 3841, quoted in ibid.
42. AA, *Turkei* 183/38, A27578, quoted in ibid., 13.
43. AA, *Turkei* 183/43, A27578, quoted in ibid.

44. Vahakn Dadrian, "Genocide as a Problem on National and International Law; the World War I Armenian Case and Its Contemporary Legal Ramifications," *Yale Journal of International Law,* 1989, vol. 14, no. 2, 266; for the English text of the law see R. Hovannisian, *Armenia on the Road to Independence* (Berkeley: University of California Press, 1967), 51.
45. *Takvimi Vekayi,* no. 2189 (May 19/June 1, 1915), quoted in Dadrian.
46. AA, Turkei 183/39, A29127 Oct. 7, 1915 report. The French text of the eleven articles is listed in Auswärtiges Amt. Turkei 183/39, A29127, and Lepsius, *Germany and Armenia,* 1914–1918, 84, quoted in Dadrian, 267.
47. Y. Bayur. *Turkiyede* [n.22], p. 46, quoted in Dadrian, 269.
48. *Kabinelerinin Isticvabi* (The War Cabinets hearings) 81 (1933), quoted in ibid, 270.
49. Jackson to Morgenthau, Aleppo, Syria, August 19, 1915, U.S. State Department Record Group 59, 867. 4016/148, serial no. 346.
50. D. Avcioglu, *Milli Kurtulus Tarihi* (History of national liberation) (1974), 1137, 1141. Sina Aksin also maintains that the Armenian deportations were implemented in pursuit of economic goals which elimated minority dominance and competition in business and industry. See Sina Aksin, *100 Soruda Jon Turkler Ve Ittihat Ve Terakki* (Ittihad ve Terakki in the context of 100 questions, 283), 1980, quoted in Dadrian, "Genocide as a Problem," 271.
51. Henry H. Riggs, *Days of Tragedy in Armenia: Personal Experiences in Harpoot, 1915–1917* (Ann Arbor, Mich.: Gomidas Institute, 1997), 88.
52. Morgenthau, *Ambassador Morgenthau's Story,* 311.
53. For an in-depth analysis of the document see Vahakn N. Dadrian "The Secret Young-Turk Ittihadist Conference and the Decision for the World War I Genocide of the Armenians," in *Holocaust and Genocide Studies* 7, no. 2 (Fall 1993), 173–74. The document is FO 371/4172/31307, 383–91, February 10, 1919, 388–89.
54. Ibid.
55. Terrence Des Pres, *The Survivor: An Anatomy of Life in the Death Camps* (Oxford University Press, 1975), 53.
56. Hilmar Kaiser, "The Baghdad Railway and the Armenian Genocide 1915–1916: A Case Study in German Resistance and Complicity" in *Remembrance and Denial: The Case of the Armenian Genocide,* ed. Richard Hovanissian (Detroit: Wayne State University Press, 1998) 75.
57. Ibid., 75, 70. See also National Archives RG 59, 867.4016/137, Dodd to Morgenthau, August 15, 1915.
58. Ibid., 75.
59. Ibid., 76.
60. Ibid., 76.
61. Ibid., 76.
62. Ibid., 72.
63. Ibid., 78.
64. Ibid., 78–79.
65. Ibid., 79, 104.
66. Jackson to Morgenthau, U.S. State Department Record Group 59, 867.4016/219, Serial No. 382, in *United States Official Documents on the Armenian Genocide,* vol. 1, *The Lower Euphrates,* compiled and introduced by Ara Sarafian (Watertown, Mass.: Armenian Review, 1993), 94–98.
67. Ibid., 95–96.

68. Bryce, *The Treatment of the Armenians in the Ottoman Empire*, 407.
69. Ibid., 419.
70. Ibid., 420.
71. Ibid., 417.
72. Ibid., 423.
73. Ibid., 427.
74. See "Armenian Genocide Resolution Unanimously Passed by the Association of Genocide Scholars of North America, June 13, 1997," which states the genocide scholarly community's assessment that "over a million Armenians perished."

CHAPTER 15: VAN, SPRING 1915

1. Robert H. Hewsen, " 'Van in This World: Paradise in the Next: The Historical Geography of Van/Vaspurakan,' " in *Armenian Van/Vaspurakan*, ed. Richard G. Hovannisian (Costa Mesa, Calif.: Mazda Publishers, 2000), 16–25.
2. Ibid., 34; see also Der Nersessian, *The Armenians*, 14–16; Walker, *Visions of Ararat*, 102–3.
3. Melson, *Revolution and Genocide*, 58.
4. Hovannisian, *Armenia on the Road to Independence*, 40–42; Walker, *Armenia: The Survival of a Nation*, 197–98.
5. Arnold Toynbee, *Turkey: A Past and a Future* (New York: George H. Doran Co., 1917), 31.
6. Uriel Heyd, *Foundations of Turkish Nationalism* (London: Luzac & Co., The Harvill Press, 1950), 128.
7. Walker, *Armenia: The Survival of a Nation*, 198.
8. Ibid.
9. Krikoris Balakian, *Armenian Golgotha*, 71.
10. Ibid., 3.
11. Landau, *Pan-Turkism*, 52; Walker, *Armenia: The Survival of a Nation*, 199.
12. Liman von Sanders, *Five Years in Turkey*, (Annapolis, Md.: United States Naval Institute, 1927), p. 31.
13. "Some biographical notes on Djeved Bey, Vali of the Vilayet of Van," *Edition de la revue "Droschak,"* Geneva, 1916. An Austrian Vice Marshal with duties in Ottoman General Headquarters during the war called Jevdet Bey "a monster in human casing." J. Pomiankowski, *Der Zusammenbruch des Ottomaschen Reiches* (The collapse of the Ottoman Empire) (Graz, Austria: 1969), 199–200, quoted in Dadrian, *German Responsibility in the Armenian Genocide*, 211.
14. Walker, *Armenia: The Survival of a Nation*, 206.
15. Ussher, *An American Physician in Turkey*, 5.
16. Ibid., 32–36.
17. Ibid., 73–75.
18. Ibid., 236–38, 241.
19. Ibid., 238.
20. Ibid., 239–43.
21. Ibid., 243–44.
22. Grace H. Knapp, *The Tragedy of Bitlis* (New York, London, Chicago: F. H. Revell, 1919), 15. For Knapp's own account see Bryce, *The Treatment of the Armenians in the Ottoman Empire*, 32–47.
23. Ussher, *An American Physician in Turkey*, 247.

24. John Otis Barrows, *In the Land of Ararat* (New York: F. H. Revell, 1916), 128, 134.

25. Ussher, *An American Physician in Turkey,* 248.

26. Ibid., 250–53.

27. Ibid., 250–55.

28. Ibid., 253.

29. Ibid., 265.

30. Ibid., 274.

31. Ibid., 275.

32. Ibid., 279.

33. Ibid., 286–88, 265.

34. Ibid., 296–99.

35. Ibid., 314.

36. Pomiankowski, *Der Zusammenbruch* [30], 160, quoted in Dadrian, "The Armenian Question," 66.

37. *Botschaft Konstantinopel,* vol. 168, No. 9, May 1915, report, in Vahakn Dadrian, "The Role of the Turkish Military in the Armenian Genocide," manuscript, 109.

38. Raphael de Nogales, *Four Years Beneath the Turkish Crescent* (London: Scribner's, 1926), 60.

39. Ibid., 80.

40. Ibid., 76.

41. Ibid., 65.

42. Ibid., 85–86.

43. Ussher, *An American Physician in Turkey,* 328–29.

44. Robert Melson, "Provocation or Nationalism," in *The History and Sociology of Genocide: Analysis and Case Studies,* eds. Frank Chalk and Kurt Jonassohn (Yale University Press, 1994), 274–75.

45. Roderick Davison, "The Armenian Crisis 1912–1914," *American Historical Review 53,* no. 3 (1948), 483.

46. Ibid., 484.

47. AA *Turkei* 183/40, or R14093 in the new system. The quotation is on page 14 of the very comprehensive seventy-two-page report quoted in Dadrian, "The Armenian Question," 67.

48. Melson, p. 276.

CHAPTER 16: APRIL 24

1. Robert H. Hewsen, *Armenia: A Historical Atlas* (University of Chicago Press, 2001), 184; Hewsen discusses the major writers of Constantinople.

2. Balakian, *Armenian Golgotha,* 108. trans. Peter Balakian, Anahid Yeremian, Aris Sevag (unpublished manuscript).

3. Ibid.

4. Ibid., 109.

5. Ibid.

6. Khachig Boghosian, "My Arrest and Exile on April 24, 1915," trans. Aris Sevag, in *Armenian Reporter,* April 21, 2001.

7. Balakian, *Armenian Golgotha,* 110.

8. Ibid., 112.

9. Ibid., 114.

10. Ibid., 115.

11. Ibid., 116.
12. Ibid., 120.
13. Ibid., 120–30.
14. Ibid., 198.
15. Ibid., 199–200.
16. Ibid., 200.
17. Ibid.
18. Boghosian, "My Arrest and Exile."
19. On May 4, 2000, PEN American Center held a tribute to honor the memory of the eighty-two Armenian writers killed in the Armenian Genocide. The event was held at the New York Public Library; among those participating were Agha Shahid Ali, Anthony Appiah, Peter Balakian, Robert Jay Lifton, Robert Pinsky, Rose Styron. (A list of the murdered writers is included in the program.)

CHAPTER 17: THE AMBASSADOR AT THE CROSSROADS

1. Morgenthau, *Ambassador Morgenthau's Story*, 4.
2. Henry Morgenthau III, *Mostly Morgenthau* (New York: Ticknor & Fields, 1991), 40–41, 55–63.
3. Ibid., 63.
4. Ibid., 71.
5. Ibid., 93.
6. Henry Morgenthau, *All in a Lifetime* (New York: Doubleday, Page, & Co., 1921), 128.
7. Henry Morgenthau III, *Mostly Morgenthau*, 95.
8. Ibid., 101.
9. Ibid., 103.
10. Ibid.
11. Ibid.
12. Ibid., 106.
13. Ibid., 107.
14. Ibid.
15. Ibid., 119.
16. Ibid., 117.
17. Ibid., 122.
18. Ibid., 123.
19. Morgenthau, *Ambassador Morgenthau's Story*, 11.
20. Ibid., 170.

CHAPTER 18: THE NEWS FROM THE AMERICAN CONSUL IN HARPUT

1. Leslie Davis, *The Slaugherhouse Province: An American Diplomat's Report on the Armenian Genocide, 1915–1917*, ed. Susan K. Blair (New Rochelle, N.Y.: Aristide D. Caratazas, 1989), 8–15.
2. Ibid., 8.
3. Leslie A. Davis, "Report of Leslie A. Davis, American Consul, Formerly of Harput, Turkey on the Work of the American Consulate at Harput Since the Beginning of the Present War" (prepared for Mr. Wilbur J. Carr, Director of the Consular Service), U.S. State Department Record Group 59, 867, 4016/392, 5.
4. Ibid., 7–8.
5. Ibid., 18.

6. Mae M. Derderian, *Vergeen: A Survivor of the Armenian Genocide* (Los Angeles, Calif.: Atmus Press, 1996), 37, 38–39.
7. Keroup Bedoukian, *Some of Us Survived* (New York: Farrar, Straus & Giroux, 1979), 15.
8. Abraham Hartunian, *Neither To Laugh Nor To Weep* (Boston: Beacon Press, 1968), 56–58.
9. Ibid., 51.
10. Davis, "Report," 19.
11. Nafina Hagop Chilinguirian, "Application for the Support of Claims Against Foreign Governments," issued by Department of State, Washington, D.C., May 15, 1915, filed by Mrs. Chilinguirian, March 1920.
12. Davis, "Report," 22.
13. Alice Muggerditchian Shipley, *We Walked, Then Ran* (Phoenix, Ariz.: A. M. Shipley, 1983), 53.
14. Ibid., 57–58.
15. Morgenthau, *Ambassador Morgenthau's Story,* 306–7.
16. Davis, "Report," 22.
17. Interview with Alice Muggerditchian Shipley in J. Michael Hagopian, "Voices from the Lake: A Film About the Secret Genocide," Armenian Film Foundation, Thousand Oaks, Calif., 2000.
18. Davis, "Report," 23.
19. Leslie A. Davis to Henry Morgenthau, June 30, 1915, U.S. State Department Record Group 59, 867.4016/269, 1–3.
20. Davis, "Report," 23.
21. Muggerditchian Shipley, 52.
22. Davis, "Report," 27.
23. *United States Official Documents of the Armenian Genocide,* vol. 2, *The Peripheries,* ed. Ara Sarafian; see map on page xvi, which shows Armenian schools and monasteries throughout Turkey according to the 1913–14 census of the Armenian patriarchate.
24. Ibid.; see map on page xiv, which shows Armenian churches throughout Turkey according to the 1913–14 census of the Armenian patriarchate.
25. Morgenthau, *Ambassador Morgenthau's Story,* 305.
26. Davis, "Report," 27.
27. Riggs, *Days of Tragedy in Armenia,* 85.
28. Davis, "Report," 28.
29. Jesse B. Jackson to Henry Morgenthau, Aleppo, Syria, August 19, 1915, U.S. State Department Record Group 59, 867.4016/148.
30. Davis, "Report," 29.
31. Bedoukian, *Some of Us Survived,* 11–12.
32. Serpouhi Tavoukdjian, *Exiled* (Washington, D.C.: Review and Herald Publishing Association, 1933), 25.
33. Antranig Vartanian, video interview by Carol Margossian, February 1, 2001, New Vernon, N.J.
34. Davis, "Report," 31, 32.
35. Ibid., 32.
36. Ibid., 34.
37. Ibid., 38.
38. Ibid., 35, 36.
39. Bedoukian, *Some of Us Survived,* 17–18.
40. Ibid., 19.

41. Ibid., 38.
42. Ibid., 21–22.
43. Patrick Allitt, "Disobedient Diplomats and Other Heroes," *Foreign Service Journal,* (October 1995), 25.
44. Leslie A. Davis to Henry Morgenthau, Mamouret-ul-Aziz (Harput), Turkey, July 11, 1915, U.S. State Department Record Group 59, 867.4016/127.
45. Davis, "Report," 48–49.
46. Ibid., 48.
47. Ibid., 49.
48. Riggs, *Days of Tragedy in Armenia,* 80–82.
49. Ibid., 52, 53.
50. Ibid., 53, 54, 55.

CHAPTER 19: LAND OF DEAD
1. Davis, "Report," 62.
2. Ibid., 62, 63.
3. Ibid., 63; most of the village names were changed after the massacre in an attempt to further cover up the crimes and obliterate the Armenian presence in the region; see *United States Official Documents on the Armenian Genocide,* vol. 3, *The Central Lands,* introduction with maps, xxiv.
4. Davis, "Report," 63–64.
5. Ibid., 65.
6. Ibid., 65–66.
7. Hewsen, *Historical Atlas of Armenia,* 199.
8. Davis, "Report," 66.
9. Ibid., 68.
10. Ibid., 66–67.
11. Ibid., 67.
12. Ibid., 67–68.
13. Ibid., 69.
14. Balakian, *Armenian Golgotha,* 177.
15. Davis, "Report," 69–70.
16. Ibid., 70–71.
17. Ibid., 72.
18. Ibid., 74.
19. Ibid., 74–75.
20. Ibid., 75–76.
21. Ibid., 76.
22. Donabed Lulejian, "A Handful of Earth," in *New Armenia,* April 1918, trans. Garabed H. Papazian.

CHAPTER 20: FROM JESSE JACKSON IN ALEPPO
1. Derderian, *Vergeen,* 55.
2. Jesse B. Jackson, formerly at Aleppo Syria, now in Washington, to Secretary of State, March 4, 1918, "Report Entitled 'Armenian Atrocities,' " to The Honorable Secretary of State, U.S. State Department Record Group 59, 867.4016/373.
3. Ibid, 1.

4. Hartunian, *Neither To Laugh Nor To Weep,* 55–60.
5. Jackson to Secretary of State, "Armenian Atrocities," 3, 5.
6. Ibid., 6–7.
7. Ibid., 7.
8. *Ravished Armenia and the Story of Aurora Mardiganian,* ed. Anthony Slide, (Lanham, Md: Scarecrow Press, 1997), 71, 85–89, 113.
9. Jackson to Secretary of State, "Armenian Atrocities," 8.
10. Jesse B. Jackson to Henry Morgenthau, Aleppo, Syria, June 28, 1915, U.S. State Department Record Group, 59, 867.4016/92, 1–3.
11. F. H. Leslie in Jackson to Morgenthau, Aleppo, Syria, August 10, 1915, U.S. State Department Record Group 59, 867.4016/139.
12. F. H. Leslie to Jackson, Urfa, Mesopotamia, August 6, 1915, U.S. State Department Record Group 59, 867.4016/139.
13. Ibid.
14. Jackson to Secretary of State, "Armenian Atrocities," 10.
15. Jackson to Henry Morgenthau, Aleppo, Syria, August 19, 1915, U.S. State Department Record Group 59, 867.4016/148.
16. Ibid.
17. Jackson to Henry Morgenthau, Aleppo, Syria, September 29, 1915, U.S. State Department Record Group 59, 867.4016/219.
18. Derderian, *Vergeen,* 64.
19. Jackson to Henry Morgenthau, Aleppo, Syria, August 19, 1915.
20. Ibid.
21. Jackson to Morgenthau, Aleppo. Syria, September 29, 1915.
22. Jackson to Henry Morgenthau through Mrs. Jesse B. Jackson, excerpt from letter dated September 3, 1915, but sent by Mrs. Jackson, October 13, 1916. U.S. State Department Record Group 59, 867.4016/298.
23. Jackson to Secretary of State, "Armenian Atrocities," 13.
24. Derderian, *Vergeen,* 65–66.
25. *Armin T. Wegner and the Armenians in Anatolia, 1915* (Milan: Guerini e Associati, 1996), 61–63.
26. Ibid., 35–36, 51.
27. Jackson to Morgenthau, Aleppo, Syria, September 29, 1915.
28. Curti, *American Philanthropy Abroad,* 247; *New York Times,* October 9, 1915.
29. Jackson to Secretary of State, "Armenian Atrocities," 13.
30. Ibid., 14
31. Ibid., 18.
32. Ibid., 23.
33. Ibid., 19–20.
34. Morgenthau, *Ambassador Morgenthau's Story,* 335, 339.
35. Hoffman Philip to Secretary of State, September 15, 1916, U.S. State Department Record Group 59, 867.4016/301.
36. Jackson to Hoffman Philip (Chargé d'Affaires), September 21, 1916, U.S. State Department Record Group 59, 867.4016/302.
37. Hoffman Philip to Secretary of State, September 15, 1916.
38. Auguste Bernau to Jesse B. Jackson, Aleppo, September 10, 1916, U.S. State Department Record Group 59, 867.4016/302, 1–2.

39. Ibid., 2.

40. ed. Anthony Slide, *Ravished Armenia,* 150.

41. Bernau to Jesse Jackson, Aleppo, Syria, September 10, 1916, 3–4.

42. Ibid., 4–5.

43. Ibid., 8.

44. Ibid., 9.

CHAPTER 21: "SAME FATE": REPORTS FROM ALL OVER TURKEY

1. Thea Halo, *Not Even My Name* (New York: St Martin's Press, 2000); she estimates that 750,000 Greeks, living on their ancient homeland in Anatolia along the Black Sea with Trebizond as their cultural center, were deported or killed.

2. Oscar Heizer to Henry Morgenthau, July 28, 1915, U.S. State Department Group 59, 867.4016/128, 1.

3. Ibid., 1–4.

4. Leon Z. Surmelian, *I Ask You Ladies and Gentlemen* (New York: Dutton & Co., 1945), 77, 79–81.

5. Heizer to Morgenthau, ibid., 3.

6. Ibid., 3–4.

7. John F. Pollard, *The Unknown Pope: Benedict XV (1914–1922) and the Pursuit of Peace* (London and New York: Geoffrey Chapman, 1999), 115–116; the pope's letter to the sultan of September 10 asking for a halt to the Armenian massacres was reported in the *New York Times* on October 10, "Spare Armenians Pope Asks Sultan."

8. Heizer to Morgenthau, 4; Vahakn Dadrian, "Documentation of Armenian Genocide in Turkish Sources," in *Encyclopedia of Genocide,* vol. ed. Israel Charny (Santa Barbara, CA, and Oxford, UK: 1999).

9. Ibid., 6.

10. Ibid.

11. Surmelian, *I Ask You, Ladies and Gentleman,* 86.

12. Ibid., 146–50.

13. Heizer to Morgenthau, 7.

14. Ibid., 7–8.

15. W. Peter to Henry Morgenthau, July 10, 1915, Morgenthau Papers, Reel 7/619, 1.

16. Surmelian, *I Ask You, Ladies and Gentleman,* 112–24.

17. W. Peter to Henry Morgenthau, 1–2.

18. W. Peter to Henry Morgenthau, August 26, 1915, American Consular Service, Samsoun, Turkey, U.S. State Department Record Group 59, 867.4016/220, 5–6.

19. Ibid., 6.

20. Charles E. Allen to G. Bie Ravndal, Esquire, American Consul General, Constantinople, March 5, 1916, U.S. State Department Record Group 59, 867.00/786, 1–2.

21. Tavoukdjian, *Exiled,* 25–27.

22. George Horton to Secretary of State, Smyrna, Turkey, February 4, 1915, U.S. State Department Record Group 59, 867.00/739, in *United States Official Documents on the Armenian Genocide,* 103–105.

23. Edward I. Nathan to Henry Morgenthau, Mersina, Turkey, July 26, 1915, Dispatch no. 464, Morgenthau Papers, Reel 7/639, 1.

24. Aghazarian, *The Cilician Armenian Ordeal,* 4.

25. Edward I. Nathan to Henry Morgenthau, 1.

26. Ibid., 2.

27. Hartunian, *Neither To Laugh Nor To Weep*, 73.

28. Harry Yessaian, *Out of Turkey: The Life Story of Donik "Haji Bey" Yessaian*, ed. Dennis Papazian (Dearborn, Mich., Armenian Research Center, 1994), 143.

29. Nafina Hagop Chilinguirian, "Claims Against Foreign Governments," filed March 20, 1920, see answer to question 55.

30. Ibid.

31. Edward I. Nathan to Henry Morgenthau, Mersina, Turkey, September 11, 1915, Dispatch no. 484, U.S. State Department Record Group 59, 867.4016/193, 1.

32. Ibid.

33. Edward I. Nathan to Henry Morgenthau, Mersina, Turkey, October 30, 1915, Dispatch no. 501, U.S. State Department Record Group 59, 867.4016/238, 1.

34. Edward I. Nathan to Henry Morgenthau, Mersina, Turkey, November 4, 1915, Dispatch no. 502, U.S. State Department Record Group 59, 867.4016/239, 1–2.

35. *Armin T. Wegner and the Armenians of Anatolia*, 62–63.

36. Antranig Vartanian, video interview conducted by Carol Margossian, February 1, 2000, New Vernon, N.J.

37. Morgenthau, *Ambassador Morgenthau's Story*, 333–34, 337–38, 342.

CHAPTER 22: AMERICA'S GOLDEN RULE:
WORKING FOR ARMENIA AGAIN

1. Morgenthau, *Ambassador Morgenthau's Story*, 328–29, 327. Morgenthau to Secretary of State, August 11, 1915 in *Papers Relating to the Foreign Relations of the United States, 1915*, supplement. *The World War* (Washington, D.C., Government Printing Office, 1928), 986.

2. Ibid., 328.

3. Henry Morgenthau to Secretary of State, September 3, 1915 (telegram) Dept. of State Record Group 59 867.4016/117.

4. James L. Barton, *Story of Near East Relief*, 40

5. Curti, *American Philanthropy Abroad*, 230–44.

6. Ibid., 240–44.

7. Barton, *Story of Near East Relief*, 4.

8. Ibid., 4–5; Moranian, *The American Missionaries*, 197–98.

9. Barton, 58.

10. Barton, 11.

11. Curti, 246.

12. Woodrow Wilson to M. Paul Hymans, 30 November 1920, ABC 16.9.1 vol. 2 #174. ABCFM archives, quoted in Moranian, 193–94.

13. Albert Shaw to James L. Barton, 12 February 1930, ABC Personal: Barton Papers, 6:2, ABCFM archives quoted in Ibid., 193–94.

14. Calvin Coolidge, Introduction to James L. Barton's *Story of Near East Relief*, vii–x.

15. Moranian, *The American Missionaries*, 191–93.

16. Barton, *Story of Near East Relief*, 39.

17. *The Armenian Genocide: News Accounts from the American Press 1915–22*, ed. Richard D. Kloian (Berkeley, Calif.: Anto Publishing, 1987).

18. Ibid.; see pages 19–88 for *New York Times* articles from summer and fall of 1915.

19. Herbert Hoover, *Memoirs—Years of Adventure* (New York: Macmillan, 1957), 385.

20. Deborah Lipstadt, *Beyond Belief: the American Press and the Coming of the Holocaust 1933–1945* (New York: Free Press, 1986).

21. Kloian, *The Armenian Genocide: News Accounts,* 18–88.

22. "Armenians Are Sent to Perish in Desert," *New York Times,* August 18, 1915, 5.

23. *New York Times,* October 4, 1915, 1.

24. Ibid., October 7, 1915, 3.

25. Morgenthau, p. 118.

26. *New York Times,* September 14, 1915, 2.

27. Ibid., September 16, 1915, 1.

28. Gust, "The Armenian Genocide," Documents from German State Archives, ed. Wolfgang Gust, 18.01.01, 22/141. For more on German involvement in the Armenian Genocide, see Dadrian, *German Responsibility and the Armenian Genocide* (Watertown, Mass.: Blue Crane Books, 1996).

29. Morgenthau, *Ambassador Morgenthau's Story,* 375.

30. *New York Times,* September 28, 1915, 2.

31. Ibid., September 29, 1915, 1.

32. Barton, *Story of Near East Relief,* 10.

33. James L. Barton, "Relief in the Near East," ABC Personal: Barton papers, 8:5, ABCFM archives, quoted in Moranian, *The American Missionaries,* 199–200.

34. James L. Barton, "Relations with Governments," ABC Personal: Barton Papers, 12:2, 252, ABCFM archives, quoted in ibid., 210.

35. Ibid., ABC Personal: Barton Papers, 12:2, 252, ABCFM archives, quoted in ibid.

36. *New York Times,* September 27, 1915, 5.

37. Ibid., October 7, 1915, 3.

38. Eliot Wadsworth and Jeremiah Smith, "War Relief Report, 1915–16," Rockefeller Foundation, GR1.1 Series 100N, box 76, folder 719, Rockefeller Family Archives.

39. Edward Stoever at War Relief Commission to Jerome D. Green, Secretary of Rockefeller Foundation Record Group 1.1 Series 100N, Box 76, folder 719, Oct. 2, 1916; RG1.1 Series 100N, Box 76, folder 719m, report from War Relief Commission June 19, 1916; Rockefeller Family Archives.

40. Charles Vickery to John D. Rockefeller Jr., January 16, 1920. 98.3. Rockefeller Family Archives.

41. *New York Times,* "Thousands Protest Armenian Murders," October 18, 1915, 3.

42. Barton, *Story of Near East Relief,* 16–17.

43. Howard M. Sachar, *The Emergence of the Middle East: 1914–1924* (New York: Alfred A. Knopf, 1969), 342–43.

44. Alvey Adee to W. W. Peet, quoted in Moranian, *The American Missionaries,* 201.

45. Jesse Jackson via Mrs. Jesse B. Jackson to the Department of State, October 13, 1916, U.S. State Department Record Group, 59, 867.4016/298.

46. Morgenthau, *Ambassador Morgenthau's Story,* 332.

47. James Bryce to James Barton, 30 September 1916, ABCFM 16.5, vol. 6, #195, ABCFM archives, quoted in Moranian, *The American Missionaries,* 201–02.

48. Moranian, ibid., 201–23.

49. Woodrow Wilson, 66th Congress, 2nd Session, proclamation in *The Statutes at Large of the United States of America,* vol. 34, pt. 2, 1802.

50. James L. Barton to W. W. Peet, 17 October 1916, ABC 3.1 vol. 296, #593, ABCFM archives, quoted in Moranian, 216.

51. Louise Franklin-Ramirez, interviewed by Peter Balakian, July 24, 2000.

52. Ibid; see also *Washington Post, Prince William Extra,* Sunday, June 7, 1997.

53. Ruth M. Hartshorn, interviewed by Peter Balakian, July 16, 2002, Hamilton, N.Y.

54. Ezra Pound, *New Age,* October 1915; also Walter Kalaidjian, "The Edge of Modernism: Genocide and the Poetics of Traumatic Memory," in *Modernism, inc.* (New York University Press, 2001).

55. Kalaidjian, "The Edge of Modernism," 108.

56. H. L. Mencken, "Who Can Save Armenia," in *Literary Digest* 51 (October 30, 1915).

57. Theodore Roosevelt, *Fear God and Take Your Own Part* (George H. Doran, New York, 1916); letter to Samuel Dutton, November 24, 1915, 377–383.

58. Henry F. Pringle, *Theodore Roosevelt* (New York: Harcourt, Brace & World, 1956), 408–16.

59. Roosevelt, *Fear God and Take Your Own Part,* 377–83.

60. *The Letters of Theodore Roosevelt,* ed. Elting E. Morison (Cambridge, Mass.: Harvard University Press, 1952); vol. 5, 536–38.

61. Ibid., vol. 5, 345.

62. Bertrand Russell, *Prophecy and Dissent 1914–16,* ed. Richard A. Rempel (London: Unwin Hyman, 1988), 266.

63. Ibid.

64. Russell, *Pacifism and Revolution,* 89.

65. *The Nation,* October 14, 1915, 449. W. E. B. Du Bois took this issue further when he noted after the war that "America's heart bleeds for Poland, Armenia, and Palestine but as for the 12 million Black Americans, he is silent." (*The Crisis,* March 1918).

CHAPTER 23: WILSON'S QUANDARY

1. *New York Times,* December 3, 1918.

2. Herbert Hoover, *The Ordeal of Woodrow Wilson* (Washington, D.C.: The Woodrow Wilson Center Press, 1958), 68.

3. John Milton Cooper, "A Friend in Power? Woodrow Wilson and Armenia," 4 (paper presented at The American Response to the Armenian Genocide conference, Library of Congress and U.S. Holocaust Memorial Museum, September 27–28, 2000). When Wilson and House revisited this issue, Wilson again wanted to make point 12 more specific by mentioning "Armenia, Mesopotamia, and Syria," but House convinced him to keep point 12 general.

4. Harley Notter, *The Origins of the Foreign Policy of Woodrow Wilson* (Baltimore: The Johns Hopkins Press, 1937), 69.

5. Woodrow Wilson, *Self-Determination and the Rights of Small Nations* (Dublin: Candle Press, 1918), 18–19, 9.

6. Hoover, *Ordeal,* 222.

7. For a more in-depth discussion of Wilson's mandatory system, see Atom Egoyan, "The New Diplomacy and National Self-Determination: A Comparison of Wilsonian and Leninist Attitudes" (Master's thesis, 25–26).

8. David Lloyd George, *Memoirs of the Peace Conference* (New Haven: Yale University Press, 1939), 810.

9. Hoover, *Ordeal,* 226.

10. Kendrick A. Clements, *Woodrow Wilson: World Statesman* (New York: Twayne and Co, 1987), 214.

11. Ibid.; Grayson, *Woodrow Wilson,* 95.

12. *New York Times,* Sunday September 7, 1919.

13. Ibid.

14. Ibid., Wednesday, September 24, 1919.

15. Grayson, *Woodrow Wilson,* 99–100; Robert H. Ferrell, *Woodrow Wilson and World War I, 1917–1921* (New York: Harper & Row, 1985), 169; Clements, *Woodrow Wilson,* 215–16.

16. Cooper, "A Friend in Power?" 2.

17. Ibid., 3.

18. Ibid.

19. Alexis de Tocqueville, *Democracy in America,* vol. 1 (New York: Vintage Books, 1962), 317.

20. Moranian, *The American Missionaries,* 242.

21. Walter Lippmann to Newton D. Baker, December 5, 1917, box 2, Newton D. Baker papers, quoted in ibid., 245.

22. Daniel Thom to James L. Barton, January 8, 1915, ABC 16.9.7. vol. 25e. #28. ABCFM archives, quoted in ibid., 246.

23. James Barton to W. W. Peet, August 28, 1918, ABC 3.1, vol. 306, #232, ABCFM. Barton wrote: "It would easily swing our country into war with Turkey if the Administration would favor it," quoted in ibid., 249–50.

24. "Why the Democrats Defeated the Turkish Treaty," *Literary Digest* 92 (1927), 10, in ibid, 250.

25. Clarence D. Ussher, *Boston Transcript,* 23 April 1918, ABC, 14.2, vol. 3, #357, ABCFM archives, quoted in ibid., 257.

26. Moranian, *The American Missionaries,* 253–54.

27. Stephen S. Wise to James L. Barton, October 23 1918, ABC Personal: Barton papers, 6:11, ABCFM archives, quoted in Moranian, *The American Missionaries,* 260.

28. Ibid., 260–61.

29. H. C. Lodge to James L. Barton, December 12, 1917, ABC Personal papers, 5:4, ABCFM archives; Henry Cabot Lodge, "The Essential Terms of Peace," August 23 1918, 6, *Collection of Speeches and Addresses,* 1892–1919, Henry Cabot Lodge papers, quoted in Moranian *The American Missionaries,* 263–264.

30. Roosevelt to Dodge, May 11, 1918. *Letters of Theodore Roosevelt,* vol. 8, 1316–18.

31. James L. Barton to William W. Peet, August 28, 1918, ABC 3.1, vol. 306, no. 650, ABCFM archives; Barton to Peet, July 17, 1918, ABC, 3.1 vol. 306, no 232, ABCFM archives, quoted in *The American Missionaries,* 251.

32. Barton to Peet, August 28, 1918, quoted in Moranian, 252.

33. For a biography of Cardashian see James H. Tashjian, "Life and Papers of Vahan Cardashian," and John Mardick, "Life and Times of Vahan Cardashian," in *Armenian Review,* vol. 10, no. 1 (Spring 1957).

34. Gregory Aftandilian, *Armenia, Vision of a Republic: The Independence Lobby in America* (Boston: Charles River Books, 1981), 22–25.

35. Henry Cabot Lodge, Senate Res. 378, December 10, 1918, Congressional Record, v. 59, pt. 1, 65th Congress, 3rd Session.

36. Arpena S. Mesrobian, *"Like One Family": The Armenians of Syracuse* (Ann Arbor, Mich.: Gomidas Institute Press, 2000), 65–68.

37. Ibid., Mesrobian's account of the guest list comes from Koolakian family papers and collection.

38. "The Pro-Armenian Campaign," *Armenian Herald* 2, nos. 3–5 (1919), 238–240.

39. Ibid., 239.

40. "'Ravished Armenia' in Film," *New York Times*, February 15, 1919, 4; "Show 'Ravished Armenia': First Public Exhibition of Official Motion Picture Today," *New York Times*, February 17, 1919, 11.

41. *Ravished Armenia and the Story of Aurora Mardiganian*, 5–8.

42. Ibid.; Howard Davies, Hector Dion, Frank Clark, Miles McCarthy, Lillian West, and Eugenie Besserer filled out the cast.

43. Ibid., 8–9.

44. Ibid., 5.

45. Ibid., 6.

46. Ibid., 13–14.

47. Ibid., 9–17.

48. Robert Jay Lifton, Preface, in Henry Morgenthau, *Ambassador Morgenthau's Story* (Detroit: Wayne State University Press, 2003), xix.

49. A review in the *New York Times* (November 24, 1918) called *Ambassador Morgenthau's Story* "a work of commanding interest and importance, remarkably readable, significant and instructive." In underscoring the importance of Morgenthau's account of the Armenian massacres, the reviewer excerpted the ambassador's testimony: " 'Of all the famous politicians whom I met [says Mr. Morgenthau] I regarded Talaat as the only one who really had extraordinary native ability.' This was the man who later was chiefly responsible for the massacre of hundreds of thousands of Armenians. He once said to Mr. Morgenthau, 'I do not expect to die in my bed.' He ought not to." *Outlook* (December 1918) called the memoir "one of the most vigorous volumes the war has produced." In January 1919 the reviewer in *Survey* (January 11, 1919, 508–9) noted that "better than any other writer he has made the Young Turk leaders to stand forth in all their duplicity, selfishness and cruelty. As he was fearless in his dealing with them, so he has not hesitated to tell the world how grossly unfit these men were to govern." And the *American Historical Review* (vol. 25, issue 2 [January 1920], 287–88) called it "one of the outstanding books of the four years of the Great War," and noted that Morgenthau's portraits of Enver, Talaat, and Wangenheim "are masterpieces of vivid expression."

50. Moranian, *The American Missionaries*, 218–9.

51. Ibid., 213.

52. Armin T. Wagner, "Open Letter to the President of the United States of America, Woodrow Wilson," *Berliner Tageblatt*, February 23, 1919, in *Armin T. Wegner and the Armenians in Anatolia, 1915*, 137–46.

CHAPTER 24: THE RISE OF A NEW TURKISH NATIONALISM AND THE CAMPAIGN AGAINST ARMENIA

1. Hovannisian, *Armenia on the Road to Independence*, 63–68; Walker, *Armenia: The Survival of a Nation*, 243.

2. Hovannisian, *Armenia on the Road to Independence*, 98.

3. Walker, *Armenia: The Survival of a Nation*, 244.

4. Hovannisian, *Armenia on the Road to Independence*, 107–8; 190–93; Walker, *Armenia: The Survival of a Nation*, 256–57.

5. Hovannisian, *Armenia on the Road to Independence*, 114–15.

6. Ibid., 248–49.

7. Ibid., 176.

8. Walker, *Armenia: The Survival of a Nation*, 254, Hovannisian, *Armenia on the Road to Independence*, 176.

9. Hovannisian, *Armenia on the Road to Independence,* 191

10. Walker, *Armenia: The Survival of a Nation,* 274.

11. Ibid., 263; FO 371/3657, 10607.

12. Lord Kinross, *Ataturk: The Rebirth of a Nation* (London: Weidenfeld & Nicolson, 1964), 139.

13. Ibid., 147–48; 174–75.

14. Lewis, *The Emergence of Modern Turkey,* 239–40.

15. Ibid., 243. Furthermore, in July 1919, the Kemalists held a congress in Erzurum in an Armenian schoolhouse—abandoned after the massacre—in which they dedicated themselves to fighting for the boundaries of the Turkish state, see Kinross, 179.

16. Kinross, *Ataturk,* 169.

17. Ibid., 175–77.

18. Ibid., 187–88.

19. Ibid., 189.

20. James B. Gidney, *A Mandate for Armenia* (Oberlin, Ohio: Kent State University Press, 1967), 106–8.

21. Marjorie Housepian Dobkin, *Smyrna 1922: the Destruction of a City* (London: Faber & Faber), 21–26.

22. Gidney, *A Mandate for Armenia,* 116. Although there was much disagreement about the wisdom of a Greek occupation of Smyrna, Prime Minister Lloyd George was most enthusiastic about the idea and a forceful champion of President Venizélos.

23. Maj. Gen. James G. Harbord, Harbord Report, in Senate Documents, 66th Congress, 2nd Session (Washington, D.C.: U.S. Government Printing Office, 1920), 15, no. 266, 11.

24. Lewis, *The Emergence of Modern Turkey,* 241.

25. Ibid., 247.

26. Walker, *Armenia: The Survival of a Nation,* 276.

27. Lewis, *The Emergence of Modern Turkey,* 247–49.

28. *Major Peace Treaties of Modern History, 1648–1967,* ed. Fred Israel, with an introduction by Arnold Toynbee (New York: McGraw-Hill, 1967), 2084–88.

29. Walker, *Armenia: The Survival of a Nation,* 279.

30. Ibid., 279–80.

31. Ibid., 305.

32. Kazim Karabekir, *Isitkal Harbimiz,* 2nd edition (Istanbul, 1969), 736–37, quoted in ibid.

33. Ali Fuat (Cebesoy), *Moskova Hairalari* (Istanbul, 1955), 70, quoted in ibid.

34. Walker, *Armenia: The Survival of a Nation,* 306–8.

35. Dadrian, *History of the Armenian Genocide,* 357–59.

36. Walker, *Armenia: The Survival of a Nation,* 310–11; Richard Hovannisian, *The Republic of Armenia,* vol. 4 (Berkeley: University of California Press, 1996), 253–61.

37. Walker, *Armenia: The Survival of a Nation,* 316; Hovannisian, *Republic of Armenia,* 40–44.

38. Hovannisian, *Republic of Armenia,* 390–98; Walker, *Armenia,* 317.

39. Hovannisian, *Republic of Armenia,* 389.

40. Ibid., 391, 398–402.

CHAPTER 25: TURKISH CONFESSIONS: THE OTTOMAN COURTS-MARTIAL

1. Gostan Zarian, *Bancoop and the Bones of the Mammoth,* trans. Ara Baliozian (New York: Ashod Press, 1982), 18.

2. Gostan Zarian, *The Traveller and His Road*, trans. Ara Baliozian (New York: Ashod Press, 1981), 16, 19, 21.

3. Gary Jonathan Bass, *Stay the Hand of Vengeance: The Politics of War Crime Tribunals* (Princeton University Press, 2000), 117–21.

4. Akaby Nassibian, *Britain and the Armenian Question, 1915–1923* (London: Croom Helm, 1984), 44–47.

5. FO 371/21488/58387, 12 May 1915; in Sharp to Bryan, 28 May 1915, Foreign Relations of the United States, 1915 Supplement, 981. The statement read: "For about a month the Kurd and Turkish population of Armenia has been massacring Armenians," and "in view of these new crimes of Turkey against humanity and civilization, the Allied governments announce publicly to the Sublime Porte that they will hold personally responsible [for] these crimes all members of the Ottoman Government, and those of their agents who are implicated in such massacres" quoted in Bass, *Stay the Hand*, 116–17.

6. FO 371/2488/148493, Oct. 6, 1915; FO 371/2488/172811, Nov. 17, 1915, quoted in ibid., 113.

7. David Lloyd George, *Memoirs of the Peace Conference* (New Haven, Conn.: Yale University Press, 1939), vol. 1, 117.

8. Ibid., vol. 2, 811–12.

9. CAB 23/24, part 2, 19 May 1918, 3 P.M. meeting, quoted in Bass, *Stay the Hand*, 113.

10. Lloyd George, *Memoirs of the Peace Conference*, vol. 2, 651.

11. Bass, *Stay the Hand*, 119.

12. FO 371/4172/12905, 7 January 1919, quoted in ibid, 120.

13. Bass, *Stay the Hand*, 121–22.

14. Record Group, 59, M-353, roll 7, 867.00/861, enclosure in Heck to Lansing, 11 March 1919, U.S. National Archives, quoted in ibid., 122.

15. Bass, *Stay the Hand*, 122.

16. Ibid., 123.

17. Ibid., 124.

18. Vahakn Dadrian, "The Turkish Military Tribunal's Prosecution of the Authors of the Armenian Genocide: Four Major Court-Martial Series," in *Holocaust and Genocide Studies* 7 (Spring 1997), 32–33.

19. Vahakn Dadrian, "A Textual Analysis of the Key Indictment of the Turkish Military Tribunal Investigation the Armenian Genocide," in *Armenian Review* 44, no. 1/173 (Spring 1991), 3–4.

20. Dadrian, "The Turkish Military Tribunal's Prosecution," 33.

21. Dadrian, "A Textual Analysis of the Key Indictment," 4, 6.

22. Dadrian, "The Turkish Military Tribunal's Prosecution," 35.

23. Mazhar Affidavit of Radi, one of Ankara's notables, pages 1, 3, quoted in Dadrian, "A Textual Analysis of the Key Indictment," 7.

24. Dadrian, "A Textual Analysis of the Key Indictment," 8–9.

25. *Takvimi Vekayi* no. 3540, 5; pretrial interrogation papers, 15. Testimonies from the key indictment—such as this one—were included in the regional hearings, quoted in ibid., 9.

26. Dadrian, "The Turkish Military Tribunal's Prosecution," 35.

27. The Ottoman-Turkish text of this affidavit is in the Jerusalem Armenian Patriachate Archive, series 21, file M, doc. no. 469, quoted in ibid., 36.

28. Series 21, file M, docs. 574–77. There is confirmation of the use of these implements in the 4th, 6th, 15th sessions, Feb. 11 and 15, and March 27, 1919, quoted in ibid., 37.

29. Dadrian, "The Turkish Military Tribunal's Prosecution," 37.

30. Ibid., 39.

31. Haigazn K. Kazarian, "A Turkish Military Court Tries the Principal Genocidists of the District of Yozgat," *Armenian Review* 25 (summer 1972), 36.

32. Bass, *Stay the Hand*, 125–26.

33. FO 371/4173/61185, 22 April 1919, quoted in ibid., 126.

34. FO 371/4173/61185, 17 April 1919, quoted in ibid, 125.

35. Balakian, *Armenian Golgotha*, chap. 22, "The Confessions of a Slayer Captain," 228.

36. Ibid., 231; see also Dadrian, "A Textual Analysis of the Key Indictment," 4.

37. Ibid., 230.

38. Balakian, *Armenian Golgotha*, 213, 215–17. Sergeant Sukru is cited as a supervisor of the area massacres in the written testimony of Maj. Mehmet Salim, the Military Commandant of Yozgat cited above. He is cited at the 5th session (Feb. 12) and at the 16th (March 29, 1919) by witnesses reciting their experiences.

39. Ibid., 220–22; 225–26.

40. Ibid., 227.

41. Dadrian, "The Turkish Military Tribunal's Prosecution," 44–45; Kazarian, "Turkey Tries Its Chief Criminals," 10.

42. Dadrian, "The Turkish Military Tribunal's Prosecution," 40.

43. Ibid., 41.

44. Ibid.

45. *Takvimi Vekayi*, no. 3616, published 6 August 1919, quoted in Vahakn Dadrian, ed., "Armenian Genocide in Official Turkish Records," *Journal of Political and Military Sociology* 22, no. 1 (summer 1994), 45.

46. Dadrian, "The Turkish Military Tribunal's Prosecution," 42.

47. *Takvimi Vekayi*, no 3589, 168 and 169 right column, and 210 left column, quoted in Dadrian, "Turkish Military Tribunal's Prosecution," 42–43. Almost all of them were charged with crimes against the Armenians, and among those who were indicted were prominent CUP leaders such as Ahmed Midhat, the responsible secretary for Bolu, a large district of Kastamonu Province, whose propaganda work incited the Muslim population to engage in massacring Armenians, Abdul Gani, the responsible secretary of Sivas Province, the largest center of deportation and massacre west of the Euphrates, and Hasan Fehmi, the powerful responsible secretary of Kastamonu.

48. Dadrian, "The Turkish Military Tribunal's Prosecution," 43.

49. *Takvimi Vekayi*, no. 3772, published February 1920, quoted in Dadrian, "Armenian Genocide in Official Turkish Records," p. 75.

50. Dadrian, "The Turkish Military Tribunal's Prosecution," 44.

51. Bass, *Stay the Hand*, 128.

52. Ibid., 135–40; Dadrian, *The Turkish Military Tribunal's Prosecution*, 46. See also James Willis, *Prologue to Nuremberg: The Politics and Diplomacy of Punishing War Criminals of the First World War* (Westport, Conn.: Greenwood Press, 1982), 153–157.

53. Dadrian, *The Turkish Military Tribunal's Prosecution*, 45. Among them Said Halim, party general secretary, Midhat Sukru, Ittihad central committee member Kucuk Talat, Foreign Minister and President of the Chamber of Deputies Halil Mentese, chief party propagandist Ziya Gökalp, head of national security office Isamil Canbolat, two sheikhs-ul-Islam, *seyhulislams* Musa Kazim and Mustafa Hayri, Foreign Minister Ahmet

Nesimi, Minister for Food Supplies Mustafa Kemal, Special Organization administrator Kambur Atif, and Ittihad central committee member Yusuf Riza. Those tried in absentia included the party leaders, Minister of War Ismail Enver Pasha, Minister of the Interior Memhet Talat Pasha, Minister of the Marine Ahmet Jemal Pasha, Special Organization directors Behaeddin Sakir and Mehmet Nazim, and National Security Chief Erzurumlu Aziz.

54. Ibid., 44–46. Since most of the CUP's files and records disappeared after the war, these forty-two documents comprised the major evidence; Dadrian, "Genocide as a Problem of National and International Law: The World War I Armenian Case and Its Contemporary Legal Ramifications," *Yale Journal of International Law* 14, no. 2 (1989), 298; the forty-two documents are cataloged in Dadrian, "The Armenian Genocide in Official Turkish Records," 156–59.

55. *Takvimi Vekayi,* no. 3571, 130–31, no. 3540, 5–6, quoted in ibid., 46.

56. *Takvimi Vekayi,* no. 3571, 130, quoted in ibid., 47.

57. *Takvimi Vekayi,* no. 3540, 6, quoted in Dadrian, "The Armenian Genocide in Official Turkish Records," 64.

58. *Takvimi Vekayi,* no. 3540, 5, 6, 7, quoted in Dadrian, "The Armenian Genocide in Official Turkish Records," 59–60. Vehib first gave his testimony to the Mazhar Commission in December 1918, and it was then read into the record at the second session of the Trebizond trials on March 29, 1919, and portions of it were published in the key indictment and in the Harput trials verdict.

59. Dadrian, "The Turkish Military Tribunal's Prosecution," 49–50.

60. Bass, *Stay the Hand,* 135–36.

61. Ibid., 127.

62. Ibid., 142–43.

63. Dadrian, "A Textual Analysis of the Key Indictment," 3.

64. Samantha Power, *A Problem from Hell: America and the Age of Genocide* (New York: Basic Books, 2002), 1–3.

65. For an account and transcript of the trial, see *The Case of Solomon Tehlirian,* ed. and trans. Vartkes Yeghiayan (Los Angeles: ARF, Varantian Gomideh, 1985).

66. George R. Montgomery, "Why Talaat's Assassin Was Acquitted," *Current History: A Monthly Magazine of the New York Times,* July 1921, 272–274. For an in-depth analysis of these documents, see Vahakn N. Dadrian, "The Naim-Andonian Documents of the World War I Destruction of Ottoman Armenians: the Anatomy of a Genocide," *International Journal of Middle East Studies,* 18 (1986), 311–360.

CHAPTER 26: THE AMERICAN MANDATE FOR ARMENIA

1. Harry N. Howard, *The King–Crane Commission* (Beirut: Khayats, 1963), 38–39.

2. Ibid., 39–41.

3. James B. Gidney, *A Mandate for Armenia* (Oberlin, Ohio: Kent State University Press, 1967), 148–52.

4. Howard, *The King–Crane Commission,* 164–67.

5. Ibid., 184.

6. Ibid., 187.

7. *Papers Relating to the Foreign Relations of the United States: The Paris Peace Conference, 1919,* vol. 12 (Washington, D.C.: United States Government Printing Office, 1947), 821–22.

8. Ibid., 211–212.

9. PPC, 12, 810–13.

10. Ibid., 814.
11. Howard, *The King–Crane Commission*, 237; The commission went on to recommend that Turkey should also be accorded its right to self-determination, with a homeland in Anatolia with outlets to the sea, and this would constitute "a territory larger than France, with a population of about 10 million, about 8 million of whom would be either Turks or other Muslims, who would be held responsible for "sacredly guard[ing] the rights of all minorities, whether racial or religious." It affirmed the creation of a greater Syrian kingdom, including Lebanon and Palestine; a British mandate for Mesopotamia, which would by 1927 become Iraq, but felt the Zionist plan in Palestine was not yet feasible. As for Constantinople, European Turkey, the Straits, and the Sea of Marmora—they should become an international mandate overseen by the League of Nations. The ancient capital of Byzantium they envisioned as an international city—a place "free to all people for any legitimate interest." It would be, as well, a city for the many religions of the world, and although it would no longer be the capital of Turkey, the sultan would be still able to reside there. In conclusion the King-Crane report asserted its belief that the United States would be the best country to bring order and peace to the Near East. And the commission believed wholeheartedly that the United States had the resources to carry out the program; Gidney, *A Mandate for Armenia*, 161.
12. Gidney, *A Mandate for Armenia*, 163.
13. *Editor and Publisher 55*, no. 27, section 2, quoted in ibid., 165.
14. Gidney, *A Mandate for Armenia*, 169.
15. Ibid., 169–70.
16. Ibid., 170.
17. Ibid., 170–72.
18. James G. Harbord, "Investigating Turkey and Trans-Caucasia," *World's Work* 40 (May 1920), 36.
19. Ibid.
20. Ibid., 39.
21. Ibid., 40–41.
22. Ibid., 41–44.
23. James G. Harbord, "Mustapha Kemal Pasha and His Party," in *World's Work* 40 (June 1920), 176–80.
24. Ibid., 180–81.
25. Ibid., 186–87; Sachar, *The Emergence of the Middle East*, 354.
26. Harbord., 189.
27. Ibid.
28. Susan Billington Harper, "Mary Louise Graffam: Witness to Genocide" (paper presented at the conference "The U.S. Response to the Armenian Genocide," Library of Congress, September 18, 2000); Billington Harper's essay is an excellent, detailed account of Graffam's life and work.
29. Harbord, "Mustapha Kemal Pasha and His Party," 191–92.
30. Maj. Gen. James G. Harbord, "Conditions in the Near East: Report of the American Military Mission to Armenia," 66th Cong. 2nd Sess., Document no. 266, printed April 13, 1920, 6.
31. Ibid., 7.
32. Ibid.
33. Ibid., 19.

34. Ibid., 24.
35. Ibid., 25–28.
36. Ibid.
37. Ibid., 28.
38. Gidney, *A Mandate for Armenia,* 189.
39. Sachar, *The Emergence of the Middle East,* 357–60.
40. Ibid., 222; thousands of citizens and dozens of organizations, such as ABCFM, Near East Relief, the Armenian National Union, and the House of Bishops of the Protestant Episcopal Church, all requested aid and immediate protection for Armenia; see also Aftandilian, *Armenia,* 21–41; Moranian, *The American Missionaries,* chaps. 5–6.
41. *Congressional Record,* 66th Cong., 1st Sess., vol. 58, 7353; Gidney, *A Mandate for Armenia,* 222.
42. *New York Times,* April 4, 1920, 4.
43. Aftandilian, *Armenia,* 46.
44. Thomas Byrson, "John Sharp Williams: An Advocate for the Armenian Mandate, 1919–1920," *Armenian Review* 26 (1973), 32.
45. Gidney, *A Mandate for Armenia,* 231.
46. Ibid., 240.
47. Congressional Record, 66th Cong., 2nd Sess., vol. 69, 7533–34.
48. *New York Times,* May 26, 1920, 2.
49. Thomas A. Baily, *World War I and the Great Betrayal* (New York: Macmillan Company, 1945), 296.
50. Congressional Record, 66th Cong., 2nd Sess., vol. 69, 7877.
51. Gidney, *A Mandate for Armenia,* 237.
52. Ibid., 239.
53. Lewis Einstein, "The Armenian Mandate," *The Nation* 110, no. 2866 (June 5, 1920), 762.

CHAPTER 27: THE NEW U.S. OIL POLICY IN THE MIDDLE EAST AND THE TURNABOUT ON THE ARMENIAN QUESTION

1. Christopher Simpson, *The Splendid Blonde Beast* (New York: Grove Press, 1993), 23–26.
2. Ibid., 24–25.
3. Ibid., 18.
4. Ibid. 23; also Edward M. House Diary, entry for July 24, 1915, quoted in James Willis, *Prologue to Nuremberg: The Politics and Diplomacy of Punishing War Crimes of the First World War* (Westport, Conn.: Greenwood Press), 41.
5. Simpson, *The Splendid Blonde Beast,* 27–28.
6. Ibid., 24
7. Dobkin, *Smyrna 1922,* 81.
8. Ibid., 82–83.
9. Simpson, *The Splendid Blonde Beast,* 32.
10. Dobkin, *Smyrna, 1922,* 83.
11. Ibid., 75.
12. Ibid., 74. An expanding United States Chamber of Commerce now began a Levant division and advertised that "the opportunities for the expansion of American interests in the Near East are practically unlimited" (ibid., 72). By 1919 Standard Oil Co. was doing its best to exert influence on the peace process, and the company's president, Walter Teagle, made his position clear and then sent company representatives to Paris: "In the

settlement of the division of Turkey, consideration should be given to the oil possibilities . . . I am wondering if there is any way we can get into the oil producing end of the game in Mesopotamia" (ibid., 82).

13. Bristol to C. F. Gates, December 12, 1919, Bristol papers, quoted in ibid., 74.

14. Dobkin, *Smyrna, 1922*, 74.

15. Bristol to W. S. Benson, June 3, 1919, Bristol papers, Washington, D.C., quoted in ibid.

16. Bristol to Admiral W. S. Sims, 5 May, 1920, NR, quoted in ibid., 76.

17. Diary, May 25, 1919, Bristol papers, quoted in ibid.

18. Eugene P. Trani and Daniel L. Wilson, *The Presidency of Warren G. Harding* (University Press of Kansas, 1985), 168.

19. Dobkin, *Smyrna, 1922*, chs. XVII–XX.

20. Allen Dulles to Mark Bristol, April 21, 1922, Bristol papers, RG 45, National Archives, Washington D.C., in Simpson, 34.

21. Aftandilian, *Armenia*, 58.

22. "Report of Barton to Constituency," 3 February 1923, quoted in Moranian, *The American Missionaries*, 514.

23. Joseph C. Grew, Diary—1923, vol. 22, Ms. Am 1687, Joseph G. Grew papers, quoted in ibid., 527.

24. Ibid., 524.

25. Ibid., 518.

26. Barton to Folks ABCFM, 20–27 December 1922, ABC 16.5, #209, ABCFM archives, quoted in ibid., 524.

27. Barton to Patient Readers, ABCFM, 3–7 December 1922 16.5#205, ABCFM archives, quoted in ibid., 517.

28. Moranian, *The American Missionaries*, 522–23.

29. Taner Akçam, "The Genocide of the Armenians and the Silence of the Turks," in *Dialogue Across an International Divide: Essays Towards a Turkish-Armenian Dialogue* (Toronto: Zoryan Institute of Canada, 2001).

30. "The Lausanne Conference," *New York Times Current History* 17 (February 1923), 747.

31. Aftandilian, *Armenia*, 60–61; Moranian, *The American Missionaries*, 559–64.

32. *The Treaty with Turkey: Statements, Resolutions and Reports in Favor of Ratification of the Treaty of Lausanne* (New York: General Committee in Favor of Ratification of the Treaty with Turkey, 1926), 11–17.

33. "Mr Gerard's Answer," 24 January, 1924, ABC 14.2, vol. 3, #117, ABCFM archives quoted in Moranian, *The American Missionaries*, 550–551.

34. "The Turco-American Treaty of Amity and Commerce, a report of the E.P.A. *Foreign Policy Association* 26 (1924), quoted in Aftandilian, *Armenia*, 61.

35. Joseph L. Grabill, *Protestant Diplomacy and the Near East* (Minneapolis: University of Minnesota Press 1971), 281.

36. "Senator William H. King's Resolution Bearing on the Armenian Question," *Armenian Review* 27 (summer 1974), 78.

37. "Why the Democrats Defeated the Turkish Treaty," *Literary Digest* 92 (1927), 10.

38. Aftandilian, *Armenia*, 63.

EPILOGUE: TURKISH DENIAL OF THE ARMENIAN GENOCIDE AND U.S. COMPLICITY

1. A. W. Terrell, "An Interview with Sultan Abdul Hamid," *Century Magazine*, November, 1897, 134–136.

2. Judith Herman, *Trauma and Recovery* (New York: Basic Books, 1992), 8.

3. Morgenthau, *Ambassador Morgenthau's Story*, 337–38.

4. Ibid., 351–52.

5. Talaat, "The Posthumous Memoirs of Talaat Pasha," in *Current History: a Monthly Magazine of The New York Times*, vol. XV, October, 1921–March 1922, 294–295.

6. Karabekir, *Isitkal Harbimiz*, 736–37, quoted in Walker, *Armenia*, 305.

7. Ali Fuat (Cebesoy), *Moskova Hairalari*, 70, quoted in ibid.

8. Taner Akçam, "What Are Turkey's Fundamental Problems? Viewing Turkey's Problems from the Long-Range Perspective" (paper presented at international symposium on Turkey, Lockum, Germany, March 2000), 9.

9. George A. Plimpton, "The New Turkey" in *The Treaty with Turkey: Statements, Resolutions and Reports in Favor of Ratification of the Treaty of Lausanne* (New York: General Committee in Favor of Ratification of the Treaty with Turkey, 1926), 10.

10. Ibid., 15.

11. Ibid.

12. Colby Chester, "Turkey Reinterpreted," *Current History* (September 1922), 944.

13. U.S. National Archives, Record Group 59, General Records of the Department of State, Decimal File 811.4061 *Musa Dagh*. A fuller text of Ertegun's reply reads: "I have already informed my government of the satisfactory result reached through the kind support of the State Department. In this connection it is an agreeable duty for me to extend to you my best thanks and hearty appreciation for the efforts you have been so kind to exert in this matter without which the happy conclusion which has created an excellent impression in my country could not possibly have been attained."

14. Louis P. Lochner, *What About Germany?* (New York: Dodd, Mead & Co., 1942), 2. Lochner reports Hitler's speech of August 22, 1939 in which Hitler invokes the Armenian Genocide done with impunity, as a further support for his idea of gaining more *Lebensraum* (living space) for Germany. Hitler also says in this speech that "our strength is in our speed and brutality" and goes on to extol Ghengis Kahn.

15. Altemur Kilic, *Turkey and the World* (Washington, D.C.: Public Affairs Press, 1959), 18, 141, quoted in Richard Hovanissian, "Patterns of Denial," in *The Armenian Genocide in Perspective*, ed. Richard Hovannisian (New Brunswick, N.J.: Transaction Press, 1986), 121.

16. U.S. Congress, House, Rep. Gerald Ford of Michigan, 89th Congress, 1st sess. (Congressional Record, 29 April 1965), vol. 111, pt. 6, 8890.

17. See *Hairenik Weekly*, April 22, 1965; March 11, 18, 25, 1965; May 6, 1965; for further coverage of these events see the Armenian press, notably *Armenian Reporter, Armenian Mirror-Spectator,* and *Hairenik Weekly* from January to April 1965.

18. Power, *A Problem from Hell*, devotes chaps 3–5 and other portions of her book to Lemkin's codification of the word and concept of genocide.

19. Herman, *Trauma and Recovery*, 8.

20. Dadrian, "The Niam-Andonian Documents on the World War I Destruction of Ottoman Armenians: The Anatomy of a Genocide," *International Journal of Middle East Studies* 18 (1986), 342; see also Dadrian, "Genocide as a Problem of National and International Law, 272, note 169 cites the prominent Turkish historian, Y. H. Bayur, *Turk Inkilabi Tarihi* (The history of the Turkish revolution), vol. 3, no. 4, 787.

21. Des Pres, "On Governing Narratives," 250, 251.

22. Falk, "The Armenian Genocide in Official Turkish Records," i.

23. *Setting the Record Straight: On Armenian Propaganda Against Turkey*, Assembly of Turkish American Associations, Washington, D.C., no date.

24. Des Pres, "On Governing Narratives," 253.

25. Lewis, *The Emergence of Modern Turkey*, 350; without any substantiation, Lewis dispenses of the Armenian Genocide in a couple of sentences, calling it "a struggle between two nations for a single homeland." Lewis never explains how an unarmed, Christian ethnic minority in the Ottoman Empire could be fairly called a "nation," that could engage in a "struggle" with a world power (the Ottoman Empire) for a single homeland. In a recent interview, "There Was No Genocide: Interview with Prof. Bernard Lewis," by Dalia Karpel, *Ha'aretz* (Jerusalem, January 23, 1998), Lewis asserts that the massacres of the Armenian were not the result "of a deliberate preconceived decision of the Turkish government." These evasions are aimed at trivializing the Armenian Genocide.

26. Norman Itzkowitz, speech given at "Rape of Nanking" conference, Princeton University, Nov. 20–22, videotape.

27. Hovannisian, "Patterns of Denial," 125.

28. Stanford J. Shaw and Ezel Kural Shaw, *History of the Ottoman Empire and Modern Turkey*, vol. 2, *Reform, Revolution, and Republic: The Rise of Modern Turkey, 1808–1975* (Cambridge England: Cambridge University Press, 1977), 200–205, 240–41, 281, 311–17, 322–24, 256–57.

29. Deborah Lipstadt, "Armenian Genocide," letter to *Princeton Alumni Weekly*, vol. 96, no. 4 (April 17, 1996).

30. See Roger Smith, Eric Markusen, and Robert Jay Lifton, "Professional Ethics and the Denial of the Armenian Genocide," *Journal of Holocaust and Genocide Studies* 9, no. 1 (spring 1995), 1–22.

31. Des Pres, "On Governing Narratives," 251.

32. U.S. Congress, House, "National Day of Remembrance of Man's Inhumanity to Man," H.J. Res. 148, 94th Cong. 1st session, *Congressional Record* (8 April, 1975), vol. 121, pt. 8, p. 9244.

33. Simon Payaslian, "After Recognition," *Armenian Forum* 2, no. 3 (Autumn 1999), 38.

34. *Public Papers of the Presidents of the United States:* Jimmy Carter, bk. 1, 1 Jan. to 30 June 1978 (Washington, D.C.: U.S. Government Printing Office, 1979), 916–17.

35. Payaslian, "After Recognition," 39; op. cit. USAID, Overseas Loans and Grants, 1 July 1945, 30 Sept. 1982, p. 28.

36. Ronald Reagan, Presidential Proclamation 4838, April 22, 1981, *Public Papers of the Presidents of the United States*, 1981; Ronald Reagan, Jan.–Dec. 1981 (Washington, D.C.: U.S. Government Printing Office, 1982), 375–76.

37. "Statement on the Observance of the 75th Anniversary of the Armenian Massacres," 20 April 1990, *Public Papers of the Presidents of the United States*, 1990: George Bush, bk. 1, 1 Jan. to 30 June 1990 (Washington, D.C.: U.S. Government Printing Office, 1991), 533–34.

38. "Statement on the 80th Anniversary of the Armenian Massacres," 23 April 1995, *Public Papers of the Presidents of the United States*, 1996, William J. Clinton, bk. 1, 1 Jan. to 30 June 1995 (Washington, D.C.: U.S. Government Printing Office, 1996).

39. See HR 398, The United States Training on and Commemoration of the Armenian Genocide Resolution Hearing Before the Subcommittee on International Relations House of Representatives, 106th Congress, 2nd Session, September 14, 2000.

40. Elie Wiesel to Hon. Chris Smith, Chair, House International Operations Subcommittee, September 12, 2000. Correspondence to U.S. House International Relations Com-

mittee Concerning HR 398, the United States Training on and Commemoration of the Armenian Genocide, 106th Congress, 2nd Session, September 14, 2000.

41. Deborah Lipstadt, letter to Hon. Chris Smith, September 2, 2000, ibid.

42. In the 1990s PEN International, Human Rights Watch, and Amnesty International documented Turkey's consistent record of violence and repression toward intellectuals and intellectual freedom. Turkey had in the late nineties more writers in jail than any country in the world. The number of books banned in Turkey was rising; books about the Armenian Genocide, the Greek past in Anatolia, Christian minorities, or the Kurdish problem today were often banned, and their writers often jailed. These subjects are taboo in the Turkish educational system. Amnesty International and Human Rights Watch have focused on Turkey for the high percentage of children in prison; for persistent practices of torture in prison; and for practices of genital mutilation and rape of women in prison.

43. Sechuk Tezgul, "Longing to Stop the Bleeding," *Las Vegas Review Journal,* April 28, 1996.

44. Nazim Hikmet, *Things I Didn't Know I Loved: Selected Poems of Nazim Hikmet,* trans. Randy Blasing and Mutlu Konuk (New York: Persea Books, 1975), 60.

PHOTOGRAPH AND

MAP ACKNOWLEDGMENTS

———⊗⊗⊗———

The author expresses gratitude to the following for world rights permission.

Collection of Mark A. Momjian *(Sultan Abdul Hamid II in military dress; Enver Pasha)*

Boston Athenaeum; Baldwin Coolidge, photographer *(Boston's Faneuil Hall)*

Informations-und Dokumentationszentrun Armenien, Berlin *(the Adana massacres, April 1909, from Ernst Jäckh,* The Rising Halfmoon *[Berlin, 1911]; The sheikh-ul-Islam, from* The History of the First World War *[Berlin, Union Deutsche Verlagsgesellschaft, n.d.]; Armenians in amele taburlari)*

Project SAVE archives *(Armenians being marched out of Harput under armed guard, May 1915)*

Armenian National Institute, Inc., Washington, D.C.; Armin T. Wegner, photographer; courtesy of Sybil Stevens *(Execution of Armenians in a public square; 1915: Armenian deportees walking; Armenian deportees in a concentration camp in the Syrian desert; Starved Armenian woman and two small children)*

Near East Foundation, New York; Douglas Volk, 1918 *("They Shall Not Perish" Armenian relief poster)*

Collection of Harry S. Cherken Jr. *(Sheet music sold to benefit Armenian Relief, 1920)*

Harvard College Library, Theodore Roosevelt Collection *(Theodore Roosevelt)*

Armenian National Institute, John Elder Photo Collection *(Orphans in Armenia, ca 1917–19)*

Papers of Kate Clough and William Eagle Rambo, with permission of Barbara Rambo Hoshiko *(Armenian orphans spell out "America We Thank You")*

Armenian National Institute, Washington, D.C.; map produced by ANI and Nubarian Library, Paris *(Armenian Genocide Map)*

GLOSSARY

———∞∞∞———

TERMINOLOGY

amele taburlari Labor battalions; in World War I Armenians in the Ottoman army were most often placed in these and later killed.

bashibozuk Irregular soldier (fighter not in regular army).

chete Member of a fighting band or irregular fighting force, member of an organized killing squad.

dhimmi Or *zimmi;* Jew, Christian, and member of other religions tolerated by Islam within territory ruled by Muslims.

gâvur Or *giavour;* infidel, unbeliever, heathen, non-Muslim; with negative connotations.

hümayun Or *hümayoun;* royal or imperial, as in *hatt-i hümayun,* royal edict or decree of sultan.

muhajir Emigrant, fugitive, refugee; frequently used before World War I for Muslims who emigrated from the Balkans to other parts of the Ottoman Empire.

shari'a Islamic religious law which guides the entire life of Muslims, based on the Q'uran, the sayings and acts of Muhammad, analogy, consensus, and judicial opinion.

Sublime Porte Office of the Ottoman Grand Vizier.

Teshkilât-i Mahsusa Literally "Special Organization"; irregular fighters controlled by Enver Pasha and used during World War I in the Armenian Genocide as well as against Ottoman Arabs and Greeks, and in expeditions outside the Ottoman Empire.

zaptiye Military police.

Government Administrative Divisions and Officials

vilayet	Ottoman province.
vali	Governor of a *vilayet*.
sanjak	Ottoman county or subprovince.
mutasarrif	Governor of a *sanjak*.
kaza or **kaymakamlik**	Ottoman district.
kaymakam	Governor of a *kaza* or *kaymakamlik*.
nahiye	Ottoman subdistrict or group of villages.

PLACE-NAME VARIANTS

Primary usage in book: Variant spellings, or transliterated versions from other languages (Armenian, Turkish, Azerbaijani, English, Soviet/Russian).

Alexandropol	Leninakan, Giumri
Amasia	Amasya
Ankara	Angora
Deir el-Zor	Der Zor, Deyr uz-Zor, Deyr ul-Zor
Diyarbekir	Diarbekir, Diyarbakir
Egin	Agn, Akn
Elizavetpol	Elisavetpol, Gandzak, Kirovabad, Ganja
Erzurum	Erzerum, Garin, Karin
Lake Göljük	Lake Hazargölü
Hajin	Hadjin, Hachin, Saimbeyli
Harput	Kharpert Kharberd, Mamuretü'l-Aziz, Elazig
Kayseri	Caesarea, Gesaria, Kesaria
Konia	Konya
Malatia	Malatya
Marsovan	Merzifon
Mezre	(Capital of Harput province) Mezreh, Elazig
Moush	Mush
Sasun	Sasoon, Sassoon, Sassoun, Sasoun
Sivas	Sepasdia, Sebastia
Trebizond	Trabzon
Urfa	Ourfa, Shanliurfa
Zeitun	Zeitoun, Zeytun, Süleymanli

A NOTE ON USAGE

Wherever possible I have used English-language equivalents for words and place-names rather than direct transliteration (e.g., Etchmiadzin instead of Echmiadzin, or *catholicos* instead of *gatoghigos*).

Frequently, English versions of place names are those used by contemporary American or British writers. When an alternative version has been chosen, quotations maintain the original spellings of the writers.

Turkish words have been spelled with the English alphabet for ease of access to readers of English, so that certain letters of the Turkish alphabet have been converted or modified (e.g., ç = ch, c = j, ş = sh, ı = i, ğ = g). Several vowels with diacriticals in Turkish have been maintained (ö, ü).

Transliteration tables have been only roughly followed, the guiding goal being to provide accessible and phonetic versions of foreign terms and names.

SELECTED BIBLIOGRAPHY

The following selected bibliography represents the books and texts that were the most germane to my study of the Armenian Genocide and the American response. It does not represent a complete bibliography of the Armenian Genocide, nor does it include hundreds of other books and scholarly articles that I read during the writing of this book, many of which are cited in the endnotes.

STATE AND NATIONAL ARCHIVES AND RECORDS

United States: National Archives, Record Group 59, Records of the Department of State, 867 series, Internal Affairs of Turkey 1910–1929, File 867.4016, Race Problems.

Papers Relating to the Foreign Relations of the United States: The Paris Peace Conference 1919, vol. XII, Washington, D.C.: United States Government Printing Office, 1947.

Great Britain: Blue Book Series on Turkey, 1895–1897.

Great Britain: Foreign Office (FO) Archives.

Great Britain: Parliament: *The Treatment of the Armenians in the Ottoman Empire: Documents Presented to Viscount Gray of Fallodon, Secretary of State for Foreign Affairs by Viscount Bryce with a Preface by Viscount Bryce* (compiled by Arnold Toynbee) (a major collection of witness accounts of the Armenian genocide from 1915 through summer 1916 by American and European observers in Turkey).

Turkey: *Takvimi Vekayi:* Ottoman government's official gazette, whose supplements served as a judicial journal, recording the proceedings of the Turkish Military Tribunal that tried the perpetrators of the Armenian genocide in Constantinople, 1919–20 (translated by V. Dadrian). The most extensive collection of *Takvimi Vekayi* on the Armenian genocide is found in "Armenian

Genocide in Official Turkish Records," collected essays by Vahakn N. Dadrian, in *Journal of Political and Military Sociology* 22, no. 1 (summer 1994), reprinted with corrections, spring 1995.

MANUSCRIPT COLLECTIONS

Isabel Barrows Family Papers, Houghton Library, Harvard University.
The Papers of the Blackwell Family, Library of Congress.
The Papers of Clara Barton, Library of Congress.
Rockefeller Family Archives, Record Group 2, World Affairs Series, Rockefeller Archive Center.

PHOTOGRAPHIC ARCHIVES AND DOCUMENTATION

The primary photographic evidence of the Armenian Genocide is found in photographs taken by and collected by Armin T. Wegner, housed in:
Armenian Information and Documentation Center, Berlin.
United States Memorial Holocaust Museum, Washington, D.C.
Armenian National Institute, Washington D.C. (www.Armenian-Genocide .org).
Barton, James L. *Story of Near East Relief* (New York: Macmillan, 1930) contains dozens of photographs documenting the aftermath of the Armenian Genocide and relief efforts.
Hofmann, Tessa, and Gerayer Koutcharian. "Images that Horrify and Indict: Pictorial Documents on the Persecution and Extermination of Armenians from 1877 to 1922," *Armenian Review* 45, nos. 1–2 (spring-summer 1992). This essay contains 119 pages of photographs of and about the Armenian massacres and genocide.

NEWSPAPERS AND MAGAZINES

The Graphic: An Illustrated Weekly Newspaper (this popular London magazine reported the Armenian massacres of the 1890s with major photographs and coverage).
Harper's Weekly: A Journal of Civilization (this popular American magazine reported the Armenian massacres of the 1890s with extensive coverage and extraordinary illustrations).
New York Times and its magazine supplement, *Current History*. The most comprehensive collection of *New York Times* and *Current History* coverage of the Armenian genocide is Kloian, Richard D., ed. *The Armenian Genocide: News*

Accounts from the American Press: 1915–1922, Berkeley, Calif., Anto Printing, 1988.

The Nation (coverage of the Armenian massacres from the 1890s through the 1920s, combined with astute political opinion).

Punch, or the London Charivari (covered and commented on the Armenian crisis in Turkey, with cartoons and illustrations, from the 1890s through the World War I period).

Woman's Journal (Boston, edited by Alice Stone Blackwell from 1893 to 1917; a weekly newspaper that covered the Armenian massacres with thoroughness).

Boston Globe

Boston Herald

New York Herald

Chicago Tribune

BOOKS

Adalian, Rouben Paul, comp. and ed. *The Armenian Genocide in the U.S. Archives, 1915–1918* (microfiche publication). Alexandria, Va.: Chadwyck-Healey Inc., 1991–93 [37,000 pages of documents from the United States National Archives and the Library of Congress].

———, ed. *Guide to the Armenian Genocide in the U.S. Archives, 1915–1918.* Alexandria, Va.: Chadwyck-Healey Inc., 1994.

Aftandilian, Gregory. *Armenia, Vision of a Republic: The Independence Lobby in America.* Boston: Charles River Books, 1981.

Ahmad, Feroz. *The Young Turks: The Committee of Union and Progress in Turkish Politics 1908–1914.* Oxford, England: Clarendon Press, 1969.

Alder, Lory, and Richard Dalby. *The Dervish of Windsor Castle: The Life of Arminius Vambery.* London: Bachman & Turner Ltd., 1979.

Armin T. Wegner and the Armenians in Anatolia, 1915. Milan: Guerini e Associati, 1996.

Auron, Yair. *The Banality of Indifference: Zionism and the Armenian Genocide.* New Brunswick, N.J.: Transaction Press, 2000.

Balakian, Krikoris. *Hai Koghkotan (Armenian Golgotha).* Beirut: Plenetta Printing, 1977.

Balakian, Peter. *Black Dog of Fate: A Memoir.* New York: Basic Books, 1997.

Bardakjian, Kevork. *Hitler and the Armenian Genocide.* Cambridge, Mass.: Zoryan Institute, 1985.

Barrows, Isabel, and June Barrows. *The Shaybacks at Camp.* Boston: Houghton Mifflin & Co., 1887.

Barton, Clara. *The Red Cross in Peace and War.* Washington D.C.: American Historical Press, 1899.

Barton, James, ed. *Turkish Atrocities: Statements of American Missionaries on the Destruction of Christian Communities in Ottoman Turkey, 1915–1917.* Ann Arbor, Mich.: Gomidas Institute, 1998.

———. *The Story of Near East Relief.* New York: MacMillan, 1930.

Bass, Gary Jonathan. *Stay the Hand of Vengeance: The Politics of War Crime Tribunals.* Princeton: Princeton University Press, 2000.

Bedoukian, Keroup. *Some of Us Survived.* New York: Farrar, Straus & Giroux, 1979.

Blackwell, Alice Stone. *Armenian Poems.* Boston: Robert Chambers, 1917.

Bliss, Edwin M. *Turkey and the Armenian Atrocities.* Edgewood Publishing Company, 1896.

Bryce, James, Viscount. *The Treatment of the Armenians in the Ottoman Empire, 1915–16.* Compiled by A. Toynbee. London: British Governmental Document Miscellaneous, no. 31, 1916.

Chaliand, Gerard, and Jean-Pierre Rageau. *The Penguin Atlas of Diasporas.* New York: Viking/Penguin, 1995.

Charny, Israel, ed. *Encyclopedia of Genocide,* vol. I. Forewords by Archbishop Desmond Tutu and Simon Wiesenthal, Santa Barbara, Calif.: ABC–CLIO, Inc. 1999.

Clifford, Deborah Pinkham. *Mine Eyes Have Seen the Glory: A Biography of Julia Ward Howe.* Boston: Atlantic, Little, Brown & Co., 1978.

Cooper, John M. *The Warrior and The Priest: Woodrow Wilson and Theodore Roosevelt.* Cambridge, Mass.: Harvard University Press, 1983.

Curti, Merle. *American Philanthropy Abroad.* New Brunswick, N.J.: Rutgers University Press, 1963.

Dadrian, Vahakn. *The History of the Armenian Genocide.* Providence, R.I., and Oxford, England: Berghahn Books, 1995.

———. *Warrant for Genocide.* New Brunswick, N.J.: Transaction Publishers, 1999.

———. *German Responsibility in the Armenian Genocide: A Review of the Historical Evidence of German Complicity.* Cambridge, Mass.: Blue Crane Books, 1996.

Daniel, Robert L. *American Philantropy in the Near East, 1820–1960.* Athens: Ohio University Press, 1970.

Davis, Leslie. *The Slaughterhouse Province: An American Diplomat's Report on the Armenian Genocide, 1915–1917.* Susan K. Blair, ed. New Rochelle, N.Y.: Aristide D. Caratazas, 1989.

De Nogales, Raphael. *Four Years Beneath the Turkish Crescent.* London: Scribner's, 1926.

Derderian, Mae M. *Vergeen: A Survivor of the Armenian Genocide (Based on a Memoir by Virginia Meghrouni).* Los Angeles: Atmus Press, 1996.

Der Nersessian, Sirarpie. *The Armenians.* New York: Praeger Publishers, 1970.

Dobkin, Marjorie Housepian. *Smyrna 1922: The Destruction of a City.* London: Faber & Faber, 1972.

Fesch, Paul. *Constantinople aux Dernier Jours d'Abdul-Hamid*. Paris: Marcel Riviere, 1907.

Garo, Armen. *Bank Ottoman: Memoirs of Armen Garo*. Trans. H. Partizian. S. Vratzian, ed. Detroit: Topouzian Pub., 1990.

Gidney, James B. *A Mandate for Armenia*. Oberlin, Ohio: Kent State University Press, 1967.

Gilbert, Martin. *Atlas of World War I*. New York: Oxford University Press, 1994.

———. *A History of the Twentieth Century*. New York: William Morrow, 1997.

Gladstone, W. E. *The Bulgarian Horrors and Russia in Turkistan, with Other Tracts*. Leipzig: Bernard Tauchnitz, 1876.

Grabill, Joseph L. *Protestant Diplomacy and the Near East*. Minneapolis: University of Minnesota Press, 1971.

Graves, Sir Robert Windham. *Storm Centres of the Near East, 1879–1929*. London: Hutchinson & Co., 1933.

Grayson, Cary Travers. *Woodrow Wilson: An Intimate Memoir*. New York: Holt, Rinehart & Winston, 1960.

Greene, Frederick. *Armenian Massacres, or The Sword of Mohammed*. Philadelphia and Chicago: International Publishing, 1896.

Hagopian, J. Michael. *Voices from the Lake: The Secret Genocide* (Film). Thousand Oaks, Calif.: Armenian Film Foundation, 2001.

Hanioglu, M. Sukru. *The Young Turks in Opposition*. Oxford, England: Oxford University Press, 1995.

Harris, J. Rendel, and Helen B. Harris. *Letters from the Scenes of the Recent Massacres in Armenia*. New York: Fleming H. Revell Company, 1897.

Hartunian, Abraham. *Neither To Laugh Nor To Weep: A Memoir of the Armenian Genocide*. Trans. Vartan Hartunian. Boston: Beacon Press, 1968.

Haslip, Joan. *The Sultan: The Life of Abdul Hamid II*. London: Weidenfeld & Nicolson, 1958.

Hepworth, George H. *Through Armenia on Horseback*. New York: E. P. Dutton & Co., 1898.

Hertslet, E. *The Map of Europe by Treaty*. Vol. 4. London: Her Majesty's Stationery Office, 1891.

Hewsen, Robert H. *Armenia, A Historical Atlas*. Chicago: University of Chicago Press, 2001.

Heyd, Uriel. *Foundations of Turkish Nationalism: The Life and Teachings of Ziya Gökalp*. London: Luzac, 1950.

Hoover, Herbert. *Memoirs—Years of Adventure*. New York: Macmillan, 1951.

Hovannisian, Richard. *Armenia on the Road to Independence*. Berkeley: University of California Press, 1967.

———, ed. *The Armenian Genocide in Perspective*. New Brunswick, N.J.: Transaction Press, 1986.

———, ed. *The Armenian Genocide: History, Politics, Ethics*. New York: St. Martin's Press, 1992.

————, ed. *The Armenian People from Ancient to Modern Times,* Vol. 2. New York: St. Martin's Press, 1997.

————, ed. *Remembrance and Denial: The Case of the Armenian Genocide.* Detroit: Wayne State University Press, 1998.

————. *The Republic of Armenia: Between Crescent and Sickle, Partition and Sovietization,* Vol. 4. (Berkeley: University of California Press, 1996).

Howard, Harry N. *The King-Crane Commission.* Beirut: Khayats, 1963.

Kazanjian, Paren, ed. *The Cilician Ordeal.* Boston: Hye Intentions, 1989.

Kerr, Andrea Moore. *Lucy Stone: Speaking Out for Equality.* New Brunswick, N.J.: Rutgers University Press, 1992.

Kinross, Lord. *Ataturk: The Rebirth of a Nation.* London: Weidenfeld & Nicolson, 1964.

————. *The Ottoman Centuries: The Rise and Fall of the Turkish Empire.* New York: William Morrow & Co., 1977.

Klements, Kendrick A. *Woodrow Wilson: World Statesman.* Boston: Twayne Publishers, 1987.

Kloian, Richard D., ed. *The Armenian Genocide: News Accounts from the American Press 1915–22.* Berkeley, Calif.: Anto Publishing, 1987.

Knapp, Grace H. *The Tragedy of Bitlis.* New York, Chicago: F. H. Revell, 1919.

Kouymjian, Dickran. *A Crime of Silence: The Armenian Genocide.* London: Zed Books, 1985.

Kuper, Leo. *Genocide: Its Political Use in the Twentieth Century.* New Haven, Conn.: Yale University Press, 1981.

Landau, Jacob. *Pan-Turkism: From Irredentism to Cooperation.* Bloomington: Indiana University Press, 1995.

Lepsius, Johannes. *Armenia and Europe.* London: Hodder and Stoughton, 1897.

Lewis, Bernard. *The Emergence of Modern Turkey.* London: Oxford University Press, 1961.

Link, Arthur S. *Woodrow Wilson: Revolution, War, and Peace.* Arlington Heights, Ill.: Harlan Davidson, Inc., 1979.

Lipstadt, Deborah. *Beyond Belief: The American Press and the Coming of the Holocaust 1933–1945.* New York: Free Press, 1986.

Lloyd George, David. *Memoirs of the Peace Conference, Vols. 1&2.* New Haven, Conn.: Yale University Press, 1939.

Lochner, Louis P. *What About Germany?* New York: Dodd, Mead & Co., 1942.

Matthew, H. C. J. *Gladstone, 1875–1898,* Oxford, England: Oxford University Press, 1995.

Melson, Robert. *Revolution and Genocide: On the Origins of the Armenian Genocide and the Holocaust.* Chicago: University of Chicago Press, 1992.

Merrill, Marlene Deahl. *Growing Up in Boston's Gilded Age: The Journal of Alice Stone Blackwell 1872–74.* New Haven, Conn.: Yale University Press, 1990.

Miller, Donald E., and Lorna Touryan Miller. *Survivors: An Oral History of the Armenian Genocide.* Berkeley: University of California Press, 1993.

Miller, William. *The Ottoman Empire and Its Successors, 1801–1927, with an Appendix, 1927–1936*. Cambridge, England: University Press, 1936.

Mirak, Robert. *Torn Between Two Lands, Armenians in America 1890 to World War I*. Cambridge Mass.: Harvard University Press, 1983.

Moranian, Suzanne. "The American Missionaries and the Armenian Question, 1915–27." Ph.D. diss., University of Michigan, 1994.

Morgenthau, Henry. *All in a Lifetime*. New York: Doubleday, Page & Co., 1921.

———. *Ambassador Morgenthau's Story*. New York: Doubleday and Doran, 1918.

———. *Ambassador Morgenthau's Story*. Preface by Robert Jay Lifton, introduction by Roger Smith, afterword by Henry Morgenthau III. Edited by P. Balakian. Detroit: Wayne State University Press, 2003.

Morgenthau, Henry III. *Mostly Morgenthau*. New York: Ticknor & Fields, 1991.

Morison, Elting E., ed. *The Letters of Theodore Roosevelt*. Vol. 5, Cambridge, Mass.: Harvard University Press, 1952.

———. *The Letters of Theodore Roosevelt*. Vol. 8, 1954.

Nalbandian, Louise. *The Armenian Revolutionary Movement*. Berkeley: University of California Press, 1963.

Nassibian, Akaby. *Britain and the Armenian Question, 1915–1923*. London: Croom Helm, 1984.

Pears, Sir Edwin. *Forty Years in Constantinople: The Recollections of Sir Edwin Pears, 1873–1915*. London: Herbert Jenkins, 1915.

———. *Life of Abdul Hamid*. New York: Henry Holt & Co., 1917.

Power, Samantha. *A Problem from Hell: America and the Age of Genocide*. New York: Basic Books, 2002.

Pryor, Elizabeth Brown. *Clara Barton: Professional Angel*. Philadelphia: University of Pennsylvania Press, 1967.

Ramsaur, Ernest Edmondson. *The Young Turks: Prelude to the Revolution of 1908*. Princeton: Princeton University Press, 1957.

Ramsay, William M. *Impressions of Turkey During Twelve Years' Wanderings*. New York: G. P. Putnam's Sons, 1897.

Richard, Laura E., and Elliott Maud Howe. *Julia Ward Howe 1819–1910*. Boston: Houghton Mifflin & Co., 1916.

Riggs, Henry H. *Days of Tragedy in Armenia: Personal Experiences in Harpoot, 1915–1917*. Ann Arbor, Mich.: Gomidas Institute, 1997.

Roosevelt, Theodore. *Fear God and Take Your Own Part*. New York: Doran and Co., 1916.

Rubenstein, Richard. *The Cunning of History: The Holocaust and the American Future*. New York: Harper & Row, 1975.

Russell, Bertrand. *Prophecy and Dissent 1914–16*. R. Rempel, ed. London: Unwin Hyman, 1988.

Sachar, Howard M. *The Emergence of the Middle East, 1914–1924*. New York: Alfred A. Knopf, 1969.

Sanders, Liman von. *Five Years in Turkey.* Translated by Carl Reichmann. Annapolis, Md.: United States Naval Institute, 1927.

Shannon, Richard. *Gladstone and the Bulgarian Agitation.* London: Thomas Nelson & Sons, 1963.

Shipley, Alice Muggerditchian. *We Walked, Then Ran.* Phoenix, Ariz.: A. M. Shipley, 1983.

Siamanto. *Bloody News from My Friend.* Trans. Peter Balakian and Nevart Yaghlian. Detroit: Wayne State University Press, 1996.

Sibley, Elbridge, Frank A. Ross, and C. Luther Fry. *The Near East and American Philanthropy.* New York: Columbia University Press, 1929.

Simpson, Christopher. *The Splendid Blonde Beast.* New York: Grove Press, 1993.

Slide, Anthony, ed. *Ravished Armenia and the Story of Aurora Mardiganian.* (London and Lanham, MD.: Scarecrow Press, 1997).

Staub, Ervin. *The Roots of Evil: The Origins of Genocide and Other Group Violence,* Cambridge, England: Cambridge University Press, 1989.

Stern, Madeleine B. *So Much in a Lifetime: The Story of Dr. Isabel Barrows.* New York: Julian Messner Inc., 1964.

————., ed. *We the Women.* Lincoln: University Press of Nebraska, 1974.

Stone, Frank Andrews. *Academies for Anatolia: A Study of the Rationale and Impact of the Educational Institutions Sponsored by the American Board in Turkey: 1830–1980,* Lanham, N.Y., and London: University Press of America, 1984.

Suny, Ronald G. *Looking Toward Ararat: Armenia in Modern History.* Bloomington: Indiana University Press, 1993.

Surmelian, Leon Z. *I Ask You Ladies and Gentlemen.* New York: Dutton & Co., 1945.

Tavoukdjian, Serpouhi. *Exiled.* Washington, D.C.: Review and Herald Publishing Association, 1933.

Ternon, Yves. *The Armenians: History of a Genocide,* trans. Rouben C. Cholakian. Delmar, N.Y.: Caravan Books, 1981.

The Lausanne Treaty: Turkey and Armenia, 1926. New York: American Committee Opposed to the Lausanne Treaty, 1926.

Toynbee, Arnold. *Armenian Atrocities, The Murder of a Nation.* London: Hodder and Stoughton, 1915.

————, intro. *Major Peace Treaties of Modern History, 1648–1957.* Vol. 3. Edited by Fred Israel. New York: Chelsea House Publishers, 1967.

Trumpener, Ulrich. *Germany and the Ottoman Empire, 1914–1918.* Princeton: Princeton University Press, 1968.

Twain, Mark. *Innocents Abroad.* Vol. 1. New York: Harper & Brothers, 1869.

United States Official Documents on the Armenian Genocide. Vol. 1, *The Lower Euphrates.* Collected by Ara Sarafian. Boston: Armenian Review Press, 1994.

United States Official Documents on the Armenian Genocide. Vol. 2, *The Peripheries.* Collected by Ara Sarafian. Boston: Armenian Review Press, 1994.

United States Official Documents on the Armenian Genocide. Vol. 3, *The Central Lands.* Collected by Ara Sarafian. Boston: Armenian Review Press, 1995.

Ussher, Clarence D. *An American Physician in Turkey.* Boston: Houghton Mifflin & Co., 1917.

Vambery, Arminius. *The Life and Adventures of Arminius Vambery.* London: T.F. Unwin, 1914.

Vickery, Bess P. *Mount Holyoke Courageous: A Call to the Near East.* New York: Carlton Press, 1994.

Walker, Christopher. *Armenia: The Survival of a Nation.* New York: St. Martin's Press, 1980.

———. *Visions of Ararat.* London: I.B. Taurus, 1997.

Washburn, George. *Fifty Years in Constantinople and Recollections of Robert College.* Boston: Houghton Mifflin & Co., 1911.

Wheeler, C. H. *Letters from Eden: Reminiscences of Missionary Life in the East.* Boston: American Tract Society, 1868.

Willis, James F. *Prologue to Nuremberg: The Politics and Diplomacy of Punishing War Criminals of the First World War.* Westport, Conn.: Greenwood Press, 1982.

Woods, H. Charles. *The Danger Zone of Europe: Changes and Problems in the Near East.* Boston: Little Brown, 1911.

Ye'or, Bat. *The Decline of Eastern Christianity Under Islam: From Jihad to Dhimmitude.* Translated by Miriam Kochan and David Littman. Madison, N.J.: Fairleigh Dickinson University Press, 1996.

Yeghiayan, V. *The Case of Solomon Tehlirian.* Los Angeles: ARF, Varantian Gomideh, 1985.

Yessaian, Harry. *Out of Turkey: The Life Story of Donik "Haji Bey" Yessaian.* Edited by D. Papazian. Dearborn, Mich.: Armenian Research Center, 1994.

ARTICLES

"Professor James Bruce, M.P." *Century Magazine,* Jan. 1890.

"The Armenian Crisis in Turkey." *Woman's Journal* 6, Apr. 1895.

"The Women of Armenia: The Wives, Mothers, and Daughters of an Afflicted Nation." *New York Times,* Aug. 18, 1895.

"Why the Democrats Defeated the Turkish Treaty." *Literary Digest* 92 (1927).

Akçam, Taner. "The Genocide of the Armenians and the Silence of the Turks." In *Dialogue Across an International Divide: Essays Towards a Turkish-Armenian Dialogue.* Toronto: Zoryan Institute of Canada, 2001.

Allitt, Patrick. "Disobedient Diplomats and Other Heroes." *Foreign Service Journal,* Oct. 1995.

Arkun, Aram. "Les relations arméno-turques et les massares de Cilicie de 1909." In *L'actualité du Génocide des Arméniens,* ed. Hrayr H. Ayvazian, et al. Paris: EDIPOL, 1999.

Astourian, Stephan H. "The Armenian Genocide: An Interpretation." In *History Teacher* 23, no. 2, Feb. 1990.

Balakian, Peter. "Arshile Gorky and the Armenian Genocide." *Art in America,* Feb. 1996.

Blackwell, Alice Stone. "Some Reminiscences." *The New Armenia* 5, no. 2, Feb. 1918.

Boghosian, Khachig. "My Arrest and Exile on April 24, 1915." Translated by Aris Sevag. *Armenian Reporter,* Apr. 21, 2001.

Bryce, James. "The Armenian Question." *Century Magazine,* Nov. 1895.

Bryson, Thomas. "John Sharp Williams: An Advocate for the Armenian Mandate, 1919–1920." *Armenian Review* 26 (1973).

Chester, Colby. "Turkey Reinterpreted." *Current History,* Sept. 1922.

Collette, Carolyn P., and Vincent J. DiMarco. "The Matter of Armenia in the Age of Chaucer." *Studies in the Age of Chaucer* 23 (2001).

Dadrian, Vahakn. "Genocide as a Problem of National and International Law: The World War I Armenian Case and Its Contemporary Legal Ramifications." *Yale Journal of International Law* 14, no. 2 (1989).

———. "The Armenian Genocide in Official Turkish Records." Foreword by Richard Falk, introduction by Roger Smith. *Journal of Political and Military Sociology* 22, no. 1 (summer 1994), reprinted with corrections, spring 1995.

———. "The Armenian Question and the Wartime Fate of the Armenians as Documented by the Officials of the Ottoman Empire's World War I Allies: Germany and Austria-Hungary," *International Journal of Middle East Studies* 34 (2002).

———. "A Textual Analysis of the Key Indictment of the Turkish Military Tribunal Investigation of the Armenian Genocide." *Armenian Review* 44, no. 173 (spring 1991).

———. "The Niam-Andonian Documents on the World War I Destruction of Ottoman Armenians: The Anatomy of a Genocide." *International Journal of Middle East Studies* 18 (1986).

———. "The Historical and Legal Interconnections Between the Armenian Genocide and the Jewish Holocaust: From Impunity to Retributive Justice." *Yale Journal of International Law* 23, no. 2 (summer 1998).

———. "The Role of the Special Organisation in the Armenian Genocide during the First World War." In *Minorities in Wartime.* Edited by Panikos Panayi. Oxford, England, and Providence, R.I.: Berg Publishers, 1993.

———. "The Role of Turkish Physicians in the World War I Genocide of Ottoman Armenians." *Holocaust and Genocide Studies* 1, no. 2.

———. "The Secret Young-Turk Ittihadist Conference and the Decision for the World War I Genocide of the Armenians." *Holocaust and Genocide Studies* 7, no. 2 (fall 1993).

———. "The Turkish Military Tribunal's Prosecution of the Authors of the Armenian Genocide: Four Major Court-Martial Series." *Holocaust and Genocide Studies* 7 (spring 1997).

———. "The Documents of the World War I Armenian Massacres in the Proceedings of the Turkish Military Tribunal." *International Journal of Middle East Studies* 23 (1991).

Davison, Roderick. "The Armenian Crisis 1912–1914." *American Historical Review* 53, no. 3 (1948).
————. "Turkish Attitudes Concerning Christian-Muslim Equality in the Nineteenth Century." *American Historical Review* 59 (1954).
Des Pres, Terrence. "On Governing Narratives: The Turkish-Armenian Case." In *Writing into the World*. New York: Viking Press, 1991, and in *Yale Review* 75 (1987).
Dillion, E. J. "The Condition of Armenia." *Contemporary Review* 67 (1895).
Falk, Richard. "The Armenian Genocide in Official Turkish Records." *Journal of Political and Military Sociology* 22, no. 1 (summer 1994).
Gilman, Charlotte Perkins. "International Duties." *Armenia* 1, no. 1 (Oct. 1904).
Gladstone, William E. "Bulgarian Horrors and the Question of the East." In Frederick Greene, *Armenian Massacres, Or the Sword of Mohammed*. Philadelphia and Chicago: International Publishing, 1896.
————. "On the Armenian Question" (Aug. 6, 1895). In Frederick Greene, *Armenian Massacres, Or the Sword of Mohammed*. Philadelphia and Chicago: International Publishing, 1896.
Gust, Wolfgang, "The Armenian Genocide: Documents from the German State Archives"; *www.armenocide.net*.
Harbord, James G. "Mustapha Kemal Pasha and His Party." *World's Work* 40 (June 1920).
————. "Conditions in the Near East: Report of the American Military Mission to Armenia." 66th Congress, 2nd Session, Document No. 266, printed April 13, 1920.
Hetherell, W. "Armenian Refugees Waiting for Work at the Labour Bureau of the Relief Society at Van." *The Graphic: An Illustrated Weekly Newspaper*, supplement "The Crisis in Turkey," 14 Dec. 1895.
Hofmann, Tessa, and Gerayer Koutcharian. "Images that Horrify and Indict: Pictorial Documents on the Persecution and Extermination of Armenians from 1877 to 1922." *Armenian Review* 45, nos. 1–2 (spring-summer 1992). (This essay contains 119 pages of photographs of and about the Armenian massacres and genocide.)
Housepian, Marjorie. "The Unremembered Genocide," *Commentary* 42, no. 3 (Sept. 1966).
Howard, William W. "Horrors of Armenia." *Armenian Review* 18, no. 4 (winter 1965).
Kaiser, Hilmar. "The Baghdad Railway and the Armenian Genocide, 1915–1916: A Case Study in German Resistance and Complicity." In *Remembrance and Denial: The Case of the Armenian Genocide*, edited by Richard Hovanissian. Detroit: Wayne State University Press, 1998.
Kalaidjian, Walter. "The Edge of Modernism: Genocide and the Poetics of Traumatic Memory." In *Modernism, inc.* New York University Press, 2001.
Kazarian, Haigaz K. "How Turkey Prepared the Ground for Massacre." *Armenian Review* 18, no. 4 (winter 1965).

Kouymjian, Dickran. "Confiscation and Destruction: A Manifestation of the Genocidal Process." *Armenian Forum* 1, no. 3 (autumn 1998).

Kuper, Leo. "The Turkish Genocide of the Armenians, 1915–1917." In *The Armenian Genocide in Perspective*, edited by Richard Hovanissian. New Brunswick, N.J.: Transaction Press, 1987.

Lulejian, Donabed. "A Handful of Earth." Translated by Garabed Papazian. *New Armenia*. April 1918.

Mardick, John. "Life and Times of Vahan Cardashian." *Armenian Review* 10, no. 1 (spring 1957).

Melson, Robert. "Provocation or Nationalism." In *The History and Sociology of Genocide: Analysis and Case Studies*. Edited by Chalk and Jonassohn, New Haven: Yale University Press, 1994.

Montgomery, George R. "Why Talaat's Assassin Was Acquitted," *Current History: A Monthly Magazine of the New York Times*, July 1921, 272–274.

O'Neill, Patricia. "The Sword and the Sonnet: William Watson's Poems for Armenia 1895–1896." Paper presented at "Texts in Time," University of Dublin, Nov. 2002.

Payaslian, Simon. "After Recognition." *Armenian Forum* 2, no. 3 (autumn 1999).

Pitkins, Timothy. "A Comparison of Turkish Law with Actual Conditions." *Harper's Weekly*, 18 Apr. 1895.

————. "The Sultan, Interpreted by Recent Events." *Harper's Weekly*, 29 Feb. 1896.

Smith, Roger, Eric Markusen, and Robert Jay Lifton. "Professional Ethics and the Denial of the Armenian Genocide." *Journal of Holocaust and Genocide Studies* 9, no. 1 (spring 1995).

Talaat, Memhet. "The Posthumous Memoirs of Talaat Pasha." *Current History: A Monthly Magazine of the* New York Times 15 (Oct. 1921–March 1922).

Tashjian, James H. "Life and Papers of Vahan Cardashian." *Armenian Review* 10, no. 1 (spring 1957).

Terrell, A. W. "An Interview with Sultan Abdul Hamid." *Century Magazine*, Nov. 1897.

Theldberg, Elizabeth B. "An American Heroine in the Heart of Armenia: Dr. Grace Kimball and Her Relief Work at Van." *Review of Reviews* 13 (13 April 1896).

Winter, Jay. "Under the Cover of War: Genocide in the Context of Total War." Paper presented at "The American Response to the Armenian Genocide," Library of Congress, Washington, D.C., Sept. 28, 2000.

FILM AND VIDEO

The Hidden Holocaust. Panoptic Productions, London, 1992.

Voices from the Lake: A Film About the Secret Genocide. Directed by J. Michael Hagopian. Armenian Film Foundation, Thousand Oaks, Calif., 2000.

The Great War and the Shaping of the Twentieth Century. A KCET / BBC coproduction in association with the Imperial War Museum (London); produced and directed by Carl Byker, Lyn Goldfarb et al. 1996. 8 videocassettes (see cassette 3, *Total War,* for discussion of the Armenian Genocide).

The Armenians: A Story of Survival. Directed and Produced by Andrew Goldberg. Two Cats Productions in association with National Education Telecommunications Association and Two Cats Productions.

A Wall of Silence: The Unspoken Fate of the Armenians. Produced and directed by Dorothee Forma. Humanist Broadcasting Foundation, the Netherlands; distributed by Armenian International Magazine, Glendale, Calif.

ACKNOWLEDGMENTS

So many people have been so generous with their support, aid, and professional assistance during the writing of this book. I want to express my gratitide to: Jackie Aher, Nevart Apikian, Lloyd Ambrosius, James G. Balakian, Peter Black, Harry Cherkin, John M. Cooper, Michael Coyle, Martin Deranian, Fay Dudden, Atom Egoyan, Connie Fontana, Louise Franklin-Ramirez, Joan Friedman, John Gallucci, Oliver Griffin, Wolfgang Gust, Susan Billington Harper, Ruth Hartshorne, Tessa Hoffman, Tess Jones, Walter Kalaidjian, Paul B. Kebabian, Steven Kepnes and Core 301, Richard Kloian, Robert Koolakian, Alice Lahue, Matt and Denise Leone, John Manson, Marion McCurdy, Richard Meckel, Robert Melson, David Miller, Donald Miller, Mary Moran, Henry Morgenthau III, Alice Nigoghosian, Patricia O'Neill, Dennis Papazian and Gerald Ottenbreit at the Armenian Research Center at the University of Michigan, Dearborn, Helen Pfann, Paul Pfann, Nancy Ries, Tal-ee Roberts, Capril Serabian, Christopher Simpson, Jason Soghigian, Roger Smith, Lynn Staley, Adam Strom and Mary Johnson at Facing History and Ourselves, Chuck Strozier, Alan Swensen, Ruth Thomassian, Bess P. Vickery, Keith Watenpaugh, Jay Winter, Nigel Young.

I am grateful to Elizabeth Rogers, who while working for the Red Cross sent me a copy of Clara Barton's chapter on the Red Cross mission to Armenia; to Jean H. Sutherland for sending me Fredrick Green's *The Armenian Crisis in Turkey*; and to a kind person who gave me Alice Stone Blackwell's *Armenian Poems* on the chance that I might do something with them.

I am immensely grateful to Debbie Paddock for her aid and expertise with photographs; Lou Ann Matosian for her support for generously sharing with me her knowledge of Armenians and Americans in Boston in the 1890s. I am indebted to Suzanne Moranian for the important work in her dissertation on the American missionaries. Carol Margossian, Sarah Setrakian, and Susan V. Barba were most noble gatherers of testimony, and I am deeply grateful to them for getting to me the testimony of Mr. Antranig Vartanian, one of the few survivors of Moush. Karen Murphy of Facing History and Ourselves was zestful and wonderful in the assistance she gave during times of heavy research. Vartan Gregorian's interest in Theodore Roosevelt was contagious as was his affirmative energy for which I am always grateful.

Generous support from foundations was instrumental in allowing me to work as unimpededly as possible. I am most grateful to the John Simon Guggenheim Foundation; the Dolores Zohrab Liebman Fund; the Armenian General Benevolent Union (AGBU) and staff Carol Aslanian, Anita Anserian, and Maral Ashjian; Joyce and Joe Stein and the Philobosian Foundation and its generous spirit. Seta Nazarian Albrecht and the Nazarian Family Foundation for their support and generous spirit; the Gerard F. Cafesjian Foundation for its support and the example it sets. I am indebted to the steadfast leadership and generosity of Louise M. Simone, former President of AGBU, whose vitality continues to build the bridge between Armenian culture and the world.

Colleagues and professionals at Colgate University were extraordinary in many ways at many times. I am indebted to the expert work of the ITS staff, Printing Services, especially Sue Bice and Kipp Manwarren; and the superb photography of Warren Wheeler; Jane Pinchin and Jack Dovidio, Deans and Provosts, and Linck Johnson, chairman of the English department, were continually supportive at crucial times. The staff at the Everett Needham Case Library, including Ann Kebabian, Ellie Bolland, Ann Ackerson; I am particularly grateful to David Hughes, Head of Reference Services, who always calmly found what was needed and expedited knowledge to me at any time of day; he was simply unstumpable.

Mark Momjian and his collection of Armenian and American books and artifacts provided me with new textures and understandings, and his passion for this history was always energizing.

The Armenian National Institute in Washington, D.C., was invaluable in providing documents, and its wonderful staff was always there when needed. To its director, Rouben Adalian, and staff, Jenna R. Levin and Jacob J. Toumayan, I am indebted.

Aram Arkun at the Zhorab Information Center of the Diocese of the Armenian Church was an invaluable friend and scholar with his multilingual knowledge and professional expertise.

Vahakn Dadrian was always generous and patient with my questions. His pioneering scholarship has been invaluable to opening up my understanding of the infrastructure of the Armenian Genocide. He is a rare man and scholar.

Robert Jay Lifton's comments and thoughts were always invaluable, as were our conversations about this subject and many others related to it. Marjorie Housepian Dobkin was full of keen insights, and my ongoing conversation with her helped to bring me to this history and its legacy.

I am fortunate to have an agent as intelligent and wise as Eric Simonoff at Jankow & Nesbit. My editor, Gail Winston, at HarperCollins, is the best editor a writer could have; her rigor and sharp intelligence coupled with her affirmative spirit kept me going through many currents and tides. I am also indebted to the professionals at HarperCollins who did such excellent work at the various stages of editing and production: Susan Llewellyn, Senior Production Editor, Elliott Beard, Design Manager, and Christine Walsh, Editorial Assistant.

I'm grateful to my brother and sister-in-law, Jim and Janet D. Balakian, for the gracious space of their house looking out toward the bay, where much of this book was written, and to Yaddo, where early chapters were written. Thanks to Bruce Smith, Jack Wheatcroft; to my mother, Arax Balakian, my aunts, Lucille and Gladys Aroosian, and my sisters, Pamela Balakian and Jan Balakian, and to Ed Harris, Mike Hollander, Michael Holtzman, Brian Kushner, Tom Shadek, and Bill Worth for enduring support.

I am deeply grateful to my wife, Helen Kebabian; her editorial expertise and support helped this book in immeasurable ways.

P.B. (5/15/03)

INDEX

ABOUT THE AUTHOR

Peter Balakian is the author of seven previous books, including *June-tree: New and Selected Poems 1974–2000* and *Black Dog of Fate (An American Son Uncovers His Armenian Past)*, which won the 1998 PEN/Martha Albrand Prize for memoir and was a *New York Times* Notable Book and one of the best books of the year for the *Los Angeles Times*. He holds a Ph.D. in American Civilization from Brown University and is the Donald M. and Constance H. Rebar Professor of the Humanities at Colgate University, where he was the first Director of Colgate's Center for Ethics and World Societies. He is the recipient of many awards, including a Guggenheim Fellowship and the Anahit Literary Prize. He lives in Hamilton, New York, with his wife and two children.